Municipalities in Financial Distress

Yseult would like to dedicate her contribution in this book to her mother (1950–2023)

Municipalities in Financial Distress

An Environmental, Social and Governance Critique

Eugenio Vaccari

Senior Lecturer in Law, Royal Holloway, University of London, UK

Laura N. Coordes

Professor of Law, Sandra Day O'Connor College of Law, Arizona State University, USA

Yseult Marique

Professor of Law, University of Essex, UK

Geo Quinot

Professor of Law, Stellenbosch University, South Africa

Edward Elgar PUBLISHING

Cheltenham, UK • Northampton, MA, USA

This publication was supported by the University of Essex's open access fund.

Published by
Edward Elgar Publishing Limited
The Lypiatts
15 Lansdown Road
Cheltenham
Glos GL50 2JA
UK

Edward Elgar Publishing, Inc.
William Pratt House
9 Dewey Court
Northampton
Massachusetts 01060
USA

Authorised representative in the EU for GPSR queries only: Easy Access System Europe – Mustamäe tee 50, 10621 Tallinn, Estonia, gpsr.requests@easproject.com

A catalogue record for this book
is available from the British Library

Library of Congress Control Number: 2024952819

This book is available electronically in the **Elgar**online
Law subject collection
https://doi.org/10.4337/9781035319916

MIX
Paper | Supporting responsible forestry
FSC® C013604

ISBN 978 1 0353 1990 9 (cased)
ISBN 978 1 0353 1991 6 (eBook)

Printed and bound by CPI Group (UK) Ltd, Croydon, CR0 4YY

Contents

Foreword

The existence of a flourishing system of local government is a commonly accepted pre-condition of any well-ordered democracy. As expressed by the European Charter of Local Self-Government, the principle denotes 'the right and ability of local authorities, within the limits of the law, to regulate and manage a substantial share of public affairs under their own responsibility and in the interests of the local population'. Yet, despite being universally acknowledged, this principle is invariably qualified—and, indeed, often undermined—in practice.

It is not difficult to discern the causes for the uncertain status of local government in today's world. One obvious reason is that the processes of modern government are driving inexorably towards a continuous functional differentiation of public tasks, and this is a tendency that wears down the presumption that the local authority should act as a general-purpose institution with responsibility for delivering a wide range of local public services. But an even more powerful impetus has been a persistent trajectory towards increased governmental centralisation. This becomes especially problematic with respect to the issue of public finance. The principle of local government requires that municipal authorities possess sufficient financial resources to give them the capacity of policy choice in the manner of delivery of local services. In practice, however, central government's overriding commitment to macro-economic policy management not only mandates it to maintain effective supervision over levels of local expenditure; it also drives the centre to retain a power to direct local expenditure towards the realisation of centrally determined targets and policies.

These trends of functional differentiation and increasing centralisation combine to weaken local government's capacity to act as a self-sufficient authority. The resulting weaknesses are most acutely exposed in times of fiscal stress. This is the subject of this important research study. Pursuing a multidisciplinary comparative inquiry into the topic, the authors of *Municipalities in Financial Distress* provide a comprehensive overview of the legal, financial and policy aspects of the challenges faced by local authorities in the UK, the US and South Africa that, owing to these strains, are brought to the brink of bankruptcy. *Municipalities in Financial Distress* is a perceptive account of an under-examined topic that fills a significant gap in the literature on central–local government relations.

The threat of local financial breakdown first figured prominently during the 1970s and 1980s. This was an era marked by a radical restructuring of government brought about by an apparent disintegration of a post-war consensus over the welfare state. The most high-profile episode in this scenario occurred in 1975 when New York City, having borrowed extravagantly to finance an extensive programme of social services, was facing bankruptcy once its debt obligations fell due. Following the Federal Government's refusal to provide a bailout—dramatically encapsulated in the *New York Daily News* headline: '[President] Ford to City: Drop Dead'—the City had no option but to carry out a stringent programme of cuts and service restructuring. But the US was hardly alone: during the 1980s, there were a series of similar threats of local financial breakdown in Britain that were a consequence of disputes arising from opposition to the Conservative government's imposition of strict local expenditure controls by Labour-controlled urban authorities who sought to circumvent them by various creative accounting mechanisms.

We are now in a new era of austerity, leading to a renewed threat of local financial breakdown. And whereas the strains of the 1970s and 1980s were highly politicised consequences of ideological differences between governmental tiers, the fiscal challenges facing local government would appear to be structurally embedded. The financial problems that local authorities now face arise from a wider set of factors. Ranging from local financial mismanagement, through unanticipated loss of local tax revenues, to significantly increased service demands, these problems are occurring against a general background of macro-economic shifts. One consequence is that local authorities are becoming exposed to the threat of being plunged into a vicious cycle of diminishing revenues, service cutbacks, and increasing debt levels.

Because of their fixed public service obligations, local authorities cannot simply file for bankruptcy. How, then, are these threats to be managed? This is the question that this research work addresses. Noting that states have generally failed to develop principled strategies for alleviating municipal distress, the authors have carried out a systematic analysis of the problem and surveyed the available strategies. More than this: they also outline a strategy which, having regard to environmental, social, and governance considerations, might just provide the basis for the restoration of local financial stability in the longer term. This commendable study will undoubtedly be of value to all who are concerned about the continued well-being of our local governmental systems.

Martin Loughlin
London School of Economics & Political Science

Acknowledgements

At the cost of stating the obvious, we really feel it important to reiterate that writing a book is no small feat. Such an endeavour is made even harder if the writing task does not occur during a research leave, a luxury that not all of us enjoyed. Thankfully, we were blessed with the help, support, and assistance of an amazing network of colleagues, relatives, and friends. It is, therefore, appropriate for us to spend a few lines acknowledging their essential contributions, first in our individual capacities and then collectively.

Laura N. Coordes: I would like to thank the faculty and staff at the Sandra Day O'Connor College of Law at Arizona State University for their support and for some very helpful conversations. Jonathan Hadley, a rising 2L, provided excellent research assistance. I also need to thank my fantastic co-authors, Eugenio, Yseult, and Geo. I have learnt so much from you, and it has been an honour to work with you. Finally, to my family, especially Greg, Calliope, and Aurelia, for their patience and unending support—I certainly could not have done this without you beside me every step of the way. I owe you a million thanks.

Yseult Marique: I am grateful for the encouragement I received from the Constitutional and Administrative Justice Institute at Essex Law School, John Bell, Theodore Konstadinides, Andrew Le Sueur, Sabine Michalowski, Lord Neuberger, Maurice Sunkin, and Steven Van Garsse. I also would like to thank my fellows from the Westminster Abbey Institute Programme (class 2024) for their commitment to give the best of the UK civil service to the public good. I would also thank very much my co-authors for all the excellent discussions we had while preparing this book, with a particular thumbs-up to Eugenio for keeping all of us on track. As usual my family has been incredibly supportive, for which no word of thanks would do. My father will hopefully recognise here some traces of his enthusiasm for discussing his work as an insolvency professional once upon a time.

Geo Quinot: I would like to express my gratitude to the Faculty of Law at Stellenbosch University for financial support that enabled my participation in many aspects of this project. I am very thankful to my co-authors for extremely insightful discussions of the various strands of research brought together in this book and to all other participants in the broader Research Network on Local Authorities and Financial Distress (RPAFD) for being enthusiastically receptive to bringing the divergent worlds of local government and insolvency together. A special word of thanks to Eugenio for his infectious enthusiasm and boundless energy that keep both projects moving forward. Finally, a deep gratitude to my family—Marinelle, Delinda, Célina, Jean-Luc and Alexis—for not only enduring my (physical and mental) absences during the process of writing this book, but also for indulging my (sometimes esoteric) rants about the issues touched upon in the pages that follow.

Eugenio Vaccari: I would like to thank my university and, particularly, the Head of the Department of Law and Criminology, Ravinder Barn, and one of the Subject Heads, Leonardo VP de Oliveira, for their material support to this research endeavour. I am particularly grateful to Royal Holloway, University of London, which gracefully and generously funded the creation of the Research Network on Local Authorities and Financial Distress (RPAFD) website, YouTube page, logo, and related marketing material. Additionally, I would like to thank my amazing co-authors—Laura, Geo and Yseult—for the thoughtful discussions and the steady progress in conducting this research. Finally, some words of thank to my friends—particularly Alex, Dimitris, Eden, Haim, and Marton—for their moral support over these past years. Your encouragement and camaraderie have been invaluable! I am also extremely grateful to Valentina and my family for their endless patience and understanding throughout this process.

Collectively, we are indebted to some of the leading international organizations in the field of insolvency and bankruptcy law. INSOL International generously supported a comparative study of local entities in financial distress, which led to the creation of RPAFD. We are particularly grateful to the chairs of the Academic Steering Committee, Juanitta Calitz (University of Johannesburg) first and Ray Warner (St. John's University) later, for their stalwart support of this research initiative. We are also heavily indebted to David Burdette (Head of Education, INSOL International) for his constant encouragement and supervision throughout our funded project and for his material contribution to the publication of our final report.

We are furthermore indebted to The World Bank Group (particularly Akvile Gropper, Harry Lawless, and Antonia Menezes) as well as the Insolvency Law Academy (and particularly to its president Prof Sumant Batra) for their constant push of climate-related issues in the insolvency agenda. We hope that this book can bring a positive contribution to the debate in the field by including social and governance considerations in this narrative and by expanding its focus to a frequently overlooked area of law: the treatment of local entities.

We would like to extend our heartfelt gratitude to Edward Elgar Publishing and their exceptional team for their invaluable support and guidance throughout the editing and publishing process. We extend our sincere gratitude to the

University of Essex and Stellenbosch University for their generous funding, which has enabled the publication of this book as an open access work.

Finally, we are heavily indebted to the contributors of the INSOL-funded research project on local entities in financial distress, as well as the RPAFD network, together with the other PIs in the network (Emanuele Padovani from the University of Bologna and André Lino from the University of Essex), the members of the academic steering committee and the independent advisors, for their work in the early stages of this research and for their contributions to our projects. Most of these professionals dedicated hours of their precious time to answer our questionnaires, write reports, and contribute to our virtual engagement initiatives, with little to no reward. The four of us would have never been able to write this book without you. Thank you. We look forward to engaging in further exciting initiatives, hoping that our research may positively contribute to the policy debate and reforms in this area.

The book covers literature and case law published before 30 July 2024. All weblinks have been accessed on that date. The usual disclaimers apply.

Eugenio, Laura, Yseult and Geo

1. Introduction to *Municipalities in Financial Distress*

1.1 MUNICIPAL DISTRESS

The treatment of local public entities or municipalities in financial distress is a largely under-explored area of law, especially outside the United States. The rules in the area are often unaffected by legal principles developed in insolvency and restructuring law.[1] Yet a municipal failure has a huge impact on local, regional, and national governments and economies; residents; investors; general creditors; and so forth.

In most countries, when a corporation experiences financial distress, the most likely outcome is its liquidation. Whilst it is not uncommon for financially distressed entities to be merged with neighbouring ones or for their duties to be transferred to other authorities,[2] municipalities cannot "simply"

[1] This book generally uses the expression "insolvency law" to refer to the set of rules and procedures applicable to a corporate debtor undertaking a liquidation or restructuring procedure. In the US, it is more common to refer to corporate insolvency law as "bankruptcy law". As a result, when referring to the US insolvency system applicable to corporate and municipal entities, the book makes use of the wording "bankruptcy law".

[2] In some jurisdictions, it is becoming increasingly common for councils to merge to address financial issues. See, among others: M Ncube and J Monnakgotl, 'Amalgamation of South Africa's Rural Municipalities: Is It a Good Idea?' (2017) Commonwealth Journal of Local Governance 75 (warning that mergers may not result in the expected financial advantages); S Pickering, S Tanaka and K Yamada, 'The Impact of Municipal Mergers on Local Public Spending: Evidence from Remote-sensing Data' (2020) 20(2) Journal of East Asian Studies 243; T Goto, S Sekgetle and T Kuramoto, 'Municipal Merger and Debt Issuance in South African Municipalities' (2020) 28(5) Applied Economics Letters 343 (warning of opportunistic free-riding behaviours); and D MacMillan, 'More Calls for Tees Valley Councils Mergers amid Financial Woes' *BBC News* (London, 4 February 2024) <https://www.bbc.com/news/uk-england-tees-68182160>. For a study in the area, see also: H Ogawa and T Susa, 'Municipal Merger and Tax Competition' (2015) Economic Research Centre Discussion Paper E15-5 <https://www2.soec.nagoya

be liquidated. Their public role and the need to deliver essential services to local communities, coupled with the elected and non-professional[3] nature of the governing bodies of these entities, require adequate consideration when devising strategies for addressing their financial distress.

It follows that, perhaps with the sole exception of strategically important corporations, municipal distress presents more complexities than corporate distress. Municipal financial distress invariably requires a long-term, multi-pronged strategy to ensure the sustainable resilience of the reformed entity. Unlike distressed corporations, a municipality *must* continue to exist (in some shape or form) and deliver services to its inhabitants regardless of its distress.

-u.ac.jp/wp-content/uploads/2016/04/E15-5.pdf>. In South Africa, the reform of local government following democratisation in 1994 has seen a dramatic decrease in the number of municipalities due to extensive amalgamations, although the trend has significantly slowed in recent years. In 1994, there were 1,262 municipalities in South Africa, which were reduced to 257 by 2016 and have remained at that number since. Whilst the initial amalgamations were largely a result of the overall reform of the South African state, the more recent ones, especially in respect of creating larger metropolitan municipalities, were largely driven by financial sustainability factors. See, among others: Municipal Demarcation Board, 'The Impact of Municipal Amalgamations on Service Delivery' (7 November 2019) <https://www.demarcation.org.za/wp-content/uploads/2021/07/Municipal-Amalgamtions-Seminar-Report_03Dec2019_latest.pdf>. Whilst the number of municipalities in the US has changed over the years, this is mainly due to the decline in the number of independent school districts: A Smaldone and MLJ Wright, 'Local Governments in the U.S.: A Breakdown by Number and Type' (*Federal Reserve Bank of St. Louis*, 14 March 2024) <https://www.stlouisfed.org/publications/regional-economist/2024/march/local-governments-us-number-type>. Municipal mergers in the US are extremely rare. See, among others: LN Coordes, 'When Borders Dissolve' (2018) 93 Chi-Kent L. Rev. 649.

[3] Directors and executive managers of corporations, as well as mayors and other elected officials (such as municipal council members, aldermen, or councillors), share a common key characteristic: they oversee an entity that provides goods and services to local users. However, there are significant differences between these two categories of leaders. Directors are considered professionals because they possess specialised knowledge and expertise. They are expected to manage and guide their organisations with integrity and professional competence, adhering to legal and ethical standards. While mayors have similar responsibilities towards their municipalities, they are subject to additional requirements such as maintaining integrity, transparency, and accountability. Mayors often rely on a broad network of professionals to implement their political directives. Therefore, mayors and similar elected officials fulfil their roles primarily based on their political status rather than professional qualifications. Consequently, we argue that their roles have a non-professional nature.

Local democracy needs to be protected, maintained, or restored as effectively as possible. As a result, municipal crises present critical challenges and unique opportunities to address trigger factors and lay the foundations for the entity's long-term "renaissance".

Historically, countries have failed to devise principled and comprehensive strategies to deal with municipal distress. The countries considered in this book (the US, South Africa, and the UK) are no exception. For varying reasons, which are elaborated in chapters 3 to 6, these countries' current regulatory approaches to handling municipal distress fail to promote long-term solutions for addressing the underlying causes of such distress.

The US, South Africa, and the UK have been chosen for their radically different approaches to municipal distress. The US addresses municipal distress with a variation on the approach used for corporations, and the framework for dealing with local entities in distress is included within the general US Bankruptcy Code (specifically in chapter 9 of the Code). On the opposite end of the spectrum, English law provides very limited guidance in this area. It only ensures that the elected representatives are—at least on paper—accountable for their actions, and that citizens can have free and transparent access to the councils' financial accounts. Somewhat in between, South Africa adopts a comprehensive modular approach to the treatment of local entities in distress, with different remedies available based on the severity of the entity's economic and financial situation.

Given the lack of analysis of the financial distress of local public entities and the shortcomings of the frameworks analysed in this book, we argue that municipal distress should be addressed with environmental, social, and governance (ESG) considerations in mind. This approach aims to sustainably restore the financial health of local governments for the long term.

1.2 KEY TENSIONS AND IMPORTANCE OF THE BOOK

Municipalities in financial distress face a myriad of tensions stemming from both internal and external pressures. These tensions often arise due to mismanagement, declining tax revenues, increasing service demands, and economic downturns. The inability to balance budgets, coupled with the obligation to provide essential services, creates a vicious cycle of debt and service cuts. Municipalities in financial distress are often forced to make difficult decisions such as reducing public services, laying off employees, and increasing taxes. Such measures can further exacerbate financial strain and erode public trust and support by local communities.

In the US, municipal bankruptcies are rare. Chapter 9 of the US Bankruptcy Code has mainly been used by special-purpose entities, such as utility companies and taxing districts.[4] A study across 42 fiscally distressed cities[5] identified eight possible factors that may serve as predictors of municipal insolvency in the US.[6] However, the law does not rely on predictive factors to devise a rescue strategy before the municipality becomes "service insolvent".

In South Africa, municipalities face similar yet distinct challenges. Financial distress in South African municipalities is widespread and is often linked to systemic mismanagement, inefficiencies, and poor governance.[7] The Auditor-General's reports frequently highlight issues such as unauthorised, irregular, and fruitless and wasteful expenditure.[8] In their most recent report on material irregularities in municipal finances, the Auditor-General stated: 'for many years, our audits have highlighted a systemic failure in local government to establish the systems, processes and controls required to make the constitutional principles and the requirements of municipal legislation the norm'.[9] These financial failures have led directly to service delivery failures.[10] For example, in many municipalities, low and declining levels of capital expenditure on maintaining existing infrastructure and on new construction works

---

[4] M Maciag, 'How Rare Are Municipal Bankruptcies?' (*Governing*, 23 January 2013) <https://www.governing.com/archive/municipal-bankruptcy-rate-and-state-law-limitations.html>.

[5] T Reilly, LN Coordes, E Reinisch and D Schlinkert, 'Uncovering Municipal Fiscal Distress in the United States' (2023) 21(2) Public Finance and Management 86.

[6] These are: access to municipal bankruptcy; intergovernmental aid; tax and expenditure limits; unfunded pension liabilities; fiscal home rule; public sector union density; financial mismanagement; and triggering events. See Reilly et al (n 5) 89.

[7] MD Glasser and J Wright, 'South African Municipalities in Financial Distress: What Can Be Done?' (2020) 24 Law, Democracy & Development 413, 422.

[8] Auditor-General of South Africa, 'Consolidated General Report on Local Government Audit Outcomes for 2021–22' (31 May 2023) <https://mfma-2022.agsareports.co.za/>.

[9] Auditor-General of South Africa, 'Material Irregularities in Local Government. MFMA 2021–22' (3 November 2023) <https://www.agsa.co.za/Reporting/SpecialAuditReports/Materialirregularities.aspx>.

[10] H Fourie and J Kirsten, 'SA's Municipal Challenges and Their Impact on Local Economic Development' Bureau for Economic Research Note No. 6 of 2021 (October 2021) 12 <https://www.sun.ac.za/english/faculty/economy/spl/SPL%20Library/BER%202021%20SAs%20Municipal%20Challenges_Final.pdf>, noting that 'low levels of capital spending could perhaps be seen as one of the greatest causes of municipal failure in South Africa'.

for water, roads, and sanitation services, despite available funds,[11] have led to significant breakdowns in basic services.

In the UK, austerity measures implemented over the past decade have significantly impacted local governments. Cuts in central government funding have forced municipalities to reduce spending, affecting public services such as social care, libraries, and waste management. The collapse of Carillion, a major contractor for local governments, highlighted the fragility of outsourcing essential services.[12] The struggle to maintain a balance between fiscal responsibility and service provision remains a critical challenge for English municipalities. There is increasing evidence that English local authorities are struggling financially, as indicated by the rising number of authorities requesting government help through section 114 notices, a formal procedure used to address local "bankruptcy".[13]

Overall, the common thread among the jurisdictions examined in this study is the delicate balancing act municipalities must perform in managing limited financial resources while striving to meet community needs.

These issues have not gone unnoticed. There is extensive literature on local entities and their finances[14] and, more generally, on municipal distress[15] in each of the jurisdictions considered in the study. Some publications, especially

---

[11] Ibid.

[12] Business, Energy and Industrial Strategy and Work and Pensions Committees, *Second Joint Report from the Business, Energy and Industrial Strategy and Work and Pensions Committees* (HC 2017–18, 769).

[13] Levelling Up, Housing and Communities Committee, *Financial Distress in Local Authorities* (HC 2023–24, 56).

[14] See, among others: BE Dollery, J Garcea and EC LeSage Jr, *Local Government Reform* (EE Publishing 2008); N Steytler and J de Visser, *Local Government Law of South Africa* (LexisNexis 2008); C Panara and MR Varney, *Local Government in Europe* (Routledge 2013); DP Haider-Markel (ed), *The Oxford Handbook of State and Local Government* (OUP 2014); GA Fisher, *Local Government Law* (Routledge 2021); CL Johnson, MJ Luby and TT Moldogaziev, *State and Local Financial Instruments* (2nd edn, EE Publishing 2021); M Moses, *The Municipal Fiscal Crisis: A Framework for Understanding and Fixing Government Budgeting* (Palgrave Macmillan 2022); and RC Fisher, *State and Local Public Finance* (5th edn, Routledge 2023).

[15] See, among others: LN Coordes and T Reilly, 'Predictors of Municipal Bankruptcies and State Intervention Programs: An Exploratory Study' (2017) 105 Ky. L.J. 493; E Vaccari, 'Municipal Bankruptcy Law: A Solution Which Should Not Become a Problem' (2017) 5 NIBLeJ 02; E Vaccari, LN Coordes and Y Marique, 'Global Trends in the Treatment of Local Public Entities in Distress: A Principled Approach' (2023) 32(1) Int. Insolv. Rev. 93.

in the US,[16] provide practical advice and guidance through the process. Others deal with the financial challenges associated with municipal distress[17] and the inequality and hardship that local governments face.[18]

The book examines the regulations governing distressed local entities but does not provide a practitioner-orientated perspective or cover the regulations of the financial instruments used by these entities to finance their debts.

A recent, salient book by Anderson, *The Fight to Save the Town*, profiles four troubled local communities in the US to advocate for a people-centred approach to leadership.[19] Like our book, it focuses not just on the economic causes and consequences of local government distress, but on the human impacts and responses. Our book both builds on and reinforces the groundwork laid by Anderson by exploring distress in jurisdictions outside the US through an ESG-focused lens.

In one of the most recent publications in the field,[20] Schleicher pins down a trilemma for government bodies when faced with a municipality in financial distress.[21] The trilemma is as follows: the (federal) state can pay the local debts, which can lead to moral hazard; the (federal) state can encourage local government to pay its debts, but this can lead to difficult macro-economic consequences as public services are cut and staff laid off; the (federal) state can allow local government to default, but this weakens the trust that financial institutions have in the capacity of local government to repay their debts. So federal officials are faced with the risks of moral hazard, the macro-economic consequences of dire austerity, and the reduced ability to invest in public infrastructure in the future.[22] Whatever decision they take, they can only address two issues at the same time, but not all three.

Another recent publication describes US bankruptcy law as a "legal Swiss army knife" that powerful parties use to their advantage while struggling

---

[16] JE Spiotto, AE Acker and LE Appleby, *Municipalities in Distress? How States and Investors Deal with Local Government Financial Emergencies* (2nd edn, Chapman 2016).

[17] R Bahl and P Smoke, *Restructuring Local Government Finance in Developing Countries* (EE Publishing 2003); J Mysak, *Encyclopaedia of Municipal Bonds* (Bloomberg 2012); and T Guzman and N Ermasova, *Municipal Fiscal Stress, Bankruptcies, and Other Financial Emergencies* (Routledge 2023).

[18] M Wilde Anderson, *The Fight to Save the Town* (Simon & Schuster 2023).

[19] Ibid.

[20] D Schleicher, *In A Bad State—Responding to State and Local Budget Crises* (OUP 2023).

[21] Whilst the book focuses on US cases, the trilemma is common to other jurisdictions.

[22] Ibid 7–10.

families and smaller creditors are given short shrift.[23] Although not exclusively focused on distressed local entities, Jacoby does discuss the ways in which chapter 9 municipal bankruptcy is used by cities and towns to address—and escape—liabilities for civil rights and personal injury obligations, and how the resulting impact disproportionately affects black and brown residents.[24]

Legal analysis of municipal distress has been conducted in other jurisdictions. Loughlin's seminal legal analysis of the central–local government relationship in England[25] draws attention to constitutional law issues. His analysis pertained to a previous drastic wave of austerity under the aegis of Prime Minister Thatcher in the 1980s. Like in the case of Thatcher's austerity measures, recent cuts in central funding pushed local government to turn to creative techniques bordering on financial speculation to balance their budgets.

Brand offers a comparative analysis of how local authorities handle financial distress, focusing on South Africa in comparison mainly with Germany, from a constitutional law perspective.[26] He shows how municipal financial problems are closely linked to the prevailing local government finance model as framed by multi-level systems of government. Within the constraints of these models and frameworks, local governments are often compelled to seek innovative initiatives in financial governance to mediate financial pressures.

Other publications focus on the financial aspects of municipal distress. A recent book[27] dissects the dire financial situation of English local government from the lens of public economics and the position of local officials. This forensic diagnostic focuses on the strategies developed by local government to resist a decade-long period of austerity. The book demonstrates that local authorities resort to innovation and self-sufficiency through "financialisation", meaning they adopt financial strategies that involve varying degrees of risk-taking to balance their budgets. The book highlights the differences among local governments in England based on their type, size, capacity, risk appetite, openness to commercial finance, and economic conditions. It emphasises that improving local accountability could be a solution to financial distress in these entities, focusing on the economic aspects of the issue.

---

23 MB Jacoby, *Unjust Debts: How Our Bankruptcy System Makes America More Unequal* (The New Press 2024) 112.

24 Ibid 91–121.

25 M Loughlin, *Legality and Locality—The Role of Law in Central–Local Government Relations* (Clarendon Press Oxford 1996).

26 D Brand, *Local Government Finance: A Comparative Study* (SUN MeDIA 2016).

27 A Pike, *Financialization and Local Statecraft* (OUP 2023).

Other contributions have looked at the causes of municipal distress and made recommendations for reform.[28] Whilst acknowledging the challenging prospects national or federal officials face when they must address financial distress at the local level, our book takes a different perspective on the existing literature in the field by flagging the human side of the situation. First, our book highlights the challenges faced by local officials or their substitutes and the considerations weighing in their reasoning process. This allows us to probe the place ESG considerations have, could have, or should have in local decision-making when financial distress is looming, becoming recurrent, or starts to be tackled. Secondly, our book examines whether economic logic is the only guiding principle, or if the specific nature and legitimacy of local governments, based on local elections, allow them to consider non-economic factors. This includes ESG considerations when devising a plan for moving forward. Thirdly, our book does not examine the role of the central government in relation to other levels of government within a given country. Instead, it explores the role of the state as a public body in contrast to other potential governance solutions, such as market forces or community groups providing charity in times of need.

In a nutshell, our book asks if one could not take a step back from the economic logic that leads—or risks leading—to local financial distress. As an alternative, this book argues that an appropriately designed system should contribute to ensuring the return of local government to "business" in the sense of providing important services contributing to local well-being in the long term.

To achieve this goal, the book argues that it is important to include sustainability considerations as part of the restructuring process. As sustainability in itself is difficult to assess objectively, this book turns to ESG indicators in the restructuring procedures affecting municipalities in financial distress.

Many publications have been devoted to ESG considerations in the commercial sector, and on how these considerations affect corporate behaviours and credit ratings.[29] Some articles analyse how ESG considerations influence companies facing financial challenges and underscore their growing significance

---

[28] See, among others: JE Spiotto, 'The Role of the State in Supervising and Assisting Municipalities, Especially in Times of Financial Distress' *The Pew Charitable Trust* (2013) <https://www.pewtrusts.org/~/media/assets/2013/07/23/pew_state_role_in_local_government_financial_distress.pdf>; Glasser and Wright (n 7); and E Padovani, F Porcelli and A Zanardi, 'The Determinants of the Financial Distress of Italian Municipalities: How Much Is It Due to Inadequate Resources?' (2024) 31 International Tax and Public Finance 1494.

[29] P Chodnicka-Jaworska, 'ESG as a Measure of Credit Ratings' (2021) 9(12) Risks 226.

in corporate governance and financial stability.[30] However, there is a literature gap in ESG risk analysis in relation to public sector distress. This book addresses this gap and contributes to the academic and policy discussions in the field.

1.3 THE DRIVING IDEAS SUPPORTING THIS PROJECT

Underpinning this approach is a distinctive conceptual framework on the economic role of public bodies in investing in public infrastructure and well-being that our previous research on local governments in financial distress across the world[31] has helped to shape. It takes as a starting point that local services provided to vulnerable communities can only partly be analysed with economic tools because of their complexity. Our analysis rests on the following four key assumptions about local government.

1.3.1 Essential and Just Institutions

First, local governments are integral to the just institutions Rawls identifies as essential for distributive justice.[32] Rawls' framework includes institutions responsible for transfers, allocations, stabilisation, and distribution, without distinguishing between federal and local levels. Fiscal federalism theories further explain how taxation and spending powers should be optimally allocated between central and local authorities.

In times of crisis or acute need, well-structured local institutions become vital. They provide institutionalised forms of solidarity, which are essential for an effective response to the crisis or need. Markets often fail to address public goods adequately. Alternatively, market signals can lead to resource depletion. These scenarios highlight collective action problems that necessitate local governments' intervention to manage resources sustainably and equitably.

Ostrom's work on collective action and governance underscores the importance of polycentric governance, where multiple governing bodies interact and

---

30 L Chiaramonte et al, 'Do ESG Strategies Enhance Bank Stability During Financial Turmoil? Evidence from Europe' (2021) 28(12) Eur. J. Fin. 1173; J Antunes et al, 'Do ESG Risk Scores Influence Financial Distress? Evidence from a Dynamic NDEA Approach' (2023) 15(9) Sustainability 7560.

31 E Vaccari, Y Marique and LN Coordes, *When Liquidation is Not an Option: A Global Study on the Treatment of Local Public Entities in Distress* (INSOL International 2022).

32 J Rawls, *Theory of Justice* (2nd edn, Harvard University Press 1999) 242–251.

cooperate at different levels.[33] Ostrom challenges the notion that only centralised authorities can manage common pool resources (such as utilities) effectively, showing that local communities can develop sustainable management systems with the right institutional frameworks.

Local governments, within a polycentric system, are better positioned than central authorities to understand and respond to their communities' specific needs. They have the benefit of proximity to the end users. Local governments can implement tailored solutions reflecting unique social, economic, and environmental contexts, enhancing governance responsiveness and effectiveness. This localised approach promotes community participation and engagement, which are crucial for the legitimacy and success of public policies. This is sometimes recognised under the subsidiarity principle.[34] When citizens are actively involved in decision-making processes, they are more likely to support and adhere to the resulting policies.

Local governance aligns with Rawls' principles of justice by promoting fairness and inclusivity in resource and opportunity distribution. Local governments complement central authorities by addressing specific community needs and managing public goods that the market fails to provide efficiently. Fiscal federalism and Ostrom's theories highlight the importance of a balanced and cooperative approach between different government levels. By fostering institutionalised solidarity and community participation, local governments effectively address collective action problems and contribute to a fair and just society.

1.3.2 Cognitive Limitations

Our second assumption is that we should prioritise theoretical models promoting informed decision-making based on the factual circumstances of a case and a deep awareness of our heuristics. Such an approach enables considerate and empathic judgment within humans' bounded rationality. Instead of utilitarianism, Rawls proposed grounding justice in rights and principles decided collectively under a veil of ignorance. This shift in thinking leads to developing theories about procedural fairness, particularly in insolvency.[35]

---

[33] E Ostrom, 'Beyond Markets and States: Polycentric Governance of Complex Economic Systems' (2010) 100(3) AER 641.

[34] NW Barber and R Ekins, 'Situating Subsidiarity' (2016) 61(1) Am. J. Juris. 5. The European Charter on Local Self-Government illustrates one possible expression of this subsidiarity principle.

[35] S Paterson, 'Debt Restructuring and Notions of Fairness' (2017) 80(4) MLR 600.

When it comes to local government, two key differences must be considered. Firstly, local governments are not tasked with setting general ethical principles. Instead, they make daily decisions tailored to their specific circumstances to ensure their community receives the necessary services to thrive. This distinction highlights the difference between the constitutional level, where general principles are established, and the administrative level, where these principles are applied in practical contexts.

Secondly, our understanding of human decision-making is continually refined. Bounded rationality was once seen as the primary limitation.[36] However, subsequent research has identified various heuristics and shortcuts that individuals use to simplify the complexity of their environment. These insights from behavioural economics and psychology reveal that humans often employ mental shortcuts that can lead to systematic biases and errors in judgment.[37]

Recognising these cognitive limitations is essential when designing policies that aim to enhance individual capabilities and promote fair decision-making. By accounting for these cognitive limitations, local officials can make more informed and empathic decisions that better serve their communities. This approach aligns with Rawls' emphasis on fairness and collective decision-making, translating abstract principles into practical actions that address the specific needs and circumstances of local constituencies. Through this lens, local governments can navigate financial distress and other challenges more effectively, ensuring just and equitable outcomes for their communities.

1.3.3 Individual Capability and Public Good

Our third assumption is that we should depart from the concept of fair equality of opportunity,[38] to embrace a more nuanced understanding of individual capability, as articulated by thinkers like Sen and Nussbaum.[39] Individual

---

36 HA Simon, *Administrative Behavior: A Study of Decision-Making Processes in Administrative Organization* (The Free Press 1947, 4th edn in 1997); HA Simon, *Models of Bounded Rationality, Vols. 1 and 2* (MIT Press 1984).

37 D Kahneman, O Sibony and C Sunstein, *Noise – A Flaw in Human Judgment* (William Collins 2021).

38 Rawls (n 32) 73–86.

39 MC Nussbaum, 'The Capabilities Approach and the History of Philosophy', in E Chiappero-Martinetti, S Osmani and M Qizilbash (eds), *The Cambridge Handbook of the Capability Approach* (CUP 2020) 13; I Robeyns, 'The Capability Approach: A Theoretical Survey' (2005) 6(1) Journal of Human Development 93. For a constructive critique, see: I Robeyns 'Capabilitarianism' (2016) 17(3) JHDC 397.

capability acknowledges that true empowerment requires more than just removing barriers. It involves actively enhancing people's abilities and opportunities to lead the lives they value.

Such a framework inherently raises questions of vulnerability and resilience. When we empower individuals by developing their capabilities, we not only help them achieve their personal best but also build resilience against future adversities. This empowerment has a ripple effect, benefiting not only the individuals but also local officials and the broader community. For instance, a capable and empowered citizenry can lead to more effective and responsive governance, as residents are better able to articulate their needs and participate in democratic processes.

Beyond being rational agents who seek to maximise their own utility, individuals are also ethical beings striving for a good life. This encompasses material wealth but also self-development, positive freedom, and considerations of social, environmental, and moral factors.[40] The idea of a good life, therefore, is deeply intertwined with individual and collective well-being. The promotion of such a goal is a cornerstone of our study.

Ostrom's perspective on rationality expands this view by considering people as rational beings in the broadest sense. According to Ostrom, individuals seek to optimise values important to them, such as personal identity, morality, and social connections. This holistic view of rationality includes the capacity for deliberation and ethical reasoning, acknowledging that people do not live in isolation but are part of a larger social fabric.[41]

This discussion on individual capability and rationality leads us to consider the provision of collective goods such as public health, safety, water sanitation, education, and social housing. These are essential components of a good life and require effective policies for their fair distribution and sustainable funding. Ensuring that these goods are accessible to all involves collective effort and shared responsibility, reflecting the interconnectedness of individual capabilities and societal well-being. As explained above, local governments are uniquely placed to do so. This perspective also underscores the importance of

---

[40] S Amartya, 'Capability and Well-Being', in M Nussbaum and A Sen (eds), *The Quality of Life* (OUP 1993).

[41] P Lewis and M Petersen, 'Elinor Ostrom on Choice, Collective Action and Rationality: A Senian Analysis' (2023) 9(6) JOIE 852.

localising the Sustainable Development Goals (SDGs),[42] which emphasises the synergies between local and central governance.[43]

By framing these public goods within the context of individual capability, we emphasise the importance of empowering people to contribute to and benefit from these resources. This approach not only enhances personal well-being but also fosters a resilient and inclusive society, where everyone can thrive.

1.3.4 ESG Criteria, Vulnerability and Social Interdependence

Our fourth and final assumption is that to overcome vulnerability, we must recognise our social interdependence.[44] This interdependence means local governments face polycentric issues, as described by Fuller[45] and Ostrom.[46] These are complex situations where the interests of various groups need to be prioritised, often against a backdrop of scarce resources. Our interconnectedness for social well-being coexists with the reality that resources are limited.

The constraints and negative externalities brought on by economic growth have been well-known since the early 1970s. The United Nations[47] and the Club of Rome's "Limits to Growth" report (1972)[48] highlighted the risks of a burgeoning population explosion. This spurred ideas around sustainable development,[49] SDGs, and the more recent concept of degrowth.[50] A major challenge in these efforts is effectively monitoring progress and implementation.

---

42 E Bilsky, AC Moreno and A Fernández Tortosa, 'Local Governments and SDG Localisation: Reshaping Multilevel Governance from the Bottom up' (2021) 22(4) JHDC 713.

43 M Biggeri, 'Editorial: A "Decade for Action" on SDG Localisation' (2021) 22(4) JHDC 706.

44 Rawls (n 32) 373–74.

45 L Fuller, 'The Forms and Limits of Adjudication' (1978–1979) 92 Harv. L. Rev. 353, discussed in relation to social rights by J King, 'The Pervasiveness of Polycentricity' (2008) Public Law 101–124.

46 Ostrom (n 33).

47 United Nations Conference, *Report on the Human Environment* (Stockholm, 1972) A/CONF.48/14/Rev.1.

48 DH Meadows et al, *The Limits to Growth: A Report for the Club of Rome's Project on the Predicament of Mankind* (Universe Books 1972).

49 V Barral, 'Sustainable Development in International Law: Nature and Operation of an Evolutive Legal Norm' (2012) 23(2) Eur. J. Int. Law 377; RE Kim and K Bosselmann, 'Operationalizing Sustainable Development: Ecological Integrity as a Grundnorm of International Law' (2015) 24 RECIEL 194.

50 The idea of doing away with the goal of economic growth to pursue the development of a "degrowth" society first emerged in France in the early twenty-first

Approaches to addressing the major obstacle to sustainable development can be either quantitative or qualitative. A promising example of a qualitative approach is the adoption of a vulnerability-led framework for the restructuring of financially distressed entities. A vulnerability-led approach emphasises the protection of the most vulnerable and less resilient players, ensuring that the restructuring process provides enhanced support where it is most needed. This approach aligns with the principles of fairness and equity, advocating for a fair distribution of assets to creditors and adequate funding of essential services. By focusing on the needs of the most vulnerable, the restructuring of financially distressed local entities can achieve long-term sustainable success, benefiting the entire community.

The qualitative method, whilst rich in context, can be too subjective. Quantitative methods based on measurable indicators promise objectivity, allowing for systematic monitoring and auditing within frameworks that emphasise internal control and compliance.[51] International organisations like the International Financial Reporting Standards Foundation make these quantitative indicators conditions for funding.[52] They also acknowledge that sustainability factors are becoming a mainstream part of investment decision-making processes.[53]

ESG indicators can help bridge the gap between qualitative and quantitative, as well as subjective and objective, criteria. In global finance, the concept of social investment[54] evolved in the 2000s into what is now known as ESG.[55] These frameworks aim to ensure that investments are not only financially sound, but also socially and environmentally responsible. However, there is currently no single ESG standard, leading to varying interpretations. Furthermore, the three aspects of ESG—environmental, social, and

century. Its leading theorist is Serge Latouche. See, among others: S Latouche, *La Décroissance* (PUF 2019).

51 M Power, *The Audit Society—Rituals of Verification* (OUP 1999).

52 IFRS, 'About the International Sustainability Standards Board' <https://www.ifrs.org/groups/international-sustainability-standards-board/>.

53 Ibid.

54 S Waygood, 'How Do the Capital Markets Undermine Sustainable Development? What Can Be Done to Correct This?' (2011) 11 J. Sustain. Financ. Inv. 81.

55 J Holland 'A Conceptual Framework for Changes in Fund Management and Accountability Relative to ESG Issues' (2011) 1(2) J. Sustain. Financ. Inv. 159. For a discussion of the link between ESG and SDG, see (among others): G Bekaert, R Rothenberg and M Noguer 'Sustainable Investment—Exploring the Linkage between Alpha, ESG, and SDGs' (2023) 31(5) Sustain. Dev. 3831.

governance—are distinct and can sometimes be in tension with one another rather than mutually supportive.

ESG standards evaluate businesses' sustainability and impact on environmental, social, and governance issues far beyond their financial performance.[56] To ensure that companies advance long-term, sustainable, global goals, both investors and regulators have demanded corporate social responsibility (CSR) practices that reflect a commitment to balance shareholder value with ESG considerations. From a purely financial viewpoint, evidence suggests that higher ESG ratings are associated with a higher quality of financial reporting.[57] Our book builds on this narrative (developed primarily with reference to corporate entities) to suggest that, at least in the field of local entities in financial distress, ESG criteria can be used to overcome social and environmental, and not simply financial, vulnerabilities.

Critics argue that ESG ratings often function as a black box, lacking transparency and clear standards.[58] Some view the current state of ESG as utopian,[59] an ideal not yet fully realised.[60] Despite these criticisms, the continued development and refinement of ESG standards remain crucial for ensuring that our interdependent society can sustainably and equitably navigate the challenges of limited resources and complex, competing interests. Throughout the rest of this book, we will demonstrate how ESG criteria are best placed to address the polycentric issues arising in the treatment of financially distressed local entities.

Our argument is that, by integrating ESG principles, restructuring efforts can prioritise environmental sustainability, social equity, and robust governance considerations, to the benefit of the restructured entity as well as its stakeholders. For instance, environmental considerations might involve ensuring

---

[56] AF Cicchiello, F Marrazza and S Perdichizzi, 'Non-Financial Disclosure Regulation and Environmental, Social, and Governance (ESG) Performance: The Case of EU and US Firms' (2023) 30(5) Corp. Soc. Resp. Env. Ma. 1121.

[57] D Gafni, R Palas, I Baum and D Solomon, 'ESG Regulation and Financial Reporting Quality: Friends or Foes?' (2024) 61 Finance Research Letters <https://doi.org/10.1016/j.frl.2024.105017>.

[58] S Giamporcaro, 'Sustainable and Responsible Investment in Emerging Markets: Integrating Environmental Risks in the South African Investment Industry' (2011) 12 J. Sustain. Financ. Inv. 121; J Atkins, F Doni and A Gasperini, 'Exploring the Effectiveness of Sustainability Measurement: Which ESG Metrics Will Survive COVID-19?' (2023) 185 J. Bus. Ethics 629.

[59] C Lucarelli and S Severini, 'Anatomy of the Chimera: Environmental, Social, and Governance Ratings beyond the Myth' (2024) 33(5) BSE 4198.

[60] P Tettamanzi, G Venturini and M Murgolo, 'Sustainability and Financial Accounting: A Critical Review on the ESG Dynamics' (2022) 29 Environ. Sci. Pollut. Res. 16758.

that the restructured entity adopts green technologies and sustainable practices, which can reduce pollution and resource depletion, thereby mitigating negative environmental impacts and fostering long-term ecological balance. Social considerations can be addressed by implementing fair labour practices, protecting pension funds, enhancing employee welfare, and engaging with the local community to ensure that the restructuring process does not exacerbate social inequalities but instead contributes to social upliftment and cohesion. Governance improvements can involve establishing transparent and accountable management structures that reduce corruption and enhance decision-making processes, leading to more resilient and trustworthy organisations.

By focusing on ESG factors, the restructuring process can reduce economic inequalities and vulnerabilities. For example, emphasising social equity can ensure that marginalised groups are not disproportionately affected by financial distress and that there are opportunities for inclusive economic participation. Improving governance can help build stronger institutions that can better manage risks and prevent future financial crises. Moreover, sustainable environmental practices can create economic opportunities, such as green jobs and sustainable industries, that contribute to economic growth without compromising the health of the planet.

Ultimately, integrating ESG considerations into restructuring can create more resilient and sustainable local entities that are better equipped to contribute to broader economic stability and SDGs, thereby promoting a more inclusive and equitable economic system.

1.4 ORIGINALITY AND STRUCTURE OF THE BOOK

This book is the first in the field to provide a sophisticated and comprehensive overview of the restructuring landscape for local entities in distress in three jurisdictions. In doing so, it engages with an interdisciplinary field frequently overlooked in academic publications: a field at the crossroads of public and economic law, politics and law, and law and economics.

The book analyses how local governments operate in the countries considered in the study, and to what extent their locally elected members are accountable to the current public and future generations for the planning and financial decisions they make. The book identifies the statutory remedies for over-indebted municipalities. It draws on the limited literature and practice in the field to analyse how local municipalities can manage financial distress, emphasising that solutions should be inclusive and address long-term community needs. In this, we think that the law—if properly considered to design institutions and processes—can help (as much as reasonably possible) address heuristic biases, over-optimism, or short-termism.

To achieve this goal, the book is structured as follows. In chapter 2, we critique the potential application of ESG-related information in insolvency and restructuring proceedings for local public entities. This chapter develops a theoretical framework advocating the use of ESG indicators, focusing on restructuring rather than liquidation.[61] The analysis covers ESG indicators within liquidation and restructuring proceedings, foreshadowing the specific case studies of distressed municipalities yet to come in the book. It demonstrates that ESG indicators, coupled with modular and vulnerability-orientated approaches to the treatment of financially distressed local entities, highlight the human component of the financial distress of local authorities and provide a comprehensive framework to evaluate and improve the sustainability and resilience of local entities.

Chapter 3 focuses on US law, detailing the rules governing municipal distress under US law. It evaluates the inclusion (or lack thereof) of ESG criteria in chapter 9 bankruptcy proceedings and state-level interventions, using case studies like Detroit and Flint to illustrate the practical application of municipal restructuring methods. The chapter assesses to what extent these methods either encompass or fail to consider ESG principles.

Chapter 4 delves into South African law, examining the general rules and principles applicable to companies in distress and assessing the incorporation of ESG criteria. It then scrutinises the legal framework for local public entities, evaluating the extent to which South African law considers ESG factors in restructuring distressed municipalities. The practical application is illustrated through the case studies of Mangaung and Kannaland.

Chapter 5 outlines the treatment of municipalities in distress under English law.[62] It also analyses the general insolvency rules and their promotion of ESG

---

[61] Whilst mergers do result in the termination of a financially distressed entity, as they are designed to ensure the continuation of the services provided by the distressed entity, we argue that they can be classified as a form of rescue/restructuring rather than a liquidation procedure.

[62] The UK is made up of four devolved nations. Its general insolvency rules (as outlined in the Insolvency Act 1986 and the Companies Act 2006) apply to England and Wales only. The Local Government and Finance Act 1988 (LGFA 1988, which includes the provisions on "insolvent" councils) applies to Great Britain only (Scotland, England, and Wales). As it will be explained in more detail in chapter 5, section 114 LGFA 1988 (on insolvent councils) does NOT apply to Scotland (and Northern Ireland). In theory, it does apply to Wales. However, because local entities in Wales are almost entirely funded by the central government, the likelihood of one of them defaulting on their debt is very limited, as the Welsh government acts as a sort of guarantor of municipal debt. As a result, and in consideration of the fact that the only cases of municipal "bankruptcies" in the UK have affected only English councils, the chapter only refers to English law.

criteria, the specific legal framework for local public entities, and the practical implementation through case studies of Croydon, Birmingham, and Thames Water.

Chapter 6 compares the approaches of the three countries, critically assessing their differences in constitutional terms, core concerns, accountability frameworks, and judicial supervision. It suggests improvements for the regulatory frameworks to better protect vulnerable users by giving deeper consideration to ESG criteria. The concluding chapter returns to the main arguments of this book and suggests avenues for further research.

1.5 STARTING OUR JOURNEY

Local authorities perform some crucial public functions that cannot be easily interrupted or abandoned. To ensure their effective delivery despite financial distress, a flexible legal framework is essential. This framework should support a tailored, modular approach that adapts to the unique circumstances of each municipality in distress, thereby increasing the chances of sustainable success by addressing local challenges comprehensively. Traditional economic tools often fall short in explaining local authorities' operations, as they assume rational behaviour and overlook these authorities' role in distributive justice and inclusive change. Recognising local authorities as vital components of social infrastructure is crucial for promoting equity and supporting vulnerable populations.

An increasing number of local public entities are facing financial distress. Promoting local subsidiarity and community participation is crucial in addressing this issue. A participatory approach ensures that policy choices reflect community needs and aspirations, fostering ownership, accountability, and sustainable recovery. Additionally, frameworks must address cognitive limitations in decision-making by integrating alternative theoretical approaches, such as modularism and vulnerability-led frameworks. A vulnerability-led approach emphasises protecting the most vulnerable and ensuring fair distribution of assets to creditors and adequate funding for essential services. By focusing on the needs of the most vulnerable, restructuring methods can achieve long-term sustainable success, benefiting the entire community.

This book advocates for a polycentric approach to dealing with financially distressed local entities, leveraging ESG criteria to guide the restructuring process. ESG indicators provide a comprehensive framework for monitoring, evaluating, and improving the sustainability and resilience of local entities. This approach promotes equality, tailored relief measures for the vulnerable, and inclusive decision-making involving diverse stakeholders. By incorporating diverse perspectives and priorities, the restructuring process becomes more effective and inclusive.

The approach proposed in this book respects diverse social, cultural, and economic norms, offering an adaptable framework tailored to different communities rather than imposed by central governments or designed solely for the Global North. It emphasises a modular approach centred on ESG criteria to achieve sustainable and equitable recovery for financially distressed local authorities, promoting social justice, community engagement, and long-term sustainability.

This book makes a distinct contribution by approaching the issue through the complementary perspectives of administrative and insolvency law experts. By addressing the specificities of local governments—distinct from ordinary corporations or states—and prioritising interests amid limited resources, the authors aim to foster constructive discussions and contribute to concrete reforms for the benefit of local communities. The journey begins with mapping conceptual frameworks, examining each jurisdiction, drawing comparisons, and exploring avenues for academic contributions and practical reforms.

2. Theoretical framework

2.1 INTRODUCTION

This chapter introduces the theoretical notions that shape our analysis of municipalities in financial distress in the US, South Africa, and the UK (namely, England). It starts with a discussion of the background concerns underpinning our environmental, social and governance (ESG) research framework. The chapter then explains in turn each of the ESG indicators. In each section, we focus on liquidation and rescue proceedings generally. We then turn to the specific context of local public entities in financial distress and consider the potential relevance of the indicators for our specific focus. The chapter concludes by showing the need for a polycentric approach to dealing with local entities in financial distress.

2.1.1 Insolvency Theories

Insolvency law's focus has traditionally been the maximisation of returns to the debtor's creditors. Therefore, in the early days of the debate on the purposes and goals of insolvency law, most academics and commentators advocated approaches collectively described as "proceduralist".

Proceduralism, also known as the creditors' wealth maximisation approach, is based on efficiency considerations.[1] This approach has been criticised on the basis that its main proponents adopted a realist perspective, meaning they looked at the law as it was and developed a theory from practical

[1] This framework was first developed by TH Jackson, 'Bankruptcy, Non-Bankruptcy Entitlements, and the Creditors' Bargain' (1982) 91(5) Yale L.J. 857. It was further amended in the following papers, including DG Baird and TH Jackson, 'Corporate Reorganisations and the Treatment of Diverse Ownership Interests: A Comment on Adequate Protection of Secured Creditors in Bankruptcy' (1984) 51 U. Chic. L. Rev. 97; and TH Jackson and R Scott, 'On the Nature of Bankruptcy: An Essay on Bankruptcy Sharing and the Creditors' Bargain' (1989) 75 Va. L. Rev. 115.

observations.[2] This criticism is misplaced, as these scholars primarily sought to develop a method that combined the Rawlsian veil of ignorance[3] theory with efficiency considerations[4] to address the problems that insolvency laws have been designed to tackle.

From a normative standpoint, proceduralist visions assume that insolvency law is primarily a debt collection mechanism for the benefit of contractual creditors and that creditors' wealth maximisation is or should be the only legitimate goal. These assumptions are contentious, as such an approach would fail to consider the claims of a wide variety of parties impacted by a debtor's failure.[5]

The proceduralist approach also raises some practical issues. Enforcement of a collectivist approach involves as a pre-emptive condition that parties are willing to agree to freeze or postpone their individual collection rights. This generally occurs because of state-enforced safeguards and the protection of the creditors' ranking in insolvency. The proceduralist understanding of the concept of collectivity may prove difficult to apply to rescue proceedings (i.e. the most obvious outcome for procedures affecting financially distressed local authorities), where the main concern is to ensure that the interests of the general body of creditors take precedence over some claimants' individual rights.[6]

Despite these criticisms, proceduralist scholars are right in claiming that almost all insolvency cases raise the same key issue: there is not enough money to fully repay all creditors (the so-called "common pool problem").[7] To solve

---

2 N Grier, 'Well, What Would You Do? Reflections on the Need for a Theory of Bankruptcy Law' (2021) 32(4) ICCLR 221, 223.

3 J Rawls, *A Theory of Justice* (2nd edn, HUP 1999).

4 Jackson (n 1) 860–866.

5 For a summary of the most controversial theoretical criticisms raised by proceduralist theories in general and creditors' wealth maximisation visions in particular, see: E Warren, 'Bankruptcy Policy' (Summer 1987) 54(3) U. Chi. L. Rev. 775; DR Korobkin, 'Contractarianism and the Normative Foundations of Bankruptcy Law' (1992) 71 Tex. L. Rev. 541. In particular, Korobkin challenged these visions for their inability to recognise non-economic value aspects such as moral, political, social, and personal considerations: DR Korobkin, 'Rehabilitating Values: A Jurisprudence of Bankruptcy' (1991) 91 Col. L. Rev. 717, 762.

6 For an analysis of the evolution of the notion and concept of collectivity in Europe and in England: H Anderson, *The Framework of Corporate Insolvency Law* (OUP 2017) 3.09–3.12.

7 TH Jackson, *The Logics and Limits of Bankruptcy Law* (HUP 1986); Jackson (n 1); DG Baird and TH Jackson, 'Corporate Reorganizations and the Treatment of Diverse Ownership Interests: A Comment on Adequate Protection of Secured Creditors in Bankruptcy' (1984) 51(1) U. Chi. L. Rev. 97; DG Baird and TH Jackson, 'Fraudulent Conveyance Law and its Proper Domain' (1985)

this problem, proceduralist scholars virtually place a group of creditors behind a so-called "transparent veil of ignorance". These creditors know that they are creditors of the company (i.e., their legal status) and, usually, the ranking of their claim (e.g. whether their claim is secured, privileged, subordinated, or unsecured). These creditors are also free to agree on different ways to deal with their claims in insolvency. These creditors are then asked: 'If you were a creditor of a company that is important to you and it was on the brink of failure, what would you do?'. According to proceduralists, any rational person facing such a problem would choose the most efficient solution: collective liquidation.

A race to a debtor's assets upon the initiation of an insolvency procedure would favour the fastest, most skilled, and most sophisticated creditors. However, other claimants would receive nothing, and the race would not maximise the value of an insolvent debtor's assets. If someone must sell an asset as soon as possible, they might be willing to sell at undervalue, provided that the money offered is enough to repay the creditor for whose benefit it is sold.

Consequently, proceduralists argue that a proper system of insolvency rules should aim to maximise the amount received for a debtor's assets and allow the proceeds received to be allocated to that debtor's creditors in a cost-effective[8] and strictly rateable[9] manner. Scholars hold that pre-insolvency entitlements should, in general, be unaffected by a debtor's insolvency, and no new rights should be recognised as a result of a debtor's insolvency. They also contend that if any other approach was followed, the law would create a perverse incentive to file for insolvency procedures. If the distribution hierarchy in place before the opening of any insolvency proceedings was changed by insolvency rules, 'the exchange of values that took place before the insolvency proceeding (e.g. the interest rate charged by the lender for the loan) would lose its foundation'.[10]

38(4) Vanderbilt L. Rev. 829 . For a criticism, see (among others): V Finch and D Milman, *Corporate Insolvency Law: Perspectives and Principles* (3rd edn, CUP 2017), which develops a conceptual framework of "explicit values", and RJ de Weijs, 'Harmonisation of European Insolvency Law and the Need to Tackle Two Common Problems: Common Pool & Anticommons' (2012) 21(2) Int. Insolv. Rev. 67, who warns about the need to address anticommons problems, i.e. situations in which there are several owners or entitled parties, and each of the parties has it within its power to block the use by others.

[8] Jackson (n 1) 862; Anderson (n 6) 3.

[9] R Mokal, 'The Authentic Consent Model: Contractarianism, Creditor's Bargain, and Corporate Liquidation' (2001) 21 J. Leg. Stud. 400, 421.

[10] P von Wilmowsky, 'Insolvency Law: Its Roles and Principles' in A Cordes and MS Beerbühl (eds), *Dealing with Economic Failure. Between Norm and Practice (15th to 21st Century)* (Peter Lang Editions 2016) 256.

Thus, insolvency law should be understood as a set of procedures designed to deal with the collective and efficient liquidation of the debtor's assets, and the distribution of proceeds to its creditors. Its purpose is never to change the terms and conditions of existing contracts. In the end, why should companies be given a free card to sidestep contractual obligations? In addition, why should a company's failing management team rise, phoenix-like from the ashes, through the guise of a restructuring deal?[11]

It has been argued that a purely proceduralist approach would be too efficient in removing companies from the market[12] and too insensitive to the claims of other players affected by the debtor's failure. These players include the society or societies affected by the dissolution, tort claimants, and some non-adjusting creditors.[13] Proceduralism's singular focus prioritises creditors' returns at the expense of any diverging consideration, including public interest[14] or the preservation of value for creditors and the economy.[15] Therefore, especially when dealing with local authorities in financial distress, there is a need to consider the interests of parties overlooked by a purely proceduralist approach. Rather than developing a theoretical framework designed to redistribute wealth,[16] it is possible to mitigate the distortive effects of proceduralism by relying on alternative yet compatible theoretical approaches: the promotion of long-term value-maximising ESG goals during the restructuring process.

2.1.2 Protection of Vulnerable Players and Sustainability

People and companies differ in their resilience towards external disrupting factors. According to the proponents of a vulnerability approach to corporate

---

[11] C Lamont, 'Re-structuring Leasehold Estates under Chapter 11 of the US Bankruptcy Code and in England and Wales—A Comparison' (2018) 31(3) Insolv. Int. 69, 70.

[12] E Vaccari, 'A Modular Approach to Restructuring and Insolvency Law: Executory Contracts and Onerous Property in England and Italy' (2022) 31(5) Norton Journal of Bankruptcy Law and Practice (West) 534.

[13] Finch and Milman (n 7) 31–33. Non-adjusting creditors in insolvency proceedings are creditors whose claims remain fixed and cannot adapt their practices or policies in response to the debtor's increasing risk of insolvency.

[14] M Stubbins, 'What Kind of World Are We Living In? Creditor Wealth Maximisation, Contractarianism or Multiple Value in the Post-Enterprise Act 2002 Insolvency Regime' (2019) 32(2) Insolv. Int. 78, 79.

[15] Lamont (n 11) 70.

[16] Warren (n 5); E Warren, *Chapter 11: Reorganizing American Businesses* (Aspen Publishers 2008).

rescue and insolvency, legislative frameworks should be geared towards protecting non-adjusting, vulnerable creditors.

To assess people's "vulnerability", it is necessary to look at their resilience and ability to recover from losses and failure.[17] This is not the same as human vulnerability or emotional fragility. Resilience is a status that is acquired through institutional relationships regulated by the law. Vulnerability theorists hold an initial assumption that societal relationships and institutions are shaped and modified by the law in many ways. They reject the liberal *de minimis* approach to regulation because they recognise that the state is actively involved in the preservation, modification, and allocation of vulnerability amongst legal subjects.

When vulnerability approaches are applied to proceduralist frameworks, there should be minimal deviations from value-maximising and uniform rules applicable to an insolvent debtor's creditors despite an increased focus on "fairness". If a vulnerability approach leads to significant deviations from proceduralist tenets, then the resulting framework would be based on redistributive concepts that are incompatible with the tenets that underpin most of the insolvency frameworks across the world. We do not advocate for such a significant departure, because we would have to propose a new heuristic of insolvency law before tackling the issues and peculiarities affecting local entities in financial distress.

A vulnerability approach focuses on vulnerable people or a company's resilience to a debtor's failure. It focuses on the social and materially dynamic vulnerable nature of legal subjects. Whilst it is true that certain legal subjects (e.g. banks, vulture funds, etc) are more resilient than others, there is no attempt to single out groups, categories, or classes of contributors. As evidenced in 2007–2009 and again in 2023, the banking system may, at times, be vulnerable.

Local entities are as vulnerable as companies and people because they operate within the same economic ecosystems and face similar financial pressures. Like companies, local authorities rely on steady revenue streams. When these revenue streams falter, local entities experience cash flow problems and budget deficits akin to those faced by struggling businesses. Additionally, local entities are subject to external economic conditions and policy changes that can significantly impact their financial stability. Just as individuals and companies

---

17 MA Fineman, 'The Vulnerable Subject: Anchoring Equality in the Human Condition' (2008) 20(1) YJLF 1; MA Fineman, 'Vulnerability and Inevitable Inequality' (2017) 4(3) Oslo L. Rev. 133, 135. For an application of these theories to the field of corporate insolvency law, see: DR Korobkin, 'Vulnerability, Survival, and the Problem of Small Business Bankruptcy' (1994) 23(2) Capital University L. Rev. 413; JLL Gant, 'Optimising Fairness in Insolvency and Restructuring: A Spotlight on Vulnerable Stakeholders' (2022) 31(2) Int. Insolv. Rev. 1.

can become financially distressed due to job losses or market fluctuations, local authorities can suffer from reduced economic activity and increased demand for public services during economic crises. As local authorities are as vulnerable, if not more vulnerable than other economic players, it is possible to argue that vulnerability-led approaches should be extended to local authorities. A vulnerability-centred insolvency framework would prioritise identifying and addressing the specific vulnerabilities of companies, individuals, and local entities by providing tailored support and interventions aimed at their unique financial challenges. This framework would incorporate mechanisms to enhance resilience, such as targeted financial aid, restructuring options, and protective regulations, ensuring that the most susceptible entities receive the necessary resources to recover and sustain operations. Additionally, it would foster a holistic approach that considers the ESG impacts of insolvency, promoting long-term stability and minimising systemic risks across all levels of the economy.

A vulnerability-led approach is less predictable than a mechanical application of distribution rules, with limited discretion granted to either practitioners or courts to deviate from them. This is because vulnerability-informed deviations do not result in set rules applicable to uniform classes of creditors. They are based on a concrete, purposeful analysis of each claimant's situation, and they result in shared approaches to the analysis of a debtor's stakeholders' individual conditions.[18] They are founded on the need to promote equality rather than discrimination-based visions of an egalitarian society. 'Equality [is] a universal resource, a radical guarantee that is a benefit for all'.[19]

Vulnerability-led approaches in insolvency are characterised by their focus on debtors' specific needs and circumstances, emphasising flexibility and adaptability over rigid procedural rules. These approaches prioritise the identification and support of at-risk entities by considering their unique vulnerabilities and socio-economic contexts. Instead of following a one-size-fits-all procedure, vulnerability frameworks tailor interventions to mitigate the impact of financial distress. This often involves assessing the debtor's capacity for resilience, the potential social repercussions of insolvency, and the provision of customised relief measures aimed at fostering recovery and stability. Whilst these approaches may lack the predictability of procedural frameworks, they

---

[18] In insolvency, a "stakeholder" refers to any individual or group with a vested interest in the outcome of the insolvency process. For a local entity, this includes (among others) creditors, employees, suppliers, customers, shareholders, and the local community, all of whom may be affected by the entity's financial situation and its resolution.

[19] Fineman, 'The Vulnerable Subject' (n 17) 23.

offer a more nuanced and equitable means of addressing financial crises; however, they are not devoid of objectivity and predictability.

Vulnerable players in local authority insolvencies are those who, due to their economic or social position, are less capable of absorbing losses and adapting to changes. They include residents who depend on essential services provided by the local government, employees whose livelihoods depend on municipal employment, and small local businesses that rely on contracts with the authority. The framework should begin with a thorough identification process to pinpoint these vulnerable groups and assess their specific needs and dependencies. Especially for local authorities, the consultation of financial reports and a robust knowledge of the demographics of the local population allow potential investors to identify vulnerable players' key social needs, thus allowing them to conduct effective risk assessment practices before investing.

To enhance the protection of vulnerable players, it may be appropriate to rely on modular approaches when designing an insolvency framework. A modular approach to financial distress in general and in insolvency situations means employing a flexible, component-based system that can be tailored to address different aspects of financial distress based on the specific needs and circumstances of the debtor and creditors involved. This approach has been explored in relation to insolvency specifically by Davis et al[20] and indirectly by Vaccari.[21]

To understand what "modular" means, it may be helpful to think of insolvency law and procedures to address financial distress as a Lego puzzle, with many bricks. Depending on the parties involved in the procedure and the issue at stake, insolvency practitioners and relevant (*ad hoc*) managers will use some of the bricks and tailor their intervention to the affected parties' needs.

Proponents of a modular approach argue that the need for cost-effective and timely procedures requires deviating from the "one-size-fits-all" assumption that has inappropriately informed regulatory insolvency reforms in recent years. Insolvency frameworks should be flexibly and modularly designed to distinguish between viable and non-viable businesses; address issues of crossover of commercial and personal insolvency; and recognise different cultural, social, and economic norms.

A modular approach is especially promising when protecting the interests of special categories of debtors, such as sole entrepreneurs and micro and small

---

[20] RB Davis et al, *Micro, Small and Medium Enterprise Insolvency: A Modular Approach* (OUP 2017).

[21] E Vaccari, 'Insolvency Statutory Rules and Contractual Freedom: A Study on the Limits of Corporate Insolvency Law in the Anglo/American Tradition' (PhD thesis, City, University of London 2018).

enterprises (MSEs).[22] It has also been applied in the context of domestic[23] and cross-border[24] insolvencies, but only with reference to corporate disputes. A modular approach is, consequently, particularly recommended to protect the interests of vulnerable players in insolvency procedures.

Modular approaches are recognised at the international level. In 2017, the World Bank published a study on the treatment of MSEs in insolvency, acknowledging the need for tailored approaches.[25] This prompted the United Nations Commission on International Trade Law (UNCITRAL) Working Group V to start working on simplified rescue and liquidation mechanisms for MSEs; their work resulted in legislative recommendations for the treatment of such entities.[26] These recommendations adopt some of the core principles discussed elsewhere in this book (such as the debtor-in-possession framework) but fall short of providing the comprehensive modular framework advocated by the proponents of this view.

Advocating for vulnerability-informed approaches through "modularism" is, however, not the same as protecting vulnerable players. Equally, introducing a legal remedy under the law is not the same as ensuring its effectiveness.[27] Vulnerability-informed approaches are only possible in fair insolvency frameworks. Fairness is a substantive and procedural concept.[28] Procedural fairness is the propensity to rely on replicable and transparent procedures to deal with the interests of different parties in insolvency procedures. Substantive fairness

---

[22] See also: J Sarra, 'Making Insolvency Law Responsive to the Needs of Financially Distressed Micro and Small Enterprises' in PJ Omar and JLL Gant (eds), *Research Handbook on Corporate Restructuring* (EE Publishing 2021) 246. Businesses are classified into micro, small (and medium) enterprises, usually based on some combination of number of employees, gross revenue, loan size, or assets, with thresholds differing across countries.

[23] L Stanghellini, *Le Crisi di Impresa tra Diritto ed Economia. Le Procedure di Insolvenza* (Il Mulino 2007), with a particular focus on the economic impact of the implementation of law rules.

[24] AB Dawson, 'Modularity in Cross-Border Insolvency' (2018) 93(3) Chi.-Kent L. Rev. 677.

[25] World Bank, *Report on the Treatment of MSEs Insolvency* (Washington DC 2017).

[26] UNCITRAL Legislative Recommendations on Insolvency of Micro and Small Enterprises (2021) <https://uncitral.un.org/sites/uncitral.un.org/files/media-documents/uncitral/en/part_5_en.pdf>.

[27] C Ondersma, 'Overlooked Human Rights Concerns in the Restructuring and Insolvency Context' in PJ Omar and JLL Gant (eds), *Research Handbook on Corporate Restructuring* (EE Publishing 2021) 466.

[28] S Paterson, 'Debt Restructuring and Notions of Fairness' (2017) 80(4) MLR 600.

is the propensity of the system to deviate from "horizontal equity"[29] under the law or when adjudicating disputes between parties with conflicting interests in an insolvency process.

For local authorities,[30] procedural fairness involves creating inclusive decision-making processes where vulnerable players are given a voice.[31] Advisory committees or stakeholder councils, comprising representatives from vulnerable groups, can be formed to provide input on the insolvency process and ensure their concerns are addressed. This participatory approach not only enhances fairness but also improves the legitimacy and acceptance of the insolvency outcomes.[32]

In the context of local authority insolvency, this means prioritising the protection of essential services and employment over the repayment of debts to more resilient creditors such as banks or large financial institutions. For instance, a framework could mandate that before any debt repayments are made, a certain level of funding is secured to maintain critical public services and support vulnerable employees. This prioritisation ensures that the community's basic needs are met even during financial restructuring. A vulnerability approach would ensure that deviations from standard rules are restricted to a limited number of cases, and that public interests are not given general precedence over private rights.[33]

A vulnerability-informed insolvency framework should include specific relief measures tailored to the needs of vulnerable players. For small businesses, this could mean offering extended payment terms or temporary exemptions from certain taxes and fees to help them remain operational. For employees, measures could include job retention schemes, retraining programmes, and guaranteed pension schemes and severance packages. Residents, especially those dependent on social services, should be assured continued access to an

---

29 EE Zajac, *Political Economy of Fairness* (MIT Press 2001) 120.

30 Building on Habermas' deliberative theory (J Habermas, *Between Facts and Norms: Contributions to a Discourse Theory of Law and Democracy* (MIT Press 1996)), see, among others: SA Ercan and CM Hendriks, 'The Democratic Challenges and Potential of Localism: Insights from Deliberative Democracy' (2013) 34(4) PSJ 422.

31 MN Herian et al, 'Public Participation, Procedural Fairness, and Evaluations of Local Governance: The Moderating Role of Uncertainty' (2012) 22(4) JPART 815. In a similar vein, though also identifying risks for exploitation and manipulation, see RJ MacCoun, 'Voice, Control, and Belonging: The Double-Edged Sword of Procedural Fairness' (2005) 1 Annu. Rev. Law Soc. Sci. 171.

32 World Bank, *Principles for Effective Insolvency and Creditor/Debtor Regimes* (Washington DC 2017) principle C7.2.

33 Ibid principle C12.3.

adequate array of accessible essential services such as healthcare, education, and public safety. These services should ensure that those residents who cannot afford to rely on private services find a viable alternative in the public sector.

To ensure the effectiveness of these measures, robust monitoring and support mechanisms should be established. Depending on the countries and their legal traditions, measures that could be explored involve setting up independent oversight bodies tasked with ensuring that vulnerable players' interests are upheld throughout the insolvency process. These bodies could also provide ongoing support and guidance to affected stakeholders, helping them navigate the financial distress and recover more effectively.

A key tenet of the vulnerability approach is the individualised assessment of each claimant's situation. Applying this to local authority insolvency means that each case should be evaluated on its own merits, with sufficiently tailored solutions designed to address specific or group vulnerabilities. This avoids the pitfalls of a one-size-fits-all approach and ensures that each stakeholder group's unique circumstances are considered.

To encourage the correct implementation of vulnerability-informed measures, the framework should include incentives for local authorities that adopt fair practices. This could involve financial incentives from higher levels of government, such as grants or low-interest loans for authorities that successfully protect vulnerable players. Conversely, non-financial penalties for failing to adhere to these principles could be implemented to deter malpractice and ensure accountability.

The development of this framework can be informed by international examples and best practices. For instance, the UNCITRAL[34] Legislative Guide on Insolvency Law emphasises the importance of tailored approaches in handling insolvency to accommodate diverse stakeholder needs.[35] Similarly, there have been calls to incorporate social considerations into financial restructuring processes in Europe.[36]

---

34 The United Nations Commission on International Trade Law (UNCITRAL) was established by the General Assembly in 1966 (Resolution 2205(XXI) of 17 December 1966) as the vehicle by which the United Nations could play a more active role in reducing or removing obstacles to the flow of trade <https://uncitral.un.org/en/about>.

35 UNCITRAL, *UNCITRAL Legislative Guide on Insolvency Law, Parts One and Two* (2004) <https://uncitral.un.org/sites/uncitral.un.org/files/media-documents/uncitral/en/05-80722_ebook.pdf>.

36 European Trade Union Confederation (ETUC), *Overview of Restructuring in Europe* (2007) <https://www.etuc.org/sites/default/files/pdf_CES-Restructuring-EN_def-2_1.pdf>.

Protecting vulnerable players in the insolvency of local authorities requires a balanced approach that combines procedural and substantive fairness with targeted relief measures and robust oversight. By prioritising the needs of those most at risk and ensuring their active participation in the process, the framework can mitigate the adverse impacts of financial distress and promote a more equitable recovery. This approach aligns with the principles of vulnerability theory and fosters a more resilient and inclusive community, capable of withstanding future financial challenges.

2.1.3 CSR Theories and ESG Indicators

The second pillar of our theoretical framework is the reliance on corporate social responsibility (CSR) theories in general, and ESG indicators in particular.

First introduced by Bowen,[37] CSR was described as 'the obligation of businessmen to pursue those policies, to make those decisions, or to follow those lines of action which are desirable in terms of objectives and values of our society'.[38] Generally, CSR is regarded as the actions that a company takes to have a positive impact on society, often with regard to key issues such as climate mitigation and workers' rights. CSR embodies the relationship between a company and its broader context, integrating this relationship into the company's core business and objectives. CSR thus expands the company's central mandate beyond serving shareholders to take into account a wider set of stakeholder interests.[39]

These wider interests have both internal and external dimensions. Internally, CSR includes a focus on the relationship between a company and its employees, how its management takes decisions, transparency in its governance structures, and health and safety standards within its own operations. Externally, CSR focuses on a company's impact on the environment and the community within which it operates, its relationship with its customers and its suppliers, and, with respect to its products, health and safety considerations.

CSR focuses on the ethical and responsible behaviour of an entity towards its stakeholders, including employees, customers, suppliers, and the community. In the context of local public entities, CSR can enhance stakeholder

---

[37] HR Bowen, *Social Responsibilities of the Businessman* (Harper and Row 1953).

[38] Ibid 18.

[39] CSR policies should encourage companies to make socially responsible decisions with a regard to all stakeholders rather than just shareholders: A Okoye, 'Exploring Corporate Social Responsibility from a Law-Jobs Perspective' (2013) 12(1) Contemporary Issues in Law 20.

engagement and support during financial distress. For example, a local government that prioritises fair labour practices, community engagement, and transparent communication can build trust and co-operation from its employees and residents. This support is crucial during restructuring, fostering collaboration and preventing skilled officials' exodus and residents' relocation, preserving the tax base.

Since the 1950s when CSR first emerged, societal expectations have evolved, emphasising the integration of environmental, social, and governance (ESG) factors in corporate decision-making, highlighting sustainability alongside CSR. A distinct set of broad considerations related to an entity's sustainability emerged, known as ESG considerations. The turn to ESG signals an alignment between long-standing CSR business practices and the pursuit of sustainability as a prevailing societal objective, especially considering major international agendas such as the United Nations' Sustainable Development Goals. The adoption of ESG strategies is seen as a 'trending business strategy' of an 'economic transition towards a sustainable economic model'.[40]

ESG is primarily premised on institutional theory and stakeholder theory.[41] It mirrors the internal and external dimensions prevalent in CSR. In institutional theory, ESG factors are seen as influencing behaviour within a company, relating, for example, to executive decisions aimed at improving performance and preventing risk.[42] In stakeholder theory, ESG factors capture the range of stakeholder interests and relate those interests to the company's performance.[43] From these two theoretical perspectives, ESG considerations indicate that 'the production and development of enterprises depend on their legitimate activities in the international and external environments'.[44]

---

[40] Y Ang and T Lambooy, '(Re)Defining Corporate Solvency for Sustainability' (2022) 15(2) International and Comparative Corporate Law Journal 56, 57.

[41] TT Li et al, 'ESG: Research Progress and Future Prospects' (2021) 13(21) Sustainability 11663; AM Habib, 'Do Business Strategies and Environmental, Social, and Governance (ESG) Performance Mitigate the Likelihood of Financial Distress? A Multiple Mediation Model' (2023) 9 Heliyon e17847. Other relevant theories are signalling theory, agency theory, resource dependence theory, attribution theory, transaction cost theory, system justification theory, and social identity theory.

[42] I Tarmuji, R Maelah and NH Tarmuji, 'The Impact of Environmental, Social and Governance Practices (ESG) on Economic Performance: Evidence from ESG Score' (2016) 7(3) IJTEF 67, 68.

[43] Li (n 41); A Citterio and T King, 'The Role of Environmental, Social, and Governance (ESG) in Predicting Bank Financial Distress' (2023) 51 Finance Research Letters 103411.

[44] Li (n 41).

Investors and companies have considered ESG factors for over fifty years, if not always explicitly under the ESG label.[45] For instance, ESG elements are included in the Global Reporting Initiative standards, used by 73% of the world's 250 largest companies[46] to publicly report their activities' impact in a structured and transparent manner. Additionally, rating agencies such as Moody's incorporate ESG into their rating methodologies.[47] ESG considerations have recently become more prominent, influencing consumer and investor behaviour. ESG allows investors to assess the 'non-financial dimensions of a stock's performance'.[48]

ESG has accordingly become an important lens in financial markets, flowing from increased emphasis on responsible investment. The Principles for Responsible Investment describe responsible investment as 'considering environmental, social and governance (ESG) issues when making investment decisions and influencing companies or assets (known as active ownership or stewardship). It complements traditional financial analysis and portfolio construction techniques.'[49] Within responsible investment, ESG considerations serve as a non-financial measure of an entity's sustainability, its long-term, future financial performance and hence its risk profile. They are also a tangible measure of companies' CSR practices.[50] ESG risks and measurements affect finance availability through traditional risk assessments and investors' focus on ethical, socially responsible investments.[51]

---

[45] S Turner, 'Corporate Law, Directors' Duties and ESG Interventions: Analysing Pathways towards Positive Corporate Impacts relating to ESG Issues' (2020) 4 JBL 245.

[46] The Global Reporting Initiative (GRI), 'The GRI Standards—A Guide for Policy Makers' (2020) 7 <https://www.globalreporting.org/media/nmmnwfsm/gri-policymakers-guide.pdf>.

[47] Moody's, 'General Principles for Assessing Environmental, Social and Governance Risks' (28 September 2023) <www.moodys.com/research/doc--PBC_1355824>.

[48] E van Duuren, A Plantinga and B Scholtens, 'ESG Integration and the Investment Management Process: Fundamental Investing Reinvented' (2016) 138 J. Bus. Ethics 525.

[49] Principles for Responsible Investment (PRI), 'What is Responsible Investment' <https://www.unpri.org/introductory-guides-to-responsible-investment/what-is-responsible-investment/4780.article>.

[50] A Lisin et al, 'Financial Stability in Companies with High ESG Scores: Evidence from North America Using the Ohlson O-Score' (2022) 14(1) Sustainability 479.

[51] M Zioło et al, 'How Do Environmental, Social, and Governance (ESG) Factors Impact on Public Finance Performance? Risk, Efficiency, and Public

Financial market regulatory frameworks now include ESG factors, such as the EU's Sustainable Finance Disclosure Regulation[52] requiring financial market participants to disclose sustainability risk policies and adverse impacts of investment decisions on sustainability factors. The Regulation defines sustainability risks and sustainability factors.[53] Acting under the EU directive on credit institutions[54] and the Capital Requirements Regulation,[55] the European Banking Authority is developing guidelines on minimum standards and reference methodologies for the identification, measurement, management and monitoring of ESG.[56]

To date, no single set of ESG definitions or metrics has, however, found wide acceptance across all sectors. As a result, '[t]he potential credit impact of many ESG considerations is challenging to assess because it must often be inferred or estimated from multiple sources based on reporting that generally is not standardised or consistent'.[57] Some literature[58] also questions whether ESG and CSR measures should outweigh shareholders' views and there is

---

Financial System Perspectives' in A Bem et al (eds), *Sustainable Finance in the Green Economy* (Springer 2022) 262.

52 Regulation (EU) 2019/2088 of the European Parliament and of the Council of 27 November 2029 on sustainability-related disclosures in the financial services sector [2019] OJ L 317.

53 Article 2(22) defines "sustainability risk" as 'an environmental, social or governance event or condition that, if it occurs, could cause an actual or a potential material negative impact on the value of the investment' and article 2(24) defines "sustainability factors" as 'environmental, social and employee matters, respect for human rights, anti-corruption and anti-bribery matters'.

54 Directive 2013/36/EU of the European Parliament and of the Council of 26 June 2013 on access to the activity of credit institutions and the prudential supervision of credit institutions and investment firms [2013] OJ L 176.

55 Regulation EU/575/2013 of the European Parliament and of the Council of 26 June 2013 on prudential requirements for credit institutions and investment firms [2013] OJ L 176.

56 European Banking Authority (EBA), 'Draft Guideline on the Management of ESG Risks' EBA Consultation Paper (EBA/CP/2024/02, 18 January 2024) <https://www.eba.europa.eu/sites/default/files/2024-01/c94fd865-6990-4ba8-b74e-6d8ef73d8ea5/Consultation%20papaer%20on%20draft%20Guidelines%20on%20ESG%20risks%20management.pdf>.

57 Moody's (n 47).

58 C Jung, 'Sustainable Corporate Governance in the United Kingdom: Environmental Sustainability in Directors' Decision-Making' (2022) Frankfurt University of Applied Sciences Working Paper no. 25 <https://hdl.handle.net/10419/263241>.

ongoing debate about the correlation between ESG measurement and company performance.[59]

Despite the absence of a single set of ESG metrics and the need to rely on qualitative judgements, ESG presents a stable framework for measurement across its three pillars.[60] Within the corporate and financial contexts, ESG offers one of the best-developed tools for measuring an entity's pursuit of sustainability.[61]

The "environmental" pillar of ESG refers to an organisation's ecological impact and sustainability practices, emphasising a company's interaction with the natural environment, its efforts to manage resources efficiently, reduce carbon footprints, and mitigate environmental risks. Key aspects include energy use, waste management, pollution control, biodiversity conservation, and climate change mitigation strategies.[62] The environmental component assesses companies on their environmental policies and performance, such as their use of renewable energy sources, greenhouse gas emissions, and adherence to environmental regulations.[63] It also relates to the potential risks arising from regulatory or policy initiatives, that seek to reduce pollution and environmental hazards.

ESG's "social" pillar focuses on companies' interaction with their social environment. Key social considerations focus on employment such as working conditions, child and forced labour, workplace health and safety, inclusivity and diversity in employment practices, and workers' freedom of association.[64] Social factors also examine health and safety in relation to a company's products.

---

59 Li (n 41); Tarmuji (n 42); Lisin et al (n 50).

60 Among others, see: M Aluchna, M Roszkowska-Menkes and M Bogumil Kaminski, 'From Talk to Action: The Effects of the Non-financial Reporting Directive on ESG Performance' (2023) 31(7) Meditari Accountancy Research 1.

61 Tarmuji (n 42). See also the EU Taxonomy, which is a comprehensive classification system that provides definitions of what is environmentally sustainable economic activities: European Commission, 'EU Taxonomy Navigator' <https://ec.europa.eu/sustainable-finance-taxonomy/>.

62 The rating agency Moody's, for instance, classifies the environmental risks that are most relevant from a credit perspective in carbon transition; physical climate risks; water management; waste and pollution; and natural capital: Moody's (n 47) 9–10.

63 World Economic Forum, 'Measuring Stakeholder Capitalism: Towards Common Metrics and Consistent Reporting of Sustainable Value Creation' (22 September 2020) <https://www.weforum.org/publications/measuring-stakeholder-capitalism-towards-common-metrics-and-consistent-reporting-of-sustainable-value-creation/>.

64 Moody's (n 47); Li (n 41).

The third ESG pillar, "governance", encompasses factors relating to entities' internal organisation (such as board structure, executive compensation, and shareholder rights), to their external relationships with third parties (such as clients or users), and to some factors that straddle the internal/external divide (such as principles and ethical conduct, including anti-corruption measures). Effective governance ensures that companies are managed in stakeholders' best interests, including shareholders, employees, customers, and the community at large. It promotes transparency, accountability, and fairness in corporate decision-making and ideally aligns management's interests with those of the broader stakeholder group.

Strong corporate governance builds investor confidence and ensures long-term sustainability through oversight mechanisms like independent board committees, financial audits, and risk management. It includes anti-corruption, regulatory compliance, and CSR, helping companies navigate legal and ethical challenges and foster integrity. Stakeholders increasingly demand high governance standards to ensure responsible, ethical business conduct, especially after corporate and financial crises.

Some literature questions whether ESG and CSR measures should outweigh shareholders' views. Nevertheless, it is generally accepted that companies that consider both ESG and CSR factors in their decision-making process achieve more sustainable and responsible goals. Such factors feature prominently in determining investor and consumer spending.

CSR strategies and ESG factors aim to enhance sustainability, serving as valuable conceptual tools for public entities to address economic challenges. ESG indicators may impact public entities' access to private finance at a time of increasing pressure on public budgets whilst local public entities also seem particularly exposed to ESG risks.[65]

ESG indicators are critical tools in restructuring local entities in financial distress because they promote sustainable recovery and long-term viability. Integrating ESG principles into restructuring ensures financial solutions are economically sound, socially responsible, and environmentally sustainable, maintaining public trust and support.

ESG indicators offer a comprehensive framework for evaluating and improving local entities' sustainability and resilience. The environmental aspect helps mitigate risks like pollution and resource depletion, reducing costs and liabilities. Energy-efficient practices and sustainable resource management make distressed municipalities more attractive to investors and creditors.

ESG's social component emphasises the importance of social equity and community well-being. During restructuring, attention to social factors such

---

65 Zioło et al (n 51).

as public health, education, and housing can prevent exacerbating existing social issues and ensure that recovery efforts benefit all community members. Local entities that prioritise social sustainability are better positioned to maintain social cohesion and support, which are essential for successful restructuring and long-term recovery.

The governance aspect of ESG focuses on robust governance structures, transparency, and accountability. Good governance is critical during restructuring as it enhances decision-making processes, reduces corruption risks, and ensures that restructuring plans are implemented effectively. For example, transparent governance practices can improve creditor confidence and facilitate access to financing. Additionally, strong governance can help fairly distribute resources and ensure that the interests of all stakeholders are considered, reducing potential conflicts and fostering a co-operative approach to restructuring.

A final point on ESG relates to the need for variability. Turner[66] considers that to effectively implement mandatory ESG policies for businesses, it is important to distinguish between the 'overall legal construct' of different companies. Turner outlines three different types of ESG initiatives: reputational initiatives, legal compliance initiatives and legal construct initiatives. He explains that individual companies would benefit from different models depending on their size and structure. It follows that variability in mandatory ESG policies could facilitate a better fit between individual entities and ESG indicators. This argument could be extended to the way local entities operate, recognising the notable contextual differences between these entities and the ESG factors relevant to them.

2.1.4 Concluding Remarks

Incorporating vulnerability, CSR and ESG indicators into the restructuring process of local entities aligns with global best practices and regulatory expectations. Moreover, adhering to such practices can help local entities retain the critical support of local stakeholders during restructuring processes.

In conclusion, integrating these indicators into the restructuring of local entities in financial distress is essential to achieve their sustainable and equitable recovery. By focusing on ethical behaviour, environmental sustainability, social equity, and robust governance, local entities can build resilience, foster stakeholder trust, and secure the financial support needed for long-term viability.

---

66 Turner (n 45).

2.2 ENVIRONMENTAL INDICATORS

Environmental indicators are critically important because they address how an entity's operations impact the natural world. Environmental indicators include climate change adaptation and mitigation strategies,[67] carbon footprint reduction, waste management, resource depletion, and energy efficiency. Entities that prioritise environmental sustainability are not only helping to combat global issues like climate change and pollution but also positioning themselves to be more resilient in the face of regulatory changes and resource scarcity. By integrating environmental considerations into their operational models, companies and local entities can reduce costs, improve efficiency, expand their business[68] and create innovative solutions that can lead to new market opportunities.

Additionally, the emphasis on environmental responsibility can significantly boost reputation and stakeholder relations. This shift in stakeholder preferences can drive long-term financial performance and stability, as companies and local entities that manage their environmental impact are often seen as less risky and more forward-thinking. Furthermore, focusing on environmental sustainability can lead to better compliance with environmental regulations, reducing the risk of fines and legal issues, and enhancing overall corporate governance. This proactive approach not only benefits the environment, but also fosters a culture of responsibility and ethical behaviour within an entity, ultimately contributing to its success and longevity.

---

[67] "Climate adaptation" is the process of adjusting to the actual or expected effects of climate change. "Climate mitigation" refers to actions or activities that limit emissions of greenhouse gases (GHGs) from entering the atmosphere and/or reduce their levels in the atmosphere: European Environmental Agency, 'What Is the Difference Between Adaptation and Mitigation?' (30 October 2023) <https://www.eea.europa.eu/en/about/contact-us/faqs/what-is-the-difference-between-adaptation-and-mitigation#:~:text=In%20essence%2C%20adaptation%20can%20be,of%20climate%20change%20less%20severe>.

[68] For instance, the EU directive on public procurement stresses at several points that companies should comply with ESG standards, and that national and local authorities should monitor on their compliance: Directive 2014/24/EU of the European Parliament and of the Council of 26 February 2014 on public procurement and repealing Directive 2004/18/EC Text with EEA relevance [2014] OJ L 94. Article 18 (2) requires compliance with environmental and social legal requirements; corruption is dealt with in provisions such as article 57 (1).

Therefore, it is crucial to analyse the role that environmental considerations play in insolvency and restructuring procedures,[69] even if at times the goals of insolvency and environmental law seem conflicting.[70] After an overview of the role that insolvency law can play to create a robust incentive structure for companies to adapt to climate change and reduce their carbon emissions during liquidation (2.2.1) and restructuring (2.2.2) proceedings, this sub-section will refer to country-specific examples to discuss the role of environmental concerns in the restructuring of local entities in financial distress (2.2.3).

2.2.1 Liquidation Proceedings

Several insolvency provisions directly or indirectly impact a debtor's environmental footprint. This section examines the rules concerning disclaimers, asset distribution, and directors' and stakeholders' liability. These provisions, relevant during liquidation proceedings, influence how companies and local entities operate during solvent times, especially in their approach to incorporating environmental indicators into their long-term strategies.

The rules regulating disclaimers are among those that have a direct impact on a debtor's carbon footprint and on its likelihood of incorporating environmental considerations into its long-term strategies.

A disclaimer of assets refers to the formal rejection or abandonment of certain assets by the debtor. This action is typically taken when the assets in question are either onerous or of negligible value, making them a liability to the insolvent estate. By disclaiming a property, the insolvent estate relinquishes all liabilities (including clean-up costs and ongoing environmental obligations) to the collectivity and externalises costs on society at large. When countries facilitate the disclaimer of assets in liquidation, debtors have few incentives to incorporate environmental indicators into their long-term strategies.

To mitigate this risk, countries can adopt several strategies. One approach is to mandate that available funds in the insolvent estate must first be used to meet clean-up or remediation costs associated with disclaimed assets. This ensures that environmental liabilities are addressed upfront, minimising the potential for such costs to be shifted onto taxpayers or future generations. Implementing such a requirement would incentivise debtors to consider

---

[69] This has been done in the past, even if from different theoretical assumptions: KJ Koks and T Million, 'Environmental Issues in Bankruptcy' (2009/2010) 40 Texas Environmental Law Journal 43; IM Hillinger and MG Hillinger, 'Environmental Affairs in Bankruptcy' (2004) 12 ABI L. Rev. 33.

[70] HH Hill, 'Bankruptcy v Environmental Protection: A Case Study in Normative Conflict' (1998) 16 CJLJ 245.

environmental impacts early in their financial planning and could encourage more responsible behaviour towards the environment.

Another strategy involves restricting or prohibiting the disclaimer of assets with significant environmental pollution risks altogether. This approach has been exemplified by the Canadian Supreme Court,[71] which prevented trustees from disclaiming obligations to decommission oil wells and other assets requiring environmental remediation. By enforcing such restrictions, jurisdictions can uphold the principle that polluters should bear the costs of environmental damage they cause, aligning with the "polluter pays" principle and promoting accountability.

Additionally, countries can extend disclaimers to restructuring procedures. This broader application would ensure that environmental considerations remain integral across various stages of insolvency, preventing debtors from circumventing responsibilities during attempts to reorganise or recover financially.

Reforming the rules on disclaimers contributes to ensuring that financial distress does not translate into lasting environmental harm.

In terms of the rules regulating the distribution of assets, it is appropriate to focus on those establishing preferential treatments for certain categories of claims. It could be possible to grant super-priority status to environmental claims, ensuring these obligations are fulfilled and remediation effected before other debts. Responsible creditors and investors would ensure that debtors have no outstanding environmental liabilities, as otherwise such liabilities will be paid in preference to their claims. As a result, such a provision could promote compliance with environmental indicators through responsible practices and investments in cleaner technologies.

Another approach might involve climate or pollution risk insurance. However, insurers may be unwilling to cover certain climate-related risks[72]

---

71 *Orphan Well Association v Grant Thornton Ltd* (2019) SCC 5 (Sup Ct (Can)), as commented on by T Farber, 'Insolvency and Environmental Law Collide in Canada: Supreme Court of Canada Rules in Favour of Environmental Protection over the Interests of Secured Creditors' (2019) 16(4) Int. C.R. 225.

72 For instance, in the US, certain insurers are exiting certain markets due to the high risks of occurrence of certain natural events: S Delouya, 'It's Hurricane Season. Good Luck Getting Affordable Homeowners' Insurance' *CNN* (Atlanta, 1 June 2024) <https://edition.cnn.com/2024/06/01/economy/homeowners-insurance-cost-hurricane-weather/index.html>. If people, companies and local entities can insure themselves and their properties against environmental and climate-related risks, it is likely that the insurance premiums will be high and/or hardly affordable. See also footnote 268 in chapter 3 (United States).

and/or operate in developing markets.[73] Governments and creditors may compel entities to obtain insurance against climate-related risks if they operate in a certain sector (e.g. public sector).[74] Such an approach would be preferable to forms of "self-insurance",[75] where the entity guarantees—either by setting aside assets or by obtaining third-party backing—against environment-related risks. Mandatory insurance would result in more widespread compliance with environmental indicators.

Ringfencing funds for environmental costs is another effective strategy. This involves setting aside a portion of proceeds from the sale of secured assets specifically for environmental and tort liabilities.[76] Firms and local entities may also be asked to contribute to climate-remedial funds on a regular basis, thus ensuring that resources are available for remediation in case of financial distress. Whilst no-fault compensation funds may address the risk of

---

73 Insurance markets are generally underdeveloped in emerging markets and developing economies (EMDEs). See, among others: S Hallegatte et al, 'Bank Stress Testing of Physical Risks under Climate Change Macro Scenarios: Typhoon Risks to the Philippines' (2022) IMF Working Paper, WP/22/163 <https://www.imf.org/en/Publications/WP/Issues/2022/08/19/Bank-Stress-Testing-of-Physical-Risks-under-Climate-Change-Macro-Scenarios-Typhoon-Risks-to-522486>.

74 This is known as "environmental impairment liability insurance", which is at times compulsory in countries like the People's Republic of China and South Korea: A Lu et al, 'Focus: Environmental Liability' (2018) Oct 1 L.L.I.D. 4.

75 V Fogleman, *Environmental Liabilities and Insurance in England and the United States, Part A* (1st edn, Witherbys 2005) 114; C Mackie and V Fogleman, 'Self-insuring Environmental Liabilities: A Residual Risk-bearer's Perspective' (2016) 16(2) J. Corp. Law Stud. 293. See also: Department for Environment, Food and Rural Affairs (DEFRA), 'Government Response to Consultation on Enhanced Enforcement Powers and Other Measures to Tackle Waste Crime and Entrenched Poor Performance in the Waste Management Industry' (October 2015) 33 <https://assets.publishing.service.gov.uk/government/uploads/system/uploads/attachment_data/file/466879/waste-crime-consult-sum-resp.pdf>, where DEFRA noted views that '...operators and liquidators should be held responsible for ongoing compliance with an environmental permit which should not be capable of being disclaimed'; Directive 2006/21/EC on the management of waste from extractive industries [2006] OJ L102/15, art 14 (the 'Mining Waste Directive'); Council Directive 1999/31/EC on the landfill of waste [1999] OJ L182/1 (the 'Landfill Directive'), art 8(a)(iv); Directive 2009/31/EC on the geological storage of carbon dioxide [2009] OJ L140/114, art 19(1).

76 On how tort law can contribute to combatting climate change, see (among others): AG Castermans, 'The PETL and Corporate Liability for Greenhouse Gas Emissions: Duties and Remedies' (2024) 15(1) JETL 63.

uninsured and technically uninsurable losses,[77] ringfencing would arguably have limited impact in proactively pursuing any of the environmental indicators listed above.

Countries could reform their rules on directors' and stakeholders' liability to reduce the risk that insolvent entities (including local authorities) externalise environmental costs. These measures could include expanding directors' liability in insolvency procedures, lifting the corporate veil to hold parent companies accountable,[78] limiting third-party releases in insolvency, and strengthening punitive measures for misconduct. Such reforms would ensure greater accountability, foster more responsible corporate behaviour, and promote sustainable business practices aligned with climate mitigation goals.

Firstly, there is evidence that courts are moving away from a shareholder-centred approach where the debtor is insolvent or bordering insolvency.[79] In one of the most contentious wrongful trading cases of recent times, the UK High Court held that directors can be held liable for insolvency-deepening activity, and may lead to significant awards for failure to discharge their duties.[80]

By acting this way, countries can incentivise directors to prioritise environmental considerations in their decision-making processes,[81] unless they want to face the prospect of personal financial loss. Consequently, this would encourage a shift towards more sustainable operational models, aligning the entities' actions with broader climate mitigation objectives.

Secondly, lifting the corporate veil can also be a promising avenue. Often, parent entities may use subsidiaries to conduct environmentally damaging activities whilst shielding themselves from liability. By enabling courts to hold parent entities responsible—as it happened in recent landmark corporate cases

---

[77] K Watts, T Vansweevelt and B Weyts, 'Climate Change, Compensation and Unpredictable or Uninsurable Loss: A Possible Path Forward Using Compensation Funds' (2023) 14(3) JETL 316.

[78] In the public sector, this may involve holding councils accountable for the environmental damage caused by the subsidiaries they created to deliver essential public services to local communities.

[79] *BTI 2014 LLC v Sequana SA and Ors* [2022] UKSC 25.

[80] *Wright & Ors v Chappell & Ors (Re BHS Group Ltd & Ors (in liquidation))* [2024] EWHC 1417 (Ch). It is understood that the directors are seeking permission to appeal this judgment.

[81] There is evidence that such policies are being considered by lawmakers, especially when irresponsible directors' behaviour leads to environmental damage: M Bow and L Barr, 'Starmer Vows to Make Underperforming Water Bosses "Personally Responsible"' *The Telegraph* (London, 11 July 2024) <https://www.telegraph.co.uk/business/2024/07/11/thames-water-bills-rise-by-99-year/>.

in the UK[82]—regulators can ensure that these entities cannot evade their environmental responsibilities. This legal approach would promote better oversight and control over subsidiary operations, encouraging investment in greener technologies and practices, and reducing environmentally harmful activities.

In the same area, establishing that actions causing environmental damage constitutes "impropriety" justifying the piercing of the corporate veil would be effective when coupled with measures like limits to disclaimers and preferential treatment of environmental remedial costs. Moreover, governments should strengthen punitive measures for directors' misconduct. These could include revising transaction avoidance rules to target transfers made to benefit from environmentally polluting activities and restricting the scope of the *ex turpi causa* principle, allowing companies and liquidators to recover losses caused by directors' fraud or unlawful conduct.[83] Such measures would ensure that directors and stakeholders do not reap benefits from polluting activities, promoting more responsible corporate behaviour and the pursuit of the environmental goals/indicators listed at the beginning of this section.[84]

To summarise, much more can be done to ensure that corporate insolvency systems are more resilient to climate change and promote more sustainable and environmentally friendly practices. However, none of the mechanisms discussed above is sufficient, either in itself or even as a group, to ensure that corporations adopt all the necessary steps to minimise and internalise environmental risks. This is why governments should be prepared to step in to carry out remedial works, ensuring that critical actions are not delayed due to the financial incapacity of insolvent firms. This intervention should be a last resort, triggered only when no other remedies are sufficient to mitigate environmental damage. However, especially in liquidation procedures characterised by scarcity of funding, the possibility of such an intervention cannot be dismissed *ex ante*.

---

[82] *Lungowe v Vedanta Resources plc* [2019] UKSC 20; *HRH Okpabi v Royal Dutch Shell* [2021] UKSC 3.

[83] Fraud and negligence are legal concepts interpreted differently across jurisdictions. ESG indicators aim to overcome these national differences by developing transnational standards, providing consistent information for investors regardless of local laws.

[84] These questions lead to consider how humans make decisions in the face of complexity and incomplete information. They would deserve a book long analysis on their own. In particular the interactions between ethical decisions, cognitive frames and criminal law are currently gaining attention in legal scholarship (see for instance: MS Pardo and D Patterson, *Minds, Brains, and Law* (OUP 2013)). As this book focuses on local municipalities, we will not pursue this discussion here.

2.2.2 Restructuring Proceedings

Restructuring proceedings also play a crucial role in ensuring that environmental liabilities are not externalised on society at large, and that the restructuring deal promotes the long-term sustainability of the distressed entity. In restructuring processes, several techniques can be employed to achieve broader compliance with environmental indicators. In this section, we look in particular at distribution rules applicable in rescue procedures; mechanisms to ensure access to transparent and accessible information; the incorporation of ESG goals in restructuring processes; and, finally, granting a super-priority status to rescue financing.

An obvious recommendation in the area could consist of extending the restrictive rules on distribution of assets (including those on insurance, where relevant)[85] and prioritisation of creditors from liquidation to restructuring procedures. This can be achieved by requiring judicial scrutiny whenever there is a need to "cram down" environmental claims, thereby preventing firms and local entities from strategically using rescue procedures to evade their environmental obligations. Statutory securities for remedial costs can also be created, guaranteeing that specific assets are allocated for environmental remediation.

Prohibiting the restructuring of environmental liabilities ensures these obligations remain inviolable and must be fully addressed during financial restructuring. This prevents local entities from negotiating down their environmental responsibilities to benefit other creditors, maintaining the integrity of environmental remediation efforts. Such a measure discourages environmentally harmful practices. However, it should be applied carefully and flexibly, to avoid disincentivising restructuring efforts.

Restructuring rules should also promote the transfer of transparent and accessible information to all stakeholders involved in these procedures. Mandatory climate risk assessments, non-binding guidelines, and sustainability counselling in restructuring procedures are critical for global climate mitigation strategies. By mandating climate risk assessments, organisations are required to evaluate and disclose their exposure to climate-related risks, ensuring transparency and enabling stakeholders to understand the environmental impact and potential financial risks associated with corporate activities.

Rescue law applicable to local entities can promote access to transparent information by leveraging international conventions and frameworks that

---

85 As explained above *sub* 2.2.1, insurers may be unwilling to cover against some environmental risks, or they may only provide coverage subject to high premiums. Compulsory insurances may address such risks, if the state is willing to indemnify insurers against excessive losses and if the insurance market is properly regulated.

emphasise public participation and transparency in environmental matters. The Aarhus Convention,[86] to which the UK is a signatory, mandates public access to environmental information, public participation in decision-making, and access to justice in environmental matters. This ensures that during financial restructurings, local entities are held accountable to provide transparent information about their environmental obligations and initiatives, fostering public trust and compliance with environmental standards. Similarly, Latin America has adopted the Escazú Agreement,[87] which parallels the Aarhus Convention in promoting transparency and public engagement.

The importance of transparent information in environmental protection is well-documented in legal scholarship. Morrow's work on informational requirements in environmental protection underscores the critical role of transparency in ensuring effective environmental governance.[88] Furthermore, other scholars have highlighted mechanisms by which international environmental law enforces transparency and accountability.[89] These frameworks and scholarly insights illustrate how rescue laws can integrate robust transparency measures, thereby enhancing public oversight and ensuring that local entities adhere to their environmental commitments during financial restructurings.

Mandatory climate risk assessments compel entities to proactively identify and address potential climate-related hazards, enhancing their resilience against climate change. The Task Force on Climate-related Financial Disclosures (TCFD) emphasises that consistent and comparable disclosures enable better decision-making by investors and other stakeholders.[90] Additionally, compliance with stringent environmental regulations, such as the European Union's Sustainable Finance Disclosure Regulation (SFDR),

---

86 UNECE Convention on Access to Information, Public Participation in Decision-making and Access to Justice in Environmental Matters (Aarhus Convention) (1998) <https://unece.org/environment-policy/public-participation/aarhus-convention/text>.

87 <https://treaties.un.org/pages/ViewDetails.aspx?src=TREATY&mtdsg_no=XXVII-18&chapter=27&clang=_en>.

88 K Morrow, 'Informational Requirements and Environmental Protection' in E Lees and JE Viñuales (eds), *The Oxford Handbook of Comparative Environmental Law* (OUP 2019).

89 T Sparks and A Peters, 'Part VIII: Compliance, Implementation, and Effectiveness—Transparency Procedures' in L Rajamani and J Peel (eds), *The Oxford Handbook of International Environmental Law* (2nd edn, OUP 2021).

90 Task Force on Climate-related Financial Disclosure (TCFD), 'Final Report. Recommendations of the Task Force on Climate-related Financial Disclosure' (June 2017) <https://assets.bbhub.io/company/sites/60/2021/10/FINAL-2017-TCFD-Report.pdf>.

is facilitated by mandatory assessments, reducing the likelihood of legal and financial penalties.[91]

Non-binding guidelines and sustainability counselling provide a flexible framework for companies and local entities to incorporate sustainability into their operations and strategic planning. If guidelines similar to those from the United Nations Global Compact applied to local entities, they would promote better compliance with environmental indicators. Sustainability counselling during restructuring ensures that environmental considerations remain a priority even during financial or operational transitions, preventing backsliding on climate commitments. The International Labour Organization (ILO) highlights the importance of integrating sustainability into restructuring processes to achieve a just transition towards a green economy.[92]

Incorporating ESG goals into restructuring procedures can significantly advance some of the environmental indicators listed above, including particularly the promotion of climate mitigation policies. Recent restructuring proceedings have addressed large liability claims from wildfires caused by a debtor company's faulty equipment,[93] demonstrating the integration of ESG standards in distressed asset investing and restructurings. This integration involves embedding ESG into business plans, reporting requirements, board composition, executive compensation, and financial modelling. Outside of restructuring, legislative measures like the European Union's Stewardship Code for asset managers and the Corporate Sustainability Reporting Directive[94] show the importance of ESG in corporate practices, making its implementation in restructuring a logical next step.

Embedding ESG and climate mitigation policies in restructuring processes presents new opportunities, but also requires multidisciplinary expertise from restructuring professionals and investors. Despite the potential benefits, there is reluctance to apply ESG criteria in restructuring procedures, as highlighted

---

[91] Regulation (EU) 2019/2088 of the European Parliament and of the Council of 27 November 2019 on sustainability-related disclosures in the financial services sector (SFDR) [2019] OJ L 317.

[92] International Labour Organisation, 'Guidelines for a Just Transition Towards Environmentally Sustainable Economies and Societies for All' (Switzerland, 2015) 5 <https://www.ilo.org/publications/guidelines-just-transition-towards-environmentally-sustainable-economies>.

[93] *In re PG&E Corporation, Bankruptcy Case No. 19-30088* (DM) (US Bankruptcy Court for the Northern District of California, San Francisco Division).

[94] Directive (EU) 2022/2464 of the European Parliament and of the Council of 14 December 2022 amending Regulation (EU) No 537/2014, Directive 2004/109/EC, Directive 2006/43/EC and Directive 2013/34/EU, as regards corporate sustainability reporting [2022] OJ L 322.

by a study from INSOL International.[95] Some argue for unbundling climate change mitigation from ESG by introducing a net-zero transition rating (NZT Rating), which would specifically measure the debtors' efforts in addressing climate change risks, allowing for auditing and closer monitoring of the implementation of the measures contributing to reducing greenhouse gas (GHG) emissions. This approach, alongside traditional ESG ratings, could ensure that climate mitigation strategies gain prominence in the financial statements prepared by local entities on a regular basis.

Ensuring better compliance with environmental practices during the restructuring of a local entity in financial distress can be achieved by offering investors lower interest rates on loans for green initiatives. This financial incentive makes environmentally focused projects, such as reducing the energy consumption of buildings and updating the council's transport vehicles to be eco-friendlier, more attractive and feasible. By reducing the cost of borrowing, the local entity can allocate more resources towards these sustainable efforts, thereby improving its environmental impact.

Targeted investments in green projects ensure that the funds are used effectively to promote sustainability. For instance, loans with lower interest rates can be designated for upgrading buildings to improve energy efficiency, purchasing electric buses, or installing renewable energy systems. This focused allocation not only helps in achieving environmental goals but also demonstrates to investors and stakeholders a commitment to sustainability, potentially enhancing the entity's reputation and future investment prospects.

Entities undergoing restructuring must have access to sufficient funds, either as interim or new financing. Interim financing acts as a bridge fund during the negotiation period out of financial distress, whilst new financing is necessary to implement the restructuring plan. Some laws grant super-priority status to rescue financing, meaning that lenders are prioritised over existing unsecured, preferential, and sometimes secured lenders in the event of default during the restructuring process.

Certain jurisdictions, such as the US[96] and Singapore,[97] have comprehensive regulations on rescue financing. The European Union's Preventive Restructuring Directive[98] mandates member states to protect new and interim financing, ensuring a minimum level of protection, although it does not enforce US-style super priority rescue financing provisions. Despite the potential

[95] INSOL International, *ESG in Restructuring* (INSOL International 2023).

[96] 11 US Code, § 364.

[97] Insolvency, Restructuring and Dissolution Act 2018, s 67.

[98] Council of Europe, Recommendation 510 (2024) on local and regional responses to natural disasters and climate hazards <https://rm.coe.int/rec-510-2024-en-local-and-regional-responses-to-natural-disasters-jean/1680af1be5>.

benefits, no jurisdiction currently links super-priority rescue financing to the promotion of environmental indicators, even though inclusive green finance is a promising approach to mitigating climate change.

Granting super-priority status to rescue finance can significantly promote climate mitigation strategies by ensuring preferential funding for projects aimed at reducing carbon emissions and enhancing sustainability. This status elevates the repayment hierarchy of climate-focused loans, reducing financial risks for lenders and encouraging investment in green projects. International organisations like the International Monetary Fund (IMF) and the World Bank emphasise innovative financial mechanisms to tackle climate change, highlighting that targeted financial policies can mobilise capital for climate action. By lowering the risk premium on green investments, super-priority status helps reduce the overall cost of capital, facilitating greater investment in renewable energy, sustainable investments, and other climate mitigation initiatives, thus aligning with the Paris Agreement's objectives and fostering a sustainable economic transition.

It seems, therefore, that—like liquidation frameworks—current restructuring rules could be amended to promote wider compliance with environmental indicators. The next section looks at how these solutions could be successfully implemented in the management of a local authority in financial distress.

2.2.3 Municipalities in Distress

Ensuring better compliance with environmental indicators during the restructuring or liquidation of a local authority in financial distress is crucial for sustainable development. Mechanisms such as adopting climate change adaptation and mitigation strategies, reducing carbon footprints, improving waste management, managing resource depletion, and enhancing energy efficiency are essential. The Council of Europe's recent recommendations, such as those from the 46th session on local and regional responses to natural disasters and climate hazards,[99] underscore the importance of integrating resilience into local governance. These recommendations provide a valuable framework for incorporating environmental considerations into municipal restructuring processes.

Nevertheless, at the municipal level, environmental considerations generally play a very limited role in the restructuring of an entity in financial

[99] Ibid. See also document CG(2024)46-17, explanatory memorandum, co-rapporteurs Jean-Paul BASTIN, Belgium (L, EPP/CCE); Christian DEBEVE, France (R, ILDG).

distress. This is in contrast to what happens for social and governance issues, as explained below *sub* 2.4.2 and 2.5.3.

With reference to environmental indicators, one innovative approach is the issuance of environmental impact bonds, which can finance projects that directly address environmental challenges. These bonds can fund initiatives aimed at improving energy efficiency in municipal buildings, upgrading public transportation to reduce emissions, and enhancing waste management systems. By linking bond issuance to specific environmental outcomes, municipalities can attract investment from socially responsible investors who prioritise ESG criteria. This approach not only provides the necessary financial resources but also ensures that environmental performance is monitored and reported transparently, aligning with the goals of ESG frameworks.

Moreover, global trends, such as the proliferation of municipal green bonds in Africa and Latin America, highlight the importance of a climate justice approach. As noted by Herrera,[100] these bonds can address local environmental challenges whilst promoting social equity. The case of Flint (Michigan, US)[101] illustrates the potential pitfalls and benefits of using financial instruments to manage municipal distress. Ensuring proper governance, transparency, and absence of conflicts of interest in these financial mechanisms is critical to their success. This also aligns with the broader governance indicators within ESG criteria, reinforcing the integrity and accountability of the restructuring process.

Additionally, focusing on sector-specific environmental issues, such as water financing, can yield significant benefits. Investments in sustainable water management practices are crucial for municipalities facing resource depletion and climate-induced water scarcity. Innovative financing models, as discussed in various studies, can support the development of resilient water infrastructure, reducing vulnerability to climate impacts. By adopting these mechanisms, municipalities in financial distress can not only stabilise their finances but also ensure long-term environmental sustainability and compliance with international environmental standards.

In the corporate sector, we are noticing an increasing number of such cases, in which environmental concerns dictate the restructuring agenda. Yet, environmental concerns are not central in most municipal cases, although there are exceptions.

---

100 H Herrera, 'The Proliferation of Municipal Green Bonds in Africa and Latin America: The Need for a Climate Justice Approach' (2024) 36(1) Environ. Urban. 147.

101 A Murphy, 'In Service of Creditors: Emergency Financial Management and Poison Water in Flint, Michigan' (2019) 19(3) PFM 200.

Chapter 5 on English law reports a detailed analysis of the environmental concerns surrounding the restructuring of a hybrid local entity, the utility company Thames Water. This chapter highlights that years of underinvestment in critical infrastructure and uncontrolled growth of the entity's debt have resulted in poor service to customers and high levels of sewage pollution in English rivers and natural reserves. Equally, the US chapter *sub* 3.4 delves into another case of mismanagement of water services affecting the city of Flint. The magnitude and gravity of the pollution issues in the water management system of Flint were aggravated by the botched intervention of a state-appointed emergency manager. The lack of any long-term sustainability perspective in the state intervention resulted in a public health crisis and the need for the federal government to fund decontamination efforts. Finally, the South African chapter *sub* 4.1 highlights that traditionally local municipalities are late payers towards their suppliers, including utility companies. The utility companies' inability to recover the amount due for the services supplied affects their ability to provide those services to all local municipalities but also to invest in critical infrastructure designed to improve the use of natural resources and the services to local citizens.

Environmental concerns have played a key role in the restructuring of Flint and local entities in South Africa, and they are expected to be pivotal in the restructuring of Thames Water. In Flint, the severe lead contamination crisis underscored the critical need for integrating environmental health considerations into financial restructuring processes. The mismanagement and cost-cutting measures that ignored environmental and public health impacts led to widespread lead poisoning, necessitating extensive federal intervention and funding to remediate the water supply. Similarly, in South Africa, the chronic late payments by local municipalities to utility companies have stymied investments in sustainable infrastructure, exacerbating resource inefficiencies and environmental degradation. These cases highlight the importance of prioritising environmental sustainability in the financial restructuring of municipal entities. Thames Water's restructuring will most likely emphasise upgrading infrastructure to reduce sewage pollution and enhance service reliability, illustrating a growing recognition that addressing environmental issues is essential for the long-term viability and success of utility companies.

The stark consequences arising from cases where environmental concerns are not addressed as part of the entity's restructuring efforts suggest the need to include environmental considerations, and particularly climate mitigation strategies, as part of any municipal restructuring proceeding. We strongly believe that environmental issues should have equal prominence as economic, social and governance considerations in the restructuring of any financially distressed local entity.

Such a course of action would help mitigate future costs associated with climate change impacts, such as extreme weather events, and foster economic opportunities through sustainable practices and green initiatives. Additionally, addressing environmental issues can enhance the community's resilience and quality of life, attracting investment and reducing long-term financial burdens.

Europe is at the forefront in the efforts for decarbonising the economy and mitigating the human impact on climate change. The European Green Deal's ambitious goal is to ensure that the twenty-seven European member states will not produce any net emission of greenhouse gases by 2050. Countless documents have been issued to achieve this goal. One of the most significant is the European Commission's Communication on managing climate risk in Europe.[102] Such communication not only promotes climate resilience (also known as "climate adaptation strategies"), but also the adoption of policies designed to reduce vulnerability to climate change.[103] As a result, member states have adopted a series of initiatives to align with these priorities, including the adoption of National Energy and Climate Plans (NECPs).

An important financial tool to achieve this is the Resilience and Recovery Plan,[104] part of the Next Generation EU initiative. This regulation establishes the "Recovery and Resilience Facility", with article 3 outlining goals such as the green transition and social cohesion—although practically more funding has been directed towards social policies than green transition and digital transformation in some countries. Article 4 focuses on achieving net zero emissions, and the regulation also includes the "do no harm principle" to ensure that funded projects do not negatively impact environmental goals. Much of the Recovery and Resilience Facility's funds are allocated to local governments in the EU, similar to how Covid-19 relief funds were distributed in the US.[105] In the EU, this financial support must comply with the Conditionality Regulation,[106] which emphasises auditing and preventing fraud and corruption, ensuring that the funds are used effectively and transparently.

---

[102] European Commission, 'Communication from the Commission to the European Parliament, the Council, the European Economic and Social Committee and the Committee of the Regions on Managing Climate Risks—Protecting People and Prosperity COM/2024/91' (12 March 2024).

[103] Ibid [1.2.].

[104] Established by Regulation (EU) 2021/241 of the European Parliament and of the Council of 12 February 2021 [2021] OJ L 57.

[105] U.S. Dep't of the Treasury, *State and Local Fiscal Recovery Funds* (July 2024) <https://home.treasury.gov/policy-issues/coronavirus/assistance-for-state-local-and-tribal-governments/state-and-local-fiscal-recovery-funds>.

[106] Regulation (EU, Euratom) 2020/2092 of the European Parliament and of the Council of 16 December 2020 on a general regime of conditionality for the

These policies mostly apply in solvent times, and the European Union law frequently overlooks the importance of insolvency law to fight climate change. Other organisations, such as the World Bank, are working on recommendations for filling that gap and suggesting policy changes to allow insolvency law to mitigate the detrimental impact of human activity on our environment and on GHG emissions.[107]

Nevertheless, none of the countries included in this book is part of the European Union. Overall, their environmental policy goals are not as ambitious as the European ones. Looking in more details at the jurisdictions included in this study, both English and US law allow for the restructuring and discharge of environmental obligations.[108] In the US, the goal of ensuring the collective management of the insolvent estate generally prevails over competing policy objectives. However, this is not to say that environmental considerations are constantly disregarded. The US Bankruptcy Code does not allow the discharge of remediation obligations related to ongoing pollution or where remediation is necessary to prevent an imminent threat to human health or the environment.[109] Additionally, the Comprehensive Environmental Response, Compensation, and Liability Act 1980 provides a federal "superfund" to clean up uncontrolled or abandoned hazardous-waste sites as well as accidents, spills, and other emergency releases of pollutants and contaminants into the environment. It imposes liability for environmental clean-up costs on the owner of contaminated property, regardless of fault. Finally, because municipalities remain under the control of the state even during a municipal bankruptcy, such states could apply their statutory prerogatives to limit or condition abandonment of environmentally hazardous assets.[110]

---

protection of the Union budget [2020] OJ L 433I.

[107] World Bank, *Insolvency and Climate Change: Considerations for Policy Makers* (2024)—draft copy in possession of one of the authors.

[108] See Insolvency Act 1986, s 178 under English law and 11 US Code, § 554 under US law. There is voluminous literature on this topic. See, among others: DC Tay, 'Environmental Liability and the Insolvency Professional: An Issue Whose Time Has, or Will Surely Come' (1994) 3 Int. Insolv. Rev. 60; JN Lawlor, 'Toxic Tug of War: Environmental Clean-up Costs, Bankruptcy and the Administrative Expense Priority—Is It a Collision of Conflicting Policies or Just Plain Confusion?' (1991) 21 Seton Hall L. Rev. 832; E Vaccari and D Ehmke, 'Environmental Liabilities in Insolvency' in E Ghio and E Vaccari (eds), *The Perpetual Renewal of European Insolvency Law* (INSOL Europe 2024) 29–42.

[109] *Midlantic National Bank v. New Jersey Department of Environmental Protection* 474 U.S. 494 (1986). For an analysis, see (among others): LN Coordes, 'The Messiness of Midlantic' (2024) Norton Journal of Bankruptcy Law and Practice (West) (forthcoming).

[110] See chapter 3, *sub* [3.3.1].

In South Africa, article 24 of the Constitution protects the environment and establishes that every South African citizen has a right to an environment that is not harmful to their health or well-being. This statement of principle was enacted in several legislative instruments, including the National Environmental Management Act 1998[111] and several other special acts that followed. These acts create a general duty of care on all entities that cause, have caused, or may cause environmental pollution.[112] Competent local authorities have the duty and power to compel a polluter to remedy the damages caused to the environment.[113] These duties do continue in insolvency, even if competing policy considerations result in a mitigation of such duties. In fact, even if neither liquidation nor business rescue proceedings affect the obligations arising under such acts,[114] monetary claims are not enforceable in insolvency. However, the costs associated with the compliance with environmental directives can be deducted from the proceeds arising from the sale of any immovable property subject to environmental orders.[115]

Amongst the countries considered in this study, the country with the closest links with Europe is the UK. After Brexit, the UK enacted a new Environment Act.[116] Such an act grants the government new powers to set binding, ambitious, meaningful, and informed (by experts) targets on matters such as air quality, water, biodiversity, and waste reduction. The act also established a new environmental watchdog, the Office for Environmental Protection (OEP), which will hold the government and other public bodies (including local entities) to account, thus ensuring compliance with environmental laws. However, several leading environmental organisations and reports have criticised the government for failing to be sufficiently ambitious in its target-setting activity.[117]

There are signs that the tide is changing, even in the countries considered in this book. For instance, section 19 of the 2021 Environment Act (effective from 1 November 2023), imposes a duty on UK government ministers, when

---

111 Act 107 of 1998.

112 National Environmental Management Act 1998, s 28.

113 Ibid s 49A(1)(e).

114 INSOL International, *Environmental Claims and Liabilities in Insolvency and Restructuring* (2024) 242, 265.

115 Insolvency Act (South Africa), s 89.

116 Environmental Act 2021.

117 ClientEarth, 'The UK Environment Act—What's Happening Now?' (1 April 2022) <https://www.clientearth.org/latest/news/why-the-uk-environment-bill-matters/>; H Horton, 'The UK Environmental Protections Dropped Since Brexit' *The Guardian* (London, 19 January 2024) <https://www.theguardian.com/environment/2024/jan/19/the-uk-environmental-protections-dropped-since-brexit>.

making policy, to have due regard to the government's policy statement on environmental principles. Whilst being only a procedural rather than substantive duty, it is actionable in courts by any interested parties. A similar duty, effective from 1 January 2023, applies to local authorities and other public bodies by virtue of section 40 of the 2006 Natural Environment and Rural Communities Act, as amended by the 2021 Environment Act. South Africa has a robust liability regime, which also applies to insolvency practitioners, and which is able—at least on paper—to hold accountable those who have caused or aggravated environmental pollution,[118] even if the polluted land has been sold and the previous owner has lost any interest in such polluted property.[119] In particular, more rigorous rules apply with reference to sectors such as utility services and the mining industry.

There is also evidence that courts are becoming increasingly proactive in ensuring that public authorities pursue environmental policies and climate mitigation strategies as part of their everyday statutory duties. In a recent judgment delivered against the Surrey County Council,[120] the UK Supreme Court held that courts should be prepared to scrutinise and challenge the content of the environmental impact assessments (EIAs) prepared to obtain planning permission for authorised developments, especially those carried out for highly polluting activities. Whilst this judgment is technical and specific—it focuses on EIAs submitted to a council not in financial distress—we believe it sends an important message: the substantive reduction of GHG emissions is to be considered as an actionable duty against local entities, whether or not they may be financially distressed.

In the US, several decisions have reasserted the centrality of environmental concerns in bankruptcy disputes. In *Midlantic*,[121] the Supreme Court held that a bankrupt debtor's ability to abandon contaminated property is limited if the property poses an imminent and identifiable risk to public health and safety. Whilst not delivered in a municipal dispute, the recent Supreme Court judgment in *Purdue Pharma*[122] advocated for a restrictive interpretation of the provisions on third-party releases in the US Bankruptcy Code.[123] The judgment held that where third parties have neither filed for bankruptcy nor placed all their assets on the table for distribution to creditors, claims against them cannot be discharged and/or released. Furthermore, the Supreme Court went

---

118 INSOL International (n 114) 271–273.

119 *Harmony Gold Mining Company Ltd v Regional Director: Free State Department of Water Affairs* [2013] ZASCA 206.

120 *R v Surrey County Council and others* [2024] UKSC 20.

121 *Midlantic* (n 109).

122 *Harrington v. Purdue Pharma* L.P., 144 S. Ct. 2071 (2024).

123 Particularly, the catchall provision in 11 US Code, § 1123(b)(6).

on to reiterate that releases, even those of a consensual nature, cannot include claims based on "fraud" or those alleging "willful and malicious injury" by express provision of the law.[124]

Except for asbestos bankruptcies,[125] where non-consensual third-party releases are expressly provided under US law,[126] this seminal judgment has the potential to promote the implementation of climate mitigation strategies in proceedings affecting high polluting enterprises. If third parties remain liable against environmental agencies for environmental liabilities, debtors and trustees in restructuring plans may be able to gather more assets for the benefit of the insolvent estate. These assets could be used to reduce the GHG emissions of the restructured entity (and address pre-bankruptcy clean-up costs). As municipal bankruptcy law in the US builds on the chapter 11 provisions for corporate entities, such principles could be applied by courts in case of a municipal restructuring involving a request to release third party guarantors from environmental duties.

Finally, in South Africa the Supreme Court of Appeal found that it was legitimate under a broad interpretation of existing statutory powers to allow a regional authority to impose a duty to adopt anti-pollution measures on the liquidator of a mining company.[127] The reasoning of the court was that such a course of action, even if not expressly provided under the law,[128] would have been the most reasonable to achieve the constitutional and statutory anti-pollution objectives. As a result, the liquidator of the mining company had to comply with such directions.

2.2.4 Concluding Remarks on Environmental Indicators

Anyone interested in the future of the planet is aware of the detrimental impact of GHG emissions in the atmosphere. This section demonstrated that laws in the countries considered in this study are actively encouraging and/or forcing local authorities to embrace environmental indicators in the exercise of their statutory duties.

Whilst in times of distress environmental indicators are considered primarily in a limited number of proceedings affecting egregious polluters and with clear impact on the welfare of local communities, the changes in the policy attitude discussed above (and later in the substantive chapters of this book) and

---

[124] 11 US Code, §§ 523(a)(2), (4), (6).

[125] For more on this topic, see (among others): G Tweedale, *Magic Mineral to Killer Dust: Turner & Newall and the Asbestos Hazard* (OUP 2000).

[126] 11 US Code, §§ 524(e) and 524(g)(4)(A)(ii).

[127] *Harmony Gold Mining Co.* (n 119).

[128] Water Act 1998 (Act 36 of 1998), s 19(1).

the judicial interpretation of statutory provisions indicate that the importance of such indicators is bound to increase exponentially in the years to come.

Whilst most of the cases considered in this section of the book focus on corporate insolvencies, there is evidence that hybrid (e.g. Thames Water) and full (e.g. Flint) local authorities grapple with crucial environmental issues. Overlooking environmental issues in the restructuring of local entities is the byproduct of short-termism, and it is unlikely to achieve a sustainable restructuring of the affected entity.

2.3 SOCIAL INDICATORS

The social dimension of ESG focuses on the impact that an entity has on the broader society in which it operates. This broader society has both an internal and external component. Viewed internally, ESG's social dimension focuses on the relationship between the entity and its employees (and their immediate dependents). Viewed externally, the social dimension focuses on an entity's impact on and relationship with the community in which it operates as well as society at large. That is, the entity's relationship with third parties.

Social issues within the ESG framework are *par excellence* diffuse. They are highly contextual, often intertwined with (local) policy measures, and accordingly subject to significant levels of qualitative evaluation, typically within uncertain timelines.[129] Social justice is an important element of the social dimension of ESG, which includes close attention to equality. In this respect, ESG gives expression to the stakeholder theory by focusing on a wide range of stakeholders relevant to (corporate) entities' success.[130]

Given these characteristics of the social dimension of ESG, a large number of specific ESG performance indicators are used to evaluate this dimension. The main areas of focus of these indicators relate to labour, health and safety, human rights (specifically equality), litigation and regulatory exposure, political stability, and community engagement and relations.[131] For public sector entities, additional, or more specific, indicators relate *inter alia* to access to education and housing, demographic shifts, and access to basic services.[132]

---

[129] Moody's (n 47). European Banking Authority, 'EBA Report on Management and Supervision of ESG Risks for Credit Institutions and Investment Firms' (EBA/REP/2021/18, EBA 2021) 43.

[130] T Dathe and others, *Implementing Environmental, Social and Governance (ESG) Principles for Sustainable Businesses* (Springer 2024); Li (n 41).

[131] Moody's (n 47); Citterio and King (n 43); Lucy Pérez et al, 'Does ESG Really Matter—and Why?' (August 2022) McKinsey Quarterly <www.mckinsey.com/capabilities/sustainability/our-insights/does-esg-really-matter-and-why>.

[132] Moody's (n 47).

In the specific context of insolvency and restructuring, key social questions concern the treatment of employees and their benefits as well as health and safety liabilities. For corporate entities, an important social consideration, especially relating to liquidation versus restructuring options, is the potential impact of the loss of employment opportunities. In the case of public sector entities in distress, continued operations are not only important for purposes of employment, but also for provision of basic services, which adds a significant additional layer of social considerations to insolvency and restructuring in the public context.

A prime concern in relation to social indicators in insolvency is the differentiation between ordinary commercial creditors and creditors with what can be called "social claims". These "social creditors" include current and former employees with claims to wages, pensions and other benefits as well as claimants under health and safety liabilities of the insolvent, such as mass tort claimants. As Karaleu states, these claims can be viewed as 'social claims in the sense that they contribute to the social support and social fabric of countries in dealing with a more vulnerable segment of the population'.[133] From an ESG perspective, it follows that the rules applied to such social creditors vis-à-vis those applied to ordinary commercial creditors can signal a particular system's sensitivity to social considerations in managing insolvency.

2.3.1 Liquidation and Restructuring Proceedings

In the case of liquidation especially, the social impact can be severe. Two social aspects are of particular concern. The first is the involvement of and impact on (former and current) employees. The second is the effect on health and safety liability in a broad sense, including mass tort liability.

2.3.1.1 Employee interests

The insolvency of a distressed entity can have drastic consequences for employees. Accordingly, an important social indicator in dealing with insolvency is the position of employees. Procedurally, this includes their active involvement in the proceedings. Substantively, it includes the impact of liquidation or restructuring on employees and their benefits, and potentially the broader community.

The recognition of employees' distinct interests in managing their employer's insolvency typically leads to procedural mechanisms to facilitate employee input. Key questions are whether employee representatives have standing to

---

133 Y Karaleu, 'Social Responsibility Aspects of Companies' Insolvency' (2018) 5 JCR&L 7, 9.

contribute to the proceedings and whether courts (and other regulatory bodies) will take employees' views and labour issues into account when making decisions.[134] Different approaches are adopted to give employees a voice in liquidation or restructuring proceedings.[135] Employee representatives may have a seat on a creditors' committee that plays a key role in managing insolvency proceedings. Labour unions or other employee representative bodies may have rights in relation to such proceedings. Courts (or other regulatory bodies) may have the power to convene employee representation to bring employees' interests to the proceedings.

Of the systems considered in this book, the US provides an example of a combination of the first two approaches. Labour unions, as a party of interest, typically serve on official creditor committees where they can influence proceedings under the US Bankruptcy Code.[136] England and South Africa provide examples of the second approach, where the debtor must consult with employee representative bodies, such as unions, on various aspects of insolvency proceedings.[137] For example, in England under the Trade Union and Labour Relations (Consolidation) Act 1992, the insolvent employer must consult with recognised trade unions if a restructuring plan may result in redundancies above a stated number.[138] In South Africa, the Companies Act 2008 requires notice to trade unions of commencement of business rescue proceedings and of all relevant events during such proceedings. It also grants trade unions standing in any court proceedings arising from the business rescue. The act requires a business rescue practitioner to convene a meeting of employee representatives to allow them to decide on whether they want to constitute an employees' committee. This committee must be consulted by business rescue practitioners on all aspects of the proceedings. Under the Labour Relations Act 1995, the insolvent employer is obliged to consult with employee representatives, such as trade unions, when retrenchments are contemplated within insolvency proceedings.[139]

The second social aspect of particular concern in insolvency proceedings relates to the substantive impact of insolvency on employees. A range

134 INSOL International (n 95) 2.

135 Ibid 27.

136 See chapter 3, *sub* [3.2.4.1] describing the role of labour unions in chapter 11 proceedings.

137 See chapter 4, *sub* [4.2.1.2] and chapter 5, *sub* [5.2.2.1] describing the involvement of employee representative bodies in various steps of liquidation and restructuring proceedings.

138 INSOL International (n 95) 438.

139 S Van Eck, A Boraine and L Steyn, 'Fair Labour Practices in South African Insolvency Law' (2004) 121 SALJ 902.

of substantive employee interests are threatened by an employer's insolvency. The most obvious is the loss of employment itself. Continued employment is thus a major social consideration in dealing with insolvency. In the first instance, it is a major factor in deciding whether liquidation or restructuring is the optimal (or most desirable) route to take in managing employer insolvency. Furthermore, when restructuring is pursued, continued employment plays a significant role in the nature and scope of the restructuring. The extent to which continued employment is considered within any particular insolvency system is thus an important signal of that system's sensitivity to ESG factors.

The social effect of insolvency on continued employment extends beyond the immediate employees of the insolvent employer. It obviously also impacts on dependants but, even more, it may have broader social impact within the wider community. This would be especially the case where the insolvent employer is a dominant source of employment and the primary local economic driver within a particular community, such as a mining company within a mining community[140] or any other community dominated by a particular large industrial employer.[141] The insolvency of such an employer will not only have severe social impact on the income of its immediate employees, but also a potentially significant impact on income of other persons that derive their income from that of the former group.[142] That is, within the services industry existing around the dominant employer. Examples of this phenomenon abound in the US's Rust Belt region. Scranton, Pennsylvania is a pertinent example. Having once been a thriving industrial centre due to major industries such as anthracite coal mining, iron, and steel, the sharp decline of these industries for most of the twentieth century resulted in severe job losses across all sectors and subsequent decline in population.[143] In 1992, Scranton filed for

140 A 2018 survey by the International Council on Mining and Metals (ICMM) among its members found that 43% of responding operations that expected to close mining operations within 25 years were dominant economic drivers within the local or regional economy: D Brock and R Stevens, 'The Mine Closure Challenges for Government and Industry' (ICMM 14 October 2021) <www.icmm.com/en-gb/stories/2021/mine-closure-challenges-for-government-and-industry>.

141 SE Etukakpan, 'Transfer of Undertakings: The Tension between Business Rescue and Employment Protection in Corporate Insolvency' (PhD thesis, Nottingham Trent University 2012) 284.

142 V Celli, A Cerqua and G Pellegrini, 'The Long-term Effects of Mass Layoffs: Do Local Economies (Ever) Recover?' (2023) 23 J. Econ. Geogr. 1121.

143 RJ Schmidt, 'Revitalization and Its Discontents: The Political and Symbolic Economy of Post-Anthracite Scranton, PA (1945–2010)' (PhD thesis, Binghamton University State University of New York 2010).

distressed city status under Pennsylvania law, effectively being placed under State receivership.

The protection of continued employment is evident in many insolvency proceedings. The approval of restructuring schemes typically takes the impact on employment of insolvency and that of the proposed rescue scheme into account. The preservation of employment is pointedly viewed as one of the goals of restructuring as opposed to liquidation of insolvent enterprises in, for example, the US[144] and South Africa.[145] Rules on restructuring in both the US and South Africa incorporate a host of provisions directly involving employees and their representatives into the restructuring proceedings in service of this goal. Even in liquidation proceedings, South African courts have taken an expansive view of notification requirements vis-à-vis employees in recognition of the overall aim of protecting employment. For example, in *Stratford v Investec Bank Limited*,[146] the Constitutional Court interpreted the Insolvency Act's[147] requirement that a petition for sequestration must be furnished to all "employees" of the debtor to include employees working for the debtor in their private capacity (such as cleaning staff working in the debtor's home) and not just those employed in the debtor's business, as has previously been held. The court adopted this interpretation explicitly on social grounds, pointing to equality between all employees and the dignity-enhancing role of the required notice. In this respect, the court stated: '[n]otice, ultimately, signifies respect for the human dignity of employees'.[148] South African courts also directly consider continued employment when adjudicating applications to commence business rescue. For example, in *Forty Squares (Pty) Ltd v Noris Fresh Produce (Pty) Ltd t/a Golden Harvest (In Liq)*,[149] the High Court pointed to the 'loss of continued employment to some 180 workers' as "tragic", but noted that 'it would be irresponsible in the extreme to consider re-employing a workforce which would not be properly remunerated, with the prospect of their short-lived employment being terminated when the creditors vote against the plan'.

---

144 See chapter 3, *sub* [3.2.2] noting that the purpose of a business reorganisation bankruptcy under chapter 11 of the US Bankruptcy Code, as opposed to a liquidation, is 'to restructure a business's finances so that it may continue to operate, provide its employees with jobs', quoting H.R. Rep. No. 95-–595, 95th Cong., 1st Sess., at 220 (1977).

145 See chapter 4, *sub* [4.2.2] discussing the aims of the business rescue mechanism compared to liquidation.

146 [2014] ZACC 38.

147 Insolvency Act (South Africa), s 9(4A).

148 *Stratford v Investec Bank Limited* (n 146) [34].

149 [2023] ZAWCHC 78 [21], [29].

Employees commonly enjoy specific protections within restructuring proceedings and in particular in relation to redundancies.[150] These are often dealt with in terms of existing labour laws such as the Trade Union and Labour Relations (Consolidation) Act 1992, Information and Consultation of Employees Regulations 2004, and the Transfer of Undertakings (Protection of Employment) Regulations 2006 in England,[151] and the Labour Relations Act 1995 in South Africa. The latter applies (and even trumps) business rescue rules under the Companies Act in respect of employment contracts, including any dismissals.[152] In both systems it has been argued that the considerable protection granted to employees of an insolvent employer may undermine the objective of rescuing the employer. In the English context, Etukakpan has argued that the Transfer of Undertakings (Protection of Employment) Regulations 2006 provided too much protection to employees and accordingly 'have posed serious problems to sales and rescues of insolvent businesses'.[153] In his view, the regulations made it too difficult to reduce the workforce of the insolvent employer in order to facilitate a sale of the business as a going concern, which "over-deters" potential buyers of the business.[154] In South Africa, similar restrictions on reducing personnel within a business rescue process has led to the view that employees enjoy more protection in business rescue than outside of business rescue.[155]

Beyond the loss of employment, employees also have interests in payment of outstanding wages, whether arising prior or subsequent to insolvency. In relation to these interests, employees may also be creditors of the insolvent employer. These interests, which Karaleu notes are clearly both "social claims" and "economic claims",[156] are typically subject to special protections in many

150 Karaleu (n 133) 17.

151 On the topic of TUPE and insolvency, see (among others): JLL Gant, *Balancing the Protection of Business and Employment in Insolvency—An Anglo-French Perspective* (Eleven International Publishing 2017); and JLL Gant, 'Employees as Stakeholders in Restructuring and Insolvency: Acquired Rights and Business Transfers' in JLL Gant and P Omar (eds), *Research Handbook on Corporate Restructuring* (EE Publishing 2021).

152 Companies Act 2008, s 5(4)(b)(i)(bb).

153 Etukakpan (n 141) 297. See also: H Nsubuga, *Employee Rights in Corporate Insolvency: A UK and US Perspective* (Routledge 2020); C Wynn-Evans, 'TUPE, Administration and the Rescue Culture: *OTG Limited v Barke & Others* and Consolidated Appeals' (2011) 40(4) Industrial Law Journal 451; C Wynn-Evans, 'TUPE and Mothballs: *Crystal Palace FC Limited and Another v Kavanagh and Others* [2014] IRLR 139, CA' (2014) 43(2) Industrial Law Journal 185.

154 Etukakpan (n 141) 299.

155 INSOL International (n 95) 348.

156 Karaleu (n 133) 9.

insolvency proceedings. It is common to find that these employee claims are given preferential treatment in restructuring.[157] Employee claims for wages may thus enjoy preference to all other unsecured claims.[158]

A final category of employee interests that merit specific attention in insolvency proceedings includes all other employee benefits, apart from wages. The most significant of these is pension benefits, but other benefits like healthcare cover may also fall under this category. Here, the relevant stakeholders include former, retired employees. Liability to continue contributions to pension schemes as well as the level of current employees' pension benefits following a restructuring are particularly difficult issues in formulating a viable restructuring plan. It is thus not uncommon to find that countries provide a statutory guarantee fund for employee pension claims in case of employer insolvency.[159] In restructuring proceedings, employers are often also required to engage with pension fund beneficiaries where employer contributions to funds may be affected.[160]

Employees are considered a particularly vulnerable group in cases of employer insolvency given that they are unwilling creditors.[161] That is, unlike financial and trade creditors, employees have no choice in entering into a credit relationship with the employer.[162] Furthermore, with the sole exception of individual entrepreneurs and micro and small enterprises (MSEs), employees will typically be in a more precarious financial position than other unsecured

---

157 INSOL International (n 95) 27.

158 This is the position in the US and South Africa, see INSOL International (n 95) 248, 459. In England employees enjoy limited similar protections under the Employment Rights Act 1996 and Insolvency Act 1986, see chapter 5, *sub* [52.3.1].

159 PM Secunda, 'Analysis of the Treatment of Employee Pension and Wage Claims in Insolvency and Under Guarantee Schemes in OECD Countries: Comparative Law Lessons for Detroit and the United States' (2014) 41 Fordham Urb. L.J. 867, 874.

160 This is required in England, for example, under the Occupational and Personal Pensions Schemes (Consultation by Employers and Miscellaneous Amendment) Regulations 2006 and in the US under 11 US Code, § 1114.

161 Secunda (n 159) 872.

162 Financial and trade creditors have a host of mechanisms available to protect them against default and losses due to insolvency, none of which are open to employees. Financial creditors typically secure their claims by means of guarantees and various forms of real security. Trade creditors may insist on pre-payment before delivery or service, or may retain a lien over installed equipment, or may spread work among different clients to minimise their risk of one client defaulting or may carry trade-debt insurance: Karaleu (n 133) 17.

creditors given their reliance on wages as a main source of income, unlike most other creditors.[163]

Most employees do not have the same ability to diversify their income or take other measures to limit their risk to their employer's insolvency compared to other creditors. Without the ability to mitigate risk through diversification, employees are left particularly exposed, making the loss of employment and unpaid wages more devastating. Consequently, providing employees with enhanced protections in insolvency cases helps ensure they are not disproportionately harmed by their employer's financial difficulties.

With reference to public servants, the need for additional protections becomes even more compelling. Public servants often enter their roles with the expectation of job stability and fair compensation, driven by the mission to serve the community rather than to seek profit. Their work underpins essential public services, from education and public safety to healthcare and infrastructure maintenance. The financial distress of a local entity threatens not only the livelihood of these employees but also the continuity of critical public services that the community relies upon. Ensuring that public servants receive additional protection in such cases is crucial for maintaining public trust and operational stability in local governments. This protection helps safeguard the welfare of employees and ensures that essential services continue to function effectively, even during financial crises.

2.3.1.2 Liability

Liquidation or restructuring is often used by entities to manage their liabilities under health and safety litigation.[164] A key social question is thus whether health and safety liabilities (including tortious ones) can be restructured, or potentially avoided by means of insolvency proceedings.

A prime recent example of these issues is Johnson & Johnson's (J&J) high-profile attempts to restructure and settle its talc-related liabilities. Starting in 2009, J&J faced mass tort litigation in multiple jurisdictions regarding its baby powder, which several scientific studies have found contained asbestos and fibrous talc.[165] In 2013, a jury in the US found in favour of a plaintiff alleging to have developed ovarian cancer as a result of exposure to the baby powder.[166] As a result, 1,300 ovarian cancer lawsuits were filed against J&J by the end of

---

163 Karaleu (n 133) 17. Exceptions apply, such as highly skilled and paid employees, and directors operating in a dynamic job market.

164 INSOL International (n 95) 1.

165 JM Glover, 'Due Process Discontents in Mass-Tort Bankruptcy' (2023) 72 DePaul L. Rev. 535, 563.

166 Red River Talc LLC, 'Disclosure Statement for Prepackaged Chapter 11 Plan of Reorganization of the Debtor' (NAI-1539987213, OfficialTalcClaims,

2015.[167] In 2020, in similar claims, a Missouri jury awarded plaintiffs $4.69 billion against J&J (reduced to $2.2 billion on appeal).[168] By 2021, J&J and its relevant subsidiaries had spent nearly $1 billion in defending talc-related litigation and paid approximately $3.5 billion in relation to settlements and verdicts.[169] By October 2021, J&J's subsidiaries faced 'approximately 40,000 ovarian cancer cases'.[170] Even though J&J stopped selling its baby powder globally in 2022, the latency period for ovarian cancer means that the company could face talc-related litigation until the end of the century.[171] In 2021, J&J restructured the relevant subsidiary that was liable for claims in relation to its baby powder. Using what is called a "divisional merger" under Texas law, J&J split the business of its subsidiary in such a way that all its talc-liability ended up in a new corporate entity, LTL Management (LTL).[172] Within 48 hours of creating LTL, J&J put it into chapter 11 bankruptcy.[173] This move was criticised as a deliberate attempt by J&J 'to shield assets from the claims of their victims'.[174] Should it succeed, J&J would be able to shift defending its mass tort litigation into restructuring proceedings under bankruptcy law. In January 2023, the Third Circuit dismissed the petition for relief under chapter 11, holding that LTL was not in imminent financial distress despite the massive talc-related liabilities that it inherited.[175] This was because of a backstop funding arrangement in terms of which LTL could draw on J&J's 'exceptionally strong balance sheet' to settle its liabilities.[176] The court thus held that LTL was 'highly solvent' and accordingly not entitled to relief under chapter 11. Undeterred, J&J revised the backstop funding arrangement between itself and LTL (effectively placing LTL's immediate holding company between J&J and LTL) and LTL filed a second petition for chapter 11 bankruptcy in April 2023.[177] In August 2023, the Bankruptcy Court dismissed this second petition, holding that on the Third Circuit's reasoning in the first matter, LTL still had

10 June 2024) <https://officialtalcclaims.com/wp-content/uploads/2024/05/Disclosure-Statement.pdf>.

167 Ibid.

168 Glover (n 165) 563.

169 *Red River* (n 166) 14.

170 Ibid.

171 Ibid.

172 Glover (n 165) 565; INSOL International (n 114) 3.

173 Glover (n 165) 566.

174 INSOL International (n 114) 3.

175 *In re LTL Management, LLC*, 58 F.4th 738 (2023) (US Court of Appeals, Third Circuit).

176 Ibid.

177 INSOL International (n 114) 4.

sufficient access to funding to cover its talc-related liabilities and that it was accordingly still not in imminent financial distress that would justify chapter 11 relief.[178] Whilst the court felt obliged to dismiss the petition in light of the litigation history, it did note its concern regarding the effect of denying resolution of the talc-related claims by way of bankruptcy proceedings in favour of the tort system. With reference to the anticipated slow pace of finalising tort claims, the court noted:

> This glacial pace coupled with the undeniable surge in the number of new actions means that the vast majority of claimants will not get the opportunity to seek recovery for years to come, if ever. The sluggish speed of the tort system [...] continues to trouble this Court. Further, when a claimant finally gets to trial, that opportunity comes with a very meaningful risk of a defendant's verdict. On the other hand, claims reconciliation through a bankruptcy trust places reduced evidentiary and causation burdens on claimants, and resolution of claims and payments to victims can be achieved at a far more expeditious pace than through uncertain litigation in the tort system.
>
> [...]
>
> In short, the court remains unconvinced that the procedural mechanisms and notice programs offered in the tort system can protect future claimants' rights in the same manner as the available tools in the bankruptcy system.[179]

Whilst an appeal against the Bankruptcy Court's dismissal of the second petition is currently pending before the Third Circuit, J&J has issued a proposal on 10 June 2024 in which it offered to settle the bulk of the talc-related claims to the amount of $8 billion over twenty-five years.[180] If the plan is supported by 75% of claimants, J&J will effect yet another restructuring in which a new entity, Red River Talc LLC, will be created under Texas law and to which the relevant talc liabilities will be transferred. Once created, Red River Talc LLC will file for chapter 11 bankruptcy and, if granted, claimants will recover as creditors from the trust created through the bankruptcy reorganisation in lieu of their tort claims and as set out in the plan.[181] In other words, J&J will repeat the entire restructuring plan with Red River Talc LLC replacing LTL, but now with the support of the bulk of the tort claimants.

The J&J matter vividly illustrates the complexities involved in managing mass tort liabilities by way of insolvency proceedings. On the one hand, it can be argued that such use of restructuring proceedings is nothing more than an attempt to avoid (or minimise) liability and thus tantamount to an abuse

---

178 *In re LTL Management, LLC*, 652 B.R. 433 (Bankr. D.N.J. 2023).

179 Ibid.

180 *Red River* (n 166).

181 Ibid.

of the insolvency system. Like employees, tort claimants cannot be equated to other creditors given that they have not entered into the credit relationship voluntarily and do not have the same ability, or opportunity, to assess the credit risk and implement appropriate mitigation measures.[182] Since most insolvency systems do not provide tort claimants with any preferred status in insolvency proceedings,[183] such claimants may also end up in a much worse position should the debtor pursue insolvency proceedings as opposed to defending a tort claim.

On the other hand, there are seemingly cogent reasons for preferring the resolution of mass tort liability by way of insolvency proceedings instead of the tort system, also to the benefit of tort claimants. These relate to the greater level of certainty, potential lower costs and a shorter timeframe for obtaining relief. Regardless of what view one takes in any particular matter, it is undeniable that insolvency law's response to these scenarios touches on major social questions and also has upstream effects on management of risk. Such rules inevitably have an influence on how entities behave when they are solvent.[184] The possibility of managing health and safety liability through insolvency proceedings will thus inevitably impact on how entities conduct their operations with reference to health and safety. In this way, the rules on insolvency proceedings have an important impact on how social risk is managed.

2.3.2 Municipalities in Distress

Social considerations also loom large in case of municipalities in distress, arguably even more so than in the case of corporate insolvency, given the core function of municipalities in rendering many social services to residents.

Municipal employees are equally exposed, if not in a worse position compared to private-sector employees in relation to continued employment. The rules governing municipal financial distress often mandate redundancies and absolve the distressed municipality from adhering to labour agreements contrary to their private-sector counterparts.

In the US, for example, the Bankruptcy Code restricts insolvent private employers' ability to depart from collective bargaining agreements with unions. However, these special rules are not applicable in the case of municipal distress.[185] A South African municipality in distress will only be able to apply for debt relief under a financial recovery plan if it can show that all employees

182 INSOL International (n 114) 1.

183 Ibid 14.

184 Ibid.

185 See chapter 3, *sub* [3.2.4.b], noting the special rules under chapter 11 of the US Bankruptcy Code limiting insolvent employers' ability to depart from

have been discharged except those affordable in terms of reasonably projected revenues as set out in the plan.[186] Maximum discharge of employees is thus a *prerequisite* for debt relief. The distinction between municipal employees and private sector employees is stark in this context. In England, councils typically implement collective redundancies when a section 114 notice is issued.[187] Recent examples include Woking Borough Council, where all staff faced redundancy[188] and Leeds City Council, which decided to reduce staff by up to 750 posts by the end of the 2024/2025 financial year in order to avoid having to issue a section 114.[189]

A particularly thorny social issue relates to pension payments. In restructuring the insolvent municipality, the question arises whether the municipality will be able to maintain the promised levels of pension payments. This issue affects current but, most notably, former employees currently relying on such pension payments as their sole (or major) source of income. In the US, the effect of municipal insolvency on pensions has become particularly contentious, as chapter 3 discusses in detail.[190] If employees are considered a vulnerable group in employer insolvency,[191] *former* and now retired municipal employees constitute an exceptionally vulnerable group. To reduce pension benefits after retirement, when beneficiaries are no longer able to supplement their income by alternative employment, seems particularly unfair, and even more so where public employment is sought for generous retirement benefits, despite higher private-sector wages. Nevertheless, pension reductions are relatively common in municipal distress in the US. In Central Falls (Rhode Island, US) for example, retirees' benefits were cut by 55%.[192] Such pension

---

collective agreements with unions whereas those special rules are absent in chapter 9 of the US Code governing municipal distress.

186 See chapter 4, *sub* [4.3.2.1], outlining the conditions for debt relief under a financial recovery plan.

187 See chapter 5, *sub* [5.3.3.2], discussing the effect of issuing a section 114 notices on employment.

188 W Eichler, 'Woking Staff Face Redundancy' *LocalGov* (10 August 2023) <https://www.localgov.co.uk/Woking-staff-face-redundancy--/57720>.

189 D Mort and A Maclure, 'Leeds Council Budget Cuts: Job Losses, Building Closures and New Car Parking Charges Agreed' *Yorkshire Evening Post* (22 February 2024) <https://www.yorkshireeveningpost.co.uk/news/politics/council/leeds-council-budget-cuts-job-losses-building-closures-and-parking-charges-approved-4529869>.

190 See chapter 3, *sub* [3.3.1] and [3.4.3.2] on pensions.

191 Secunda (n 159) 872.

192 JM Beermann, 'Resolving the Public Pension Crisis' (2014) 41 Fordham Urb. L.J. 999. Also see chapter 3, *sub* [3.4.1] and [3.4.3.2] discussing pension fund reductions in other instances of municipal distress in the US, including in Detroit.

reductions raise larger questions about social justice.[193] In Beerman's words, the overarching question 'is about whether the US economy will support a thriving middle class, or whether it will join the many countries in the world that are divided between rich and poor',[194] because pension cuts 'would likely place large numbers of older Americans at risk of falling into poverty'.[195]

Municipal distress can severely impact public services, since local government globally are the backbone of service delivery. Worldwide, a core suite of public services[196] is provided by a local government entity, such as a municipality.[197]

Service delivery will inevitably come under pressure when a municipality experiences financial distress, with some services terminated altogether. This typically causes a ripple effect across a very broad social spectrum leading to further social problems, which the municipality is incapable to resolve given its financial distress. Financial constraints can force municipalities to cut back on essential services like water, sanitation, and garbage collection, increasing health risks. Underfunded health services struggle to manage these risks, which pressure public facilities like public transport, playgrounds, and markets and lead to potential sites of infection. The financial distress rules out increasing cleaning services. The inadequate responses can deteriorate social conditions and stability, risking community cohesion and potentially causing unrest. Such a risk is not confined to specific communities as health risks can spill over into neighbouring communities, triggering similar social pressures and exacerbating the overall crisis.

Reduced spending on public services can lead to long-term social effects, as municipalities fail to maintain infrastructure due to financial distress. This neglect results in increasing breakdowns, severely affecting dependent services. Eventually, the deterioration might reach a point where the municipality cannot provide services in the short to medium term, even if financial issues are resolved. For instance, a neglected water-supply network may become so critically damaged that effective short-term repairs are impossible, halting water services entirely.

---

193 Beermann (n 192) 1019.

194 Ibid.

195 Ibid 1020.

196 See chapters 3 *sub* [3.2.1], 4 *sub* [4.3.1.2] and 5 *sub* [5.3.1.2], discussing the public services rendered by municipalities in the US, South Africa, and England and Wales respectively.

197 *Joseph v City of Johannesburg* [2009] ZACC 30, [34]: '[t]he provision of basic municipal services is a cardinal function, if not the most important function, of every municipal government'.

These scenarios are not simply hypotheticals as all the case studies in the following chapters illustrate. In all three systems considered, examples are given of a breakdown in water services flowing from municipal financial distress—Flint, Michigan in the US,[198] Mangaung in South Africa,[199] and Thames Water in England.[200] These case studies clearly show that social considerations in municipal distress are very real and can have far-reaching social consequences for local communities.

2.3.3 Concluding Remarks on Social Indicators

It is evident that social considerations are highly relevant in the context of insolvency of all types of entities. The literature shows that a variety of social indicators are impacted by insolvency and that this impact can be mediated in different ways by various insolvency proceedings. Across all entity types, the relationship between insolvency proceedings and employment is one of the most prevalent social considerations in most legal systems. A second major social consideration is the interplay between insolvency proceedings and liability, especially of the mass tort type.

In the specific context of municipal entities facing insolvency, these identified social considerations take on an added level of significance. Such impact can extend far beyond the narrower confines of employment and liability and can adversely affect the very purpose of local government by undermining the delivery of basic services.

It follows that close attention to social indicators is highly relevant when considering the legal treatment of local public entity insolvency. As the subsequent chapters will show, social considerations are of such a nature that differentiated treatment of municipalities in distress compared to private-sector entity distress may be called for. At the very least, the high significance of social indicators in this context provides an important basis for very close attention to local public entity distress and the proceedings designed to manage such distress.

2.4 GOVERNANCE INDICATORS

Put simply, governance is about the way an entity, public or private, is run. As in the social context, governance has internal and external components. From an internal perspective, governance is about the ways in which decisions

---

198 See chapter 3, *sub* [3.4.2].

199 See chapter 4, *sub* [4.4.1].

200 See chapter 5, *sub* [5.4.3].

are made by an entity's leadership and the ways in which those decisions are enforced. From an external perspective, governance concerns the interactions between an entity's leaders and its stakeholders, including voters, residents, and taxpayers. In the restructuring or liquidation context, governance matters of particular focus may include decisions about how to use and spend money and mechanisms used to prevent fraud, or to address fraud upon discovery.

A key governance question in the insolvency and restructuring context concerns the point at which a debtor's existing management is deprived of the ability to act on behalf of the debtor and is instead replaced with outside management or oversight.[201] Relatedly, and perhaps more broadly, governance deals with the question of when an entity's management is held responsible for that entity's financial distress.[202]

Governance also concerns how an entity's leadership manages conflicts of interest, especially when it comes to matters such as management's control and compensation.[203] In liquidation and restructuring proceedings, governance focuses on resolving leadership conflicts and ensuring there are guidelines or codes of conduct for management and insolvency professionals.[204] The scope of governance also includes questions about the duties of an entity's officers and directors, to whom those duties are owed, and the extent of variance of the duties among different entities within the same industry or jurisdiction.[205]

Possibly the most "hot-button" governance issue in modern restructuring practice concerns the propriety of third-party releases in favour of a debtor entity's officers and directors.[206] If they are not consensual, meaning that all

---

[201] INSOL International (n 95) 145, discussing this concept in the context of resolving conflicts among the board and management in a restructuring.

[202] Ibid 224, discussing when directors may be held personally liable in Kenya during a liquidation.

[203] Ibid 2, including 'managing governance conflicts of interest in a restructuring' as one of the 'more pressing issues in which the fields of ESG and restructuring intersect'.

[204] Ibid, identifying another key theme as frameworks 'such as industry guidelines and best practices that serve to guide or influence conduct on ESG-related matters in a restructuring'.

[205] Ibid 59, discussing industry guidelines related to conflicts of interest for restructuring professionals in Argentina and noting that 'the precise content of the duty may vary depending on the corresponding venue'.

[206] Ibid 18: '[t]here are contentious policy issues surrounding the grant of third-party releases in favour of directors and officers of the company, particularly where the claims relate to alleged wrongdoing committed by the directors and officers'.

potential claim holders have not consented to the release,[207] these releases may be especially controversial. Critics assert that they are a way for an entity's directors and officers, who are not themselves subject to liquidation or restructuring proceedings, to reap the benefits of such proceedings whilst escaping their burdens.[208] The US Supreme Court recently held that non-consensual, non-debtor releases are not authorised by the Bankruptcy Code, injecting significant uncertainty about the future of chapter 11 practice, especially as it relates to resolution of mass torts.[209]

In spite of the controversial question of third-party releases, governance concerns are often aligned with insolvency and restructuring policies.[210] This stands in contrast with many environmental and social considerations.[211]

As one of the three components of ESG, good governance supports and reinforces considerations of environmental and social aspects. For example, a key facet of governance revolves around disclosure—disclosure of conflicts, of course, but also disclosure of information relating to other ESG indicators.[212]

---

[207] MJ Berger, 'How Nonconsensual Third-Party Releases Can Be Useful in Chapter 11 Bankruptcy Cases' *BankruptcyPower.com* (13 October 2023) <https://www.bankruptcypower.com/blog/how-nonconsensual-third-party-releases-can-be-useful-in-chapter-11-bankruptcy-cases/#:~:text=Nonconsensual%20third%2Dparty%20releases%20are,in%20a%20number%20of%20situations>.

[208] KK Going and D Thomson, 'Second Circuit Assesses Propriety of Third-Party Releases in Purdue' *MWE.com* (12 June 2023) <https://www.mwe.com/insights/second-circuit-assesses-propriety-of-third-party-releases-in-purdue/>: '[t]hese releases conflict with the notion that bankruptcy's benefits are reserved for parties who file for bankruptcy and, in doing so, subject themselves to the bankruptcy process and everything it legally entails'.

[209] *Purdue Pharma* (n 122).

[210] INSOL International (n 95) 4: 'some ESG matters, such as […] ensuring good corporative governance of the debtor-in-possession, are generally consistent and aligned with the policy objectives of restructuring law'.

[211] See, among others: Warren (n 5) 777 viewing bankruptcy 'as an attempt to reckon with a debtor's multiple defaults and to distribute the consequences among a number of different actors'; Baird and Jackson, 'Corporate Reorganizations' (n 7) 103 arguing that bankruptcy's purpose is to focus only on those 'who, outside of bankruptcy, have property rights in the assets of the firm'; LV Gelber and S Kim, 'The Intersection of Environmental and Bankruptcy Laws', in LP Schnapf (ed), *Environmental Issues in Business Transactions* (American Bar Association 2011) 339: '[a]n inherent conflict exists between the policies underlying environmental and bankruptcy laws'.

[212] INSOL International (n 95) 122, describing how the Canadian Securities Administrators published guidance on ESG practice disclosures for investment funds.

With respect to local governments in particular, for example, US law requires local governments to provide the public with access to their records.

It is thus important to pay attention to the role of governance in insolvency and restructuring procedures. This portion of the chapter is an attempt to pay governance matters their due. Questions about what it means to follow "good" governance principles and whether an entity is following those principles, within and outside of a distressed setting, are critically important to determining that entity's ultimate fate. The discussion that follows provides an overview of the role governance plays in various insolvency and restructuring contexts and foreshadows the country-specific information to follow in later chapters.

2.4.1 Liquidation Proceedings

Although governance may have played a role in an entity's need for liquidation, governance concerns often take a back seat in the insolvency or liquidation process itself. Perhaps this is for the obvious reason that an entity aiming to liquidate will soon have no need for governance. In liquidation proceedings, attention primarily shifts to liquidating the entity for the benefit of its creditors.[213] Most entities in liquidation lack the funds to pay most or all of the claims against them in full, meaning that creditors often take a front seat in liquidation proceedings, especially those creditors fortunate enough to hold priority claims or security interests in the debtor's assets.[214]

Despite the overall lack of focus on governance in liquidation proceedings, governance does have a role to play, particularly with respect to two primary areas: (1) the retention of professionals and (2) their compensation.[215] With respect to retention, an area of key importance is disclosure to the overseeing court or authority to ensure that disinterested professionals are involved in the process. This in turn benefits creditors (and possibly other stakeholders), enabling them to receive the most value from the liquidation process. With respect to compensation, disclosure again plays an important role in ensuring that those professionals hired to guide an entity are not looting the entity as they do so.

---

[213] See chapter 4, *sub* [4.2.4] describing the laws governing insolvency as primarily creditor-focused.

[214] See chapter 3, *sub* [3.2.4.4] noting the lack of priority and special treatment given to ESG-related claims in general.

[215] This is also a focus in restructuring proceedings: INSOL International (n 95) 2, listing as a key governance question, 'How are board/management conflicts addressed in a restructuring, e.g. in situations where board/management receive benefits under a restructuring plan …?'.

For example, in US liquidation proceedings under chapter 7, the management of a business debtor is replaced with a trustee, whose role is to liquidate the business's assets and distribute the proceeds to creditors (and other stakeholders, if applicable).[216] In order to maximise the liquidation value of the debtor's assets, the trustee, in turn, will often hire professionals, to help evaluate the debtor's assets, arrange sales, and otherwise conduct the process of liquidation.[217] Although chapter 7 trustees themselves are paid a percentage of the amount distributed to creditors,[218] any professionals they hire must disclose their fees to the bankruptcy court to ensure that they are only being compensated a "reasonable" amount 'for actual, necessary services rendered'.[219]

In short, although governance concerns do not generally loom large on a going-forward basis when an entity is slated for liquidation, governance matters, such as disclosure, do play a part in liquidation proceedings so that the proceedings can be conducted in a manner that is fair and value-maximising.

2.4.2 Restructuring Proceedings

Because a restructuring contemplates an entity's survival, the entity's governance—past, present, and future—takes on more significance than in a liquidation. A restructuring is an opportunity to scrutinise an entity's past governance failures,[220] as well as to construct new, "good governance" frameworks for the entity's future.

---

216 US Courts, *Chapter 7—Bankruptcy Basics* <https://www.uscourts.gov/services-forms/bankruptcy/bankruptcy-basics/chapter-7-bankruptcy-basics>: '[T]he bankruptcy trustee gathers and sells the debtor's nonexempt assets and uses the proceeds of such assets to pay holders of claims … in accordance with the provisions of the Bankruptcy Code'.

217 11 US Code, § 327; W Metzen, 'Chapter 7 Bankruptcy Fee Applications: What the 5th Circuit Has to Say to Trustee's Professionals' *Detroit Bankruptcy Lawyer* (Detroit, 23 February 2022) <https://www.detroitbankruptcylawyer.com/chapter-7-bankruptcy-trustee/2022/02/chapter-7-bankruptcy-fee-applications-what-the-5th-circuit-has-to-say-to-trustees-professionals/> (noting that professionals employed by chapter 7 trustees 'can be attorneys, accountants, realtors, appraisers, and others').

218 11 US Code, § 326(a).

219 Ibid § 330(a).

220 This is not to say that liquidation proceedings do not involve scrutiny of past governance failures; rather, when past governance is examined in liquidation proceedings, the goal is different. For example, governance may be examined in the context of determining which avoidance actions a trustee or creditors may bring in the proceedings to enhance creditors' recoveries.

In a restructuring, as in a liquidation, the same concerns about retention and compensation of professionals exist. The US Bankruptcy Code does not differentiate between restructuring and liquidation proceedings when it comes to disclosure of professionals' retention and compensation. Because these issues have been discussed above, this section will primarily focus on governance concerns that uniquely arise in the restructuring context.

The role and importance of governance in restructuring proceedings is reflected, at least somewhat, in the written laws and policies of the countries studied in this book.[221] Furthermore, in the US and the UK at least, a culture has evolved wherein the public typically does not leap to blame management for a company's financial distress. In the UK, the Cork Report advised that corporate failure should be seen as a 'fact of life';[222] similarly, in the US, corporate failure is often described merely as part of a company's life cycle, rather than as a failure of management.[223]

This culture is identifiable in the general attitude toward restructuring and, in the US in particular, in the popularity of the DIP model of chapter 11 bankruptcy. Indeed, the DIP model is the hallmark of US restructuring and in general, in a chapter 11 case, existing management remains in charge of a company. Common rationales for the DIP model are that it promotes early intervention, on the theory that management will be more likely to seek bankruptcy relief if they know they will not be displaced as a result, and that it allows for the company to rely on management's industry expertise to guide the debtor to a fresh start.[224]

---

[221] See chapter 4, *sub* [4.2.4] (noting that South African restructuring law contemplates more stakeholders than insolvency law and seeks to balance the rights and interests of all relevant stakeholders, as opposed to merely creditors); see chapter 3, *sub* [3.2.2] (explaining that, in the US, business rescue proceedings generally seek to retain current management); see also chapter 5, *sub* [5.2.2] (noting that, although England and Wales have not codified governance protections in their restructuring laws, an expansive interpretation of the concept of fairness may provide some similar protections).

[222] See chapter 5, *sub* [5.3.3.3].

[223] See chapter 3, *sub* [3.2.2]. See also: E Heaslip, 'Don't Be Afraid of Failure! 4 Smart Strategies for Learning From Your Mistakes' *U.S. Chamber of Commerce* (2 January 2024) <https://www.uschamber.com/co/start/strategy/how-to-learn-from-failure> ('[f]ailure happens fairly regularly in growing businesses'); C Nobel, 'Why Companies Fail—and How Their Founders Can Bounce Back' *Harvard Business School* (Cambridge, 7 March 2011) <https://hbswk.hbs.edu/item/why-companies-failand-how-their-founders-can-bounce-back> ('[f]ailure is the engine that causes growth', quoting Shikhar Ghosh).

[224] DJ Whaley and CG Bradley, *Problems and Materials on Debtor and Creditor Law* (Wolters Kluwer 2022) 15: '[t]he general thinking […] is that often

The DIP model is simply the default rule in a chapter 11 case. It is possible for a case trustee to be appointed to operate the debtor's business and guide the debtor through bankruptcy.[225] The bankruptcy court is required to order the appointment of a case trustee if a party in interest or the US Trustee[226] has moved for a trustee and there is "cause" for appointing a trustee, including 'fraud, dishonesty, incompetence, or gross mismanagement', as well as if a case trustee's appointment would be in the interests of creditors, equity security holders, or the estate.[227]

If, as a general matter, a legislature believes it is valuable to keep current management involved (in at least some capacity) in a restructuring proceeding, the question arises as to how to motivate management to remain involved in an entity that is suffering acute financial distress. One incentive is to offer management a release from liability. As mentioned above, third-party releases are a hot-button governance issue in many restructurings and, in the US, the question of the propriety of non-consensual third-party releases in chapter 11 plans was recently answered, in the negative, by the Supreme Court.[228] Proponents of non-consensual third-party releases claimed that such releases were a necessary component of a company's rehabilitation. They were granted 'in exchange for substantial contributions from the released parties' and were approved only when found essential to the reorganisation.[229] Opponents, however, lambasted these releases on a variety of grounds, including the claim that they were unconstitutional.[230] Others characterised them as escape valves for parties that do not themselves share in the burden of a bankruptcy

[...] managers have irreplaceable expertise'.

[225] 11 US Code, § 1106.

[226] The US trustee is part of the federal Department of Justice and acts as a watchdog, overseeing the administrative aspects of a bankruptcy case: US Courts, *Chapter 11 – Bankruptcy Basics* <https://www.uscourts.gov/services-forms/bankruptcy/bankruptcy-basics/chapter-11-bankruptcy-basics#:~:text=Although%20the%20appointment%20of%20a,in%20a%20chapter%2011%20case>.

[227] 11 US Code, § 1104(a). Case trustees are also appointed in every case filed under subchapter V of chapter 11, which deals with small business reorganisations: 11 US Code, § 1183. A full discussion of a subchapter V trustee's role is outside the scope of this book.

[228] *Purdue Pharma* (n 122).

[229] AJ Casey, 'Responding to Flawed Arguments Against Bankruptcy Releases' The Federalist Society (7 September 2023) <https://fedsoc.org/commentary/fedsoc-blog/responding-to-flawed-arguments-against-bankruptcy-releases>.

[230] R Brubaker, 'Mandatory Aggregation of Mass Tort Litigation in Bankruptcy' (2022) 131 Yale L.J. Forum 960, 965: '[t]he fundamental illegitimacy of nondebtor releases is of a constitutional magnitude'; see generally AJ Levitin, 'The Constitutional Problem of Nondebtor Releases in Bankruptcy' (2022) 91

proceeding.[231] Although the Supreme Court held that non-consensual, non-debtor releases are indeed impermissible (except when specifically authorised by Congress), many issues remain open, including, notably, what counts as "consent" to a release and whether exculpations, a narrower form of release, are permissible. Consequently, it is likely that third-party releases will continue to be attempted, in some form, in future proceedings.

In England, third-party plan releases are also "commonplace".[232] English courts scrutinise third-party releases on the basis of necessity but also look to how they are explained and disclosed.[233] A third-party release cannot be implied, a rule that reinforces the idea that disclosure is paramount when it comes to governance issues.[234] If the scheme or plan containing the releases is "fair" overall, it is possible in England for third parties to be released from liability for the debtor's breaches.[235]

In addition to third-party releases, debtors may attempt to provide financial incentives to entice management to remain in place during a restructuring. In the US, these payments are strictly limited and heavily scrutinised.[236] Debtors must satisfy the factors enumerated in section 503(c)(1) of the US Bankruptcy Code in order to pay employees a bonus under a Key Employee Retention Plan (KERP).[237] Alternatively, debtors may pay management a bonus under a Key Employee Incentive Plan (KEIP) after that employee has attained certain

---

Fordham L. Rev. 429, arguing that all non-consensual nondebtor releases are unconstitutional.

[231] G Posner and R Brubaker, 'The Sacklers Could Get Away With It' *N.Y. Times* (New York, 22 July 2020) <https://www.nytimes.com/2020/07/22/opinion/sacklers-opioid-epidemic.html>, noting that 'a full liability release would provide the Sacklers [the non-bankrupt owners of chapter 11 debtor Purdue Pharma] with more immunity than they could ever obtain in a personal bankruptcy filing'.

[232] See chapter 5, *sub* [5.2.3.1].

[233] Ibid.

[234] Ibid.

[235] Ibid.

[236] S Restagno, 'KEIPs v. KERPs: Court Shows Deference to Chapter 11 Companies to Defend Their Bonus Plans Under BAPCPA' *ABI.org* <https://www.abi.org/member-resources/blog/keips-v-kerps-court-shows-deference-to-chapter-11-companies-to-defend-their>.

[237] 11 US Code, § 503(c)(1). The factors are: the employee has a *bona fide* job offer from another employer at the same or greater rate of compensation; the employee performs functions essential to the company's survival; and the amount of the bonus is not greater than ten times the amount of bonuses given to non-management employees and not greater than 25% of the bonus paid to the employee in the previous calendar year.

milestones, such that payment is justified under the facts and circumstances of the case.[238]

However, even when the law allows management to stay in place during a restructuring, and even when it allows for the debtor to provide incentives to management, in practice, in the US at least, it is not uncommon for members of management to depart prior to or during a restructuring.[239] Even if management does not leave, debtors or prospective debtors will often seek to hire turnaround professionals[240] and/or to replace members of their boards of directors.[241]

Even if management is not replaced, in full or in part, in a restructuring, management typically hires professionals to guide them through restructuring proceedings.[242] US law imposes requirements on the retention of these professionals to ensure that they are not conflicted—namely, to ensure that they are "disinterested",[243] which is a defined term under US law.[244] However, the law

---

238 Ibid § 503(c)(3).

239 Whaley and Bradley (n 224) 15: '[o]ften particularly inept or corrupt managers have been replaced prior to the bankruptcy filing'.

240 See, among others: J Gething et al, 'When Do You Need a Chief Restructuring Officer?' *McKinsey & Co.* (13 November 2020) <https://www.mckinsey.com/capabilities/transformation/our-insights/when-do-you-need-a-chief-restructuring-officer>: '[a chief restructuring officer] is signaled for when an outside event is expected to cause a breach of covenant or missed repayment on a loan, or a liquidity crisis and overleveraged balance sheet'.

241 See generally JA Ellias, E Kamar and K Kastiel, 'The Rise of Bankruptcy Directors' (2022) 95 S. Cal. L. Rev. 1083, criticising the practice of distressed companies that appoint bankruptcy experts to their boards of directors in preparation for a chapter 11 filing.

242 Whaley and Bradley (n 224) 381: '[o]ne of the most significant areas of close court supervision is the hiring and the pay of professionals such as lawyers, accountants, consultants, brokers, and so on'.

243 11 US Code, § 327(a), providing that the debtor in possession 'may employ one or more attorneys, accountants, appraisers, auctioneers, or other professional persons, that do not hold or represent an interest adverse to the estate, and that are disinterested persons'.

244 Ibid § 101(14): '[t]he term "disinterested person" means a person that (A) is not a creditor, an equity security holder, or an insider; (B) is not and was not, within 2 years before the date of the filing of the petition, a director, officer, or employee of the debtor; and (C) does not have an interest materially adverse to the interest of the estate or of any class of creditors or equity security holders, by reason of any direct or indirect relationship to, connection with, or interest in, the debtor, or for any other reason'.

does not ensure or mandate that these professionals possess particular competencies, a theme that recurs in the context of municipal distress.

In summary, governance matters do play a significant role in restructuring proceedings. In business restructurings in particular, there appears to be less blame for management and more acceptance of management's continuing control during and after restructuring proceedings. Laws, whether directly or indirectly, provide incentives for management to stay on during a restructuring as long as governance has been generally good. The law also provides guardrails to ensure that key governance issues, such as fraud or conflicts of interest, do not derail a restructuring. At the same time, the law in practice may of course vary from the law in the books, making it difficult to assess whether the law's incentives and guardrails are doing their intended work in every case.

2.4.3 Municipalities in Distress

Municipal governance is often viewed differently than corporate governance, just as municipal distress may be viewed differently from corporate distress. When it comes to distressed municipalities, governance challenges can loom quite large. The extent to which a municipality's management (i.e. local officials and councils) are to blame for the municipality's financial distress may be viewed very differently from in the corporate context. The extent to which local officials may be removed or replaced also varies from the corporate restructuring analogue.

One of the pervading themes across this book is the hands-off nature of judicial scrutiny of municipal governance. This can be seen in South Africa, where courts are very deferential in decisions made about public funds and public spending.[245] This can also be seen in the US: even when a municipality seeks bankruptcy relief, bankruptcy courts are prohibited from interfering with a municipality's governance or the use of municipal property throughout the chapter 9 case.[246] Like their corporate counterparts, municipal debtors in the US remain "in possession" and control throughout the bankruptcy case. However, as will be described further below, the identity and selection of those in charge of the municipality during bankruptcy proceedings is often the subject of debate.

Although US law restricts bankruptcy court involvement in municipal affairs, in practice, bankruptcy courts have been highly influential in shaping

---

245 See chapter 4, *sub* [4.3.3].

246 11 US Code, § 903 (reserving the power to control municipalities to the states) and § 904 (limiting a court's jurisdiction and powers in a chapter 9 case).

a municipality's forward-looking governance.[247] Indeed, some US scholars have even advocated for bankruptcy courts to more explicitly shape municipal governance.[248]

Despite the hands-off judicial approaches to municipal distress as seen in the law in the books, governance challenges can significantly contribute to municipal financial distress.[249] In the US, at least, the hands-off judicial approach is commonly justified by the need to respect federalism and the fact that the Constitution reserves most control over municipalities to the fifty states.[250] In practice, however, tying a judge's hands may not be the most effective way to address municipal distress, especially distress that was caused by mismanagement. Consequently, in practice, in the US at least, judges have at times interfered beyond what the law appears to allow.[251]

Another theme present in cases of local government financial distress is either partial or full replacement of management. For example, in South Africa, distressed municipalities may become subject to the authority of an administrator, which steps into the shoes of the municipal council but does not displace all local management.[252] Notably, however, there are no industry standards or qualifications for these administrators, and so the administrator that takes over may be unqualified to do so effectively.[253]

Similarly, the English chapter describes several instances where management loses control of a local authority after a section 114 notice is issued.[254] As in South Africa, there are no specific qualifications for replacement

---

[247] See generally: MB Jacoby, 'Federalism Form and Function in the Detroit Bankruptcy' (2016) 33 Yale J. Reg. 55 (describing how a bankruptcy court can 'functionally exercis[e] significant influence throughout a chapter 9 case' and using the Detroit bankruptcy as a representative case study).

[248] See generally: CP Gillette and DA Skeel, Jr., 'Governance Reform and the Judicial Role in Municipal Bankruptcy' (2016) 125 Yale L.J. 1150 (arguing that bankruptcy must address governance dysfunction and that bankruptcy courts can and should effect municipal governance reform).

[249] See chapter 4, *sub* [4.4] (illustrating, through case studies, how governance challenges can cause both severe financial distress and significant public service disruptions, as well as knock-on environmental and social problems).

[250] Jacoby (n 247) 57: '[c]ommentators have asserted for decades that the municipal bankruptcy system [...] abides by Constitutional commands and federalism principles only if federal court intervention is minimized'.

[251] Ibid 60 (questioning whether the law's restraints on judicial interference in chapter 9 bankruptcy proceedings are effective and raising questions about 'the sufficiency of constraints on the federal judiciary').

[252] See chapter 4, *sub* [4.3.2]–[4.3.3]

[253] Ibid [4.3.2.2].

[254] See chapter 5, *sub* [5.3.2].

management.[255] The removal and replacement of management with leaders who are not necessarily any more qualified or competent to run the local authority than the displaced management—and who may, in fact, be less qualified and competent—seems to be a particularly ineffective approach to addressing municipal distress, even distress caused (in whole or in part) by failures of governance. If management is removed immediately or without an assessment of whether and to what extent governance problems contributed to the local authority's distress, such action may motivate leaders of distressed localities to try and hide their problems instead of seeking out early intervention and relief.

The US demonstrates a similar pattern of replacing elected officials with unelected leaders. This replacement happens, not by virtue of US bankruptcy law, but rather because of state laws, some of which require or allow the appointment of state receivers or oversight boards once a municipality exhibits signs of financial distress.[256]

Whenever management is forcibly replaced—and replacement of management is a common theme across all jurisdictions studied in this book—resentment seems to follow. If municipal leadership is not completely replaced, those left behind must co-operate with the administrators, receivers, or oversight boards that take over in order for the municipality's financial distress to be resolved smoothly. However, in practice, such co-operation can be lacking. The South African chapter, for instance, documents how municipal administrations have refused to co-operate with administrators, occasionally even blocking them from accessing information or premises.[257]

As in the corporate context, problems with governance can also result in municipal financial distress. However, the primary fixes offered by the existing laws—a hands-off judicial approach to governance, sometimes in combination with hands-on interference from a higher level of government that results in replacing local officials with new management—does not seem responsive to the root problem. Put differently, failures in governance often cause financial distress, leading a municipality to seek relief in the courts or via administrative changes.[258] But when relief arrives, in the form of replacement management, that relief is not particularly (substantively) qualified nor specially skilled in good governance techniques, even if at times good governance is critical to resolving the municipality's financial woes.

---

[255] Ibid [5.3.2.1].

[256] See chapter 3, *sub* [3.3.2.3].

[257] See chapter 4, *sub* [4.4.1].

[258] See chapter 5, *sub* [5.3.3.3] (noting that most independent reviews of section 114 notice cases showed serious governance failures in the lead-up to the issuance of the section 114 notice).

As in the other two jurisdictions studied in this book, in the US, failures of governance have led to municipal financial distress and have had knock-on effects with respect to environmental and social issues. For example, even after the US federal government allocated money to the city of Flint (Michigan, USA) so that it could rectify a growing public health crisis, poor local decision-making resulted in that money largely remaining unspent.[259] This was despite a widely publicised public health crisis that affected some of Flint's most vulnerable citizens.

In addition to thinking about governance failure, municipal distress shines a light on another critical aspect of governance: disclosure of information. How do we know when a municipality is distressed and what, exactly, has caused that distress? The answer lies, in part, in the reporting and auditing requirements a municipality is subject to. In the US, these requirements are largely the province of state law and vary widely across the country, although the federal government has recently stepped in to provide some regulation in this area.[260]

Auditing and reporting are critical components of assessing a municipality's governance, especially because merely having good structures in place does not ensure good governance outcomes. This appears to be the experience in England with the borough of Croydon.[261] Croydon experienced governance failures that led to financial difficulties despite having a governance structure in place, because senior officers were able to disregard those governance structures.[262]

Yet another governance theme in the context of municipal distress involves blame. To what extent are municipal officials blamed for the problems their municipalities experience? And do municipalities fare better under elected officials or under replacement, appointed officials? In the US, some courts have sought to allow municipal officials to distance themselves from the municipality's failures through the allowance of third-party releases in municipal debt adjustment plans.[263] In addition, chapter 9 of the US Bankruptcy Code extends the bankruptcy automatic stay to officers and inhabitants of the

---

259 See chapter 3, *sub* [3.4.2].

260 See G Miller, 'The Coming Fight Over Municipal Financial Data' *Governing* (14 November 2023) <https://www.governing.com/finance/the-coming-fight-over-municipal-financial-data> (explaining that the federal Financial Data Transparency Act requires states and localities to prepare their financial information in machine-readable forms).

261 See chapter 5, *sub* [5.4.1].

262 Ibid.

263 See chapter 3, *sub* [3.3.3.3].

debtor municipality, giving those officers and inhabitants breathing space to sort out their own connections to the municipality's failures.[264]

In the case studies analysed in the US chapter, both Detroit and Flint were under emergency management for periods of years, during which time the citizens of those cities were deprived of democratic self-governance.[265] In the case of Flint in particular, poor decisions by the emergency manager directly led to a crisis with significant environmental, social, and health impacts.[266] Is it proper to blame democratically elected officials for this crisis when the city was under the control of an unelected emergency manager? To what extent should government be to blame at all when private companies also exercised influence in the city? These questions are still being untangled in the story of Flint, and the answers remain unclear.[267] On a larger scale, the insights gleaned from all of the country-specific chapters in this book suggest that when a municipality's governance structure is changed, whether due to financial distress or otherwise, questions of accountability often remain unanswered.

In sum, governance challenges and their resolution loom large in municipal restructurings. Yet, the ways in which the jurisdictions studied resolve municipal distress do not generally provide good fixes for governance challenges. The courts remain at least superficially hands-off. Replacing local officials raises concerns about democracy, self-governance, competence, and qualifications. Punishing those officials, whether explicitly or implicitly, may lead to less disclosure overall and less proactive attention to financial distress warnings. In short, there is no easy fix to these governance challenges, but we have much to learn from the studies in the chapters to come.

2.4.4 Concluding Remarks on Governance Indicators

When financial distress occurs, it is perhaps natural to blame poor management. Indeed, poor management is often a (significant) contributing factor to an entity's financial distress. In examining the governance issues that arise in insolvency and debt restructuring processes, however, it becomes clear that merely substituting new management, without examining their qualifications and without taking other steps to promote a good governance framework (such as disclosure rules), is a solution that may create more problems than it resolves.

At bottom, we care about governance because we care about who makes the decisions that enable an entity's continued existence, as well as the process behind the decision-making. Without governance—without a system for

264 Ibid [3.2.2.2].
265 Ibid [3.3.1]–[3.3.2].
266 Ibid [3.3.2].
267 Ibid.

making and evaluating those decisions—an entity will not exist for long or very well. Thus, when examining restructuring proceedings—or any proceedings that contemplate the continued existence of a financially distressed entity—governance questions should be at the forefront. In the studies of the three jurisdictions that form the centrepiece of this book, the lack of attention paid to governance matters by these jurisdictions can at times seem surprising. Whilst critics may dismiss ESG concerns as unimportant or secondary, the fact remains that neglecting governance threatens not just an entity's existence but its ability to continue providing goods and services deemed necessary to a basic standard of living.

2.5 CONCLUDING REMARKS

The financial distress of local authorities is a complex and multifaceted issue that necessitates a principled approach beyond the proceduralist frameworks traditionally applied to insolvent individuals and companies. Whilst the US and (to a lesser extent) South Africa have developed some comprehensive rules for addressing municipal financial distress, many countries lack comprehensive and coherent frameworks. This book argues for a new theoretical foundation that addresses the unique challenges faced by local authorities, emphasising the need to maintain their public functions even during periods of financial distress. The proposed approach is flexible and modular, incorporating various strategies to enhance the likelihood of sustainable success for restructured entities.

Local authorities serve critical public functions that cannot be easily interrupted or abandoned. Their role in providing essential services such as health, safety, water sanitation, education, and social housing underscores the necessity of a legal framework that ensures these functions continue uninterrupted. This framework must be flexible, allowing for a multi-pronged and modular approach that adapts to the specific circumstances and needs of each distressed municipality. Such an approach increases the chances of achieving sustainable success by providing a tailored set of solutions that address the unique challenges faced by local authorities.

Economic tools often fall short in explaining the operations of local authorities because they assume rational behaviour, a notion that behavioural economic studies have repeatedly challenged. Moreover, these tools overlook the critical role of local authorities as agents of distributive justice and inclusive change. Local authorities are not merely economic units; they are politically elected and essential components of social infrastructure, promoting equity and providing support to vulnerable populations. Therefore, any framework for addressing their financial distress must recognise and enhance their capacity to act as forces for good within their communities.

Promoting local subsidiarity is essential in devising effective solutions for financially distressed local authorities. Community participation and engagement, alongside institutionalised solidarity, together ensure that policy choices reflect the needs and aspirations of the community. This participatory approach fosters a sense of ownership and accountability, increasing the likelihood of sustainable recovery. By involving the community in decision-making processes, local authorities can develop more resilient and responsive strategies to overcome financial challenges.

Additionally, a framework for local authorities in financial distress must address the cognitive limitations inherent in human decision-making processes. Ensuring procedural and substantive fairness in managing financially distressed entities requires mechanisms that mitigate biases and promote informed, balanced decisions. This can be achieved through the integration of alternative theoretical approaches, such as vulnerability-led frameworks, which complement proceduralism and offer a more nuanced understanding of the issues at hand.

A vulnerability-led approach emphasises the protection of the most vulnerable and less resilient players, ensuring that the restructuring process provides enhanced support where it is most needed. This approach aligns with the principles of fairness and equity, advocating for a fair distribution of assets to creditors and adequate funding of essential services. By focusing on the needs of the most vulnerable, the restructuring of financially distressed local entities can achieve long-term sustainable success, benefiting the entire community.

The book advocates for a polycentric approach to dealing with local entities in financial distress, leveraging ESG criteria to guide the restructuring process. ESG indicators—Environmental, Social, and Governance—provide a comprehensive framework for evaluating and improving the sustainability and resilience of local entities. This approach not only promotes equality and tailored relief measures for the most vulnerable but also ensures that a broad category of stakeholders can influence the decision making process. By incorporating diverse perspectives and priorities, the restructuring process becomes more inclusive and effective.

Furthermore, the approach proposed in this book respects varying social, cultural, and economic norms. It is neither imposed by central governments, nor designed solely with the priorities of the Global North or Developed World in mind. Instead, it is an adaptable framework that can be tailored to the specific needs and contexts of different communities, ensuring relevance and efficacy across diverse settings.

In conclusion, this book highlights the human component of the financial distress of local authorities in multiple jurisdictions. It suggests that the most appropriate way to devise long-term sustainable solutions is through a modular approach centred on the promotion of ESG criteria. Reliance on ESG indicators is essential for achieving the sustainable and equitable recovery of financially distressed local entities. These indicators provide a comprehensive framework to evaluate and enhance the sustainability and resilience of local authorities, ensuring that they can continue to serve their communities effectively and equitably. Through this innovative and inclusive approach, we can develop robust solutions that address the financial challenges of local authorities whilst promoting social justice, community engagement, and long-term sustainability.

3. United States of America

3.1 INTRODUCTION

As the only jurisdiction in this book with an insolvency-based framework for addressing municipal distress, the US provides an important source of comparison with the UK and South Africa when it comes to examining the treatment of distressed local public entities. The chapter begins by providing an overview and an environmental, social, and governance (ESG) critique of US bankruptcy law (2). It then turns to a discussion of US municipalities, examining and critiquing, from an ESG perspective, the two routes a municipality in distress may take to resolve severe financial difficulties: filing for chapter 9 bankruptcy or being subject to state intervention procedures (3). The chapter concludes with two case studies—Detroit and Flint, both cities in the State of Michigan—which illustrate various ESG factors in action (4). The chapter concludes by discussing what can be learnt from the case studies and suggesting that further work must be done to promote ESG criteria in municipal debt restructuring.

3.2 US BANKRUPTCY LAW

The US Constitution empowers the US Congress, the federal legislature, to enact uniform laws "on the subject of bankruptcies".[1] In common legal parlance, "bankruptcy" refers to a court proceedings used to address and resolve a debtor's financial difficulties. US bankruptcy law has a lengthy history. The first federal bankruptcy law was enacted in 1800, just 24 years after the creation of the US.[2] In its early days, US bankruptcy was primarily a creditors' remedy. Today, the law has evolved and now seeks to balance creditor remedies with debtor relief, though the extent to which this balance has been achieved is a subject of open debate.[3] Bankruptcy today is often referred to as a means

[1] US Constitution, art I, s 8, cl 4.

[2] Bankruptcy Act of 1800, ch 19, 2 Stat 19 (repealed 1803).

[3] See, among others: JR Graham, 'Institutional Capture: Why We're Overdue for a New Bankruptcy Act' (2023) 19 N.Y.U.J.L. & Bus. 409, 411 (stating that the US Bankruptcy Code 'is the most "debtor-friendly" in the world'); R Ruser,

of providing distressed debtors with a "fresh start", and this fresh start narrative is particularly salient in the context of individual (consumer) bankruptcy.[4]

There are two primary forms of relief available under US bankruptcy law: liquidation and rehabilitation (or reorganisation). In addition to the federal Bankruptcy Code, the laws of each of the 50 states contain various alternatives to the bankruptcy process, such as receiverships and assignments for the benefit of creditors. However, per the US Constitution, states cannot enact their own bankruptcy laws, and state alternatives to bankruptcy therefore cannot discharge debt and are limited in various other ways. In addition, bankruptcy cases are heard exclusively in the federal courts; Congress has created separate, specialised bankruptcy courts to hear and decide cases arising under bankruptcy law.[5]

Bankruptcy is an exclusively federal remedy because the framers of the US Constitution were concerned that if states designed their own bankruptcy laws, they would favour their own creditors over creditors in other states. Even if this did not occur, if a debtor had creditors, property, or both in multiple states, variations in state laws could create inequalities among otherwise similarly situated parties. As one of the framers stated, '[t]he power of establishing uniform laws of bankruptcy is so intimately connected with the regulation of commerce, and will prevent so many frauds where the parties or their property may lie or be removed into different states that the expediency of it seems not likely to be drawn into question'.[6]

The federal bankruptcy laws are found in Title 11 of the US Code, otherwise known as the "Bankruptcy Code".

3.2.1 The Bankruptcy Code

The US Bankruptcy Code is divided into nine chapters. Chapters 1, 3, and 5 are chapters of general application; each contains provisions that, in general,

'Analysis of the Bankruptcy Abuse Prevention and Consumer Protection Act of 2005 (BAPCPA)' 2 SPNA Rev., available at: <https://scholarworks.gvsu.edu/spnareview/vol2/iss1/6/>, finding that the 2005 amendments to the Bankruptcy Code are largely "creditor-friendly".

[4] See US Courts, *Process – Bankruptcy Basics* <https://www.uscourts.gov/services-forms/bankruptcy/bankruptcy-basics/process-bankruptcy-basics>: 'A fundamental goal of the federal bankruptcy laws enacted by Congress is to give debtors a financial "fresh start" from burdensome debts'.

[5] See US Courts, *Bankruptcy Cases* <https://www.uscourts.gov/about-federal-courts/types-cases/bankruptcy-cases>, stating that federal courts have 'exclusive jurisdiction over bankruptcy cases'.

[6] J Madison, 'The Federalist Papers No 42' (1788).

apply to each of the subsequent chapters.[7] The remaining chapters outline specific processes that apply only to particular debtors. These chapters are:

- Chapter 7 (liquidation);
- Chapter 9 (adjustment of municipal debt);
- Chapter 11 (reorganisation);
- Chapter 12 (debt adjustment for family farmers and family fishermen);
- Chapter 13 (debt adjustment for individual wage earners); and
- Chapter 15 (ancillary and cross-border cases).

Several of the above "case chapters" include subchapters, which apply in special types of cases. The subchapters are:

- Subchapter III of chapter 7 (stockbroker liquidation);
- Subchapter IV of chapter 7 (commodity broker liquidation);
- Subchapter V of chapter 7 (clearing bank liquidation);
- Subchapter IV of chapter 11 (railroad reorganisation); and
- Subchapter V of chapter 11 (small business reorganisation).

The Bankruptcy Code has been in effect since 1 October 1979.[8] It was enacted as part of the Bankruptcy Reform Act of 1978 and is the law currently in effect in the US. Although the Bankruptcy Code has undergone several revisions since it was first drafted in 1978, most notably through the Bankruptcy Abuse Prevention and Consumer Protection Act of 2005,[9] and the Small Business Reorganization Act of 2019,[10] which added the above-referenced subchapter V of chapter 11, the Code itself has not received a holistic overhaul since its enactment.

3.2.2 Purposes and Rules

The purpose of bankruptcy law depends on which type of bankruptcy proceedings, namely liquidation or reorganisation, a debtor has chosen or is otherwise eligible for.

Broadly speaking, a liquidation bankruptcy under chapter 7 has a twofold purpose: to provide (1) relief to debtors and (2) equitable treatment to creditors. Several aspects of liquidation bankruptcy are especially important for

7 Only some of these general provisions apply in chapters 9 and 15.
8 Pub L No. 95-598, 92 Stat 2549 (1978).
9 Pub L No 109-8, 119 Stat 23 (2005).
10 Pub L No 116-54 (2019).

fulfilling these purposes. First, liquidation bankruptcy is often, but not always, voluntary, meaning that the debtor itself initiates the process. Once the bankruptcy petition is filed, an automatic stay immediately takes effect, halting all debt collection actions against the debtor and giving the debtor breathing space to assess its next steps.[11] A bankruptcy trustee then proceeds to liquidate the debtor's assets for its creditors' benefit; upon doing so, the debtor receives a discharge, and creditors can no longer look to the debtor—or what is left of it—for payment. A debtor's secured creditors receive the value of their collateral and are paid before unsecured creditors. A debtor's unsecured creditors are paid according to the Bankruptcy Code's priority scheme;[12] if an unsecured creditor does not fall within any of the categories listed in that scheme, the creditor is considered a general unsecured creditor and is paid equally with other general unsecured creditors on a *pro rata* basis.[13]

Municipal debt adjustment under chapter 9 of the Code is a focal point of this chapter and will be discussed in greater detail below.

In contrast to a liquidation, the purpose of a business reorganisation bankruptcy under chapter 11 is 'to restructure a business's finances so that it may continue to operate, provide its employees with jobs, pay its creditors, and produce a return for its stockholders. The premise of a business reorganisation is that assets that are used for production in the industry for which they were designed are more valuable than those same assets sold for scrap'.[14] Similar to a liquidation, a reorganisation bankruptcy is designed to maximise the debtor's value for the benefit of its creditors, but in a reorganisation bankruptcy, it is generally recognised that the debtor is worth more as a going concern than if the business were disbanded and the assets sold piecemeal. Put slightly differently, in a reorganisation bankruptcy, the optimal use of the debtor's assets is typically their continued use in an ongoing business.

A business seeking to reorganise under bankruptcy law typically proceeds under chapter 11 of the Bankruptcy Code. In recent years, scholars and practitioners alike have criticised chapter 11 for failing to achieve its goals of value maximisation and optimal asset deployment, as well as for being too expensive and cumbersome a process.[15] Regardless of these criticisms, chapter 11 is still a popular avenue for businesses seeking to reorganise their debts and continue life as a going concern. Indeed, even international businesses have sought out

---

11 11 US Code, § 362.

12 Ibid §§ 507(a), 726(a)(1).

13 Ibid § 726(b).

14 HR Rep No 95-595, 95th Cong, 1st Sess, at 220 (1977).

15 See, among others: Commission to Study the Reform of Chapter 11, *Final Report and Recommendations* (American Bankruptcy Institute 2014).

chapter 11, rather than attempting to use restructuring procedures that may be available in their home countries.[16]

Notably, although chapter 11 is frequently characterised as the business reorganisation chapter of the Bankruptcy Code, its use is not limited to business entities. Individuals may also file for chapter 11 relief.[17] In addition, businesses sometimes use chapter 11 to liquidate their assets rather than to reorganise.[18] Although these businesses are usually eligible for chapter 7 bankruptcy as well, the main advantage to pursuing a chapter 11 liquidation is that the debtor may remain "in possession" and thus, in control of the liquidation process. By contrast, a chapter 7 liquidation is overseen by a trustee. Indeed, one of the key advantages of any chapter 11 case, at least from the perspective of management, is that the debtor's management typically remains in control during the case and operates the business as a "debtor in possession" under the bankruptcy court's supervision.[19]

The plan of reorganisation is at the heart of most chapter 11 cases. Typically, the debtor in possession puts together the plan. However, if the debtor takes too long to create a viable plan, other parties, such as creditors, may also submit plans. The plan proponent must get the plan approved by creditors and the bankruptcy court before the plan can take effect. Chapter 11 plan confirmation is largely based on the democratic principle that the majority binds the minority. Creditors are divided into classes and vote on the plan as a class.[20] If all classes accept the plan, the bankruptcy judge will review the plan and, in most cases, confirm it.[21] If one or more classes objects to the plan, however, the plan proponent may still seek to have the plan confirmed, though additional requirements apply.[22] Specifically, the bankruptcy court must find that the plan is "fair and equitable"—in the case of unsecured creditors in particular, the plan must comply with the "absolute priority rule". This rule provides that, unless senior classes consent to lesser treatment, a junior class of creditors is entitled to payment only if all classes senior to it have been paid in full.

---

[16] SA Elberg, L Laukitis and L Downing, *International Companies Turn to US Restructurings for COVID-19 Relief, Skadden* (June 2021) <https://www.skadden.com/insights/publications/2021/06/quarterly-insights/international-companies-turn-to-us-restructurings>.

[17] *Toibb v. Radloff* [1991] 501 US 157 (holding that an individual debtor not engaged in business may use chapter 11).

[18] 11 US Code, § 1123(b)(4) (providing for a liquidating chapter 11 plan).

[19] Ibid § 1107 (describing the rights, powers, and duties of a debtor in possession).

[20] Ibid § 1126.

[21] Ibid § 1129(a)(8).

[22] Ibid § 1129(b).

Chapter 12 of the Bankruptcy Code was enacted in the wake of the US farm crisis in the 1980s and was designed to make it easier for family farmers to keep their farms. Historically, chapter 12 has been rarely used, with only a few hundred chapter 12 cases filed each year.[23] Although chapter 12 was designed for family farmers and family fishermen, these debtors are also eligible to file under other chapters of the Code; they are not limited to filing under chapter 12.

Chapter 13 is the chapter of the Bankruptcy Code designed to allow wage-earning individuals to adjust their debts. Under this chapter, an individual debtor designs a plan to pay its creditors over a three- to five-year period. The plan is overseen by a trustee, and the debtor receives a discharge upon completion of the plan payments.

Finally, chapter 15 provides a mechanism for courts in the US to co-operate and communicate with courts in a foreign jurisdiction. The goal of chapter 15 is to promote fair and efficient administration of cross-border cases.[24] Chapter 15 is the US's adoption of the UNCITRAL Model Law on Cross-Border Insolvencies.

In addition to the Bankruptcy Code, the Federal Rules of Bankruptcy Procedure, along with local court rules, govern the procedural aspects of a bankruptcy case. A full discussion of these rules is outside the scope of this chapter.

3.2.3 Bankruptcy Courts and Case Management

Because US bankruptcy law is federal law, bankruptcy cases are heard exclusively in the federal courts. The US Constitution authorises the creation of a Supreme Court and inferior federal courts.[25] There are twelve circuit courts of appeal in the US, each with authority to decide appeals arising from cases decided by federal district courts within a certain geographic area.[26] A decision from the court of appeals binds all lower courts within that circuit.

There are 94 federal districts in the US, each with its own federal district court. The district court is the court of first instance for federal matters arising

[23] US Courts, *Bankruptcy Statistics Data Visualizations* <https://www.uscourts.gov/statistics-reports/analysis-reports/bankruptcy-filings-statistics/bankruptcy-statistics-data> showing that, for example, the number of chapter 12 cases filed in 2022 was 169; in 2023, only 139 chapter 12 cases were filed.

[24] 11 US Code, § 1501.

[25] US Constitution, art III, s 1.

[26] US Courts, *Geographic Boundaries of United States Courts of Appeals and United States District Courts* <www.uscourts.gov/file/document/us-federal-courts-circuit-map>.

within the district. District courts thus hear most disputes involving federal issues in the US. Per the Constitution, judges sitting on the Supreme Court, the courts of appeal, and the district courts serve life terms after appointment by the US President and confirmation by the Senate.[27]

Congress also created federal bankruptcy courts, which hear and decide bankruptcy cases.[28] Bankruptcy judges are also federal judges; however, they are differently situated from most of their federal counterparts because they are established by Congress pursuant to its Article I bankruptcy powers. Bankruptcy judges are appointed, not by the President, but by the court of appeals in the jurisdiction where they sit. They serve fourteen-year renewable terms instead of life terms.[29] Technically, the US district courts have jurisdiction over all bankruptcy cases, and such cases are referred by the district court to a bankruptcy court. In practice, however, all district courts automatically refer bankruptcy cases to the bankruptcy courts, and bankruptcy cases are thus filed directly in bankruptcy courts. These cases will remain in the bankruptcy court unless the district court decides, in its discretion, to "withdraw the reference" and hear the bankruptcy case itself.[30] Withdrawal of the reference is extremely rare, and thus, a bankruptcy judge typically hears all bankruptcy cases and all proceedings related to a bankruptcy case.[31] Parties to a bankruptcy case may also consent to have the bankruptcy court determine a matter that would otherwise be heard by a district court.[32]

If a party seeks to appeal a bankruptcy court decision, that appeal will be heard either by the district court or by a specially established bankruptcy appellate panel (BAP). Although all circuits in the US may create BAPs, only five circuits have established them. In the circuits that have BAPs, all parties must consent to having the BAP, rather than the district court, hear the appeal, and the district judge must authorise the appeal to the BAP.[33] An appeal to a district court will be heard by a single district judge. By contrast, BAPs are composed of three bankruptcy judges appointed from the districts within their circuit. Thus, for those parties that have a choice to have their appeal heard

---

[27] US Constitution, art III.

[28] 28 US Code, § 151.

[29] Ibid § 152(a)(1).

[30] Ibid § 157(d).

[31] The extent to which a bankruptcy court may enter a final order on a proceeding depends in large part, though not exclusively, on whether the proceeding is a "core proceeding" or not. See 28 US Code, § 157(b), (c); see also *Stern v. Marshall* [2011] 564 US 462 (holding that Congress unconstitutionally delegated certain core matters to bankruptcy courts).

[32] See *Wellness Int'l Network Ltd. v. Sharif* [2015] 575 US 665.

[33] See 28 US Code, § 158(b).

by either a BAP or a district judge, the choice is largely strategic and may be based on whether bankruptcy-specific expertise would be beneficial in deciding the appeal.

The judge's primary role in a bankruptcy case is to hear and decide any issues that arise in the case; the judge does not carry out administrative functions in the bankruptcy.[34] Instead, that task belongs to the US trustee. The US trustee is part of the federal Department of Justice, and the US Attorney General appoints all US trustees.[35]

The US trustee is sometimes referred to as the "watchdog" of the bankruptcy case.[36] It carries out many administrative functions, including:

- Establishing panels of private trustees to serve in bankruptcy cases;
- Appointing private and standing trustees;
- Reviewing fee applications;
- Ensuring timely filing of reports and payment of fees;
- Monitoring plans of reorganisation;
- Appointing and monitoring creditors' committees;
- Monitoring the progress of the case; and
- Conducting any required audits.[37]

Forty-eight US states use US trustees to handle the administrative functions outlined above. Two states, Alabama and North Carolina, use bankruptcy administrators rather than US trustees.[38] Apart from the fact that bankruptcy administrators are not part of the federal Department of Justice, the bankruptcy administrator serves all the same functions as the US trustee in a bankruptcy case.

---

[34] US Courts (n 4).

[35] 28 US Code, §§ 581(a), 586(c).

[36] See, among others: US Trustee Program, *About the United States Trustee Program* (12 April 2024) <https://www.justice.gov/ust/about-program#:~:text=The%20mission%20of%20the%20United,%2C%20creditors%2C%20and%20the%20public.&text=The%20Attorney%20General%20is%20charged,and%20Assistant%20United%20States%20Trustees>.

[37] 28 US Code, § 586.

[38] US Courts, *Trustees and Administrators* <https://www.uscourts.gov/services-forms/bankruptcy/trustees-and-administrators#:~:text=When%20a%20bankruptcy%20case%20is,bankruptcy%20trustee%20monitors%20the%20case>.

3.2.4 An ESG Critique of US Bankruptcy Law

When it comes to taking ESG perspectives into account, US bankruptcy law is still evolving. As in many countries, the very concept of ESG is still developing in the US.[39] As ESG perspectives take a firmer hold in the US more generally, US bankruptcy law may eventually do more to take ESG perspectives into account.

3.2.4.1 Environmental considerations

There is a tension between US bankruptcy law and US environmental law, largely because the goals of the two areas of law can come into conflict.[40] Bankruptcy law aims to restructure and/or discharge a debtor's pre-bankruptcy obligations, with an eye towards maximising the value of the debtor's assets for the benefit of all creditors.[41] Consequently, if a debtor enters bankruptcy with outstanding environmental obligations, such as clean-up responsibilities or money owed for an environmental clean-up, those obligations may be either restructured—paid out at cents on the dollar—or discharged entirely, such that the debtor is no longer responsible, financially or otherwise, for addressing those obligations.

US environmental laws are numerous and varied and exist at local, state, and federal levels, making it difficult to provide a straightforward reconciliation of bankruptcy law and environmental law.[42] In general, the liability US environmental law imposes on a polluter varies based on the type of pollutant at issue, the extent of the pollution, and several other factors, such as whether other parties may be responsible for contributing to the pollution. For example, the federal Comprehensive Environmental Response, Compensation, and Liability Act (CERCLA) designates four categories of "potentially responsible parties" (PRPs) that can be liable for clean-up costs if a PRP 'contributed any amount of hazardous substance to [a] contaminated site'.[43] Under CERCLA,

---

[39] See T Linna, 'Company Purpose in the Context of Business Sustainability and Insolvency Proceedings' (2021) 18 European Company Law 162 (noting that, for now, "sustainability" is still an underdeveloped and uncertain concept in the context of insolvency proceedings); E C Johnson, Jr., JH Stout, and AC Walter, 'Profound Change: The Evolution of ESG' (2020) 75 Bus. Law. 2567 (noting that ESG is an evolving concept).

[40] S Astringer, 'United States of America' in *ESG in Restructuring* (INSOL Int'l 2023) 455.

[41] Ibid.

[42] Ibid 456.

[43] *Quick Reference: Comprehensive Environmental Response, Compensation, and Liability Act (CERCLA)* <https://css.umich.edu/sites/default/files/2022-04

either the federal Environmental Protection Agency (EPA) may initiate clean-up actions, or the EPA may compel one or more PRPs to clean up a site.[44] Consequently, a company's liability under CERCLA may be asserted by the EPA, another PRP, or even a private citizen.[45]

Given the array of PRPs and the nature of environmental damages, if a debtor in bankruptcy has environmental liabilities, it is not uncommon for those liabilities to be contingent, meaning that the full extent of the debtor's liability is undetermined at the time of bankruptcy and is dependent on other events either occurring or not occurring.[46]

One of the thorniest issues involving environmental claims in bankruptcy concerns timing, namely when the claim arose for purposes of determining whether the claim was discharged in the bankruptcy proceedings. If a bankruptcy court determines that an environmental claim arose pre-petition (pre-bankruptcy), that claim is generally treated as a general unsecured claim in bankruptcy and provided a distribution that is shared pro rata with other general unsecured creditors.[47] This distribution is typically a mere fraction of the claim amount asserted against the debtor. By contrast, if the court determines that a claim arose post-petition (after the debtor has filed for bankruptcy), that claim may not be discharged in the bankruptcy, and in some cases may have to be paid in full as a condition of the debtor exiting bankruptcy. Courts have used various tests to determine when a claim arose for purposes of a discharge analysis; there is no single standard applicable across all fifty states.[48]

/CERCLA.pdf>. The four categories of PRPs under CERCLA are: '(1) current owners or operators of the site at which hazardous substances were disposed; (2) past owners or operators of a site at the time hazardous substances were disposed of at the site; (3) anyone, including generators, who arranged for the disposal, transport or treatment of hazardous substances found at the site; [and] (4) transporters or anyone who arranged for transport of hazardous wastes to the facility. The liability imposed by Section 107(a) of CERCLA is strict, joint and several, and retroactive'.

44 Ibid.

45 Ibid (noting that under CERCLA's "citizen suit" provision, private citizens can 'initiate civil action against parties that violate CERCLA').

46 Astringer (n 40) 456.

47 Ibid. Although it is not always the case, in most cases environmental claims will be treated as a general unsecured claim. See Comment, 'Environmental Claims in Bankruptcy: It's a Question of Priorities' (1995) 32 San Diego L. Rev. 221, 254.

48 See, among others: *Signature Combs, Inc. v. United States* [WD Tenn 2003] 253 F. Supp. 2d 1028 (describing four approaches for determining when a contingent environmental claim arose for purposes of discharge). The four approaches are: (1) the right to payment approach, where a claim does not arise until all

Other aspects of bankruptcy law clash with environmental enforcement. For example, if an environmental agency or private party sues another party that then becomes a debtor in bankruptcy, the bankruptcy automatic stay halts the litigation.[49] Nevertheless, many courts have held that an exception to the automatic stay applies, allowing a governmental action for clean-up orders to continue, notwithstanding the debtor's bankruptcy or the possible depletion of the debtor's estate.[50]

In addition, bankruptcy law permits debtors to abandon property that is burdensome or of inconsequential value to the bankruptcy estate, meaning that debtors can sometimes abandon environmentally contaminated property.[51] For example, in the case of *In re Exide Holdings Inc.*, a debtor was allowed to abandon contaminated property to state regulators as part of a settlement.[52] Although the US Supreme Court has determined that a debtor cannot abandon property that would pose an immediate threat to the public's health and safety, this rule does not prohibit the abandonment of environmentally contaminated property that does not pose such a threat.[53] Courts are divided over how to determine the scope and applicability of this rule.[54]

Any environmental authority may assert a claim in a bankruptcy case, and environmental authorities are considered parties in interest that may appear

---

CERCLA elements exist; (2) the underlying act approach, which provides that a claim exists as long as the underlying polluting act occurred prepetition; (3) the debtor-creditor relationship approach, where CERCLA liability is discharged if the creditor and debtor began a relationship prepetition *and* the underlying act occurred prepetition; and (4) the fair contemplation approach, which provides that a claim arises prepetition only if that claim was based on prepetition conduct that can fairly be contemplated by the parties at the time of the bankruptcy: Ibid 1033–37.

[49] Astringer (n 40).

[50] J Bender, DL Beier and JA Lesser, 'Environmental Liability in Bankruptcy: The Comprehensive Environmental Response, Compensation, and Liability Act Perspective' (*Nat'l Law Review*, 22 May 2024) <https://natlawreview.com/article/environmental-liability-bankruptcy-comprehensive-environmental-response?utm_campaign=2024-6-28+NLR+Bankruptcy+News&utm_content=0d4dce02c26eccb06f265b6895063725&utm_medium=email&utm_source=Robly.com >.

[51] 11 US Code, § 554.

[52] *In re Exide Holdings, Inc.* [D Del 26 July 2021] 2021 WL 3145612.

[53] *Midlantic Nat. Bank v. New Jersey Dept. of Envtl. Prot.* [1986] 474 US 494.

[54] Compare *In re Howard* [Bankr SD Miss 2015] 533 B.R. 532 (allowing abandonment in violation of environmental laws unless there is imminent and identifiable public harm) with *Lancaster v. Term. (In re Wall Tube & Metal Prods. Co.)* [6th Cir 1987] 831 F.2d 118, 122 (refusing to allow abandonment of property in violation of environmental laws, regardless of public harm).

and be heard on issues in the case. However, in general, environmental authorities do not receive any deference or special treatment in bankruptcy, and, especially if they are seeking monetary compensation, they are generally treated no differently from other unsecured creditors.

A debtor that is seeking to liquidate in bankruptcy raises particular concerns about lingering environmental damage. A debtor that has run out of money cannot be forced to pay more than it has, regardless of the seriousness of the environmental concern(s) the debtor may have caused or contributed to.[55] Even if a liquidating debtor is able to provide some amount of money towards clean-up, that money is often inadequate to compensate for the environmental damage caused, leaving the state or municipal government to expend the funds to clean up the damage.[56]

Despite the various opportunities for conflict outlined above, it is important to recognise that bankruptcy and environmental law are not always at odds. Indeed, companies can even use bankruptcy to mitigate environmental damage. For example, when Pacific Gas & Electric (PG&E), a California electric utility, filed for bankruptcy, a private investment company, Inherent Group, invested in the company to try to improve its environmental risk mitigation strategies.[57] After Inherent's investment, these strategies indeed improved, and that improvement in turn aided PG&E's profitability.[58] Particularly if a debtor is using bankruptcy to reorganise and emerge on a stronger financial footing, it may be necessary for the debtor to adopt environmentally-friendly practices in order to become competitive or successful in the future.

In short, although bankruptcy law and environmental law need not always be at odds, when the two areas of law do conflict, bankruptcy law and practice very often do not take environmental considerations into account to the extent that environmental advocates would prefer.

3.2.4.2 Social considerations

In recent years, social considerations have become increasingly important in the chapter 11 arena in particular. Numerous large companies have sought relief under chapter 11 of the Bankruptcy Code to resolve mass tort issues that

---

55 Linna (n 39).

56 Ibid.

57 Nandini Shenai, 'Sustainably Aligned: The Interplay between ESG and Restructuring' (*Fordham Journal of Corporate & Financial Law Blog*, 20 January 2022) <https://news.law.fordham.edu/jcfl/2022/01/20/sustainably-aligned-the-interplay-between-esg-and-restructuring/>.

58 Ibid.

often have a significant impact on a large portion of the public.[59] Consequently, one of the biggest social debates in modern US bankruptcy practice involves the propriety of using chapter 11 bankruptcy to resolve a company's mass tort liabilities.[60]

As previously explained, the bankruptcy automatic stay halts all pending actions against a company in bankruptcy and centralises all disputes within the bankruptcy court. The debtor uses bankruptcy as a means of restructuring and discharging its pre-petition obligations.[61] The Bankruptcy Code contains a specific provision allowing debtors with mass asbestos liability to channel claims away from the company itself and into a trust established and funded through the debtor's plan of reorganisation.[62] In this way, the debtor can continue operations post-bankruptcy, whilst the trust handles all asbestos-related claims and payments to creditors. Although the Code's provision applies by its terms only to asbestos cases, many debtors with other types of mass tort liabilities have sought to use a similar channelling injunction and trust combination to address mass tort claims whilst allowing the company to operate post-petition.[63] Although many courts had allowed this injunction-trust arrangement in practice, on the grounds that it is necessary for the debtor's reorganisation, the Bankruptcy Code itself does not sanction this arrangement except in asbestos cases. Indeed, the US Supreme Court recently struck down a significant component of these arrangements—the use of non-consensual, non-debtor releases—on the grounds that they were prohibited by the Bankruptcy Code.[64] Unless and until Congress chooses to modify the Code to include provisions like the asbestos provision for all types of mass tort cases, there is now significant uncertainty about the extent to which chapter 11 bankruptcy will continue to be an attractive mechanism for companies to sort out their mass tort liability.

In general, social liabilities, including tort claims relating to health and safety, are treated as unsecured claims in a bankruptcy case.[65] This treatment gives the debtor an advantage in bankruptcy, allowing the debtor to discharge these liabilities whilst often paying victims only cents on the dollar for the harms they have suffered.

---

59 See JC Lipson, 'The Rule of the Deal: Bankruptcy Bargains and Other Misnomers' (2023) 97 Am. Bankr. L.J. 41.

60 Astringer (n 40) 457.

61 11 US Code, § 1141.

62 Ibid § 524(g).

63 Astringer (n 40) 457 ('Bankruptcy courts may allow for channelling injunctions in other cases as well').

64 *Harrington v. Purdue Pharma L.P.* [27 June 2024] Case No. 23-124.

65 Astringer (n 40) 458.

Tort victims are considered parties in interest in a mass tort bankruptcy case and may appear and be heard on any issue. However, these victims are often numerous and scattered across the country, and scholars have raised concerns about the adequacy of the bankruptcy system for vindicating tort victims' rights.[66]

Other entities that represent large groups of individual claimants, such as labour authorities and unions, are also considered parties in interest in a bankruptcy case.[67] The debtor's employees typically receive some special treatment in a bankruptcy case: claims for employee wages and contributions to employee benefit plans are given priority up to a certain amount, and special rules apply before a debtor in chapter 11 can reject a collective bargaining agreement with a labour union or reject retiree benefits.[68] In addition, assets in certain retirement plans of a debtor's employees may not be used to satisfy creditors' claims in a bankruptcy case.[69] The US government also has a pension insurer, the Pension Benefit Guaranty Corporation, which seeks to protect employee pensions if a company files for bankruptcy or experiences distress, and other federal agencies investigate and work to protect pensions for employees of the debtor company.[70]

In sum, the Bankruptcy Code itself provides some protection for social interests, whilst balancing the need for that protection with a debtor's need to achieve its desired outcomes in a bankruptcy proceeding. In recent years, however, chapter 11 practice in particular has evolved to open the door to extra-statutory procedures that may further insulate debtor companies from the social harms of their products and behaviour. The extent to which those procedures will continue to thrive in some form after the Supreme Court's recent decision in *Purdue Pharma* is yet to be seen.

3.2.4.3 Governance considerations

In terms of governance, one of the most hotly debated issues in US bankruptcy law today involves the propriety of a bankruptcy plan providing for

---

66 See, among others: C McCarthy, 'Creditors' Committees: Giving Tort Claimants a Voice in Chapter 11 Bankruptcy Cases' (2015) 31(2) Emory Bankr. Dev. J. 431.

67 Astringer (n 40) 459.

68 Ibid.

69 B Miller, '401(k) Assets Caught in Limbo: Plan Sponsor Bankruptcy Explained' (*Bloomberg Law*, 27 June 2024) <https://news.bloomberglaw.com/daily-labor-report/401k-assets-caught-in-limbo-plan-sponsor-bankruptcy-explained>.

70 Ibid.

third-party releases, most often to a debtor's officers, directors, or affiliates.[71] These releases allow non-debtors to reap a benefit of bankruptcy—a release from liability for pre-petition claims—without actually filing for bankruptcy themselves. Non-consensual third-party releases, which seek to bind all creditors, even those who did not vote to accept the release, have been the focus of particular scrutiny and were recently struck down by the US Supreme Court.[72] The Court's decision was momentous and leaves several open questions, including what it means to "consent" to a third-party release.

In addition to (or in lieu of) non-debtor releases of liabilities, debtors have other means available to them to protect, attract, and retain their management. This is particularly important if the debtor is seeking to remain a going concern after bankruptcy, as management will be needed to guide the debtor on its post-bankruptcy path. If a debtor wants to retain certain employees, it may implement a key employee incentive or retention plan.[73] These plans are subject to specific, detailed rules and may only be implemented after notice and a hearing and approval by the bankruptcy judge.

In addition to retaining current management in a chapter 11 case, debtors often seek to hire a chief restructuring officer (CRO), either during or prior to bankruptcy.[74] A CRO may be an accountant, manager, or former chief financial officer with specific experience advising and restructuring distressed businesses.[75] It is also common practice for debtors to appoint independent members to their boards of directors prior to commencing a chapter 11 case.[76] Leadership and management must disclose any conflicts and any self-dealing in the plan and disclosure statement that accompanies the plan.

All professionals who assist the debtor in bankruptcy must be "disinterested", which is a defined term in the Bankruptcy Code. A "disinterested" person:

- Is not a creditor, equity security holder, or insider of the debtor;
- Has not been an officer, director, or employee of the debtor within two years of the petition date; and

71 Astringer (n 40) 458.

72 *Harrington* (n 64).

73 Astringer (n 40) 459.

74 Ibid 460.

75 J Gething et al, 'When Do You Need a Chief Restructuring Officer?' (*McKinsey & Co.*, 13 November 2020) <https://www.mckinsey.com/capabilities/transformation/our-insights/when-do-you-need-a-chief-restructuring-officer>.

76 Astringer (n 40) 459; see JA Ellias, E Kamar and K Kastiel, 'The Rise of Bankruptcy Directors' (2022) 95 S. Cal. L. Rev. 1083 (describing the troubling role of some of these directors).

- Does not have any interest “materially adverse” to the debtor or any class of creditors or equity security holders.[77]

Disclosure of any and all conflicts or relationships is key for restructuring professionals and helps maintain the integrity of the bankruptcy process.

In sum, whilst bankruptcy provides perhaps a greater opportunity to scrutinise the debtor’s management and professionals, it also provides an opportunity for those individuals—especially management—to be released from liability without undertaking their own bankruptcy filing. The Supreme Court’s decision in *Harrington v. Purdue Pharma* in the summer of 2024 curtailed this opportunity, holding that non-consensual releases of non-debtors are not permissible, but questions remain about how chapter 11 practice will adapt to this ruling. It is possible that future creative efforts will find workarounds to the Court’s decision.

3.2.4.4 Summary: An ESG critique of US bankruptcy law

Although, as mentioned, the concept of ESG itself continues to evolve, a few key observations can be made about US bankruptcy law from an ESG perspective.

First, bankruptcy law does an incomplete job of resolving the tension between holding debtors responsible for social and environmental harms and providing them with a discharge and fresh start. There are numerous practical challenges that arise with the resolution of claims that involve long-term or developing harms, including identifying those claims, pinpointing when they arose, and determining where those claims should fall in bankruptcy’s general priority scheme. Although US case law provides some guidance for dealing with these challenges, they are by no means resolved, and many of the long-running debates about US bankruptcy law revolve around environmental, social, and governance issues.

For example, although bankruptcy provides a powerful tool to debtors by allowing them to abandon property from which they can no longer benefit, case law in the US has imposed restrictions on a debtor’s ability to abandon environmentally contaminated property.[78] However, these restrictions are judge-made and are particularly vulnerable to modification over time as they

---

[77] 11 US Code, § 101(14).

[78] See ‘Recent Developments at the Intersection of Bankruptcy and Environmental Law’ (*Weil Restructuring*, 8 August 2022) <https://restructuring.weil.com/environmental/recent-developments-at-the-intersection-of-bankruptcy-and-environmental-law/> (discussing these restrictions).

are not enshrined in a statute.[79] Similarly, various circuits in the US have developed different tests for evaluating the propriety and scope of third-party releases. These tests are not part of the Bankruptcy Code but rather represent the development of judge-made rules that may eventually be overridden by amendments to the Code. Indeed, many of these tests have now been overruled by the Supreme Court's recent decision in the *Purdue Pharma* case, injecting uncertainty into chapter 11 practice and specifically about whether it will remain an effective tool for resolving mass tort liability.

Although there has been some debate about whether ESG-related claims should receive special treatment in a bankruptcy case, debtors in bankruptcy often simply do not have the funds available to pay these claims in full. Even if they do, money often cannot adequately compensate for the harms caused by, for example, environmental damage or past abusive behaviour. Thus, it is unclear whether giving ESG claimants priority treatment in bankruptcy would be effective in terms of actually reducing environmental, social, or governance harms.

Further to the social perspective, scholars, commentators, jurists, and practitioners have taken divergent views over whether bankruptcy is the proper forum for the resolution of social ills such as mass torts.[80] Bankruptcy does provide certain advantages to mass tort defendants—namely, bankruptcy's collective approach provides a common forum for all parties to address their issues. However, scholars have raised concerns that mass tort defendants have taken matters a step too far, exploiting the bankruptcy system to deprive mass tort claimants of rights they would receive if their claims were addressed in a different forum. An ever-present worry, both in bankruptcy and outside of it, is whether tort victims can be adequately compensated for the harms inflicted upon them.

Finally, from a governance perspective, the practice of granting third-party releases to non-debtor affiliates, officers, and directors of a debtor has recently come under fire. There is debate over whether such releases are necessary for a company's rehabilitation or whether they are get-out-of-jail-free cards for

---

[79] See DW Houston, IV, KE Waits and AC Wyatt, 'Bankruptcy Treatment of Environmental Liabilities' (2021) 40(7) Am. Bankr. Inst. J. 18 (discussing a split in courts over when a debtor can permissibly abandon environmentally contaminated property).

[80] See, among others: SD Parikh, 'Mass Exploitation' (2022) 170 U. Pa. L. Rev Online 53 (generally agreeing that bankruptcy is a proper forum for resolution of mass tort issues but criticising the "unprecedented techniques" mass tort defendants have used in bankruptcy); TA McKenzie, 'The Mass Tort Bankruptcy: A Pre-History' (2012) 5 J. Tort L. 59 (describing the historical antecedents of modern mass tort bankruptcy cases).

parties who have not themselves submitted to the scrutiny of bankruptcy proceedings. Although the Supreme Court has recently held that non-consensual third-party releases are impermissible, thus lending some clarity to this question, other questions remain about what chapter 11 can be used to accomplish, especially for non-debtors.

In general, although bankruptcy undoubtedly invokes concerns in the environmental, social, and governance arenas, the Bankruptcy Code itself is not overly focused on ESG. To the extent the law takes ESG considerations into account, it is often through practice and case law development rather than through the application of a particular statutory provision. Given that ESG issues involve some of the most controversial topics in modern bankruptcy practice, Congress may in the future consider revising the Bankruptcy Code to take ESG considerations into greater account.

3.3 MUNICIPALITIES

Municipal governments play a critical role in the day-to-day lives of US residents. This portion of the chapter examines and critiques the laws specific to municipal financial distress and bankruptcy in the United States.

3.3.1 Principles and Purposes

To understand the role of municipalities in the US, it is important to understand the country's federal system of government. The US Constitution provides that powers not granted to the federal government are reserved to the states.[81] For their part, states distribute these reserved powers between state-level governments and various local governments.[82]

State and local governments are those closest to the American people, meaning that Americans have more frequent contact with these governments than they do with the federal government.[83] State and local governments oversee many of the resources, programmes, and facilities that Americans interact with in their daily lives, including police departments, libraries, and schools, to name just a few.[84]

Elected officials manage both state and local governments in the US. The head of the state is an elected governor, and each state also has a legislature

---

[81] White House, *State and Local Government* <https://www.whitehouse.gov/about-the-white-house/our-government/state-local-government/>.

[82] Ibid.

[83] Ibid.

[84] Ibid.

composed of elected representatives.[85] All states except Nebraska have a bicameral legislature consisting of an upper and a lower house.[86] Nebraska, the lone exception, has a unicameral, or one-house, legislature.[87] The bicameral structure of most state legislatures mirrors that of the federal government, which has a Senate (the upper house) and a House of Representatives (the lower house) that together make up the US Congress. Finally, state judicial systems are composed of a series of lower courts as well as a high court, usually denominated the supreme court.[88]

For their part, local governments generally consist of higher and lower tiers. With respect to the former, all states except for Alaska and Louisiana designate their higher-tier local governments as counties.[89] In Alaska, the higher-tier governments are called boroughs, and in Louisiana, they are parishes.[90] The higher-tier government (i.e., the county in most states) is then divided into lower-tier governments, called municipalities.[91] Municipalities can take many forms—at a general level, they may be called towns, cities, townships, boroughs (not to be confused with the higher-tier boroughs in Alaska), or villages.[92] Municipalities may also be created to provide specific services to residents, such as water, sewer, and utility services, or school and safety services. These "special-purpose" municipalities may provide services that span multiple counties or general-purpose municipalities, or they may be confined to a more limited geographic area.

Most municipal governments are organised around a population centre that corresponds to the geographical designations the US Census Bureau uses to report housing and population statistics.[93] Municipalities vary greatly in size, from, for example, a large city such as New York (made up of over 8 million people)[94] to a small town such as Cannon Beach, Oregon (population around 1,500).[95]

---

85 Ibid.
86 Ibid.
87 Ibid.
88 Ibid.
89 Ibid.
90 Ibid.
91 Ibid.
92 Ibid.
93 Ibid.
94 United States Census Bureau, *Quick Facts New York city, New York; New York; United States* <https://www.census.gov/quickfacts/table/3651000,36,00>.
95 Data Commons <https://datacommons.org/place/geoId/4110850?utm_medium=explore&mprop=count&popt=Person&hl=en>.

In the US, local governments are responsible for a wide variety of services, including parks and recreation, police and fire safety, housing services, emergency medical services and transport, municipal courts, transportation services and public transit, and public works, including street and sewer maintenance and snow and garbage removal.[96] Consequently, municipal finance and policy are critically important to ensuring that US residents receive an acceptable level of basic services.

Importantly, municipalities have only the power that the state in which they are located grants to them.[97] However when it comes to leadership, although the state may appoint some municipal officials, most municipal governing bodies, such as a mayor or city council, are directly elected by the people who live in the municipality.[98]

3.3.2 Legal Framework for Municipalities in Distress

A distressed municipality in the US may seek relief at the state level, the federal level, or both. This portion of the chapter first outlines the federal bankruptcy relief available to distressed municipalities before turning to a discussion of state intervention mechanisms.

3.3.2.1 Chapter 9: Functions, mission, and key players

As previously mentioned, chapter 9 is the portion of the US Bankruptcy Code that provides for the adjustment of municipal debt. Congress first enacted chapter 9 in response to the Great Depression in the 1930s; however, in 1936, the US Supreme Court struck down the law as an unconstitutional federal government infringement on state sovereignty.[99] Undeterred, Congress revised chapter 9, and the Supreme Court subsequently upheld the revised version just two years later, in 1938.[100] With some revisions, the version of chapter 9 that was upheld in 1938 is largely what is in effect today.

Chapter 9 is one of the least frequently used chapters of the Bankruptcy Code. Fewer than 500 chapter 9 cases have been filed since its enactment nearly a century ago.[101]

---

96 White House (n 81).

97 Ibid.

98 Ibid.

99 US Courts (n 4); *Ashton v. Cameron County Water Improvement Dist. No. 1* [1936] 298 U.S. 513, 532.

100 US Courts (n 4); *United States v. Bekins* [1938] 304 U.S. 27, 54.

101 US Courts (n 4).

Chapter 9's goal is to protect a financially distressed municipality from its creditors and give it time to develop and negotiate a plan to adjust its debts.[102] A municipality may adjust its debts in any number of ways, most commonly by extending maturity dates, reducing the amount of principal or interest owed, or engaging in other refinancing techniques.[103]

Notably, chapter 9 is distinct from other chapters of the Bankruptcy Code in that it does not permit a municipality to liquidate its assets or to dissolve.[104] This limitation exists in large part due to concerns about federal bankruptcy law unconstitutionally infringing on state sovereignty.[105] Because US municipalities are under state control, it is thought that only a state should be able to force a municipality to liquidate or dissolve.[106] At the same time, because states cannot impair contractual obligations non-consensually, municipalities will need federal bankruptcy relief if they wish to impair their contractual obligations in order to adjust their debt.

Bankruptcy judges overseeing chapter 9 cases are also more limited than they would be if overseeing a case under a different Code chapter. A bankruptcy court may not interfere with the municipality's governance or the way it uses its property.[107] As a general rule, the bankruptcy court has a smaller role to play in a chapter 9 case than in other types of bankruptcy cases, such as chapter 11. At least as delineated by statute, the bankruptcy court's role in chapter 9 is largely limited to approving the bankruptcy petition, confirming the municipal debtor's plan of adjustment, and ensuring that the plan is implemented according to its terms.[108]

3.3.2.2 Chapter 9: Key provisions and processes

A municipal debtor's eligibility for chapter 9 is strictly limited. In practice, when a municipality files a chapter 9 case, its eligibility for bankruptcy is often a source of litigation.[109]

Section 109(c) of the Bankruptcy Code provides that only a "municipality" is eligible for chapter 9 relief. "Municipality" is defined in the Code as a

---

[102] Ibid.

[103] Ibid.

[104] Ibid.

[105] Ibid.

[106] Ibid.

[107] Ibid.

[108] Ibid.

[109] See LN Coordes, 'Gatekeepers Gone Wrong: Reforming the Chapter 9 Eligibility Rules' (2017) 94 Wash. U. L. Rev. 1191 (discussing and critiquing this litigation).

'political subdivision or public agency or instrumentality of a State'.[110] Though not further defined in the Code itself, scholars have generally further classified municipalities as either general-purpose or special-purpose entities. General-purpose municipalities include cities, towns, townships, counties, and similar entities. Special-purpose municipalities are created by the state to provide a particular, specific service and may include entities such as school districts, public improvement districts, transportation authorities, water districts, and the like.

In addition to meeting the Bankruptcy Code's definition of "municipality", a prospective chapter 9 debtor must satisfy four other criteria before it is deemed eligible for chapter 9:[111]

1. The municipality must be specifically authorised to be a debtor by the state in which it is located;
2. The municipality must be "insolvent", as defined in the Code;[112]
3. The municipality must desire to effect a plan to adjust its debts; and
4. The municipality must:
   a. Obtain the agreement of creditors holding at least a majority in the amount of the claims of each class that the debtor intends to impair under a chapter 9 plan;
   b. Negotiate in good faith with creditors and fail to obtain the requisite agreement outlined in subsection (a);
   c. Be unable to negotiate with creditors due to impracticability; or
   d. Reasonably believe that a creditor may attempt to obtain a preference.

To commence a chapter 9 case, a municipality must voluntarily file a petition in bankruptcy court.[113] Unlike, for example, in a chapter 11 case, only the municipality itself can commence a chapter 9 case; a municipality's creditors are ineligible to force the municipality into bankruptcy. Along with the petition, the municipal debtor should file a list of its creditors.[114] Once a chapter 9 petition is filed, the chief judge of the court of appeals for the circuit that

[110] 11 US Code, § 101(40).

[111] Ibid § 109(c).

[112] Ibid § 101(32)(C): 'The term "insolvent" means … financial condition such that the municipality is (i) generally not paying its debts as they become due unless such debts are the subject of a bona fide dispute; or (ii) unable to pay its debts as they become due.'

[113] Ibid §§ 303, 901(a).

[114] Ibid § 924.

includes the district where the case is commenced will assign a bankruptcy judge to oversee the case.[115]

Once the case is assigned to a bankruptcy judge, the clerk of the court will issue a notice that a case has been commenced.[116] Parties in interest, such as creditors, may object to the filing of the case; as noted above, objections about the debtor's eligibility for bankruptcy are common, particularly in cases involving general-purpose municipalities such as Detroit.[117] If the court determines that the debtor is ineligible for chapter 9 relief, or if the court determines that the debtor is eligible but has filed the petition in bad faith, the court may dismiss the case.[118] On the other hand, if a debtor can overcome objections to its eligibility, the court will allow the case to proceed.[119]

Once a debtor is in chapter 9 bankruptcy, as in other chapters under the Code, the automatic stay applies to halt all collection actions against the debtor and its property.[120] Uniquely to chapter 9, the automatic stay also prohibits all actions against officers and inhabitants of the debtor if those actions seek to enforce a claim against the debtor.[121] Notably, however, the automatic stay does not apply to the application of pledged special revenues to the payment of debt secured by those revenues.[122] Put slightly differently, and as explained further below, special revenue bonds remain largely unaffected by a chapter 9 case.

The court in a chapter 9 case will set a time within which parties may file proofs of claim or interest.[123] A creditor need only file a proof of claim if its claim is disputed, contingent, or unliquidated, or if the debtor fails to include the claim when it files its list of creditors with the court.[124]

As mentioned above, a court in a chapter 9 case has limited power over the municipal debtor. Unless the debtor consents or the plan so provides, the court may not interfere with '(1) any of the political or governmental powers of the debtor; (2) any of the property or revenues of the debtor; or (3) the debtor's use or enjoyment of any income-producing property'.[125] These restrictions are

115 Ibid § 921(b).

116 Ibid § 923; Fed. R. Bankr. P. 9007, 9008.

117 11 US Code, § 921(c); LN Coordes (n 109) (describing chapter 9 eligibility disputes).

118 11 US Code, § 921(c).

119 Ibid § 921(d).

120 Ibid §§ 362(a), 901(a).

121 Ibid § 922(a).

122 Ibid § 922(d).

123 Fed. R. Bankr. P. 3003(c)(3).

124 11 US Code, § 925.

125 Ibid § 904.

designed to ensure that chapter 9 does not conflict with federal constitutional provisions giving states (and, by extension, state and local elected officials) authority over their municipalities' affairs. In addition, chapter 9 explicitly provides that it 'does not limit or impair the power of a State to control, by legislation or otherwise, a municipality of or in such State in the exercise of the political or governmental powers of [the] municipality, including expenditures for such exercise', with limited exceptions.[126]

As with the judge, the US trustee's role in a chapter 9 case is also more limited than in other types of bankruptcy cases. The US trustee does not examine a municipal debtor, nor may the US trustee move for the appointment of a case trustee or examiner.[127] The US trustee may not move to convert the case to a different chapter and, in general, the US trustee does not supervise the administration of the case, monitor the debtor's financial operations, or review professionals' fees, the way it would in a chapter 11 case.[128] Instead, the US trustee's primary role in a chapter 9 case is to appoint a creditors' committee.[129]

A creditor's role is likewise limited in chapter 9. Unlike in a chapter 11 case, a creditor may not propose a competing plan of debt adjustment for a municipal debtor.[130] However, creditors are generally represented in chapter 9 cases by creditors' committees, and those committees may be active in helping to shape the debtor's plan and otherwise negotiating with the debtor.[131]

In addition, chapter 9 explicitly provides that certain other parties may appear and be heard in a case. These other parties include the US Secretary of the Treasury,[132] state representatives,[133] the US Securities and Exchange Commission, and other parties in interest, such as the municipality's employees and residents.[134]

For its part, the municipal debtor has significant powers in a chapter 9 case. A municipal debtor has great freedom to use its property as it wishes, to raise taxes, and to make expenditures.[135] It may assume or reject executory contracts and unexpired leases, and it may borrow money during the case, giving

---

126 Ibid § 903.
127 US Courts (n 4).
128 Ibid.
129 Ibid.
130 Ibid.
131 11 US Code, §§ 903, 1103.
132 Fed. R. Bankr. P. 2018(c).
133 Ibid.
134 11 US Code, §§ 901(a), 1109.
135 US Courts (n 4).

its lender priority of payment as an administrative expense.[136] As alluded to above, a municipal debtor may also employ professionals, such as lawyers, accountants, and financial advisors, without court approval.[137] Although these powers are indeed significant, in practice, as discussed below, a municipality in bankruptcy may already be run, not by elected local officials, but by a state-imposed emergency manager or financial control board. Thus, although the law provides "the municipality" with significant powers in bankruptcy, the key people seeing the municipality through its bankruptcy case may well be different from the elected officials that were running it prior to bankruptcy.

Municipal bonds often make up a significant portion of a chapter 9 debtor's debt. Broadly speaking, these bonds can be divided into two types: general obligation bonds and special revenue bonds. Both bonds are rated by the three major rating agencies in the US: Moody's Investors Service, S&P Global, and Fitch Ratings.[138] General obligation bonds are largely what they sound like: bonds issued to allow the municipality to fulfil its general obligations to the public. These bonds are treated in bankruptcy as general unsecured debt, and the municipal debtor need not make payments on these bonds during the case.[139] By contrast, special revenue bonds are bonds dedicated to specific municipal projects and are often secured by special revenues that the municipality brings in from those projects. Thus, special revenue bonds are treated as secured debt and are serviced throughout the chapter 9 case.[140] Notably, the different treatment of general obligation bonds and special revenue bonds means that a chapter 9 debtor often cannot fully adjust its debt through the bankruptcy process.

The goal of chapter 9 is debt adjustment; consequently, a critical part of a chapter 9 debtor's job is to file a plan of debt adjustment.[141] The debtor is the only entity that may file such a plan.[142]

Once the debtor files its plan, the bankruptcy court must examine the plan to ensure that it meets the standards outlined in the Bankruptcy Code for plan confirmation.[143] The court must confirm a plan if all of the following conditions are met:[144]

---

136 11 US Code, §§ 364, 503, 901(a).

137 US Courts (n 4).

138 WM Financial Strategies, *Municipal Bond Ratings* <https://www.munibondadvisor.com/rating.htm>.

139 US Courts (n 4).

140 11 US Code, § 928.

141 Ibid § 941.

142 See *Ashton* (n 99); *Bekins* (n 100).

143 11 US Code, §§ 943(b), 1129.

144 Ibid § 943(b).

1. The plan complies with the applicable provisions of the Bankruptcy Code;
2. The plan complies with the provisions of chapter 9 specifically;
3. All amounts to be paid for services or expenses have been fully disclosed and are reasonable;
4. The debtor is not prohibited by law from taking any action necessary to carry out the plan;
5. Except to the extent that a holder of a claim has agreed to different treatment, the plan provides that on the effective date, each holder of a priority claim will receive, on account of such claim, cash equal to the allowed amount of such claim;
6. Any regulatory or electoral approval necessary under applicable non-bankruptcy law in order to carry out any provision of the plan has been obtained, or such provision is expressly conditioned on such approval; and
7. The plan is in the best interests of creditors and is feasible.

A municipal debtor can receive a discharge after:

1. Confirmation of the plan;
2. Deposit of any consideration to be distributed under the plan with a court-appointed disbursing agent; and
3. A determination by the court that securities deposited with the disbursing agent will constitute valid legal obligations of the debtor and that any provision made to pay or secure payment of such obligations is valid.[145]

Chapter 9 contains two important discharge exceptions. First, either the plan itself or the court's order confirming the plan may except debt from discharge.[146] Second, if an entity does not receive notice or have actual knowledge of the case prior to plan confirmation, any debt owed to that entity is not discharged.[147] The bankruptcy court may also revoke an order confirming a plan of debt adjustment if it determines that the order was procured by fraud.[148]

3.3.2.3 State-level interventions

In addition to, or in lieu of, seeking federal bankruptcy relief, a municipality in distress may also be the recipient of state intervention. However, the types and availability of state intervention vary widely across the 50 states. Accordingly,

---

145 Ibid § 944(b).
146 US Courts (n 4); 11 US Code, § 944(c)(1).
147 11 US Code, § 944(c)(2).
148 Ibid §§ 901(a), 1144.

this section of the chapter will attempt to paint a high-level summary of some of the most notable types of state intervention.

Fewer than half of the states in the US have laws explicitly allowing them to intervene in municipal finances.[149] In the 19 states that do have intervention programmes, specific interventions vary.[150] However, a common theme is that most interventions are reactionary in nature rather than preventative.[151] State interventions may provide an alternative pathway out of financial distress, or they may serve as a barrier, prohibiting the distressed municipality from filing for federal bankruptcy relief before specific steps are completed.[152]

A 2013 study found that states intervene in the affairs of their distressed municipalities for several reasons, including to protect their own financial standing, to protect the financial standing of other municipalities in the state, to enhance economic growth, and to maintain public health and safety.[153] For their part, local officials and residents often resent this interference, viewing it as an infringement on their powers and rights rather than needed assistance.[154] For example, several cities in the state of Michigan pushed back against what they perceived to be undue state interference in distressed localities' affairs, and in November of 2012, Michigan residents voted to strike down the state's mandatory emergency manager system for distressed local governments.[155] The state government subsequently replaced the mandatory system with a menu of options for local officials to choose from; however, shortly thereafter, then-Governor Rick Snyder opted for the appointment of an emergency manager to take over Detroit's day-to-day operations, a decision that further entrenched resentment among local residents of perceived state interference.[156]

Because state intervention programmes vary, there is no single model state intervention programme. However, there are some common themes. For instance, many states designate a person or group of people to intervene, such as a receiver, an emergency manager, a state agency head, or a financial control board.[157] The state then provides the designated intervenor with one or more options to address local financial distress, including the power to renegotiate

149 'The State Role in Local Government Financial Distress' (*The Pew Charitable Trusts*, July 2013) <https://www.pewtrusts.org/-/media/assets/2016/04/pew_state_role_in_local_government_financial_distress.pdf>.

150 Ibid.

151 Ibid.

152 Ibid.

153 Ibid.

154 Ibid.

155 Ibid.

156 Ibid.

157 Ibid.

debt and labour contracts, the ability to raise taxes, the ability to offer state-backed loans or grants, the ability to provide technical advice, or even, on occasion, the power to dissolve the local government entity.[158] In this way, a municipality's "management"—local officials—can be displaced by mandate of a state intervention programme. If they are not outright replaced, their role in municipal decision making is at least minimised.

The list below describes some representative examples of the varying intervention programmes adopted by the states:[159]

- Some states, including Alabama and California,[160] do not provide state intervention programmes at all.
- By contrast, the oldest state intervention programme is North Carolina's, which emphasises state-level monitoring of local government finances to detect early signs of trouble. North Carolina's is a rare example of an intervention programme that is preventative rather than reactionary. North Carolina's system has produced mostly good results, as the state 'has managed to escape serious local government budget problems'.[161]
- Some states, including Michigan, Pennsylvania, and Rhode Island, allow for significant involvement in local government finances when the local government becomes financially distressed. For example, as mentioned above, Michigan provides a menu of options for the state to intervene in a distressed locality, including an emergency manager. Pennsylvania has a comprehensive receivership programme for distressed municipalities.
- Finally, some states, including Connecticut, New York, and Massachusetts, take a more *ad hoc* approach to intervention, deciding on the level of state involvement based on the severity of a city's financial emergency.

Although a full explanation of the variances among state intervention programmes would itself be a book-length project, it is believed that some states have more limited intervention programmes because their localities have not yet experienced significant levels of financial distress (or specific causes of financial distress) that would warrant more invasive state intervention.[162]

---

158 Ibid.

159 Ibid.

160 California does, however, have legislation requiring a municipality to mediate (in most cases) prior to filing for chapter 9 bankruptcy relief. See RJ Winthrop, 'New Requirements for Municipal Bankruptcies' (*Brownstein Hyatt Farber Schreck*, 2 November 2011) <https://www.bhfs.com/Templates/media/files/insights/AB%20506.Client%20Alert_Karol%20names%20removed.pdf>.

161 *State Role* (n 149).

162 Ibid.

3.3.3 An ESG Critique of US Laws on Municipalities in Distress

Although this chapter will delve into particular issues with respect to ESG and municipal distress, two general matters are worthy of note now. First, ESG outcomes matter to both residents in a municipality and to investors, making ESG an important part of any municipal credit risk analysis.[163] Second, from the perspective of promoting long-term sustainability, preventive restructuring and intervention measures are considered preferable to late-stage, reactionary measures.[164] This is because, by the time a municipality reaches a point of financial distress, it may resort to cutting services that are necessary for public health, safety, and enjoyment in order to save money.

Despite the sustainability benefits of early intervention, most state intervention programmes, to the extent they exist at all, are primarily reactionary in nature. A notable exception is North Carolina's programme, which emphasises monitoring and early warnings.[165] However, North Carolina is an outlier, and one of the barriers to enacting preventative programmes on a broader geographic scale is the concern that municipalities in other states will either resent what they perceive to be an intrusion into their affairs or will not be prepared to provide the detailed information necessary for monitoring to be effective.

At the federal level, chapter 9 poses structural barriers to early intervention because a municipality is required to be "insolvent" under the Bankruptcy Code before it is eligible for chapter 9 relief.

3.3.3.1 Environmental considerations

As previously discussed, there is a tension between US environmental law and US bankruptcy law, in large part because bankruptcy law allows for the restructuring and discharge of many environmental obligations. This same tension also applies in the context of municipal bankruptcies.

In some ways, however, the tension may be augmented in municipal bankruptcy. For example, because a bankruptcy court may not interfere with a municipal debtor's use of its property, the bankruptcy court arguably could not prevent a municipal debtor from abandoning property that is environmentally hazardous. However, as municipalities are subject to the control of the state where they are located, state law could apply to limit or condition abandonment in such cases.

---

[163] C Bruno and W Henisz, 'ESG Factors in Municipal Finance' (*Principles for Responsible Investment*, 24 February 2022) <https://www.unpri.org/pri-blog/esg-factors-in-municipal-finance/9550.article>.

[164] Linna (n 39).

[165] *State Role* (n 149), also mentioning New York as a state that monitors its local government's finances proactively.

3.3.3.2 Social considerations

As previously discussed, in a chapter 11 bankruptcy, special rules apply to protect certain social groups, such as unions, employees, and retirees. A chapter 11 debtor must take specific steps to negotiate with a union before it can reject a collective bargaining agreement,[166] and similar rules apply to a debtor's rejection of retiree benefits.[167] However, in chapter 9, these special rules do not apply, and a municipal debtor is free to reject such agreements without engaging in any special process, although municipal debtors may of course voluntarily choose to engage with these groups.

Notably, chapter 9 does provide some protection for creditor groups more generally. One of chapter 9's entry requirements is, broadly speaking, that a municipality must either negotiate with its creditors in good faith or show that such negotiation is impracticable. Although this is a general creditor protection, not targeted toward specific groups, in practice, this requirement may spur the municipality to try to reach an agreement with labour and retiree groups prior to entering bankruptcy, especially if those groups represent a significant portion of the municipality's debt.

With respect to retirees specifically, the city of Detroit has used chapter 9 to cut its pensions, and bankruptcy courts in Michigan and California have held that a municipal debtor may use chapter 9 to cut even those pensions that have already accrued. In the case of Detroit, such cuts were upheld despite explicit protections for these pensions in Michigan's constitution, on the grounds that, in bankruptcy, pension-related claims are no different from ordinary contract claims.[168] By contrast, the city of Vallejo, California chose not to pursue pension cuts in bankruptcy, even though its pension debt was significant. Thus, Vallejo found itself facing a new budget crisis just two years after exiting bankruptcy, as pension costs ate up an increasing share of the city's tax revenues.[169] The law will likely continue to develop in the area of the legality of pension cuts in bankruptcy, and municipal officials may be placed in the uncomfortable position of either having to make unpopular pension cuts or prolonging municipal financial distress.

---

[166] 11 US Code, § 1113.

[167] Ibid § 1114.

[168] *In re City of Detroit* [Bankr ED Mich 2014] 524 B.R. 147, 211; 'pension claims are unsecured contract claims under the Michigan constitution and are therefore subject to impairment in bankruptcy.'

[169] T Reid, 'Two Years After Bankruptcy, California City Again Mired in Pension Debt' (*Reuters*, 1 October 2013) <https://www.reuters.com/article/world/us/two-years-after-bankruptcy-california-city-again-mired-in-pension-debt-idUSBRE9900Z8/#:~:text=(Reuters)%20%2D%20Less%20than%20two,growing%20share%20of%20tax%20revenues.>.

Finally, as Professor Melissa Jacoby has extensively documented, municipal bankruptcy may be used to eliminate a municipality's responsibilities for civil rights violations, along with the obligations of individual police officers within the municipality.[170] Professor Jacoby has found that, in Detroit's bankruptcy in particular, civil rights and personal injury claimants received "the weakest treatment."[171]

3.3.3.3 Governance considerations

As discussed above, the propriety of non-consensual third-party releases of a debtor's officers, directors, and affiliates was, until recently, one of the most hotly contested issues in US bankruptcy practice. In a municipal bankruptcy, third-party releases may be viewed as especially necessary to allow certain municipal officials, who themselves are not debtors in bankruptcy, to continue serving in their roles.[172] Consequently, some courts have allowed municipal debtors to include third-party releases in their debt adjustment plans. Such third-party consideration is consistent with chapter 9's extension of the automatic stay to officers and inhabitants of the debtor municipality, even though these releases are not otherwise explicitly provided for in the Bankruptcy Code.[173] Time will tell whether these releases continue to be permitted in chapter 9 in the aftermath of the Supreme Court's *Purdue Pharma* decision, which struck down such releases in the chapter 11 context.

From a governance perspective, however, probably the most significant issue in the municipal distress context is the replacement of elected officials with unelected ones. State programmes that mandate the intervention of an unelected receiver, emergency manager, or financial control board have been criticised by scholars and citizens alike for their replacement of elected officials.[174] Further, although chapter 9 of the Bankruptcy Code does not allow the bankruptcy court to manage a municipality's governance aspects, in practice, bankruptcy courts have been very influential in the governance of a

---

170 MB Jacoby, *Unjust Debts: How Our Bankruptcy System Makes America More Unequal* (The New Press, 2024).

171 Ibid 110.

172 For a discussion and critique of third-party releases in the municipal bankruptcy context, see C Morbidelli, 'Third-Party Relief for Municipal Debtors: "Necessity" in the Chapter 9 Context' (2019) 35 Emory Bankr. Dev. J. 225.

173 11 US Code, § 922(a).

174 See, among others: D Skeel, 'Reflections on Two Years of P.R.O.M.E.S.A.' (2018) 87 Rev. Jur. U.P.R. 862, 865–66 (describing the public perception of oversight boards as initially "undemocratic and highly unpopular" though noting that 'initial hostility later gave way to acceptance and in some cases enthusiastic endorsement').

municipality, and some scholars believe that bankruptcy courts could do even more to alter municipal governance structures.[175]

Finally, it is worth noting that retention and payment of professionals receives less scrutiny in a chapter 9 bankruptcy than in chapter 11. Despite the relatively lower level of scrutiny, it is widely considered a best practice for all professionals to disclose any actual or potential conflicts of interest in a chapter 9 case.

3.4 MUNICIPALITIES—LAW IN PRACTICE

As a general matter in bankruptcy cases, the law in practice can differ significantly from the law as written. Experiences with municipal bankruptcy and state intervention programmes are no exception. Because the structure, purposes, and functions of municipalities vary, the practice of municipal restructuring can be very *ad hoc*, with chapter 9 dubbed the "wild west" of bankruptcy practice.[176] This section presents two case studies examining the law in practice before critiquing that law from an ESG perspective.

3.4.1 Case Study 1: Detroit (Chapter 9 Bankruptcy)

On 18 July 2013, Detroit became the largest US city to file for municipal bankruptcy protection.[177] Approximately four months after it filed, in November 2013, Detroit appointed a new Chief Financial Officer, whose task was to work with the previously appointed emergency manager to stabilise the city's finances.[178] Ultimately, the bankruptcy was successful, resulting in Detroit's elimination of $7 billion of long-term debt obligations.[179] This financial freedom, in turn, has arguably enabled the city to re-invest in its citizens, and, all being well, setting the city up for a more sustainable future.

Although Detroit's exit from bankruptcy came relatively quickly for a city of its size, its entry into bankruptcy was quite rocky. As the largest US city ever to take advantage of chapter 9 proceedings, Detroit was met with several challenges to its bankruptcy filing, including allegations that the city was not,

---

175 CP Gillette and DA Skeel, Jr, 'Governance Reform and the Judicial Role in Municipal Bankruptcy' (2016) 125(5) Yale L. J. 1150.

176 See, among others: L Farmer, 'City Bankruptcies: The Wild West of Financial Law' (*Governing*, 23 January 2013) <https://www.governing.com/archive/gov-city-bankruptcies-the-wild-west-of-financial-law.html>.

177 'How a City Transformed From Bankruptcy to Renewal' (*EY*) <https://www.ey.com/en_it/growth/how-a-city-transformed-from-bankruptcy-to-renewal>.

178 Ibid.

179 Ibid.

in fact, insolvent.[180] The bankruptcy judge overseeing the case, Judge Steven Rhodes of the US Bankruptcy Court for the Eastern District of Michigan, ultimately determined that Detroit was indeed insolvent, due in part to the city's inability to provide basic health and safety services to its residents.[181] Judge Rhodes's decision received widespread attention due to this novel approach to insolvency—dubbed "service delivery insolvency"—whereby the judge likened the city's inhabitants to creditors who were owed a debt of minimally acceptable services.[182] This decision consequently opened the door to consideration of taxpayer interests in municipal bankruptcy, despite taxpayers previously being viewed as lacking party-in-interest standing at the eligibility stage of a case.[183]

Public safety was a significant issue in Detroit and just one of a set of factors, including blight, population decline, pension underfunding, the decline of the automotive industry, and infrastructure problems, that led the city to the doorstep of the bankruptcy court.[184] However, Detroit emerged from bankruptcy fewer than eighteen months after it entered; Judge Rhodes confirmed Detroit's plan of debt adjustment on 7 November 2014.[185] That plan eliminated over $7 billion of the city's debt and legacy liabilities and deferred the repayment of the principal of most of the city's remaining unsecured debt for at least nine years.[186] The plan was also forward-looking, making approximately $1.7 billion available over the next 10 years for restructuring and reinvestment initiatives to address blight, restore infrastructure, and improve service delivery to residents, notably in the area of public safety.[187] In this way, the plan sought to both put Detroit on firmer financial footing and allocate resources to address the problems that led the city to file for bankruptcy in the first place.

---

180 *In re City of Detroit, Mich.* [2013] 504 B.R. 97, 168 ('Several individual objectors and [a union] challenge the City's assertion that it is insolvent').

181 For a discussion of this decision and its potential impacts, see CS Chung, 'Rising Tides and Rearranging Deckchairs: How Climate Change is Reshaping Infrastructure Financing and Threatening to Sink Municipal Budgets' (2020) 32 Geo. Envtl. L. Rev. 165.

182 Ibid.

183 Ibid.

184 D Kurtzleben, 'Everything You Need to Know about the Detroit Bankruptcy' (*Vox*, 15 December 2014) <https://www.vox.com/2014/12/15/18073574/detroit-bankruptcy-pensions-municipal>.

185 'Nine Lessons From Detroit's Chapter 9 Case' (*Jones Day*, November 2014) <https://www.jonesday.com/en/insights/2014/11/nine-lessons-from-detroits-chapter-9-case>.

186 Ibid.

187 Ibid.

The centrepiece of Detroit's plan of adjustment was the so-called "Grand Bargain". A critical issue in Detroit's bankruptcy was whether the Detroit Institute of Arts (DIA) should sell its valuable artwork collection to help pay off the city's debts.[188] Although the funds raised from any sale of the artwork would have aided the city's goals of repaying creditors and protecting pensions, public outcry ensued, as the DIA was an important cultural institution in Detroit, with a valuable art collection carefully amassed over decades.[189] The Grand Bargain allowed the DIA's art collection to remain in place and consisted of donations by foundations, private donors, and the State of Michigan.[190] Pursuant to the terms of the deal, the donated funds would be dispersed to the state's pension systems to ameliorate pension cuts.[191] The Grand Bargain was a significant factor in persuading retirees to accept Detroit's plan (which included the pension cuts), and the DIA became an independent institution, meaning the City of Detroit no longer owned the artwork.[192] The Grand Bargain was the product of multiple rounds of contentious mediation overseen by US District Chief Judge Gerald Rosen.[193]

From a financial perspective, the bonds that fared the worst in Detroit's bankruptcy were general obligation (GO) bonds. Many bondholders had previously viewed these bonds as the safest type of municipal bonds; however, Judge Rhodes's decision confirmed that such bonds could be impaired in bankruptcy as unsecured obligations.[194] Indeed, these bonds had to be impaired, according to Judge Rhodes, so that Detroit could provide essential services to its residents. In other words, the need to provide these services outweighed the interests of GO bondholders, exposing them to more risk in the bankruptcy than they had previously expected.[195]

Detroit's bankruptcy also exposed a broader truth about municipal bonds: many lack protections that would be standard in the corporate context, thus subjecting bondholders to avoidable risks.[196] For example, Detroit's bonds, consistent with many municipal bonds, did not include "make whole" provisions protecting its bondholders from interest rate reductions.[197] Consequently,

---

188 'Grand Bargain' (*Detroit Historical Society*) <http://detroithistorical.org/learn/encyclopedia-of-detroit/grand-bargain>.

189 Ibid.

190 Ibid.

191 Ibid.

192 Ibid.

193 Ibid.

194 *Nine Lessons* (n 185).

195 Ibid.

196 Ibid.

197 Ibid.

Judge Rhodes was able to approve the resetting of the interest rates on Detroit's bonds during plan confirmation.[198]

Detroit's bankruptcy raised other concerns for creditors as well. For example, some of the city's lenders had structured their loans creatively so as to avoid blatantly running afoul of state-imposed debt limits.[199] In bankruptcy, however, these structures were scrutinised, and loans that were in fact in excess of the debt limit were found to be unenforceable.[200]

Detroit's bankruptcy was not just painful for traditional creditors, however. For example, the city's pensioners faced cuts in bankruptcy even though the Michigan constitution protected accrued pensions from impairment.[201] Because Detroit had never fully funded its accrued pensions, the bankruptcy judge found that the accrued but unfunded portions were subject to reduction in bankruptcy.[202] Specifically, Judge Rhodes held that the Michigan constitution's pensions clause, which provided that accrued pensions are "contractual obligations" that cannot be "diminished or impaired" by the state or its political subdivisions, was no obstacle to the impairment of pension claims in bankruptcy and merely conferred contractual status on pension claims.[203] This meant that pension claims could be impaired like any other contract in bankruptcy.[204] Although Judge Rhodes's decision was noteworthy, he was not the first judge to have held that pensions could be cut in bankruptcy despite state law protections; Judge Christopher Klein had made a similar decision a few months earlier in the bankruptcy of Stockton, California.[205]

Although Judge Rhodes held that Detroit could cut its pensions, the ultimate arrangement in Detroit was one of shared sacrifice.[206] Rather than slashing pensions with impunity, Detroit worked with retiree interest groups to reach an agreement, as part of the Grand Bargain, and pensions were not cut as much as they legally could have been.[207] Like much of Detroit's bankruptcy plan, these agreements were forward-looking as well as backward-looking, providing for the establishment of hybrid pension plans to deliver future pensions for current

---

198 Ibid.
199 Ibid.
200 Ibid.
201 Ibid.
202 Ibid.
203 Ibid.
204 Ibid.
205 Ibid.
206 Ibid.
207 Ibid.

employees.[208] Commentators have praised these hybrid plans as a potential "blueprint" for broader pension reform.[209]

Broader pension reform is widely viewed as necessary in the US, as US pension plans historically have subscribed to 'a policy that essentially believes that investment gains [are] permanent and losses [are] temporary'.[210] Notably, Judge Rhodes praised city leaders in Detroit for working with labour leaders to bargain for more appropriate funding of pension benefits.[211] At the same time, he admonished all parties and the state of Michigan to use more 'honest and realistic accounting and actuarial' assumptions when it came to disclosure of liabilities and pension funding shortfalls.[212]

As a result of its agreements with labour leaders, Detroit ended up treating pensions differently from the claims of other unsecured creditors, leading some objectors to raise claims of "unfair discrimination".[213] For example, one class of unsecured pension claims received a recovery of approximately 60%, whilst a class of general unsecured creditors received only 13% under Detroit's plan of adjustment.[214] Despite this significant difference in recovery, Judge Rhodes held that Detroit's plan did not discriminate unfairly for at least three reasons. First, Detroit had a 'strong interest in preserving its relationships with its employees and in enhancing their motivation, consistent with its financial resources'.[215] Second, the discrimination was directly tied to Detroit's mission of providing adequate services to its residents.[216] And third, Detroit's more favourable treatment of its pension claims was consistent with creditors' reasonable expectations given the protections for pensions enshrined in Michigan's constitution.[217]

Evaluating Detroit post-bankruptcy is complicated, as the city has seen both successes and failures in the years since its emergence from bankruptcy proceedings. For example, numerous construction projects have sprung up across much of downtown Detroit; however, the city still lacks a comprehensive plan for addressing its 40,000 blighted buildings and 70,000 vacant lots.[218] Even

---

208 Ibid.
209 Ibid.
210 Ibid.
211 Ibid.
212 Ibid.
213 Ibid.
214 Ibid.
215 Ibid.
216 Ibid.
217 Ibid.
218 'The Road to Rebuilding Detroit' (*JPMorgan Chase*, 2019) <https://www.theatlantic.com/sponsored/jpmc-city-makers-2015/the-road-to-rebuilding-detroit

after exiting bankruptcy, Detroit continued to use the bankruptcy as a shield against civil liability lawsuits.[219]

On the positive side, in 2016, Detroit became the first city in the nation whose voters approved a community benefits agreements ordinance.[220] This law, which applies to projects greater than $75 million in value or that receive over $1 million in city support, requires developers to proactively engage with the community to identify benefits and address negative consequences of their development projects.[221] In another concrete sign of the city's turnaround, Detroit recently sold $46 million of investment grade-rated general obligation bonds at a lower interest cost, driven by competitive bidding.[222] These bonds will support further changes in Detroit, including public lighting, transportation, and public safety improvements.

Although many lessons can be learnt from Detroit's bankruptcy, it is important to recognise that chapter 9 municipal bankruptcies are still quite rare. It is also important to keep in mind that municipalities vary significantly from each other, meaning that what worked in Detroit may not cleanly translate to success for a different municipality. Nevertheless, Detroit's bankruptcy stands out as an example of a swift and remarkable chapter 9 case for a large and complicated city.

3.4.2 Case Study 2: State Intervention in Flint

Whilst Detroit went through a highly publicised chapter 9 bankruptcy, the nearby city of Flint, Michigan, was undergoing its own crisis. Located just 70 miles from Detroit, Flint did not ultimately file for bankruptcy; instead, Flint serves as a counterexample to Detroit of a city where only state, rather than federal, intervention was used.

Flint's troubles began receiving significant national attention when heavy metal contamination of the city's water supply caused a public health crisis.[223] The roots of the crisis can be traced to 2011, when Flint began to explore whether it could save money by switching water suppliers, from the Detroit

---

/374/>.

219 Jacoby (n 170) 112 ('Because of the breadth of the bankruptcy law's definition of claim, Detroit's bankruptcy affected not only civil right lawsuits that had already been filed but also those filed years later').

220 CJ Tyson, 'The Impact of Municipal Fiscal Crisis on Equitable Development' (2021) 48 Fordham Urb. L.J. 883.

221 Ibid.

222 E Hudson, *Revived Detroit Draws Enough Bidders to Sell Debt at Lower Cost* (Bloomberg Law, 18 July 2024).

223 Chung (n 181).

Water and Sewerage Department (DWSD) to the Karegnondi Water Authority (KWA).[224] To make the switch, Flint needed to build a pipeline to connect its water system with the KWA's.[225] Flint terminated its relationship with the DWSD before the new pipeline was built, however. To bridge this gap in services, Flint temporarily switched the city's water supply to the Flint River.[226]

Notably, at the time Flint made this switch, it was under the control of a state-appointed emergency manager, and this manager made the ultimate decision to switch the water supply to the Flint River. Then-Governor Rick Snyder had declared Flint to be in financial emergency in 2011, resulting in the appointment of several emergency managers over the ensuing years.[227]

Under Michigan law, emergency managers have significant intervention powers with respect to municipalities. Although Michigan voters initially repealed the expansion of emergency manager power proposed by Governor Snyder, Snyder ultimately enacted legislation that has been contested as 'disproportionately target[ing] black communities and continu[ing] a narrative of structural and strategic racism'.[228] Among other things, Governor Snyder's legislation gives emergency managers the power to alter collective bargaining agreements.[229]

Soon after Governor Snyder named Michael Brown as Flint's emergency manager in November of 2011, he eliminated pay for the mayor and city council, laid off several city officials, and shut down two city offices: the ombudsman and the civil service commission.[230] A judge subsequently found that the state had violated an open meetings law when appointing Brown, and he was removed from office in March of 2012, but then reappointed after an appeals court reversed the decision.[231]

Darnell Earley was subsequently appointed as Flint's emergency manager in September of 2013.[232] It was Earley who oversaw the decision to change the water source to the Flint River in April of 2014.[233]

---

224 Ibid.

225 Ibid.

226 Ibid.

227 O Goodin-Smith, 'Flint's History of Emergency Management and How it got to Financial Freedom' (*MLive*, 16 January 2018) <http://mlive.com/news/flint/2018/01/city_of_the_state_flints_histo.html>.

228 Ibid (internal quotations omitted).

229 Ibid.

230 Ibid.

231 Ibid.

232 Ibid.

233 Ibid.

Almost immediately after the switch, Flint residents noticed a change in the colour and odour of the city's water and began to express concerns.[234] The Flint River water was contaminated with *E. coli* and coliform bacteria, so the city increased the chlorine levels in its water, which contributed to the corrosion of the city's old lead pipes.[235] Flint residents soon reported foul-smelling, brownish water coming from their taps.[236]

Notably, in October 2014, General Motors decided to stop using water from the Flint River, citing concerns about the corrosive effects of chlorine on its equipment.[237] Still, Flint officials continued to allow the Flint River to supply the city's residents with water. By early 2015, tests had detected elevated levels of heavy metals in the water supply, and some children in the city had elevated levels of lead contamination in their blood.[238] By one estimate, the increased lead concentrations in Flint's water caused a 58% increase in foetal deaths over a two-year period.[239]

Making matters worse, Flint had never implemented corrosion controls at its water treatment facility.[240] The combination of river water and lack of anti-corrosion additives corroded the city's pipes, causing more heavy metals to leach into the city's water system.[241] More broadly, climate change had threatened the city's infrastructure, exacerbating an already challenging situation in a community that was particularly vulnerable.[242] In 2015, Flint was found to be violating the federal Safe Drinking Water Act.[243] The city subsequently issued a public health advisory to its residents.[244] Although Flint ultimately switched back to the DWSD for its water supply, that action was too little, too late: the damage had been done.[245]

As mentioned, Flint was under the control of an emergency manager when the city decided to switch its water supply to save money. This emergency

---

234 Chung (n 181).
235 R DeBaecke, 'Flint Michigan Water Crisis, 2014–2020' (*Sustainable Rev.*, 6 February 2023) <https://sustainablereview.com/flint-michigan-water-crisis-continues/>.
236 Ibid.
237 Chung (n 181).
238 Ibid.
239 DeBaecke (n 235).
240 Chung (n 181).
241 Ibid.
242 Ibid.
243 DeBaecke (n 235).
244 Ibid.
245 Ibid.

manager was state appointed rather than elected by the citizens of Flint.[246] Notably, in testimony before the Michigan Civil Rights Commission, Professor Hammer observed that, although Flint's financial crisis was due to structural financial problems associated with population decline and the loss of the city's manufacturing base, the state of Michigan's response to that crisis precipitated the very distress that the state used to justify the appointment of an unelected emergency manager.[247] In particular, Professor Hammer pointed out that Michigan had decreased its revenue sharing with Flint by 61% over the six-year period from 2006 to 2012.[248] Although the Flint water crisis was caused largely by human error, the lead-up to the crisis was characterised by years of disinvestment by the state of Michigan into one of its poorest cities.[249] Put differently, had Flint not been under pressure from the state and under the thumb of an emergency manager, city officials may not have decided to shift the source of Flint's drinking water from the DWSD, a well-established public water system, to the highly contaminated Flint River simply to save money.[250]

Years after Flint made the switch, the predominantly African-American town of 100,000 was still suffering the consequences of the public health crisis.[251] Notably, Flint attracted attention from the federal government as well: at the end of 2016, the US Senate approved a $100 million bill to fund decontamination efforts in the city's water supply grid.[252] The federal Environmental Protection Agency (EPA) subsequently expedited this funding to remove and restore Flint's lead service lines.[253] The Michigan Civil Rights Commission has alleged that the emergency manager's decision to switch the water supply to contaminated river water was grounded in racism.[254]

At the end of 2017, Flint signed a 30-year lease deal with the Great Lakes Water Authority, which guaranteed the city's access to clean water from Lake Huron, as well as a greater portion of the federal funding designated by the EPA for an overhaul of its water infrastructure.[255] By the end of that year, Flint

246 Chung (n 181).

247 Ibid.

248 Ibid.

249 Tyson (n 220).

250 DC Esty, 'Red Lights to Green Lights: From 20th Century Environmental Regulation to 21st Century Sustainability' (2017) 47 Envtl. L. 1.

251 DeBaecke (n 235).

252 Ibid.

253 Ibid.

254 Ibid.

255 Ibid.

had located and reinstituted over 6,000 lead service lines, but more work was still to be done.[256]

On 4 April 2018, the state of Michigan put an end to Flint's period in state receivership.[257] After six years, the city was at last freed from state control.[258] Just two days later, then-Governor Snyder announced that the state would stop giving free bottled water to Flint residents, despite thousands of residents continuing to drink water from lead-contaminated pipes.[259] The message seemed to be that the state was withdrawing completely from Flint, despite having precipitated many of the events that had caused problems for the city.

Today, Flint residents remain wary of local officials' decisions when it comes to water.[260] Although lead levels in the city's water supply are now below levels considered dangerous by the federal government, some medical professionals contend that no amount of lead in water is healthy for domestic use.[261] In addition, the bulk of the federal government's $100 million allocation for water infrastructure improvements has remained unused, raising questions about whether city management is organisationally equipped to get the city back on track.[262]

The years following the Flint water crisis have been marked by finger-pointing and blame-shifting. The engineering firm that Flint originally hired to evaluate its water system has been fighting a multimillion-dollar civil lawsuit over its role in the crisis.[263] The firm, Veolia, contends that the blame for the water crisis rests solely on government officials who oversaw and, allegedly, covered up the botched switch.[264] Although Veolia's executives privately told government officials that Flint should switch back to the DWSD for its water supply, the firm made no public recommendations to that effect.[265] However, Flint, for its part, had been recording incorrect data and submitting inaccurate

---

[256] Ibid.
[257] Ibid.
[258] Ibid.
[259] Ibid.
[260] Ibid.
[261] Ibid.
[262] Ibid.
[263] K Ruble, 'Company Sued Over Flint's Water Crisis Wages Digital PR War During Trial' (*The Detroit News*, 8 September 2022) <https://www.detroitnews.com/story/news/local/michigan/2022/09/09/veolia-north-america-flint-water-crisis-google-advertising/7959344001/>.
[264] Ibid.
[265] Ibid.

reports to state environmental regulators, suggesting that both government and private interests were to blame for the crisis.[266]

In 2021, the Michigan Attorney General's Office announced criminal charges for eight former state officials, including former Governor Rick Snyder and emergency manager Darnell Earley, as well as one current official for their alleged roles in the water crisis.[267] Charges included perjury, misconduct in office, and involuntary manslaughter.[268] In total, Flint's water crisis has been linked to at least 12 deaths and 80 illnesses.[269]

The State of Michigan itself is at least partially responsible for the crisis. Michigan restricts how tax dollars can be spent to sustain clean, affordable water in its cities.[270] However, Flint's water crisis has also resulted in changes to laws regulating lead and other contaminants in drinking water at both the state and federal levels.[271]

3.4.3 An ESG Critique to Law in Practice

There are, of course, differences between Flint and Detroit in terms of, among other things, city size, the different nature of the crisis each city experienced, and the fact that one city filed for bankruptcy and one did not. But the two cities, just 70 miles apart, are both examples of the different ways in which municipal financial distress has environmental, social, and governance impacts.

3.4.3.1 Environmental impacts

Flint is a prime example of the negative environmental impacts of the law in practice. Flint's deteriorating infrastructure, combined with a belief by its emergency managers that cost-cutting was necessary, resulted in heavy metal contamination of the public water supply. This switch put an already vulnerable city into a significantly worse situation. The shift in the water supply to the contaminated Flint River was directly precipitated by the city's fiscal crisis and the state of Michigan's influence over the process via the imposition of an unelected emergency manager.

---

[266] Ibid.

[267] M Joffe, 'Government Failures, Not Privatization, Are to Blame for Flint's Water Crisis' (*Reason*, 16 June 2022) <https://reason.org/commentary/government-failures-not-privatization-are-to-blame-for-flints-water-crisis/>.

[268] Ibid.

[269] Ibid.

[270] J Orr, 'Ask the Expert: Flint Water Crisis and Its Impact' (*MSU Today*, 22 September 2022) <https://msutoday.msu.edu/news/2022/Ask-the-expert-Flint-water-crisis-and-its-impact>.

[271] Ibid.

Moreover, although the federal government has supplied money to Flint to decontaminate its water supply grid, governance issues at the local level have resulted in most of the money not being used, even years after the money was allocated. This suggests that there is a need for capacity building and an underlying governance problem, on top of the overt environmental issues just discussed.

As a more general matter, climate change and rising sea levels have increased costs and undercut property tax bases throughout the US, resulting in a direct hit to local governments' financial resources. According to one study,[272] over half of the state of Florida's 410 municipalities will be affected by 6.6 feet of sea-level rise. Almost 30% of the revenues currently generated by these 211 affected municipalities come from buildings in areas that will become chronically flooded due to this rise in sea level. This change could happen as early as the end of this century. Fire-prone areas are similarly affecting municipalities and their financial bottom lines.[273]

Cities throughout the US are often heavily reliant on property taxes as a source of revenue. However, this reliance has encouraged development in flood zones, in a short-sighted attempt to make money. Over time, there is a concern that climate change will increasingly threaten these areas, as well as the property taxes they generate. This threat is present in some form today, as insurance companies and property markets have begun downgrading property values in acknowledgement of climate impacts.

Climate change may also make it more difficult and expensive to provide other municipal services, such as water, sewage, and road maintenance. If cities decide to cut back on these services, or on development in vulnerable areas

---

[272] L Shi, T J Holmes and W Butler, 'Climate Change is a Fiscal Disaster for Local Governments—Our Study Shows How It's Testing Communities in Florida' (*PreventionWeb*, 5 October 2023) <https://www.preventionweb.net/news/climate-change-fiscal-disaster-local-governments-our-study-shows-how-its-testing-communities#:~:text=But%20climate%20disasters%20and%20sea,for%20reducing%20long%2Dterm%20risks>.

[273] L Parshley, 'In Wildfire-Prone Areas, Homeowners are Learning They're Uninsurable' (Yale Climate Connections, 26 October 2023) <https://yaleclimateconnections.org/2023/10/in-wildfire-prone-areas-homeowners-are-learning-theyre-uninsurable/> noting that the indirect costs of US wildfires in 2018, including health care costs and "disruption to the broader economy", totalled nearly $150 billion. See M Chediak, 'Wildfire Threats Make Utilities Uninsurable in US West' (*Bloomberg*, 24 June 2024) <https://www.bnnbloomberg.ca/wildfire-threats-make-utilities-uninsurable-in-us-west-1.2088716> discussing insurers' reluctance to cover utilities for wildfires and how the lack of insurance could force utilities to go bankrupt if they are forced to pay for damages caused by fires started by their electrical lines.

more generally, property taxes will continue to decline, potentially spurring a downward spiral of financial distress.

3.4.3.2 Social impacts

From a social perspective, it is notable that, in the Detroit bankruptcy, the bankruptcy judge treated taxpayers as the functional equivalent of parties in interest in the bankruptcy by finding that the city was "service-delivery insolvent". In other words, the judge recognised that municipalities owe a minimum level of services to their residents; as Detroit was unable to provide even this minimum level, it was insolvent in that sense. This concept of service-delivery insolvency is nowhere to be found in the Bankruptcy Code itself and is a judge-made innovation that, whilst remarkable, may not be replicated in future cases because of its lack of foundation in the written law.

Detroit's plan of debt adjustment, which it put together whilst in chapter 9 bankruptcy, made money available to address blight, restore infrastructure, and improve service delivery. In this respect, Detroit's bankruptcy was perhaps more forward-looking than other municipal bankruptcies. In particular, Judge Rhodes's decisions throughout the bankruptcy case seemed aimed at prioritising long-term sustainability for the city.[274] He used the powers he had in Detroit's bankruptcy to try and set the city on a sustainable future path by, for example, encouraging more transparency in both pension funding and liability disclosure more specifically. Judge Rhodes's decisions also indicated that pension claims could receive a greater recovery in bankruptcy due to Detroit's interest in preserving employee relationships and due to the city's need to provide adequate services to its residents. The Grand Bargain, an integral piece of Detroit's bankruptcy plan, was also highly unusual and spurred in part by public outcry over the potential loss of a cultural icon, the DIA.

Detroit's bankruptcy raises the possibility of including a broader concept of "stakeholder" in bankruptcy law. Taxpayers and residents of the City of Detroit, even if they were not "creditors" in the traditional sense, were owed obligations by the city and were recognised by the court as being owed those obligations. This raises the broader question of the extent to which other interests can be considered "stakeholders" in a bankruptcy case and the degree to which bankruptcy can and should protect interests outside of the traditional debtor–creditor relationship.[275]

To some extent then, Detroit's bankruptcy illustrates that ESG-related goals need not always be in tension with bankruptcy and insolvency law. For example, Detroit's relatively favourable treatment of pension claims was consistent,

---

[274] Linna (n 39).

[275] Ibid.

to some degree, with other creditors' reasonable expectations of their treatment, given that Michigan's constitution holds specific protections for public pensions.

As much as Detroit's bankruptcy brought about some positive developments in the ESG arena, both Detroit and Flint also represent a somewhat cautionary tale about the incursion of private entities into public welfare.[276] Both Detroit and Flint were under the leadership of emergency management appointed by the state, rather than elected by the citizens. Both illustrate the trade-offs associated with this leadership choice: although emergency managers are more insulated from the whims of the public, such insulation risks breeding public resentment and threatens the democratic foundations upon which municipal government is based. In Flint in particular, some observers raised concerns about racism as the impetus for the emergency manager's decision to switch the city to a contaminated water supply. And in Detroit, although the city did engage with many stakeholders, it left civil rights and personal injury claimants out in the cold.[277]

3.4.3.3 Governance impacts

As just mentioned, both Detroit and Flint were under emergency managers during periods of extreme financial distress, raising concerns about the role of democratic self-governance in local financial affairs. In Flint in particular, the state of Michigan's response to Flint's financial crisis was to decrease revenue sharing with the city. This in turn precipitated additional financial distress that the state then used to justify the appointment of unelected emergency managers, who then made the fatal decision to divest Flint from the DWSD and use the Flint River as a temporary water source.

The story of Flint is also a story about assigning accountability. There has been significant blame-shifting between government officials and private water treatment professionals, though, to date, only the former have been charged with crimes in connection with the crisis. Flint's story also reminds us of the difficulty of retroactively assigning blame. Were the receivers' hands truly tied because elected officials had made decades' worth of poor decisions prior to their appointment? Or should the receivers have done more due diligence when deciding to switch the water supply? To what extent is the state government to blame for the city's predicament? These questions may not be answerable in a book, let alone a book chapter, but they are important questions, and questions

---

276 See A Atkinson, 'Commodifying Marginalization' (2022) 71 Duke L.J. 773.

277 Jacoby (n 170) 112.

about accountability should be taken into consideration whenever a municipality's governance structure is changed.

These questions also raise the issue of whether and how restructuring can be used to address (or even prevent) fraud and mismanagement in a locality. In the case of Flint, the state's emergency managers arguably inflicted harm on the city, even as they sought to mitigate Flint's desperate financial situation.

3.4.4 Conclusion: An ESG Critique of US Treatment of Distressed Local Public Entities

US municipal bankruptcy law has existed for nearly a century, and the states' relationship with their municipalities is a complex and shifting story. To distill this history and try to learn from it is a daunting task. Still, several observations can be made about the ways in which the US deals with its distressed localities and the environmental, social, and governance impacts of that treatment.

First, a key problem with both chapter 9 municipal bankruptcy and state intervention programmes is getting the timing right. Most states react to municipal fiscal crises rather than attempting to proactively prevent them. On the federal side, chapter 9 is largely viewed as a "last resort", and is designed to rectify old problems and address existing ones at least as much as it seeks to prevent new ones. Finding the "right" time to intervene in municipal fiscal distress is a complicated and uncertain endeavour. Yet, more focus could be given to the development of proactive monitoring and budgeting measures.

Second, there is a need to better link our "solutions"—whether bankruptcy or state intervention—to the persistent problem of pension underfunding in the US. Two federal bankruptcy judges have now held that accrued pensions can be cut in chapter 9 bankruptcy, giving municipalities a potentially significant bargaining chip in negotiations with retirees and employees. Pension underfunding is a huge social issue, however, and relying on bankruptcy to "solve" the underfunding crisis will not be effective, in essence, because a bankruptcy comes too late in the process.

Third, the extent and type of displacement of local officials is a key theme in both state-level and federal-level programmes. At the state level, we have seen receivers or emergency managers appointed to displace local elected officials in times of crisis. At the federal level, although a bankruptcy court in chapter 9 is not supposed to interfere with governance matters, in practice, the court holds significant sway over government officials, as seen in the Detroit bankruptcy. This is especially true with respect to the Grand Bargain, a product of extensive mediation overseen by another federal judge in a largely out-of-court process. Indeed, some scholars believe that more court interference in governance is desirable to get a municipality back on its feet in a chapter 9 bankruptcy.[278]

Fourth, and on a more positive note, municipal debt restructuring is an area where creativity can flourish, and if creative measures take hold, perhaps they will extend to other areas of the law. Because chapter 9 is used so rarely, judges do not have a significant body of precedent to examine, and judicial discretion can therefore play a larger role. For example, Judge Rhodes's determination that Detroit was "service-delivery insolvent" opened the door to consideration of a broader range of interests in the case than simply examining the debtor's relationship with its financial creditors. At the same time, creativity can work against the protection of social interests, as, for example, when municipalities use the bankruptcy process to escape liability for civil rights violations, as Professor Jacoby has documented.[279]

Fifth, the effectiveness of both chapter 9 and various state intervention programmes remains an open question. Often, these programmes and laws are not specifically designed with ESG goals and concerns in mind. However, giving a municipality an opportunity to put its financial house in order may, in the long run, allow the municipality in question to better address ESG issues that arise.

Sixth, municipal distress brings the question of the state–local government relationship to the forefront. The case studies of both Detroit and Flint raise the question of the degree of responsibility the state of Michigan has for the financial status of its distressed localities. The case studies also shed light on public–private relationships. To what extent are private entities—consultants, foundations, professional firms, and so forth—to blame for a city's financial issues?

Finally, the day-to-day operations of a municipality are intricately intertwined with ESG concerns. Any time a municipality is facing financial distress or failure, these concerns—and the public-facing, service-delivery aspects of municipal governance—come to the forefront. In this way, ESG considerations in municipal distress and bankruptcy may be more pronounced than in the context of, for example, the financial distress of a private corporation. Thus, considering the ESG implications and impacts when a municipality experiences financial distress provides a valuable perspective and an invitation to consider the ESG implications and impacts of financial distress writ large.

These concluding reflections indicate that, if anything, the work is only beginning when it comes to ESG and financial distress. Hopefully, the

---

278 Gillette and Skeel (n 175).

279 Jacoby (n 170) 112.

information in this chapter will encourage further study into how to recognise and rectify the impact financial distress has on a local public entity's citizens, leaders, and surrounding communities. If local governments can become leaders in addressing ESG issues, they can pave the way for broader acceptance of ESG considerations in the commercial context as well.

4. South Africa

4.1 INTRODUCTION

South African insolvency law, corporate law, administrative law, local government law, and judicial structures have historically all been significantly influenced by English law. South Africa thus shares with England and the US a broad common-law legal language in dealing with municipalities in distress. However, in contrast with the US and England, South Africa is a developing country with an emerging, upper-middle-income economy. It became a democracy only in 1994 and faces major developmental challenges with unemployment above 30% and significant income inequality.[1] Simultaneously, South Africa's Constitution[2] contains extensive justiciable fundamental rights, including rights to dignity and equality, socio-economic rights, labour rights, property rights, rights to administrative justice and access to courts, and environmental rights. These provide a comprehensive legal basis for an ESG framework in financial distress rules. In fact, the constitutionality of South African insolvency rules has repeatedly been challenged.[3] Whilst South Africa is often influenced by corporate and legal developments in the UK and US,[4] it, in turn, asserts notable influence on other African countries.

[1] D Francis and E Webster, 'Poverty and Inequality in South Africa: Critical Reflections' (2019) 36 Dev. South. Afr. 788.

[2] Constitution of the Republic of South Africa, 1996.

[3] A Boraine et al, 'The Pro-Creditor Approach in South African Insolvency Law and the Possible Impact of the Constitution' (2015) 3 NIBLeJ 59; KE van der Linde and MJ van Staden, 'Judicial Development (and Activism) in Insolvency Law. *Sarrahwitz v Maritz* 2015 4 SA 491 (CC)' (2017) SALJ 414, 415–417; A Smith, K van der Linde and J Calitz, *Hockly's Law of Insolvency, Winding-up and Business Rescue* (10th edn, Juta 2022) 18–19.

[4] This is quite evident in the reform of South African company law in the early 2000s that resulted, among others, in the introduction of business rescue as an alternative to the liquidation of companies and in which process developments in the UK and US clearly played a notable role. See, among others: The Department of Trade and Industry, *South African Company Law for the 21st Century: Guidelines*

South Africa is a useful jurisdiction to study municipalities in distress from a law-in-context approach. South African law contains an extensive, dedicated regulatory and administrative framework on municipal finance management. The framework's rules on financial problems constitute one of the most comprehensive, dedicated sets of rules on local entities in distress globally and exist largely parallel to insolvency law. However, financial distress of South African municipalities is a common phenomenon. The South African National Treasury's *2022 State of Local Government Finances and Financial Management Report* indicated that most municipalities' financial situation deteriorated in the preceding five years. In 2015/16, 37.7% of municipalities were in financial distress, growing to 61% in 2021/22. The report showed that 15% of all municipalities were under intervention in 2022 with a further nine municipalities seeking voluntary Financial Recovery Plans due to governance failures. One of the municipalities placed under intervention is Mangaung, one of the eight metropolitan municipalities in the country and the capital city of one of the nine provinces (the Free State).

Our discussion starts by briefly setting out insolvency law and business rescue in South Africa generally (2). Then we discuss what constitutes a local entity in South Africa (3). The frameworks governing local entities in distress are consequently explored, including the dedicated set of rules focusing on municipal finance management (4). Finally, the frameworks' application is analysed in two case studies, focusing particularly on environmental, social, and governance (ESG) considerations (5). We conclude that the dedicated set of rules governing local entities in distress, primarily municipalities, has largely failed to effectively address ESG challenges (6).

4.2 SOUTH AFRICAN LAW ON INSOLVENCY AND REORGANISATION

The legal rules governing financial distress generally, and in relation to local public entities specifically, exist in three almost completely siloed, parallel legal frameworks in South Africa. For private entities,[5] the two primary mechanisms are liquidation and business rescue, each with its own regulatory framework. For local public entities, a separate regulatory framework exists under municipal finance law.

Insolvency in South Africa is mainly governed by the Insolvency Act 24 of 1936 and the Companies Act 71 of 2008. South Africa has a fragmented legal

---

for Corporate Law Reform (Government Notice 1183, May 2004) <https://www.gov.za/sites/default/files/gcis_document/201409/26493gen1183a.pdf>.

[5] The focus in this chapter is on juristic persons rather than natural persons.

framework on insolvency, with the law distinguishing between insolvency of companies and of natural persons.

The Insolvency Act has governed the insolvency of natural persons since 1936. Company insolvency is primarily governed by the 2008 Companies Act. However, the previous Companies Act of 1973 continues to apply to the winding-up and liquidation of companies.[6] This transitional arrangement was included in the 2008 Companies Act, given ongoing law reform on the consolidation of insolvency rules in a single statute. This reform process has been ongoing for years.[7] The South African Law Reform Commission has published various working and discussion papers and draft bills in this regard.[8] However, no law to this effect has been introduced into Parliament to date. Consequently, the "transitional" 1973 Companies Act rules continue to apply to insolvent companies. In addition to these statutes, there are also insolvency rules emanating from common law supplementing the legislation.[9]

4.2.1 Procedures

Liquidation and business rescue are the main procedures governing companies in distress.[10] Liquidation results in the removal of the company from the companies register and the winding up of its activities. Business rescue procedures are aimed at the continuation of all or part of the debtor's activity, either under the existing or (more frequently) a new owner, in terms of a business rescue plan designed to address the distress.

---

[6] Prior to the 1973 Companies Act, the winding up of companies was provided for in chapter VII of the Companies Act 1926.

[7] A Keay, 'To Unify or Not to Unify Insolvency Legislation: International Experience and the Latest South African Proposals' (1999) 32 De Jure 62; M Havenga, 'Simplification and Unification in Corporate and Insolvency Law—Are We Making Any Progress?' (2001) 13(3) SA Mercantile LJ 408; J Calitz, 'Historical Overview of State Regulation of South African Insolvency Law' (2010) 16(2) Fundamina 1; A Boraine and M Roestoff, 'Revisiting the State of Consumer Insolvency in South Africa after Twenty Years: The Courts' Approach, International Guidelines and an Appeal for Urgent Law Reform (2)' (2014) 77(4) THRHR 527; A Boraine, 'Formal Debt-Relief, Rescue and Liquidation Options for External Companies in South Africa' (2020) 7(4) BRICS Law J 85, 121–122.

[8] See South African Law Commission, Project 63, Commission Paper 582 *Review of the Law of Insolvency* (2000) Vols 1 & 2.

[9] *Du Plessis NO v Rolfes Ltd* [1996] ZASCA 45 26; Callitz (n 7) 25.

[10] The Companies Act 2008 also provides for other arrangements between a company and creditors, such as compromise (s 155). Our analysis omits reference to compromise between a company and creditors due to the hybrid, contractual, and corporate nature of that mechanism.

4.2.1.1 Liquidation

Insolvent companies can be either voluntarily or compulsorily wound up.[11] The company, a creditor, any of the company's members, or all of these parties jointly can apply to the court for the company's compulsory winding up.[12] Such applications must be served on the Master of the High Court, who may report any relevant facts to the court.[13]

South Africa has no dedicated insolvency regulator. The Master of the High Court and the Companies and Intellectual Property Commission (CIPC) fulfil certain regulatory insolvency functions.[14] The Master of the High Court is a statutory office within the Department of Justice, staffed by civil servants, with regulatory authority over several matters in the administration of justice.[15] It is not a judicial office. The CIPC is likewise a statutory body, created by the Companies Act, to provide regulatory oversight over all matters relating to companies.[16] Neither of these offices has a dedicated insolvency mandate.

Once a winding-up order is granted, the company's property comes under the Master's control until the Master has appointed a liquidator.[17] The Master exercises oversight over the work of liquidators.[18] Liquidators are nominated by creditors and members at their respective first meetings following the order.[19] The court and the Master have the power to summon any party with a relationship to the liquidated company for examination to obtain relevant information.[20]

A voluntary winding up is done by way of resolution by the company itself.[21] The resolution must be registered with the CIPC and takes effect once registered.[22] As with a compulsory winding up, the Master summons meetings of creditors and members once the winding up takes effect and appoints a liquidator.[23]

---

[11] Companies Act 61 of 1973, s 346(1), s 343, s 349.

[12] Ibid s 346(1).

[13] Ibid s 346(4).

[14] *Motala v Master, North Gauteng High Court* [2019] ZASCA 60 [72]–[74]; J Calitz and A Boraine, 'The Role of the Master of the High Court as Regulator in a Changing Liquidation Environment: A South African Perspective' (2005) SALJ 728.

[15] Ibid.

[16] Companies Act 71 of 2008, s 185.

[17] Ibid s 361.

[18] Ibid s 381.

[19] Ibid s 369.

[20] Ibid s 417.

[21] Ibid s 349.

[22] Ibid ss 350–352.

[23] Ibid s 369.

In all instances, the liquidator takes full control of the company and its assets.

4.2.1.2 Business rescue

The Companies Act of 1926 introduced judicial management as a mechanism to reorganise companies in distress and avoid liquidation. Under narrowly framed circumstances, courts could order a judicial manager to assume control over the company and return it to solvency, whilst also granting a moratorium against the company's creditors. The mechanism was not a success. In *Le Roux Hotel Management (Pty) Ltd v E Rand (Pty) Ltd (FBC Fidelity Bank Ltd (under curatorship) intervening)*,[24] the court called it a "moribund old horse" and 'a system which has barely worked since its initiation in 1926'.

The 2008 Companies Act replaced judicial management with a modern business rescue regime with effect from 2011. A company can be placed in business rescue voluntarily by a resolution of the company's board of directors or compulsorily by a court.[25]

Any affected person, that is a creditor, shareholder, trade union, employee, or employee representative, may apply to the court to place a company in compulsory business rescue.[26] The application must also be served on the CIPC.[27] The applicant must nominate the business rescue practitioner in the court papers, but the creditors must ratify the nomination if the order is granted.[28] For voluntary business rescue, the board resolution must be filed with the CIPC and the company must appoint a business rescue practitioner.[29]

A company's board of directors may commence business rescue if it reasonably believes that the company is financially distressed and there are reasonable prospects of rescuing the company.[30] The Companies Act defines "financially distressed" as when 'it appears to be reasonably unlikely that the company will be able to pay all of its debts as they become due and payable within the immediately ensuing six months; or it appears to be reasonably likely that the company will become insolvent within the immediately ensuing six months'.[31] The courts have confirmed that companies that are currently insolvent will also qualify as "financially distressed" and not only those that are likely to

24 2001 (2) SA 727 (C) (at paras 55, 60).
25 Companies Act 71 of 2008, s 129, s 131.
26 Ibid s 128, s 131.
27 Ibid s 131.
28 Ibid.
29 Ibid s 129, s 132.
30 Ibid s 129.
31 Ibid s 128.

become insolvent.[32] For currently insolvent companies, business rescue will be a true alternative to liquidation. However, the further requirement that there must be reasonable prospects for rescuing the company may bar recourse to business rescue where the company is already hopelessly insolvent.[33] The test is whether there are reasonable prospects that any of business rescue's aims could be achieved, namely that the company be returned to solvency or that a better outcome be achieved for creditors and shareholders than under liquidation.[34] Sufficient grounds showing the reasonableness of the prospects of achieving one of the aims on the facts must be submitted.[35]

At the heart of the business rescue process is the business rescue plan. The Companies Act prescribes what a business rescue practitioner must address in the plan.[36] More than 75% of the creditors' voting interests that voted must support the plan and, where relevant, also at least 50% of the independent creditors' voting interests that voted.[37] A plan proposing to alter rights attached to any class of the company's securities must also be supported by a majority of such voting rights that voted.[38] Once the plan has been adopted, it is binding on the company, all creditors, and all holders of the company's securities.[39]

4.2.2 Purposes and Rules

The primary object of South Africa's insolvency system under the Insolvency Act is the benefit of creditors.[40] Evans called this 'the golden rule in South African insolvency law'.[41] South Africa's insolvency system is thus pointedly

[32] *Oakdene Square Properties (Pty) Ltd v Farm Bothasfontein (Kyalami) (Pty) Ltd* [2013] ZASCA 68 [7]; *Tyre Corporation Cape Town (Pty) Ltd v GT Logistics (Pty) Ltd* [2016] ZAWCHC 124 [15].

[33] *Swart v Beagles Run Investments 25 (Pty) Ltd* [2011] ZAGPPHC 103.

[34] *Oakdene* (n 32).

[35] Ibid.

[36] Companies Act, s 150.

[37] Ibid s 152(2). An independent creditor refers to a creditor that is not related to a director of the company or the business rescue practitioner, or that does not directly or indirectly control the company.

[38] Ibid s 152(3).

[39] Ibid s 152(4).

[40] *Ex parte Pillay; Mayet v Pillay* 1955 (2) SA 309 (N) 311; *Marshall Industrials Ltd v Pillay* 1956 (4) SA 580 (N) 581; *R v Meer* 1957 (3) SA 614 (N) 619; *Epstein v Epstein* 1987 (4) SA 606 (C) 611; Smith et al (n 3) 5.

[41] R Evans, 'Insolvency' (2021) 2(1) YSAL 631, 642.

a pro-creditor one.[42] In *Marshall Industrials Ltd v Pillay*,[43] the court noted that 'the Insolvency Act was passed [...] not for the relief of harassed debtors'.

In contrast with the insolvency regime, the fairly recently introduced rules on business rescue are aimed at rehabilitating a company in distress.[44] Whilst the aim of the Insolvency Act is to benefit creditors above all, the purpose of business rescue is to find a balanced solution to financial distress for all involved. One of the 2008 Companies Act's purposes is to 'provide for the efficient rescue and recovery of financially distressed companies, in a manner that balances the rights and interests of all relevant stakeholders'.[45]

Business rescue is an alternative to liquidation for a financially distressed company, and the Companies Act reflects 'a legislative preference for the restoration of viable companies rather than their destruction'.[46] In *Diener NO v Minister of Justice and Correctional Services*,[47] the Constitutional Court stated: '[t]he primary goal of business rescue is to avoid liquidation and its attendant negative consequences on stakeholders'. However, business rescue does not preclude liquidation. If business rescue fails, liquidation may still follow.

Courts have recognised the wider interests served by business rescue rules. In *Koen v Wedgewood Village Golf & Country Estate (Pty) Ltd*,[48] the court pointed to the economic and social 'collateral damage' caused by liquidation, noting the public interest in avoiding 'such adverse socioeconomic consequences' through business rescue. In *Oakdene Square Properties (Pty) Ltd v Farm Bothasfontein (Kyalami) (Pty) Ltd*,[49] the court juxtaposed the narrow purpose of insolvency rules with the broader purpose of business rescue, stating that business rescue 'attempts to secure and balance the opposing interests

---

[42] RD Sharrock, 'Insolvency' in M Kühne (ed), *The Law of South Africa* (Vol 11, 2nd edn, LexisNexis 2008) para 199; R Bradstreet, 'The New Business Rescue: Will Creditors Sink or Swim?' (2011) 128(2) SALJ 352; FHI Cassim (ed), *Contemporary Company Law* (2nd edn, Juta 2012) 866; E Levenstein, *South African Business Rescue Procedure* (LexisNexis 2020) paras 2.1 and 2.3; Boraine et al (n 3) 60.

[43] 1956 (4) SA 580 (N) 581.

[44] Companies Act 71 of 2008, s 128(1)(b); Smith et al (n 3) 318–319.

[45] Companies Act 71 of 2008, s 7(k).

[46] *Ferrostaal GmbH v Transnet SOC Ltd* [2021] ZASCA 62 [17]; *FirstRand Bank Ltd v KJ Foods CC* [2017] ZASCA 50 [77], endorsed in *Diener NO v Minister of Justice and Correctional Services* [2018] ZACC 48 [54].

[47] [2018] ZACC 48 [54].

[48] [2011] ZAWCHC 464 [14].

[49] [2012] ZAGPJHC 12 [12].

of creditors, shareholders and employees. It encapsulates a shift from creditors' interests to a broader range of interests'.

4.2.3 Case Law and Management

The ordinary High Court exercises general oversight over both liquidation and business rescue proceedings.

In applications for a company's winding up, courts may grant either a provisional or final winding-up order.[50] Courts typically first grant a provisional order, allowing all interested parties to be heard on a return date whilst protecting creditors' interests in the interim.[51] Companies may be wound up on a statutory list of grounds.[52] The most general ground is where the court considers it 'just and equitable that the company should be wound up'.[53] This ostensibly creates a wide judicial discretion.[54] However, courts have adopted a narrow approach, recognising only a limited number of "just and equitable" scenarios to grant a winding-up order.[55] Following a pro-creditor approach, courts have held that a winding-up order is justified where 'it is just and equitable that the creditors should be protected from further losses and that it should be prevented from disposing of assets and incurring further liabilities'.[56]

Courts also retain broad discretionary powers to intervene in liquidation proceedings after the winding-up order.[57] Liquidators, creditors, or shareholders may apply for such judicial intervention, which may include staying or setting aside the winding-up order or the continuation of the process on any terms the court may state.[58]

Courts may grant an order commencing compulsory business rescue proceedings if they are satisfied that the company is financially distressed or has failed to pay any contractual or regulatory employment-related obligations, or it is otherwise just and equitable to do so for financial reasons. There is accordingly a similarly broad "just and equitable" jurisdiction to order business rescue. *Additionally*, the court must be satisfied that there are reasonable

---

[50] Companies Act 61 of 1973, s 347.

[51] Smith et al (n 3) 292.

[52] Companies Act 1973, s 344.

[53] Ibid s 344(h).

[54] *Moosa NO v Mavjee Bhawan (Pty) Ltd* 1967 (3) SA 131 (T).

[55] *Rand Air (Pty) Ltd v Ray Bester Investments (Pty) Ltd* 1985 (2) SA 345 (W).

[56] *Kia Intertrade Johannesburg (Pty) Ltd v Infinite Motors (Pty) Ltd* [1999] 2 All SA 268 (W).

[57] RC Williams, 'Companies' in M Kühne (ed), *The Law of South Africa* (Vol 4(3), 2nd edn, LexisNexis 2014) para 136.

[58] Companies Act 61 of 1973, s 354.

prospects for rescuing the company.[59] Alternatively, the court may order liquidation if, for example, it is unconvinced of reasonable prospects of rescue.[60]

4.2.4 Rules on Financial Distress through an ESG Lens

The Insolvency Act evidently has a narrow focus compared to the broader approach to business rescue under the Companies Act. The Insolvency Act, read with the insolvency provisions of the 1973 Companies Act, is weak on ESG considerations, while business rescue under the Companies Act 2008 incorporates more ESG considerations.

The Insolvency Act's strong pro-creditor stance, trumping almost all other factors, implies that very limited governance factors influence insolvency proceedings and virtually no social or environmental factors. The latter considerations only come into play where a creditor's claim has environmental or social dimensions. Even then, the insolvency regime's aim is the advantage of such a creditor rather than the environmental or social nature of the claim. However, since the 2000s, shifts away from a strict or harsh pro-creditor position have emerged. In particular, consumer debtors are increasingly statutorily protected through the National Credit Act 34 of 2005 and the Consumer Protection Act 68 of 2008.[61] These have introduced a wider range of factors into financial distress proceedings, albeit only to the benefit of natural-person debtors. Courts have softened the strict pro-creditor approach by inserting social considerations such as equality and dignity into the Insolvency Act by means of interpretation. In *Stratford v Investec Bank Limited*,[62] the Constitutional Court interpreted the Insolvency Act[63] to require furnishing a petition for sequestration also to domestic employees and not just those employed in the debtor's business, as had previously been held. The court based its reasoning on equality between all employees and the dignity-enhancing role of the required notice, stating: '[n]otice, ultimately, signifies respect for the human dignity of employees'.[64]

Despite these developments, insolvency rules remain weak on ESG factors.

---

59 Companies Act 71 of 2008, s 131.

60 Ibid.

61 See J Calitz and A Boraine, 'Some Consequences of the National Credit Act 34 of 2005 on the Proof of Claims in Insolvency Law' (2010) SALJ 797.

62 [2014] ZACC 38.

63 Insolvency Act, s 9(4A).

64 *Stratford v Investec Bank Limited* [2014] ZACC 38 [34].

South African law experiences the same tension between insolvency rules and environmental protection rules familiar to many legal systems.[65] There are no special rules in either insolvency or environmental law to mediate the tension between insolvents' environmental-protection liabilities and discharge of liabilities under insolvency proceedings. Any civil claims regarding environmental protection, for example, by a regulatory agency tasked with enforcement of specific environmental-protection rules, are subject to the same stay and discharge arrangements applicable to all other claims. Entities can thus potentially escape environmental-law duties, such as rehabilitation duties, via insolvency and/or subsequent dissolution. This gap in environmental protection should arguably be filled by allowing enforcement actions by regulatory agencies against the insolvent estate to address serious environmental harm that poses a threat to public health and safety.[66] Additionally, Stander argues that the costs of effecting environmental obligations *whilst* the entity is in liquidation must be viewed as part of the administration costs and thus be paid from the proceeds of liquidation ahead of all creditors.[67] Where enforcement of environmental law takes the form of criminal or administrative proceedings, rather than civil claims, insolvency should not affect the insolvent's obligations.[68] This undoubtedly hinges on the entity's continued existence and would also be discharged when the entity is finally wound up and dissolved.

Social considerations are also not appreciably protected in South African insolvency law. For example, debtors' primary homes are not robustly protected in insolvency proceedings. Unlike comparative jurisdictions, such as the US and UK, South African insolvency law includes debtors' primary dwellings in the insolvent estate and does not protect the insolvent's continued use of the dwelling.[69] This is troubling given the strong protection of housing in sections 26 and 28 of the South African Constitution.[70]

---

[65] AL Stander, 'Die Opskorting van Omgewingsgedinge in insolvensie' (2014) 25 Stell. LR 511.

[66] Ibid 534.

[67] AL Stander, 'Some Thoughts on Environmental Claims in Liquidation' (2013) 76 THRHR 436, 438, 443.

[68] Ibid.

[69] RG Evans, 'Does an Insolvent Debtor Have a Right to Adequate Housing?' (2013) 25 SAMLJ 119; A Boraine, 'Does the Prevention of Illegal Eviction and Unlawful Occupation of Land Act of 1998 Provide Adequate Family Home Protection to Insolvent Debtors or Is It Still Pie in the Sky? (part 2)' (2020) 41 Obiter 871; Boraine et al (n 3) 83–89.

[70] Constitution of the Republic of South Africa, 1996.

The introduction of business rescue by the 2008 Companies Act represents the most significant step, from an ESG perspective, away from a narrow creditor-focused approach to financial distress.[71]

The 2008 Companies Act positions financial distress in a much broader context than the Insolvency Act. Several social and governance considerations are apposite when dealing with companies' financial distress. This is clear from the Companies Act's aim of balancing interests of *all* relevant stakeholders[72] and the special provision for employees' interests in business rescue.[73] The courts likewise consider the impact on the labour market and communities more broadly in business-rescue applications. For example, in *Forty Squares (Pty) Ltd v Noris Fresh Produce (Pty) Ltd t/a Golden Harvest (In Liq)*,[74] the court pointed to the 'loss of continued employment to some 180 workers' as 'tragic', but noted that 'it would be irresponsible in the extreme to consider re-employing a workforce which would not be properly remunerated, with the prospect of their short-lived employment being terminated when the creditors vote against the plan.'

Unlike liquidation, business rescue proceedings largely aim to retain current management and the workforce. The Companies Act 2008 prohibits termination of employment contracts during business rescue, except as allowed under ordinary labour law.[75] Likewise, the Act confirms the continued functions of directors, albeit subject to the business rescue practitioner's authority.[76]

4.3 LOCAL PUBLIC ENTITIES IN DISTRESS

Against the background of the rules governing financial distress generally, we now turn to the specific context of local public entities. The rules governing financial distress of local public entities stand in stark contrast to the general rules on insolvency in South Africa.

4.3.1 Local Public Entities—Legal Framework

Following the principle of constitutionalism, as expressed in section 2 of the Constitution, all public entities in South Africa owe their existence to the Constitution and the law flowing from the Constitution. That is also true for local public entities, which are all creatures of the Constitution and statute.

71 Bradstreet (n 42); Cassim (n 42) 866; Levenstein (n 42) paras 2.1 and 2.3.
72 Companies Act 71 of 2008, s 7(k).
73 Ibid s 131, s 136.
74 [2023] ZAWCHC 78 [21], [29].
75 Companies Act 71 of 2008, s 136(1).
76 Ibid s 137(2).

4.3.1.1 Local authorities

South Africa has a weak federal system of government, called co-operative government, consisting of three spheres: national, provincial, and local. Plenary power resides in the national sphere, while the nine provinces and 257 local authorities only have those powers explicitly assigned to them by the Constitution or legislation.[77] The Constitution describes the three spheres of government as 'distinctive, interdependent and interrelated'.[78] The free-standing constitutional status of local government was confirmed by the Constitutional Court in *Fedsure Life Assurance Ltd v Greater Johannesburg Transitional Metropolitan Council*,[79] where the court noted the fundamental shift from the pre-constitutional era where 'the very existence of local government depended entirely on superior legislatures'.

Local government structures fall within the broad concept of an "organ of state", which is the most common constitutional structure for public entities in South Africa. The concept of an "organ of state" is defined in section 239 of the Constitution to include 'any department of state or administration in the national, provincial or local sphere of government'.

Section 151 of the Constitution states that the 'local sphere of government consists of municipalities' and that there are three categories of municipalities, namely Categories A, B, and C:

> (a) Category A: A municipality that has exclusive municipal executive and legislative authority in its area.
> (b) Category B: A municipality that shares municipal executive and legislative authority in its area with a category C municipality within whose area it falls.
> (c) Category C: A municipality that has municipal executive and legislative authority in an area that includes more than one municipality.

These three categories of municipalities are labelled as metropolitan municipalities (category A), local municipalities (category B), and district municipalities (category C) by the Local Government: Municipal Structures Act 117 of 1998, which terminology is consistently applied throughout the legal framework.[80]

The Local Government: Municipal Systems Act 32 of 2000 (the Systems Act) provides a more detailed definition of a municipality as follows:

> A "municipality"—

---

77 Constitution, s 40, s 43, s 44.

78 Ibid s 40(1).

79 [1998] ZACC 17 [38].

80 Local Government: Municipal Structures Act 117 of 1998, s 1.

(a) is an organ of state within the local sphere of government exercising legislative and executive authority within an area determined in terms of the Local Government: Municipal Demarcation Act, 1998;
(b) consists of—
  (i) the political structures and administration of the municipality; and
  (ii) the community of the municipality;
(c) functions in its area in accordance with the political, statutory and other relationships between its political structures, political office bearers and administration and its community; and
(d) has a separate legal personality which excludes liability on the part of its community for the actions of the municipality.[81]

Municipalities, as the paradigm local public entity in South Africa, are primarily governed by the elected municipal council, led by the mayor.[82] The administration of the municipality is headed by the municipal manager, who is an appointed official accountable to the council.[83]

The Systems Act also defines the concept of a "municipal entity".[84] This can be a private company established by one or more municipalities, or in which one or more municipalities hold an interest as set out in the Act; a service utility, or a multi-jurisdictional service utility. A municipality may, by way of by-law, create a service utility for a specific, stated purpose.[85] Multi-jurisdictional service utilities may also be created jointly by multiple municipalities.[86] Municipalities do not have to hold all or even majority interest in a company they create, but effective control of such companies must always be in the hands of an organ of state, whether local or in provincial or national spheres.[87] If the effective control of the company is held by one or more municipalities, that company will qualify as a municipal entity.[88]

The Systems Act also defines a "parent municipality" as the municipality holding effective control over a company. Additionally, the Companies Act 2008 defines the concept of a "state-owned company" to include a company registered under the Companies Act and owned by a municipality. It follows from these definitions that a "municipal entity" that is registered as a company will simultaneously be a "state-owned company".

Municipal entities are subject to the control of the parent municipalities. Such control is typically exercised through the board of directors of the

---

81 Systems Act, s 2.
82 Constitution, s 151(2).
83 Systems Act, s 54A, s 55.
84 Ibid s 1.
85 Ibid s 86H.
86 Ibid s 87.
87 Ibid s 86C.
88 Ibid s 86D.

relevant municipal entity, which is the direct controlling body over the entity.[89] The board of directors in turn appoints the chief executive officer to head the administration of the entity.[90]

4.3.1.2 Mission and functions

There is no single mission statement for local public entities in South African law. The Constitution provides the following broad objects for municipalities:

(a) to provide democratic and accountable government for local communities;
(b) to ensure the provision of services to communities in a sustainable manner;
(c) to promote social and economic development;
(d) to promote a safe and healthy environment; and
(e) to encourage the involvement of communities and community organisations in the matters of local government.[91]

The powers of municipalities are restricted to the administration of those subject matter areas or functions listed in schedules to the Constitution.[92]

Courts have held that the provision of basic municipal services is the key mission of local government. In *Joseph v City of Johannesburg*,[93] the Constitutional Court held that,

> [t]he provision of basic municipal services is a cardinal function, if not the most important function, of every municipal government. The central mandate of local government is to develop a service delivery capacity in order to meet the basic needs of all inhabitants of South Africa.

The specific powers allocated to municipalities in the Constitution show that this core mission of service delivery extends across a wide range of areas. They include economic development functions relating *inter alia* to local tourism, municipal planning, trading regulations, and control over liquor sales.[94] They include environmental matters such as air pollution, electricity and gas reticulation, parks, refuse removal, and stormwater management.[95] They also include social development functions relating *inter alia* to child-care facilities,

---

[89] Ibid s 93E.
[90] Ibid s 93J.
[91] Constitution, s 152.
[92] Ibid sch 4B and sch 5B.
[93] [2009] ZACC 30 [34].
[94] Constitution, sch 4B, sch 5B.
[95] Ibid.

health services, water and sanitation services, and parks and recreation.[96] In fulfilling these functions, municipalities must 'give priority to the basic needs of the community',[97] 'conduct its business in an open manner',[98] be accountable and transparent,[99] provide services 'impartially, fairly, equitably',[100] and be governed by democratic principles reflecting 'a high standard of professional ethics'.[101]

When a municipality creates a service utility, the by-law creating that entity must specify its mandate. The Systems Act restricts activities of municipal entities that are private companies to 'the purpose for which it is used by its parent municipality' and determines that a municipal entity (of any type) 'has no competence to perform any activity which falls outside the functions and powers of its parent municipality'.[102] The Act provides that a municipality may only establish a municipal entity in the form of a private company 'if there is a need to perform that function or power in accordance with business practices in order to achieve the strategic objectives of the municipality more effectively; and the company would benefit the local community'.[103]

4.3.1.3 Funding and financial management

Municipal finances are primarily governed by the Constitution and Local Government: Municipal Finance Management Act 56 of 2003 (the MFMA), which sets out detailed rules on financial management. Municipalities are obliged to prepare and table annual budgets for approval by their municipal councils. The roles, responsibilities, and procedures for drafting, finalising, tabling, approving, and implementing the annual budget are prescribed in detail.

At a high level, the Constitution prescribes that municipal budgets and budgetary processes must promote transparency, accountability, and the effective financial management of the economy, debt, and the public sector.[104] The Constitution mandates the national Parliament to prescribe further detailed rules for municipal finance.[105] Based on this mandate and to achieve the constitutional principles for municipal finances, the MFMA requires that budgets

---

96 Ibid.
97 Ibid s 153.
98 Ibid s 160(7).
99 Ibid s 195(1)(f), (g).
100 Ibid s 195(1)(d).
101 Ibid s 195(1)(a).
102 Ibid s 86D.
103 Ibid s 86E.
104 Ibid s 215.
105 Ibid.

must be realistic and credible and must include comparisons with previous years' budget and actual expenditure.[106] The budget must be aligned with the municipality's key strategic plan, known as the integrated development plan, and be accompanied by a service delivery and budget implementation plan.[107] Municipalities must publish monthly budget statements reporting against the implementation plan and must table quarterly budget implementation reports to their council.[108] Municipalities must submit financial reports to the relevant provincial treasury, including monthly budget statements[109] and reports on failures by a municipal council to adopt or implement budgetary policies.[110] Any serious financial problems that emerge must be reported to the provincial government.[111]

The municipal manager is the municipality's accounting officer, carrying primary responsibility for financial management in terms of the law.[112] The chief executive officer is the accounting officer of a municipal entity, responsible for financial management of the entity.[113]

Compliance with the local government financial management rules is annually audited by the Auditor-General in terms of section 188 of the Constitution, the MFMA, and the Public Audit Act 25 of 2004. The Auditor-General submits its findings in an annual audit report to the national Parliament, including findings on irregular expenditure by municipalities and the state of local government finances.

The regulatory framework prescribes consequences for failures to comply with the municipal finance management rules. One of the most extreme measures is intervention by either the relevant provincial government or national government,[114] which may involve placing the municipality under administration.

Where the Auditor-General finds material irregularities in the finances of a municipality, it must issue recommendations to the municipality to address such irregularities.[115] If the municipality fails to implement these, the Auditor-General must take appropriate remedial action, which, in the case of such irregularities involving financial loss to the state, must include a directive to

106 MFMA, s 17.
107 Ibid s 17, s 21, s 53.
108 Ibid s 52, s 71.
109 Ibid s 71.
110 Ibid s 73.
111 Ibid s 54.
112 Ibid s 60.
113 Ibid s 93.
114 Ibid s 139.
115 Public Audit Act 25 of 2004, s 5A.

the municipal manager to recover the loss from the responsible person.[116] If the municipal manager fails to implement such a directive, the Auditor-General may issue a certificate of debt to the municipal manager requiring the manager to repay such an amount as determined by the Auditor-General.[117]

Local public entities' sources of income are restricted by law and derive primarily from an equitable share of revenue raised nationally, additional allocations made by national and provincial governments, and income generated by rates on property and surcharges on fees for services provided.[118] In stark contrast to provincial government, local government receives only a small percentage of its overall income from the equitable share. The logic behind this difference is that local government is empowered to raise its own funds through rates and fees to cover its expenditure, whereas provincial governments are not. Between 2017/18 and 2021/22, an average of 82% of local government income originated from its own income.[119] The equitable share is annually determined by national legislation in the form of the Division of Revenue Act. For the 2023/24 financial year, the Division of Revenue Act 5 of 2023 allocated only 5% of the total revenue raised nationally to local government directly, compared with 29% allocated to provincial government.[120] The Act also estimated a similar 5% allocation in 2024/25 and 2025/26.[121] An additional 2.9% of the total revenue raised nationally was allocated to local government in 2023/24 by way of conditional allocation from the national equitable share in terms of the Act.[122] Further allocations from national and provincial equitable shares brought local governments' total share up to 10% of the revenue raised nationally.[123]

Additional municipal taxes may be authorised by national government, but these may not include income tax, value-added tax, general sales tax, or customs duty.[124] The Municipal Fiscal Powers and Functions Act 12 of 2007 provides for national approval, by way of regulations, of additional municipal taxes. To date, only a limited number of pre-existing municipal taxes have

---

116 Ibid.

117 Ibid s 5B.

118 Constitution, s 227, s 229.

119 National Treasury of South Africa, *2023 Budget Review* 75 <https://www.treasury.gov.za/documents/national%20budget/2023/review/FullBR.pdf>.

120 Division of Revenue Act 5 of 2023, s 5 read with sch 3.

121 Ibid.

122 Ibid s 8 read with ss 4, 5, 6, and 7.

123 National Treasury of South Africa (n 119) 71.

124 Constitution, s 229(1)(b); Municipal Fiscal Powers and Functions Act 12 of 2007, s 4.

been approved under this regime. Property taxes and surcharges on fees may be capped by national government.[125]

The powers of local public entities to take loans or subscribe to financial instruments are also restricted. Generally, municipalities may only raise loans for capital expenditure.[126] Municipalities may only incur short-term debt for non-capital expenditure and must repay such debt within the financial year and may not refinance such debt.[127] Municipalities may only incur long-term debt for capital expenditure or to refinance existing long-term debt.[128] In terms of the Municipal Regulations on Debt Disclosure 2007, municipalities have extensive and ongoing disclosure obligations regarding all debt. These include simple loan agreements as well as municipal debt instruments, which are defined as 'any note, bond, debenture, or other evidence of indebtedness issued by a municipality or municipal entity, including dematerialised or electronic evidence of indebtedness intended to be used in trade'.[129] These disclosure obligations serve to ensure that municipalities do not take on any debt if they are not in good financial standing. Disclosure furthermore enables prospective lenders to confirm that all statutory requirements were met prior to entering the transaction. A bona fide failure in disclosure will not impact the validity of the lending transaction.[130] A failure to adhere to the substantive statutory requirements, especially the limits, on lending, may, however, lead to the invalidity of the transaction. Organs of state are generally 'constrained by the principle that they may exercise no power and perform no function beyond that conferred upon them by law'.[131] When they do act beyond the limits of statutory power, such action is open to review and setting aside by the High Court.[132] Whether the transaction will in fact be set aside by the court upon an application for review is within the court's discretion.[133] Since the court has a wide discretion to 'make any order that is just and equitable',[134] the court may set the transaction aside *ex tunc, ex nunc*, or keep the transaction in place. The

---

125 Local Government: Municipal Property Rates Act 6 of 2004, s 20; Municipal Fiscal Powers and Functions Act 12 of 2007, s 8.

126 Constitution, s 230A; MFMA, s 18, s 19, s 46.

127 MFMA, s 45.

128 Ibid s 46.

129 Municipal Regulations on Debt Disclosure 2007, reg 1.

130 Ibid reg 25.

131 *Fedsure Life Assurance Ltd v Greater Johannesburg Transitional Metropolitan Council* [1998] ZACC 17 [58].

132 Ibid.

133 *Bengwenyama Minerals (Pty) Ltd v Genorah Resources (Pty) Ltd* [2010] ZACC 26 [85].

134 Constitution, s 172.

default remedy where a municipality entered a contract contrary to statutory prescripts is, however, invalidation.[135]

4.3.2 Dealing with Local Public Entities in Distress—Legal Framework

Just like almost all other aspects of local public entities in South Africa, the financial distress of municipalities is exhaustively dealt with in a detailed set of dedicated legislative provisions. These rules form part of the statutory framework governing municipalities and not the statutory regime governing insolvency.

4.3.2.1 Principles, purposes and procedures

Municipal financial distress is primarily governed by the MFMA, which contains a chapter (chapter 13) on "Resolution of Financial Problems", applying to municipalities and municipal entities. The main rules governing municipalities in financial distress in South Africa thus do not form part of general insolvency law but constitute a bespoke set of rules for this particular purpose. However, there are distinct points of intersection between these dedicated rules and general insolvency rules.

The legal point of departure is that a municipality is itself primarily responsible for identifying and resolving financial problems.[136] Only if municipalities are truly unable to resolve their own financial distress will provincial governments intervene or, failing such provincial intervention, national government step in.[137]

With municipal entities, the board of directors is primarily responsible for addressing any financial distress. If the board fails to do so, the parent municipality must step in.[138] The parent municipality may impose a financial recovery plan, equivalent to the recovery plan that a provincial government may impose on a municipality in distress.[139] Alternatively, the parent municipality may liquidate the municipal entity.[140]

Municipalities cannot be liquidated under South African law,[141] but can at most be placed under administration. Municipal entities may, however,

---

[135] *Eskom Holdings v New Reclamation Group* [2009] ZASCA 8.

[136] MFMA, s 135.

[137] Constitution, s 139.

[138] MFMA, s 109.

[139] Ibid.

[140] Ibid.

[141] R Roos and L Stander, 'Insolvent Municipalities? An Analysis of the Debt Relief Mechanisms at the Disposal of Municipalities and the Disappearance of the

be liquidated under ordinary insolvency law governing liquidation.[142] There is some doubt whether municipalities can be sequestrated in terms of the Insolvency Act, like individuals, but it seems highly unlikely that this is possible.[143] Both municipalities and municipal entities may be subjected to financial recovery plans under the MFMA.

The core aim of the legislative framework dealing with municipalities in distress is to secure the continuation of public services despite the financial distress.[144] Several elements of the legislative framework confirm this aim. Section 142 of the MFMA states that the aim of a municipal financial recovery plan is 'securing the municipality's ability to meet its obligations to provide basic services'. Accordingly, a mandatory provincial intervention into the affairs of a municipality in distress may only come to an end when 'the municipality's ability to meet its obligations to provide basic services or its financial commitments is secured'.[145] This aim is also illustrated in the rule that entities may not dispose of a capital asset needed to provide the minimum level of basic municipal services, regardless of its financial distress. Such assets are excluded from the entire framework dealing with financial distress, such as those providing for financial recovery plans and restructuring of debt.[146]

The primary objective of this legislative framework is thus distinct from the objective of general insolvency law in South Africa. Whereas the latter is primarily aimed at the benefit of creditors (South African insolvency law's "golden rule"),[147] the rules on the resolution of municipal financial problems are aimed at the restoration of the municipality. As Roos and Stander argue, references to creditors in these rules illustrate that 'their interest is not paramount'.[148] The purpose of these rules is, in fact, diametrically opposite to those of insolvency law generally. Whereas the court stated in *Marshall Industrials Ltd v Pillay*[149] that 'the Insolvency Act was passed [...] not for the relief of harassed debtors', the MFMA rules on municipal financial distress are precisely aimed at the relief of the debtor municipality.

"Advantage of Creditors"' (2007) 22 SA Public Law 166, 182.

142 MFMA, s 109; Systems Act, s 93B, s 93C.

143 Roos and Stander (n 141) 188.

144 MZ Makoti and OK Odeku, 'Intervention into Municipal Affairs in South Africa and its Impact on Municipal Basic Services' (2018) 10(4) African Journal of Public Affairs 68, 77.

145 MFMA, s 148(2)(b).

146 Ibid s 48(3)–(5), s 142(1)(b), s 154(b), s 155(1)(b).

147 See above, *sub* [4.2.2].

148 Roos and Stander (n 141) 173.

149 1956 (4) SA 580 (N) 581.

The MFMA framework dealing with municipalities in distress is only applicable to entities in the local government sphere. The courts have held that there is no duty on other spheres of government (national or provincial government) to provide funds to local governments to service debts.[150]

Municipal entities that are companies are also subject to the provisions governing business rescue of all corporate entities under the 2008 Companies Act. The board of a municipal entity in distress may thus place the entity in business rescue, just like business rescue of private corporate entities. These entities will furthermore be subject to the normal rules governing winding-up of companies.

4.3.2.1.1 Interventions

Both municipalities and municipal entities are subject to special rules regarding provincial or national intervention as a way of dealing with financial distress. For municipalities, this is the only mechanism for dealing with financial problems, whereas municipal entities may alternatively be liquidated under ordinary insolvency laws.

Comparable to sequestration by voluntary surrender or by compulsory sequestration under the Insolvency Act, the MFMA, read with the Constitution, provides for discretionary and mandatory interventions in cases of municipal financial problems.[151]

Provincial governments have a discretion to intervene in a municipality experiencing serious financial problems flowing from or leading to the failure of the municipality to comply with its executive obligations.[152] Factors that may point to serious financial problems include:

(a) the municipality has failed to make payments as and when due;
(b) the municipality has defaulted on financial obligations for financial reasons;
(c) the actual current expenditure of the municipality has exceeded the sum of its actual current revenue plus available surpluses for at least two consecutive financial years;
(d) the municipality had an operating deficit in excess of 5% of revenue in the most recent financial year for which financial information is available;
(e) the municipality is more than 60 days late in submitting its annual financial statements to the Auditor-General [...];

---

150 *Member of the Executive Council for Local Government, Mpumalanga v Independent Municipal and Allied Trade Union* 2002 (1) SA 76 (SCA).

151 MFMA, s 136 read with the Constitution, s 139.

152 MFMA, s 136(2), s 137.

(f) the Auditor-General has withheld an opinion or issued a disclaimer due to inadequacies in the financial statements or records of the municipality, or has issued an opinion that identifies a serious financial problem in the municipality;
(g) any of the above conditions exist in a municipal entity under the municipality's sole control, or in a municipal entity for whose debts the municipality may be responsible, and the municipality has failed to intervene effectively; or
(h) any other material condition exists which indicates that the municipality, or a municipal entity under the municipality's sole control, is likely to be unable, for financial reasons, to meet its obligations.[153]

A municipality may also request intervention as an attempt to address its financial problems.

A provincial government is obliged to intervene in a municipality when that municipality is (or admits that it is) in serious or persistent material breach of its obligations to provide basic services or to meet its financial commitments because of a financial crisis.[154] Should the provincial government fail to intervene, or intervene inadequately, the national government must intervene.[155] Factors that may point to a serious material breach of a municipality's obligations to meet its financial commitments include:

(a) the municipality has failed to make any payment to a lender or investor as and when due;
(b) the municipality has failed to meet a contractual obligation which provides security in terms of [MFMA] section 48;
(c) the municipality has failed to make any other payment as and when due, which individually or in the aggregate is more than an amount as may be prescribed or, if none is prescribed, more than 2% of the municipality's budgeted operating expenditure; or
(d) the municipality's failure to meet its financial commitments has impacted, or is likely to impact, the availability or price of credit to other municipalities.[156]

153 Ibid s 138.
154 Ibid s 136(4), s 139.
155 Constitution, s 139(7); MFMA, s 150.
156 MFMA, s 140(2).

4.3.2.1.2 Financial recovery plan

Intervention may involve the preparation of a financial recovery plan.[157] The aim of a financial recovery plan must be to secure the entity's ability to meet its obligations to provide basic services or its financial commitments.[158] The plan must identify the financial problems and the strategy for addressing those problems to place the entity in a sound and sustainable financial condition.[159] The plan may provide for debt restructuring or debt relief and for the liquidation of specific assets, excluding assets needed for the provision of the minimum level of basic municipal services.[160]

Any suitable person may prepare the financial recovery plan in a voluntary intervention,[161] whereas only the Municipal Financial Recovery Service, a unit within the National Treasury, may prepare the plan in a mandatory intervention. The person drafting the plan must consult with the municipality, the municipality's principal suppliers and creditors, the relevant provincial member of the executive council (MEC) for finance and the MEC for local government, and with organised labour.[162] Whilst the category "principal suppliers and creditors" is not defined in the MFMA, it signals that not all creditors need to be consulted in the preparation of the plan. Consultation with the "principal suppliers and creditors" is further qualified with the condition, 'to the extent they can reasonably be contacted'.[163] A draft of the plan only needs to be served on creditors 'on request'.[164] This limited involvement of creditors provides yet another example of the differentiation in purpose between the rules governing municipal financial distress compared to ordinary business rescue and insolvency rules.

The relevant MEC for local government must approve a financial recovery plan. The MEC has discretion to approve the plan and to make amendments in voluntary interventions.[165] In mandatory interventions, the MEC must approve the plan if the statutory prescripts are met.[166] Once approved, the financial recovery plan is binding on the municipality, and it is statutorily obligated to implement it.[167]

---

157 Ibid s 137(1)(c), s 139(1)(a).
158 Ibid s 142.
159 Ibid s 142(1)(a).
160 Ibid s 142(1)(b).
161 Ibid s 141(1), (2).
162 Ibid s 141(3)(a).
163 Ibid s 141(3)(a)(ii).
164 Ibid s 141(3)(c)(i)(ee).
165 Ibid s 143(1).
166 Ibid s 143(2).
167 Ibid s 145(1), s 146(1).

4.3.2.1.3 Administration

As the most extreme step under an intervention, the provincial or national government may dissolve a local council and place the municipality under administration.[168] That is, the term of the current councillors constituting the local council will come to an end, and new councillors must be elected. In such an instance, an administrator is appointed to take over the functions of the municipal council until a new council is elected.[169] Placing a municipality under administration is evidently an extraordinary measure since it encroaches upon the principle of co-operative government under the Constitution, which recognises local government as a distinct sphere of government.[170] Such a step is accordingly only permissible in serious instances of financial distress, primarily when a council fails to adopt the necessary legislative measures to give effect to a financial recovery plan.[171]

In *Premier, Gauteng v Democratic Alliance*,[172] involving a challenge to a provincial decision to put the capital city, Pretoria, under administration, the Constitutional Court held that while such a decision will not automatically be reviewed when there are other, less invasive measures available to deal with the problem at hand, the existence of such alternative measures will be a relevant consideration. As the Court stated: '[r]esorting to dissolution may very well be inappropriate in circumstances where there was another step that could have been taken which was reasonably capable of resolving the issue and would have been less invasive of local government autonomy'.[173] The Court added that the power to dissolve a council and place the municipality under administration must be used 'sparingly'.[174]

4.3.2.1.4 Debt restructuring

The MFMA allows a municipality in distress to apply to court for an order:

- staying (up to a maximum of 90 days at a time) of all legal process (including execution) by creditors;
- suspending the entity's financial obligations to creditors (or any portion thereof) until the entity can meet those obligations; or

---

[168] Constitution, s 139(1)(c), (5)(b); MFMA, s 145(3), 146(3)(a); Local Government: Municipal Structures Act 117 of 1998, s 34(4).

[169] MFMA, s 137(1)(c), s 139(1)(a)(iii).

[170] *Mnquma Local Municipality v Premier of the Eastern Cape* [2009] ZAECBHC 14.

[171] Constitution, s 139(5)(b).

[172] [2021] ZACC 34.

[173] Ibid [88].

[174] Ibid [126].

- terminating the entity's financial obligations to creditors and settling claims in terms of a distribution scheme.[175]

The suspension or termination of debt may only be ordered if a financial recovery plan has been implemented, is unlikely to succeed without such order, and liquidation of all non-essential assets will be insufficient to cover the debt.[176] For a termination order, it must also be shown that all employees have been discharged except those affordable in terms of reasonably projected revenues under the financial recovery plan.[177]

For termination, the relevant MEC for finance must appoint a trustee to prepare a distribution scheme to settle all legitimate claims against the municipality.[178] Claims must be settled proportionally, in the following order:

(i) rights of secured creditors as to the assets with which they are secured in terms of a resolution of the council, provided the security in question was given in good faith and at least six months before the mandatory intervention began;
(ii) preferences provided for in the Insolvency Act; and
(iii) non-preferent claims.[179]

The distribution scheme must be approved by the court.[180]

If a local entity that is a company is liquidated, the ordinary rules governing enforcement actions apply and all civil proceedings against the entity shall be suspended until a liquidator is appointed.[181] All attachment or execution proceedings instigated after the commencement of the winding-up will be void.[182] Creditors wishing to pursue claims against the entity post-commencement of the winding-up must notify the liquidator within four weeks after their appointment or will be considered to have abandoned the proceedings.[183] Similar provisions apply in the case of business rescue proceedings under section 133(1) of the 2008 Companies Act, applicable to municipal companies placed under business rescue. The special rules on local entities in distress do not provide for the automatic stay of enforcement actions. The MFMA provides that its

---

175 MFMA, s 153(1).
176 Ibid s 153(2).
177 Ibid s 155(1).
178 Ibid s 155(2).
179 Ibid s 155(3)(c).
180 Ibid s 155(4).
181 Companies Act 61 of 1973, s 359.
182 Ibid.
183 Ibid.

debt restructuring measures do not affect the rights of any creditor against an entity, any person's access to ordinary legal process; or the rights of a municipality, municipal entity, or of the parties to a contract with a municipality or municipal entity, to alternative dispute resolution mechanisms, notice procedures, and other remedies.[184] As noted above, a court may grant upon application either a stay or suspension of legal process against an entity.

There are no special rules governing new and interim financing for municipalities in distress. South African courts have held that there is no duty on other spheres of government to provide funds to local governments to enable them to pay their debts. The general rules on business rescue under the 2008 Companies Act provide for post-commencement finance to be secured against any assets of the company not already encumbered and to be repaid as a preferential claim.[185] This may only occur after payment of the business practitioner's remuneration and expenses and other business rescue costs and of claims by employees for services rendered during the business rescue proceedings.

4.3.2.2 Parties

The primary responsibility for dealing with distress resides with the municipal council or municipal entity's board of directors. Only when they fail to take appropriate action would either the provincial or national government step in and effectively take over the process through an intervention under section 139 of the Constitution.

The preparation of a financial recovery plan for a municipality under intervention must involve consultation with the municipality, the municipality's principal suppliers and creditors, the relevant provincial government, and organised labour, which consultation must consider any plans proposed by such parties.[186] The proposed plan must also be submitted to these parties for comment before finalisation.[187] The final plan must be approved by the provincial government and submitted to the municipality, national government, the Auditor-General, and organised local government in the province.[188]

Once approved, the municipality must implement the financial recovery plan and report monthly to the provincial government on implementation.[189] Where a financial recovery plan involves an application to court for restructuring of debt, notice of such application must be served on the relevant provincial government, national government, organised labour, and all persons to whom

---

[184] MFMA, s 151.
[185] Companies Act 71 of 2008, s 135.
[186] MFMA, s 141.
[187] Ibid.
[188] Ibid s 143.
[189] Ibid s 145, s 146.

the municipality owes an amount exceeding R100,000 (approximately £5,000) and that can reasonably be located.[190]

Creditors enjoy no special powers in relation to dealing with municipalities in distress. This differs significantly from the rules governing business rescue proceedings under the 2008 Companies Act and winding-up proceedings under the 1973 Companies Act. Where a local entity is a private company and is subjected to business rescue or winding up in terms of the Companies Act, creditors enjoy the same powers as those of all other creditors in relation to corporations in insolvency or business rescue proceedings. Creditors are directly involved in the appointment of either the business rescue practitioner or the liquidator under either of those frameworks. Under the business rescue regime, all affected parties have a right to participate in the court hearing to place a company in compulsory business rescue.[191]

Creditors play a prominent role in business rescue proceedings under the Companies Act. They must be notified of all relevant events and may formally and informally participate in all proceedings.[192] Creditors may form a creditors' committee and formally engage with the business rescue practitioner via such committee throughout the proceedings.[193] Creditors can vote to amend, approve, or reject a proposed business rescue plan and, if rejected, can propose the development of an alternative plan.[194] There is no distinction between different classes of creditors regarding participation in business rescue proceedings. The 2008 Companies Act sets out the voting rights of creditors on the business rescue plan.[195] Secured creditors do not have special voting rights in approving or rejecting the business rescue plan. They are, however, protected in that their security interest cannot be disposed of without their consent unless their interest can be fully discharged by such disposal. Once a business rescue plan has been approved, dissenting creditors (or those who did not vote) are bound by the plan.[196] The plan is thus "crammed down" on the company, all creditors, and shareholders. If a plan is voted down, any affected person may make a binding offer to purchase the voting interests of one or more persons who opposed adoption of the business rescue plan, at liquidation value.[197] In the case of such an offer, the business rescue practitioner is obliged to put

---

[190] Ibid s 152.

[191] *Cape Point Vineyards (Pty) Ltd v Pinnacle Point Group Ltd* [2011] ZAWCHC 306.

[192] Companies Act 71 of 2008, s 145; Cassim (n 42) 902–904.

[193] Ibid.

[194] Ibid.

[195] Companies Act 71 of 2008, s 145(4).

[196] Ibid s 154.

[197] Ibid s 153.

the plan to the vote again with the vote now based on the changed voting interests.[198] This forced sale of voting interests is another way in which a business rescue plan can be "crammed down" on dissenting voters.

When a company is wound up, the Insolvency Act provides for a fixed order of payment of claims over which creditors have no power. As is the case with creditors, employees do not enjoy any special protection in financial recovery procedures under the MFMA. In fact, the MFMA contemplates the "discharge" of all municipal employees 'except those affordable in terms of reasonably projected revenues as set out in the approved financial recovery plan' as part of debt restructuring.[199] This provision is evidently aimed at forcing a municipality to reduce its expenditure to within its means. Reducing its labour costs is an important element of such expenditure control, given that the wage bill is often the single largest annual financial commitment on most municipalities' budgets and the tendency for municipalities to carry bloated staff complements for political and developmental reasons.[200] In contrast, both the business rescue framework and winding-up rules make specific provision for the protection of employees.

In business rescue proceedings, employees are treated as preferred creditors in relation to remuneration and other money due to them for services rendered during business rescue proceedings.[201] Employees are preferred unsecured creditors in respect of all remuneration and other monies due to them for services rendered before the commencement of business rescue proceedings that have not been paid.[202] Like creditors, employees of a company under business rescue have specific rights of participation.[203] They must be notified of all relevant events, may participate in court proceedings, form a committee of employees' representatives to formally engage with the business rescue practitioner, and must be consulted on the development of the business rescue plan.[204]

---

198 Ibid.

199 MFMA, s 155(1).

200 Stats SA, 'Falling Inside the Norm: Municipal Remuneration and Contractor Spending' (7 July 2023) <https://www.statssa.gov.za/?p=16466>; Stats SA, 'Municipalities Experience a Rise in Employee-Related Costs' (P9114, 15 June 2015) <https://www.statssa.gov.za/publications/P9114/P9114June2014.pdf>; National Treasury, '2011 Local Government Budgets and Expenditure Review: 2006/07-2012/13' (RP103/2011, 14 September 2011) <https://www.treasury.gov.za/publications/igfr/2011/lg/default.aspx>.

201 Companies Act 71 of 2008, s 144; Cassim (n 42) 899–902.

202 Ibid.

203 Ibid.

204 Ibid.

Affected parties' legal entitlement to participate in business rescue proceedings under the Companies Act 2008 is much more extensive than those provided for in the framework for dealing with municipalities in distress under the MFMA.

There are also marked differences between the positions of the persons in charge of the various mechanisms to deal with municipalities in distress and ordinary business rescue and insolvency cases. In less serious cases of financial distress, the MFMA provides that "any suitably qualified person" may be appointed by the provincial government to prepare the financial recovery plan.[205] No further rules exist regarding the qualifications, appointment, or remuneration of such a person. In cases of serious financial distress, the financial recovery plan must be prepared by the Municipal Financial Recovery Service (MFRS),[206] a unit under the National Treasury.[207] The head of the MFRS is appointed by the Minister of Finance and is accountable to the Director-General of the National Treasury. It thus constitutes a unit within the public administration. The MFMA sets out its basic powers and functions.[208] There are no prescripts governing who may be appointed as an administrator to ensure implementation of a financial recovery plan where a municipal council has failed to do so or who may be appointed as trustee to prepare a distribution scheme in a debt restructure. The administrator is appointed by the provincial government, and their powers are set out by way of notice in the relevant provincial gazette.[209] The administrator subsumes the assigned powers of the municipal council. The administrator does not replace the municipal administration, which remains in the hands of the municipal manager.[210] The administrator must thus steer the implementation of the financial recovery plan via the municipal manager.

In stark contrast with the scant regulation of the persons involved under the MFMA framework, business rescue practitioners are regulated in significant detail in the Companies Act 2008.[211] These rules include prescripts on the qualifications of practitioners, including the licensing of persons to act as practitioners by the CIPC,[212] their appointment and removal,[213] their powers

205 MFMA, s 141.
206 Ibid.
207 Ibid s 157.
208 Ibid s 158.
209 Local Government: Municipal Structures Act 117 of 1998, s 35.
210 *Ngaka Modiri Molema District Municipality v Moto-Tech (Pty) Ltd* [2017] ZANWHC 54.
211 Companies Act 71 of 2008, ch 6, pt B.
212 Ibid s 138; Companies Regulations 2011, regs 126–127.
213 Companies Act 71 of 2008, s 139.

and duties,[214] and their remuneration.[215] Similarly, liquidators for the winding up of entities are regulated in detail under the Companies Act 1973 (read with relevant provisions of the Insolvency Act). These rules include provisions on the appointment and removal of liquidators,[216] costs and remuneration,[217] their powers and duties.[218] Business rescue practitioners are remunerated in terms of a tariff prescribed under the Companies Act.[219] This is a time-based remuneration fee as opposed to the commission-based fee structure paid to liquidators in the case of winding up.[220] The remuneration of business rescue practitioners for state-owned companies is set at the same level as that for large companies, that is, at the highest level.[221]

Courts play distinct roles in all three frameworks governing municipalities in distress. South Africa has a unitary judicial system so that the same courts deal with all matters, regardless of the cause of action (with a few exceptions that are not relevant here). The High Court thus deals with all proceedings relating to municipalities in distress in the same way that it deals with corporate entities in distress. The High Court has specific powers in relation to the general liquidation and business rescue legal frameworks and the specialised framework for municipal entities in distress.

In the case of winding up a company under the general rules governing liquidation in the Companies Act 1973, the Master of the High Court retains an oversight function over the work of the liquidator and needs to provide consent for certain actions of liquidators, for example, the termination of lease agreements or the sale of immovable property prior to convening a general meeting of creditors.[222] A liquidator is obliged to file with the Master an account of receipts and payments and a distribution plan.[223] Objections to this account may be lodged with the Master, and the Master may sustain a complaint and direct the liquidator to amend the account.[224] The Master may also, in the absence of a complaint, direct the liquidator to adjust the account.[225] Once all

---

214 Ibid ss 140–142.

215 Ibid s 143; Companies Regulations 2011, reg 128.

216 Companies Act 61 of 1973, ss 367–380.

217 Ibid ss 383–384.

218 Ibid ss 386–411.

219 Companies Regulations 2011, reg 128.

220 Regulations for the Winding-up and Judicial Management of Companies 1973, reg 24.

221 Companies Regulations 2011, reg 128.

222 Companies Act 61 of 1973, s 381, s 386.

223 Ibid s 403.

224 Ibid s 407.

225 Ibid.

adjustments have been made, the Master must confirm the account, and such confirmation has the effect of a final judgment.[226] Only after such confirmation may the liquidator distribute the assets.[227] Once the entire process has been finalised, that is, the company has been finally wound up, the Master must lodge a certificate with the CIPC to that effect, and the CIPC must record the dissolution of the company.[228]

4.3.3 An ESG Critique of South African Laws on Local Entities in Distress

The MFMA rules governing municipalities in financial distress take an evidently broader approach to balancing various interests at stake than insolvency law does. Most pertinently, the MFMA regime adopts the opposite objective from that of the Insolvency Act in placing the protection of the municipality at the centre of the process. However, unlike rules on business rescue, the MFMA regime provides very limited protection to creditors. Scholars such as Roos and Stander have thus pointedly criticised the MFMA rules for what they call "a shortcoming" in that 'the interest of creditors is not taken into account during the processes that are designed to offer protection to municipalities'.[229] Whilst Roos and Stander object to this lack of protection of creditors, stating that:

> [m]unicipalities as organs of state that exercise governmental or state authority in the public sphere, ought not be placed in a stronger position than an ordinary debtor in the context of non-compliance with financial obligations.[230]

The special legal regime governing municipalities in financial distress is less aimed at protecting municipalities as debtors and more at the protection of the public interest. It is the public interest that is placed in a stronger position *vis-à-vis* creditors in the case of municipal distress when compared to the position of ordinary debtors. Given the material differences between municipalities in financial distress and ordinary debtors, when viewed through an ESG lens, such differentiation in treatment seems rational.

The discussion of the special legal regime governing municipalities in distress illustrates that the continuation (or in many cases, the restoration) of public services stands at the heart of the rules. These rules do not focus on

226 Ibid s 408.
227 Ibid s 409.
228 Companies Act 71 of 2008, s 82.
229 Roos and Stander (n 141) 189.
230 Ibid.

financial distress *per se*, but rather on the link between such financial distress and public services. It is this link that serves as the precondition for many of the processes, such as the commencement and termination of interventions, financial recovery plans, and administration. The special rules on municipalities in financial distress thus accommodate a much broader range of ESG considerations than ordinary insolvency law in South Africa.

This sensitivity to ESG considerations was, for example, recognised in *Unemployed Peoples Movement v Premier Province of the Eastern Cape*,[231] where the court noted the link between the trigger for provincial intervention and the environmental and socio-economic rights guaranteed in the Constitution. The case involved an application to force the provincial government to intervene in a municipality by dissolving the council and appointing an administrator to implement a financial recovery plan. The court noted that the application was 'based in essence on the constitutional rights of the people of Makhanda to a healthy environment, health care, food, water and social security'.[232]

This link between environmental and social rights and managing municipal financial distress emerges most clearly in the MFMA's definition of 'basic municipal service', a concept which stands at the core of the MFMA regime. The Act defines a "basic municipal service" as 'a municipal service that is necessary to ensure an acceptable and reasonable quality of life and which, if not provided, would endanger public health or safety or the environment'.[233]

It is especially the social dimension of the ESG framework that comes into focus when the rules governing municipal financial problems under the MFMA are considered within the context of the rights guaranteed in the South African Constitution. Municipalities' core function of providing basic services to residents, the continuation of which is the primary objective of the rules on municipal financial problems, is informed by everyone's right to have access to adequate housing,[234] the right to have access to health care services, sufficient food and water, and social security.[235] It also encompasses the right of children to family or parental care or to appropriate alternative care, to basic nutrition, shelter, basic health services, and social services.[236] Basic municipal services in this context link to everyone's right to basic education and further education.[237] All these rights can be viewed as constitutionally defining what an "acceptable

231 2020 (5) BCLR 573 (ECG).
232 Ibid [6].
233 MFMA, s 1.
234 Constitution, s 26.
235 Ibid s 27.
236 Ibid s 28.
237 Ibid s 29.

and reasonable quality of life" should be in South Africa. These rights play an important role in giving content to the services to be protected and maintained (or restored) in specific instances of municipal financial problems. This would, for example, determine which capital assets may not be disposed of by the municipality since they are needed to provide the minimum level of basic municipal services. In determining what this "minimum level of basic municipal services" is in a given case, it is important to note that the duty on the state to progressively realise the socio-economic rights in the Constitution includes an injunction against retrogressive measures. In the important judgment in *Government of the RSA v Grootboom*,[238] the Constitutional Court endorsed the general comment of the United Nations Committee on Economic, Social and Cultural Rights that 'any deliberately retrogressive measures [...] would require the most careful consideration and would need to be fully justified by reference to the totality of the rights provided for [...] and in the context of the full use of the maximum available resources'. Whilst retrogressive measures, i.e., a reduction in services already provided, would not be impossible, Liebenberg points out that 'weighty justifications should be required where the retrogressive measures result in depriving marginalised and vulnerable groups of access to basic social services'.[239]

The courts' endorsement of a reasonableness approach to the realisation of socio-economic rights within the paradigm of the progressive realisation of such rights also points to an important restraining governance consideration in the legal framework dealing with municipal financial distress. That is the courts' general reluctance to become too closely involved in decisions relating to the spending of public money. South African courts have adopted a highly deferential approach in evaluating executive and legislative decisions on public spending.[240] In its very first socio-economic rights judgment, the Constitutional Court set the tone for such deference when it stated that the public administration,

> has to make decisions about the funding that should be made available for health care and how such funds should be spent. These choices involve difficult decisions to be taken at the political level in fixing the health budget, and at the functional level in deciding upon the priorities to be met. A court will be slow to interfere with

---

[238] 2001 (1) SA 46 (CC) [45].

[239] S Liebenberg, *Socio-Economic Rights Adjudication under a Transformative Constitution* (Juta 2009) 190.

[240] S van der Berg, 'The Need for a Capabilities-Based Standard of Review for the Adjudication of State Resource Allocation Decisions' (2015) 31 SAJHR 330.

> rational decisions taken in good faith by the political organs and medical authorities whose responsibility it is to deal with such matters.[241]

Thus, whilst courts play an important role in defining the substantive content of services to be provided by municipalities at the base of the MFMA regime governing municipal financial distress, the courts are simultaneously highly unlikely to become closely involved in scrutinising substantive financial choices made in managing distress. The courts are inclined to grant executive and legislative decision-makers wide discretion in this respect.

A final important governance consideration in evaluating the rules governing municipal financial distress relates to fraud and corruption. It is no secret that fraud and corruption play a major role in the dysfunction of many South African municipalities and are root causes of financial distress in many instances.[242] It is notable that the dedicated rules governing municipal financial problems do not pertinently deal with fraud and corruption. It is also notable that the intervention mechanisms only provide for the replacement of political office bearers (councillors) and not professional staff, such as senior management. This limitation on the intervention power makes it particularly difficult to directly address fraud and corruption within the municipal administration. This is not to suggest that fraud and corruption cannot be addressed. The MFMA contains extensive provisions dealing with financial misconduct generally,[243] whether the municipality is in distress or not. An intervention may thus include the utilisation of these provisions to address fraud and corruption, including disciplinary steps against offending officials and criminal charges. Where the intervention involves the replacement of the council by an administrator, that administrator may institute such steps given that they step into the shoes of the council until a new council is elected.

4.4 DEALING WITH LOCAL PUBLIC ENTITIES IN DISTRESS—LAW IN PRACTICE

Financial distress is a very common phenomenon among municipalities in South Africa. In 2004, the Auditor-General questioned the ability of municipalities to continue as going concerns in the face of massive increases in

---

241 *Soobramoney v Minister of Health, Kwazulu-Natal* 1998 (1) SA 765 (CC) [29].

242 T Ledger and M Rampedi, *Mind the Gap: Section 139 Interventions in Theory and in Practise* (Public Affairs Research Institute 2019) 1.

243 MFMA, ch 15.

municipal debt, rising between 2002 and 2003 alone by 12%.[244] The position has only worsened since. In the 2019–2020 general audit report on local government, the Auditor-General stated that

> local government finances continue to be under severe pressure [...] The financial position of just over a quarter of municipalities is so dire that there is significant doubt that they will be able to continue operating as a going concern in the near future [...] Almost half of the other municipalities are exhibiting indicators of financial strain, including low debt recovery, an inability to pay creditors, and deficits.[245]

In its most recently published financial data on local governments (quarter 3 of 2020/21), the National Treasury reported that 85.2% of municipalities met at least one trigger for determining serious financial problems under the MFMA.[246] It is accordingly not surprising that municipalities are heavily indebted. National Treasury indicated that municipalities owed their creditors R67.3 billion (approximately £2.85 billion) on 31 December 2020, up by R19.8 billion (approximately £0.84 billion) from the first quarter of 2020/21.[247] National aggregated municipal revenue stood at R484 billion (approximately £20.51 billion) on 31 December 2020, whilst national aggregated municipal expenditure stood at R489 billion (approximately £20.72 billion).[248] It is furthermore not surprising that interventions into local entities, especially municipalities, have become common in South Africa.[249] Between 1998 and 2017, there were 140 instances of interventions in 143 municipalities under section

---

[244] C Peel and A Issa, 'Municipal Debts Are Rising' (2004) 6(5) Local Government Bulletin 4.

[245] Auditor-General of South Africa, 'Consolidated General Report on the Local Government Audit Outcomes MFMA 2019–20' (2021) 8 <https://www.agsa.co.za/Reporting/MFMAReports/MFMA2019-2020.aspx>.

[246] National Treasury, 'Municipalities Meeting Criteria for Determining Serious Financial Problems in Terms of Section 138 and 140 of the MFMA—Q3 2020/21' (2021) <http://mfma.treasury.gov.za/Media_Releases/s71/2021/3rd_2021/Pages/pdf.aspx>. See also: MD Glasser and J Wright, 'South African Municipalities in Financial Distress: What Can Be Done?' (2020) 24 LDD 413, 419 for a discussion of what these triggers entail.

[247] National Treasury, 'Media Statement—Local Government Revenue and Expenditure: Second Quarter Local Government Section 71 Report for The Period: 1 July 2020–31 December 2020' (2021) <http://mfma.treasury.gov.za/Media_Releases/s71/2021/2nd_2021/Pages/default.aspx>.

[248] Ibid.

[249] J De Visser and J November, 'Overseeing the Overseers. Assessing Compliance with Municipal Intervention Rules in South Africa' (2017) 9 HJRL 109, 114.

139 of the Constitution.[250] In 2020 alone, about one in five municipalities was under administration.[251] A large proportion of these interventions was premised on financial distress.[252] The use of financial recovery plans to address municipalities in distress has accordingly become a common feature of South African local government. These interventions are not restricted to smaller, less well-resourced local entities but have included major cities.

Two case studies are presented below. These represent two ongoing instances of financial distress from two very different contexts. The first case study focuses on Mangaung Metropolitan Municipality, which is a major city and one of the provincial capitals. The second case study looks at Kannaland Local Municipality, which is a small rural municipality.

4.4.1 Case Study 1: Mangaung

Mangaung is one of eight metropolitan municipalities in South Africa, the largest type of municipality. It includes the city of Bloemfontein, which is the capital city of the Free State province. According to 2022 census data, its population was 811,431 people, comprising just under one-third of the population of the entire province.[253] The municipality faces significant socio-economic challenges. In 2019, the average monthly household income was R2,683 (approximately £113.70), whilst the Gini coefficient stood at 0.655.[254] The unemployment rate is estimated at 25.3%.[255]

Following serious financial distress, a voluntary financial recovery plan was prepared for Mangaung in 2018. However, the council repeatedly failed to effectively implement the plan, and the provincial government consequently

---

250 Ledger and Rampedi (n 242) 4. Also see De Visser and November (n 249).

251 J Griffiths, 'The Decline and Fall: One in Five Municipalities in a State of Collapse' *Daily Maverick* (6 October 2020) <https://www.dailymaverick.co.za/opinionista/2020-10-06-the-decline-and-fall-one-in-five-municipalities-in-a-state-of-collapse/>.

252 De Visser and November (n 249) 117–118.

253 Statistics South Africa, *Census 2022 Mangaung* <https://census.statssa.gov.za/#/province/4/2>.

254 National Treasury, *Municipal Socio-Economic Profiles—Mangaung* <https://lg.treasury.gov.za/ibi_apps/rs/ibfs//WFC/Repository/Public/Municipal_Socio-Economic_Profiles/Profiles/Municipal_Profiles/Free_State/Mangaung.pdf?IBIRS_action=run>.

255 National Treasury, 'Mangaung Metropolitan Municipality Updated Status Quo Assessment' (August 2023) <www.treasury.gov.za/comm_media/press/2023/MangaungFRP/Mangaung_Final_SQA_15_Aug_2023.pdf>.

undertook a mandatory intervention under section 139 of the Constitution.[256] This involved the appointment of a team of administrators to guide the process of developing and implementing a revised financial recovery plan. The council was, however, not dissolved. While the team was appointed in January 2020, their terms of reference were only finalised in May 2020, and a plan only finalised by December 2020.[257] The plan consisted of three phases: a rescue phase, which was to last for 6 to 8 months, a stabilisation phase, lasting 9 to 18 months, and a sustainability phase, lasting for 18 to 24 months.[258] The overall intervention in terms of the plan was thus estimated to last between 33 and 50 months.

The South African Local Government Association (SALGA) questioned the efficacy of the provincial intervention, including the intervention mechanism under section 139 of the Constitution.[259] SALGA, for example, pointed out that whilst the provincial government decided to intervene in Mangaung in December 2019, the provincial government owed Mangaung about R630 million (approximately £26.77 million) at the end of June 2020.[260] SALGA accordingly pointedly asked, 'Has provincial government not contributed to the financial collapse of Mangaung Metro?'[261] These comments reflect the ostensible disconnect between the *powers* of provincial governments to intervene in municipalities in distress and the *obligations* of provincial governments to financially assist municipalities in distress.

The intervention experienced significant challenges from the start. In November 2020, the national Department of Cooperative Governance reported to Parliament that there were significant governance conflicts, including the ousting of the executive mayor in a motion of no confidence, continuous

---

[256] Ministry of Finance Republic of South Africa, 'Media Statement—Mangaung Intervention in terms of section 139(5)(a) & (c)' (2020) <www.treasury.gov.za/comm_media/press/2020/2020021101%20Media%20Statement%20-%20GOVERNMENT%20INTERVENTION%20IN%20MANGAUNG.pdf>.

[257] South African Local Government Association, 'A SALGA Reflection on Section 139 Interventions' (2020) <www.parliament.gov.za/storage/app/media/Pages/2020/september/02-09-2020_National_Council_of_Provinces_Local_Government_Week/docs/session5/A_SALGA_reflection_on_Section_139_interventions.pdf>.

[258] M Macheli, 'State of Mangaung Metropolitan Municipality. Presentation to Portfolio Committee on Cooperative Governance and Traditional Affairs' (24 November 2020) <https://pmg.org.za/committee-meeting/31573/>.

[259] Ibid.

[260] Ibid.

[261] Ibid.

conflict between the intervention team and municipal management, and a lack of financial and governance support for the intervention team.[262]

The intervention team also reported a dispute between the municipality and Bloemwater, a water utility providing bulk water services to Mangaung, that continued to impact adversely on Mangaung's financial distress and the implementation of the recovery plan. This dispute involved alleged non-payment by the municipality for water services provided by Bloemwater, resulting in significant outstanding debt and the consequent implementation of water restrictions by the utility.[263] Bloemwater reported that the municipality owed it a total of R1.1 billion (approximately £47 million) on 31 August 2020.[264] Since Mangaung is Bloemwater's anchor client, the municipality's non-payment impacted Bloemwater's ability to service other municipalities in the area.

Two years after the provincial intervention in December 2019, no real progress had been made in implementing the financial recovery plan. In the report on the audit of the consolidated financial statements of Mangaung as of 30 June 2021, the Auditor-General noted that the municipality's "long overdue" outstanding debt 'indicate that a material uncertainty exists that may cast significant doubt on the municipality's ability to continue as a going concern'. The audit report raised various concerns about deficient governance practices, including inadequate performance management systems and a complete lack of consequence management for irregular expenditure.[265] These matters were reported almost identically in the 2020 audit report.[266] Between the 2019–2020 and 2021–2022 financial years, the audit outcome of the municipality in fact regressed from an unqualified audit opinion with findings to a qualified opinion.[267]

---

262 Ibid.

263 Mangaung, 'Media Statement: Response to Statement as Issued by Bloem Water' (15 July 2019) <www.mangaung.co.za/2019/07/15/response-to-statement-as-issued-by-bloem-water/>.

264 Bloemwater, 'Business Plan Entered into between Bloemwater and the Department of Water and Sanitation' (2021) 36 <www.bloemwater.co.za/wp-content/uploads/2021/07/2021-26-BLOEM-WATER-BUSINESS-PLAN-with-Updated-BP-SHC-with-tariff-11-approval-as-at-30-April-2021.pdf>.

265 Auditor-General of South Africa, 'Report of the Auditor-General to the Free State Legislature and the Council on Mangaung Metropolitan Municipality. Report on the Audit of the Consolidated Financial Statements 2019/2020 <https://lg.treasury.gov.za/supportingdocs/MAN/MAN_Audit%20Report_2021_Y_20220226T132354Z_5405.pdf>.

266 Ibid.

267 Auditor-General of South Africa, 'Consolidated General Report on Local Government Audit Outcomes MFMA 2021–22' (2023) 111 <https://mfma-2022.agsareports.co.za/>.

Consequently, the national government implemented a mandatory intervention under section 139(7) of the Constitution in April 2022, taking over from the provincial government.[268] The national intervention involved the development of a new financial recovery plan, which was approved in August 2023, while also assuming responsibility for implementing the plan. The council was not dissolved, but a national technical team was deployed to the municipality to oversee the implementation. This team acted alongside the existing administration by taking over as acting heads of all departments. A key and immediate challenge facing the national intervention was the continued political and administrative instability that undermined the effective functioning of both the council and the municipal administration. The council was largely non-functional due to political infighting and a hung council.[269] This instability was one of the main causes for the failure of the provincial intervention and the previous financial recovery plan, most of which was never implemented.[270]

> Following the national intervention some stability seems to have returned with the election of a Speaker, Executive Mayor and Chief Whip. Most senior administrative positions had also been vacant for extended periods of time. The previous municipal manager resigned in 2021 and the position was only filled again on a permanent basis on 1 December 2023. At the same time, permanent heads of departments were also appointed after all departments were headed by acting heads for more than a year. The Auditor-General had previously highlighted high vacancy rates as a key concern, noting that the municipality regressed in audit outcome, because of the failure to fill key leadership vacancies.[271]

The August 2023 status quo assessment noted that the continued high level of vacancies (standing at 50.58%) poses a material risk to the successful implementation of the financial recovery plan. Uncontrolled overtime payments were identified as a major challenge contributing to the financial distress. The lack of appropriate and permanently appointed senior staff in key management positions contributed largely to this challenge. The status quo assessment accordingly noted that the failure to address this issue by means of appropriate appointments posed a risk to the financial sustainability of the municipality and hence the success of the intervention.

Debt remains a significant problem for Mangaung. Between June 2021 and June 2022, creditors increased by R216.3 million (approximately £9.2 million) year on year. The average term for payment of trade creditors during

[268] National Treasury (n 255).
[269] Ibid.
[270] Ibid.
[271] Auditor-General of South Africa (n 267) 111.

2021–2022 was 115 days compared to the prescribed 30-day period.[272] At the same time, the municipality's annual debt collection rate between 2020–2021 and 2021–2022 was 80%, whilst the norm is 95%.

The municipality's financial distress, characterised by major governance challenges, led to severe disruption in public services. The dispute with Bloemwater resulted in water restrictions being implemented. Services across virtually all departments were affected by the financial problems, which resulted in (often violent) protests by disgruntled residents over poor service delivery. These failures in service delivery are exacerbated by and likely to increase in the future due to poor maintenance of critical infrastructure. In 2021–2022, the municipality only spent 46% of its capital budget.[273] Underspending on maintenance of infrastructure occurred across all service areas, with only 23% spent on electricity, 25% on the built environment, 27% on sanitation, 32% on water, and 43% on roads and stormwater.[274] Poor financial and project management furthermore resulted in grant funding for infrastructure development, among others, being reduced, further placing pressure on the already-stretched infrastructure. Since local government relies heavily on income from infrastructure-related services, these infrastructure challenges greatly reduce the municipality's revenue. The decreased revenue in turn intensifies the financial distress, which again adversely affects infrastructure maintenance, leading to a vicious cycle.

Finally, Mangaung's financial distress also resulted in adverse environmental impacts. One effect of the municipality's failure to properly maintain infrastructure, due to its financial distress, was that wastewater discharges did not adhere to prescribed standards and reasonable steps were not taken to prevent pollution of the adjacent environment.[275] As part of its audit of infrastructure for service delivery, the Auditor-General found in her 2021–2022 audit that the municipality's failure to maintain equipment at its Botshabelo wastewater treatment works resulted in 'raw, untreated sewage being discharged into the neighbouring environment, including the groundwater and the Klein Modder River and its extended watercourse'.[276] Similar findings were made in relation to two other wastewater treatment works.[277]

Dealing with Mangaung's financial distress in terms of the rules on financial problems under the Constitution and MFMA cannot be viewed as a success to date. Despite the third intervention currently being underway, with the third

[272] National Treasury (n 255).
[273] Ibid.
[274] Ibid.
[275] Auditor-General of South Africa (n 267) 74.
[276] Ibid.
[277] Ibid 59.

financial recovery plan in six years being implemented, there is little progress in restoring Mangaung to financial stability. As the Auditor-General stated in her most recent report on audit outcomes for local government, '[a]lthough several interventions are still underway, the situation at the metro is unlikely to improve in the short term' and 'the provincial and national interventions in terms of the Constitution did not have the desired outcome as they were not supported by both the council and municipal officials'.[278] This assessment is borne out by the progress report on the intervention to Parliament in October 2023, indicating that only 44% of the activities identified in the 2021 second financial recovery plan had been completed by October 2023.[279] It also shows that Mangaung's outstanding debt remains high, specifically in relation to its indebtedness to the water board, which stood at R821 million (approximately £35.08 million) at 30 June 2023. There has thus been only a small decrease in this debt since 2020. The revenue collection rate decreased to 73% at 30 September 2023.[280]

4.4.2 Case Study 2: Kannaland

Kannaland is a rural local municipality in the Western Cape province, encompassing the towns of Calitzdorp, Ladismith, Vanwyksdorp, and Zoar. It has a population of 31,986 people according to 2022 census data, making it the smallest of the seven municipalities in the Garden Route District.[281] Income inequality has increased from a Gini coefficient of 0.54 in 2014 to 0.59 in 2020.[282]

In 2016, Kannaland experienced serious financial difficulties and on 2 December 2016, the council passed a resolution requesting the provincial government to intervene in terms of section 139(5) of the Constitution.[283] The

---

278 Ibid 48, 112.

279 Department of Cooperative Governance, 'Progress on the Implementation of Section 139(7) Interventions in Lekwa, Mangaung and Enoch Mgijima Municipalities' (18 October 2023). Document not publicly available in possession of the authors.

280 Ibid.

281 Statistics South Africa, *Census 2022 Kannaland* <https://census.statssa.gov.za/#/province/4/2>.

282 National Treasury, *Municipal Socio-Economic Profiles—Kannaland* <https://lg.treasury.gov.za/ibi_apps/rs/ibfs//WFC/Repository/Public/Municipal_Socio-Economic_Profiles/Profiles/Municipal_Profiles/Western_Cape/Kannaland_Municipality.pdf?IBIRS_action–run>.

283 *Executive Council of the Western Cape Province v Kannaland Local Municipality* [2021] ZAWCHC 208.

provincial government accepted the invitation and instructed the provincial treasury to develop a financial recovery plan. The council was not dissolved, and an administrator was not appointed. A financial recovery plan was consequently imposed on the municipality on 17 March 2017.[284] Implementation of the plan was left in the hands of the municipal council.

By December 2018, the provincial government formed the view that the council had not adequately implemented the financial recovery plan and resolved to implement the plan itself.[285] An administrator was appointed to ensure the implementation of the plan and vested with all executive powers necessary to do so. However, neither the council nor the administration was dissolved. The council retained its legislative powers, and the administration was required to work alongside, and subject to the supervision of, the administrator. The administrator made progress in implementing the recovery plan, and the council adopted a revised organisational structure in May 2020 that would result in savings of about R8.9 million (approximately £380,000).[286] Despite this progress, the municipality remained under financial distress.

In November 2020, the council adopted a resolution that purported to terminate the provincial intervention and the implementation of the financial recovery plan.[287] Despite the administrator and provincial government indicating to the council that it was not at liberty to unilaterally terminate a provincial intervention, the municipal manager informed all municipal staff on 3 December 2020 that the administrator's term had come to an end and that the administrator was no longer considered part of the municipal administration. Staff were accordingly instructed not to take instructions from the administrator.[288]

The provincial government consequently sought a court order enforcing the intervention and restraining the municipality from obstructing the implementation of the financial recovery plan. In response, the municipality argued that the imposition of the financial recovery plan was void *ab initio* and sought an order declaring the imposition of the plan invalid. In October 2021, the court found in favour of the municipality, holding that the provincial government had not adhered to the strict requirements for mandatory interventions under the Constitution and the MFMA. The court held that it was a peremptory requirement under the MFMA that a financial recovery plan in the case of mandatory interventions be prepared by the MFRS in National Treasury.[289] Since the plan in the current instance was prepared by the provincial treasury,

---

[284] Ibid.
[285] Ibid.
[286] Ibid.
[287] Ibid.
[288] Ibid.
[289] Ibid.

the court held that the imposition of the plan was unlawful. The court emphasised the importance of the checks and balances built into the MFMA for instances where one sphere of government intervenes in another. The involvement of National Treasury by means of the MFRS was an essential check on the exercise of intervention powers by the provincial government. The latter's failure to adhere to this important check meant that the intervention, and particularly the financial recovery plan, could not be sustained.

The court also held that the appointment of an administrator to fulfil certain functions in implementing the financial recovery plan alongside the council was unlawful.[290] It found that a provincial government may only impose an administrator with the required powers to implement the plan if the relevant council had been dissolved. Alternatively, the council had to implement the plan. The court reasoned that this clear distinction between the two routes to implementation was essential to avoid 'perpetual squabbling between [...] competing centres of power'.[291] The court thus ruled that the 'use of an Administrator to take over the executive functions of the municipality whilst the council is still in office is no remedy'.[292]

The court criticised the extended nature of the intervention in Kannaland. In this respect, the court stated that

> the prolonged intervention infringes on the autonomy of the local government. It was certainly not temporary or to the extent necessary as contemplated in the Constitution. National and provincial spheres are not entitled to usurp the functions of the municipal sphere except in exceptional circumstances, but only temporarily and in compliance with strict procedures.[293]

Despite the judicial condemnation of the prolonged intervention in Kannaland in October 2021, the provincial executive resolved to implement a new mandatory intervention in December 2023. It accordingly requested the MFRS to develop a financial recovery plan. This latest development means that the municipality has effectively been subject to intervention for close to eight years with no end in sight. This is the better part of two municipal council terms.

By 2024, the situation in Kannaland remained dire. Its financial position had not improved, and the provincial government considered mandatory intervention due to financial crises to be justified. The Department of Cooperative Governance reported to Parliament in March 2024 that the municipality experienced persistent failure of infrastructure and that several directives had been

---

290 Ibid.
291 Ibid [63].
292 Ibid [64].
293 Ibid [71] (footnotes omitted).

issued for non-compliance with waste and wastewater delivery processes.[294] Water losses stood at 24% across the entire municipality in the 2022–23 financial year, and as high as 40% in particular towns.[295] From a governance perspective, the position of municipal manager continued to be occupied on an acting basis. During the briefing to the Parliamentary committee, the committee chair noted that they were 'dealing with a municipality that has got no leadership'.

The Kannaland matter illustrates the challenges of multi-level governmental approaches to municipal financial distress. The *Kannaland* judgment leaves open the question of whether a provincial government may impose a financial recovery plan and leave it to the council to implement, but later decide to dissolve the council and appoint an administrator if the council proves unable or unwilling to implement the plan. The case study shows the unique constitutional questions raised by rules governing municipal distress compared to ordinary insolvency and business rescue rules. It also shows the fundamental challenge in dealing with distress without the possibility of liquidating the entity in case rescue attempts fail. One lesson from the Kannaland matter is that a more robust use of the power to dissolve a council may be required to effectively address severe financial distress.

4.5 CONCLUSIONS – AN ESG CRITIQUE OF THE LAW IN PRACTICE

The two case studies suggest that the dedicated rules on municipalities in financial distress are not achieving significant ESG improvements in practice.

A notable lack of governance improvements lies at the heart of the problem in both cases, and the failure to resolve the governance deficits seems to have an adverse knock-on effect on environmental and social considerations. The regulatory regime's ostensible inability to resolve the governance problems underlying the financial distress acts as a barrier to improving environmental and social conditions.

The challenges in addressing governance concerns are tied to issues with the appointment and role of administrators. Specifically, the lack of qualification requirements can lead to the appointment of inappropriate, inexperienced, and

---

[294] Department of Cooperative Governance, 'State of Kannaland Local Municipality Presentation to the Portfolio Committee Cooperative Governance and Traditional Affairs, Parliament of the Republic of South Africa' (12 March 2024). Document not publicly available in possession of the authors.

[295] Ibid.

unqualified individuals in these positions.[296] This stands in stark contrast to the extensive qualification criteria for business rescue practitioners and liquidators. This parallelism extends to their organisational separation: insolvency is managed by the Department of Justice, whilst municipal financial distress is overseen by National and Provincial Treasuries, with no practical interaction between the two from the highest level of policy formulation to the street level of implementation.

Another governance problem is municipal administrations' refusal to cooperate with administrators, denying them access to premises and information.[297] This issue arises because administrators replace the municipal council, whilst the existing municipal administration, led by the municipal manager, remains.[298] Successful interventions, like in Cederberg Municipality, involved appointing an acting municipal manager,[299] unlike ineffective interventions in Mangaung, Kannaland, Masilonyana, and Nala.[300] This suggests that retaining failed leadership in the administration hampers addressing financial problems in municipalities.

Provincial interventions often face criticism for being politically motivated rather than addressing financial distress.[301] Whilst these claims are certainly contested, Ledger and Rampedi found the legislative framework unevenly

---

[296] Ledger and Rampedi (n 242) 11; DM Mohale, 'Placement of Municipalities under Administration. A Comparative Case Study of Masilonyana and Nala Local Municipalities in the Free State Province in South Africa' (MMPP thesis, University of the Witwatersrand 2013) 114–116 <https://wiredspace.wits.ac.za/server/api/core/bitstreams/dfc4e154-5e2f-4dcc-97b2-51de8420d93c/content>.

[297] Ibid; *Western Cape Province v Kannaland* (n 283).

[298] See South African Local Government Association, 'Municipal Support and Intervention Framework' (2020) 53 <www.salga.org.za/event/nma20/documents/LG%20Publications/SALGA%20%20Framework%20for%20Municipal%20Support%20and%20Intervention.pdf>.

[299] Western Cape Provincial Government Department of Local Government and Housing, 'Case Study of a Provincial Intervention at a Municipality as a Result of a Financial Crisis' (2006) <www.westerncape.gov.za/text/2006/4/bestpracticecederberg_web.pdf>.

[300] Mohale (n 296).

[301] Ledger and Rampedi (n 242) 9; NCOP Cooperative Governance & Traditional Affairs, Water and Sanitation and Human Settlements Select Committee, 'Joint Workshop with National and Provincial Legislatures on the Application of Section 139 of the Constitution and the need for legislation in terms of Sections 139(8)' (2010) <https://pmg.org.za/committee-meeting/12254/) 74; W Greffrath and G Van der Waldt, 'Section 139 Interventions in South African Local Government, 1994–2015' (2006) 75 New Contree 135.

applied and at the discretion of provincial executives.[302] De Visser and November also noted significant uncertainty about the basis for interventions.[303]

Governance failures negatively impact environmental and social conditions. Mangaung illustrates how prolonged financial distress results in insufficient funding for infrastructure maintenance and payments to bulk service providers. This neglect makes short- or medium-term reversal nearly impossible. Deteriorating infrastructure in turn reduces municipal income, as volumes of income-generating services fall, residents seek alternative services (such as solar power installations in lieu of buying electricity from the municipal grid), and property values decrease, leading to lower taxes.

The dedicated legal framework for assisting distressed municipalities appears ineffective. Ledger and Rampedi found that most interventions under section 139 of the Constitution were not long-term successes, based on financial analyses before, during, and two years after interventions.[304] From an ESG perspective, municipalities in severe distress—financial collapse, governance breakdown, infrastructure collapse—are unlikely to regain stability.[305] This suggests the regulatory framework fails for seriously distressed municipalities, akin to insolvent enterprises. Unlike insolvent enterprises, municipalities cannot be wound up, indicating a gap in South Africa's legal framework, which creates significant ESG risks due to municipalities' crucial role in implementing constitutional socio-economic and environmental commitments.

---

302 Ledger and Rampedi (n 242) 10. Also see Makoti and Odeku (n 144) 76.
303 De Visser and November (n 249) 125.
304 Ledger and Rampedi (n 242) 13.
305 Ibid.

5. United Kingdom

5.1 INTRODUCTION

This chapter outlines the rules governing the treatment of local authorities/entities[1] in (financial) distress in England and links them to the central argument advanced in this book, namely that the current framework for dealing with local entities in financial distress needs reform to better align with environmental, social and governance (ESG) criteria.

The chapter is divided into three parts. The first part describes the general framework applicable to companies in distress under English law. It assesses to what extent these rules consider ESG in rescue procedures. Whilst "traditional" insolvency rules do not apply to local authorities, a modified version of these rules applies to entities providing essential services to local citizens, such as utility and water companies. This part outlines what lessons can be learnt from corporate practice.

The second part describes the rules applicable to local public entities in England, and analyses to what extent (if any) English law on restructuring local entities in distress considers ESG criteria. The final part looks at the law in practice, to assess whether the law, coupled with the practice of municipal restructuring, promotes ESG.

The treatment of local public entities differs across the four UK nations.[2] Therefore, the chapter focuses primarily on English rules. Section 114 of the Local Government and Finance Act 1988 also applies to Wales. However, Welsh authorities are funded in a different way from English local entities, thus making them more reliant on central government funding and less prone to financial distress.[3] To date, no Welsh authority has issued a section 114 notice.

---

[1] The terms local authority, municipality, and local entity are used interchangeably in this part of the book.

[2] For Northern Ireland: Local Government Act (Northern Ireland) 1972; for Scotland: Local Government etc. (Scotland) Act 1994; for Wales: Local Government (Wales) Act 1994.

[3] See, among others: N Thomas, 'Caerphilly Finance Boss Confident Council Can Avoid Section 114 Notice' *South Wales Argus* (Newport, 7 February 2024)

5.2 ENGLISH INSOLVENCY LAW—INCREASING LEEWAY FOR FAIRNESS

Corporate debtors who are struggling financially can liquidate or rescue their business in England in various ways. This section details these options, as well as the role that key actors play in prioritising certain interests. This section also explains the constraints under which these actors make such prioritisations.

The English framework includes three types of liquidation procedure, one of which is available to solvent debtors. The Insolvency Act 1986 (IA 1986) outlines two rescue mechanisms,[4] the traditional practitioner-in-possession administration procedure (IA 1986, Schedule B1) and the US-inspired debtor-in-possession company voluntary arrangement (CVA–IA 1986, Part IA). Administration can be tailored to the needs of specific debtors thanks to flexible rules that allow debtors to retain possession of insolvent companies (light touch administrations),[5] and/or to arrange a fire sale of the business and its assets ahead of the formal opening of the insolvency procedure (pre-packaged administrations).[6] Finally, the Companies Act 2006 (CA 2006) envisages further rescue-orientated mechanisms such as schemes of arrangement[7] and restructuring plans.[8]

None of these remedies are available to municipalities experiencing financial distress. It is, however, important to briefly discuss these procedures to assess if and to what extent they promote ESG goals and, consequently, whether any lessons can be applied to the treatment of local authorities in financial distress.

The promotion of ESG goals is possible primarily where debtors undertake non-terminal procedures designed to turn their companies and/or their businesses around.[9] In the past, liquidation has been used to hive down a business

---

<https://www.southwalesargus.co.uk/news/24102321.caerphilly-finance-boss-confident-council-can-avoid-section-114-notice/>; S Stowers, 'Local Government in England, Scotland and Wales' (*UK in a Changing Europe*, 2 April 2024) <https://ukandeu.ac.uk/explainers/local-government-in-england-scotland-and-wales/>.

[4] Liquidation procedures are those that result in the removal of the company from the Company's Registry and in the cessation of its activities. Rescue procedures are those that result in the continuation of all or part of the debtor's activity, either under the existing or (more frequently) a new owner.

[5] For an outline, see (among others): E Vaccari and E Ghio, *English Corporate Insolvency Law: A Primer* (EE Publishing 2022) 154–164.

[6] Ibid 138–154.

[7] Ibid 185–191.

[8] Ibid 191–208.

[9] "Business rescue" refers to the practice of rescuing the corporate activity without necessarily preserving the corporate shell. This is usually achieved

whilst allowing the discharge of debt (e.g. *British Steel*).[10] Despite this, English liquidation rules are statutorily geared towards terminating the debtor's business activity. Critically assessing the ESG potential of liquidation procedures would, therefore, be most inappropriate.[11] As a result, our analysis focuses on the ESG potential of the other restructuring procedures available under English law except for schemes of arrangement due to the hybrid, contractual nature of these proceedings.[12] As established in *Gategroup*,[13] only restructuring plans hold the status of "proper" restructuring procedures available to financially distressed corporations.

5.2.1 A Complicated Set of Procedures

Administration[14] is the most well-known formal rescue procedure available under English law. First introduced by the IA 1986, it allows a financially

---

through a sale of the profitable or promising part of the debtor's business to a new buyer through an insolvency procedure. "Corporate rescue" refers to the practice of restructuring the company's financial or contractual (e.g. tenancy agreements, supply contracts, etc.) obligations whilst making minimal changes to the debtor's business. This is usually achieved through debtor-in-possession procedures such as CVAs. Such an option is preferable for companies that have a solid business but have become over-leveraged over time.

[10] A Keay and P Walton, 'British Steel—Is It a Wind Up?' (2019) 12(4) C.R. & I. 125.

[11] This is except for the environmental impact of liquidation procedures. When a company shuts down, any unsold or unusable real estate assets are left abandoned. This includes polluted assets. Liquidation may itself lead to pollution if real estate is not maintained. Over the years, local councils and private companies may redevelop the abandoned sites for the benefit of local communities. ESG criteria may form part of these redevelopment projects, as in the case of the Parkside Colliery site in Warrington, a town located between Liverpool and Manchester: G Skentelbery, 'Full Planning Permission Being Sought to Regenerate Former Parkside Colliery Site' *Warrington Worldwide* (Warrington, 20 July 2023) <https://www.warrington-worldwide.co.uk/2023/07/20/full-planning-permission-being-sought-to-regenerate-former-parkside-colliery-site/>.

[12] A scheme is a compromise or arrangement between the debtor and its creditors, which becomes legally binding if it is approved by all classes of creditors with the majority thresholds prescribed by the law *and* it is sanctioned by a court.

[13] *Re Gategroup Guarantee Ltd* [2021] EWHC 304 (Ch).

[14] IA 1986, sch B1.

distressed or insolvent[15] debtor to conceive a rescue plan whilst trading. During this period, a company is protected by a moratorium against creditor actions.

To make an administration order, a court must be satisfied that a company is, or is likely to become, unable to pay its debts[16] and that an administration order is reasonably likely to achieve the intended purpose of the administration.[17] When an administrator is appointed out of court by a debtor or a qualifying floating charge holder, it is not necessary to prove the applicant's insolvency. After entering a formal insolvency procedure, a company is typically managed by an administrator, who is a licensed insolvency practitioner.[18]

A *sui generis* form of administration that has continued to gain popularity[19] is the pre-pack procedure.[20] Pre-packs are arrangements for the sale of a debtor's business. They are negotiated with prospective purchasers and agreed upon by major creditors prior to the formal commencement of a statutory administration procedure. The sale is completed shortly after an administration order is made. Significant reforms to this procedure have been introduced

---

[15] IA 1986 uses two definitions of insolvency, namely cash-flow and balance-sheet insolvency. The statutory definitions can be found in IA 1986, s 123(1) and (2).

[16] The "inability to pay debts" is defined by IA 1986, s 123 as both want of liquidity (i.e. cash flow insolvency) and balance sheet insolvency. In assessing the latter, the court is required to have regard to prospective and contingent liabilities (*BNY Corporate Trustee Services Ltd v Eurosail-UK 2007-3BL plc* [2013] UKSC 28).

[17] *Re AA Mutual International Insurance Co Ltd* [2004] EWHC 2430 (Ch).

[18] There are, however, examples of debtor-in-possession administrations, known as "light touch administrations", where the existing management continues to run the company during administration under the supervision of the administrator.

[19] J Armour, 'The Rise of the "Pre-Pack": Corporate Restructuring in the UK and Proposals for Reform' in RP Austin and FJG Aoun (eds), *Restructuring Companies in Troubled Times: Director and Creditor Perspectives* (Law Publishing Unit, 2012). See also the introductory analysis in T Graham, 'Graham Review into Pre-pack Administration: Report to the Rt Hon Vince Cable MP' (*The Insolvency Service*, 2014) <https://www.gov.uk/government/publications/graham-review-into-pre-pack-administration>.

[20] For an analysis, see (amongst others): E Vaccari, 'English Pre-Packaged Corporate Rescue Procedures: Is there a Case for Propping Industry Self-Regulation and Industry-Led Measures such as the Pre-Pack Pool?' (2020) 31(3) ICCLR 169.

by the Administration (Restrictions on Disposal etc. to Connected Persons) Regulations 2021.[21]

Another procedure available to companies in financial distress is CVA.[22] This is an agreement between a registered company (that may or may not be insolvent), its shareholders, and its creditors. The use of a CVA does not result in a statutory moratorium being granted automatically. The Corporate Insolvency and Governance Act 2020 (CIGA 2020) made it possible for companies undertaking a restructuring procedure to rely on a short stay, known as a Part A1 moratorium. This stay initially lasts for 20 business days, but it can be extended for up to one year. Whilst CVAs can be used as autonomous procedures, they are frequently complemented by an administration, a winding-up, or a scheme of arrangement.

Only available to companies in financial difficulty that are not yet insolvent, restructuring plans were introduced by CIGA 2020. They have been used in high-profile cases,[23] such as the restructuring of Virgin Atlantic Airways.[24] Drawing extensive inspiration from schemes of arrangement, restructuring plans are flexible court-supervised restructuring procedures. Unlike schemes, restructuring plans can be imposed on a dissenting class of creditors ("cross-class cram-down") if certain conditions are met.[25]

---

21 Administration (Restrictions on Disposal etc. to Connected Persons) Regulations 2021.

22 IA 1986, Part I, ss 1–7B; and Insolvency Rules 2016, Part II, rules 2.1–2.45.

23 *Re Deep Ocean 1 UK Ltd* [2021] EWHC 138 (Ch); *Re Virgin Active Holdings* [2021] EWHC 1246 (Ch); *Re National Car Parks* [2021] EWHC 1653 (Ch); and *Re Hurricane Energy plc* [2021] EWHC 1759 (Ch), where the High Court refused to sanction a restructuring plan because the dissenting creditors would not be better off under it than in the alternative corporate liquidation procedure. On the importance of this judgment, see K Stephenson and Z Stembridge, 'Sanctioning a Restructuring Plan: Not a Port for Every Storm' (2021) 32(7) PLC Mag. 10.

24 *Re Virgin Atlantic Airways Ltd* [2020] EWHC 2376 (Ch). For an assessment of the effectiveness of the measures introduced by CIGA 2020, see: P Walton and L Jacobs, 'Corporate Insolvency and Governance Act 2020—Final Evaluation Report' *The Insolvency Service* (November 2020) <https://www.gov.uk/government/publications/corporate-insolvency-and-governance-act-2020-evaluation-reports/corporate-insolvency-and-governance-act-2020-final-evaluation-report-november-2022>.

25 These are that the dissenting creditors are not treated worse than in the relevant alternative, and that the plan has been voted by a class of impaired creditors: CA 2006, s 901G.

Traditionally, the English framework has mainly been creditor-friendly,[26] largely due to various management displacement procedures, and also due to the secured creditors' and financers' protections in each of these procedures. The reduction in the privileges granted to floating charge holders by reason of the Enterprise Act 2002, the introduction of both debtor-in-possession restructuring plans[27] and short interim moratoria,[28] and new restrictions on the use of certain clauses in corporate contracts[29] have progressively softened the pro-creditor stance taken by English law. The next sections assess to what extent these new debtor-friendly rules have resulted in the promotion of fair results and ESG considerations in rescue procedures.

5.2.2 Fairness in English Restructuring Law

Courts have adopted a certain degree of flexibility in adapting insolvency law to the circumstances of individual cases by relying on the notions of "fairness" and "discretion". This leaves leeway for ESG considerations in restructuring procedures.

Scholarship[30] has provided an analytical framework for the fairness debate in debt restructuring. Finch suggests that insolvency law could be explained and developed using four basic benchmarks: efficiency, expertise, accountability, and fairness.[31] Paterson explores the quality of fairness in debt

---

[26] S Shandro and B Jones, 'Bankruptcy Jurisdiction in the US and Europe: Reconsideration Needed!' (2005) 18(9) Insolv. Int. 129; and K Akintola, 'Pro-commerce Outlooks: The Bane of English Corporate Insolvency Law?' (2021) 34(1) Insolv. Int. 6.

[27] See below *sub* [5.2.2.1].

[28] IA 1986, Part A1. For a comment on the impact on the creditor-friendly attitude of the English corporate framework, see L Doyle, 'Part A1 Moratorium Monitorship: Some Practical Problems and Pitfalls' (2020) 33(4) Insolv. Int. 107.

[29] IA 1986, s 233B. On the risks associated with the introduction of this debtor-friendly mechanism: F Toube and J Rumley, 'A Brave New World? Should the UK Ban Ipso-Facto Clauses in Non-Executory Contracts?' (2018) 31(3) Insolv. Int. 78, 81.

[30] Some minority scholarship argues that reliance on these notions is misplaced. According to economic efficiency purists, fairness considerations amount to undesirable arbitrariness, inconsistency and lack of predictability in enforcement. DA Crane, 'Chicago, Post-Chicago, and Neo-Chicago' (2009) 76 U. Chi. L. Rev. 1911. These views are not followed by English mainstream scholarship or by English case law.

[31] V Finch and D Milman, *Corporate Insolvency Law: Perspectives and Principles* (CUP 2017) 41; V Finch, 'The Measures of Insolvency Law' (1997) 17(2) Oxford J. Legal. Stud. 227.

restructuring, and conceives of different (substantive) principles of fairness, in addition to various procedural factors, to assess the outcome of each case.[32] Vaccari argued for the need to distinguish between procedural and substantive fairness.[33]

English courts exercise their discretion within this theoretical framework but in a statutory vacuum, as terms such as "unfair" are not defined in the law. This does not result in the courts using the concepts of "fairness" and "discretion" haphazardly. Their meaning is left to the courts to elucidate, which they do on a case-by-case basis.

In the absence of a single or universal test, this part discusses how courts have interpreted the concept of fairness. It also investigates if and to what extent the concept of fairness has accommodated or can accommodate ESG considerations.

5.2.2.1 Restructuring plans

Restructuring plans are restructuring procedures available to companies that are experiencing financial distress and have a sufficient connection with England. They are designed to achieve an arrangement or composition with the majority of the debtor's creditors. When the statutory requirements are met, these plans can be imposed on dissenting creditors and their classes.

One of the most widely debated topics has revolved around the courts' "absolute" discretion to refuse the sanctioning of a restructuring plan under CA 2006, sections 901F and 901G.[34] The legislator provided the courts with the power to assess the merit of the plan, and to potentially refuse its sanctioning even if the procedural statutory prerequisites and voting thresholds have been satisfied.[35] Courts have taken the "fairness test" from schemes of arrangement and adapted it to the different context and procedure of a restructuring plan.[36] Courts have refused to sanction a plan whenever it operates unfairly against a

---

32 S Paterson, 'Debt Restructuring and Notions of Fairness' (2017) 80(4) MLR 3.

33 E Vaccari, 'Broken Companies or Broken System? Charting the English Insolvency Valuation Framework In Search for Fairness' (2020) 35(4) JIBLR 135.

34 Explanatory Notes to the Corporate Insolvency and Governance Act 2020, paras 15 and 190.

35 P de Vries and M Trottier, 'Fair's Fair: The Concept of Fairness in Part 26A Restructuring Plans' (2023) 16(6) C.R. & I. 199.

36 *Re Amicus Finance plc (in administration)* [2021] EWHC 3036 (Ch) [40]–[45]; *Re Hong Kong Airlines Ltd* [2022] EWHC 3210 (Ch) [48]–[50]; *and Re SGB-SMIT GmbH* [2023] EWHC 2551 (Ch) [15], [26].

(group of) creditors.[37] Fairness has been used as a mechanism to challenge a plan,[38] but also as a prerequisite to sanction it.[39] Courts require proof that the statutory majority of members and creditors are acting *bona fide*, and are not coercing the minority into promoting interests adverse to those of the class they represent (the so-called "fairness and reasonable" test).[40] This means that the proposal must be one that a competent and honest person could fairly endorse.[41]

In the context of schemes, courts apply a rationality test in which they ask whether an intelligent and honest man, who is a member of the class concerned and is acting in respect of its interests, might reasonably approve the plan. This rationality test is not applied mechanically. As evidenced in the *Noble Group* case,[42] courts need to be satisfied that the parties who voted in favour at the meeting were a true reflection of the class as a whole. Additionally, the court needs to ensure that the majority in each class did not vote in favour purely to promote personal—as opposed to collective—interests.[43] In other words, even where a cross-class cram-down is not a contentious matter, courts cannot simply rely on the simple majority achieved in each voting class and apply the rationality test mechanically.

However, at times, courts have used their powers in a light touch manner. For instance, in *Smile Telecoms*, they refused to investigate if a plan was fair towards an in-the-money creditor simply because the creditor failed to attend the hearing to make representations.[44] Courts have been reluctant to exercise their discretion to sanction a plan if a significant majority voted in favour (even if this majority was below the statutory threshold), if none of the opposing creditors appeared to oppose the sanctioning of the plan, and if none of them

---

[37] *Re Nasmyth Group Ltd* [2023] EWHC 988 (Ch); *Re The Great Annual Savings Co Ltd* [2023] EWHC 1141 (Ch); and *Re AGPS Bondco plc* [2024] EWCA Civ 24.

[38] *Re Houst Ltd* [2022] EWHC 1941 (Ch); *Nasmyth Group* (n 37); and *Great Annual Savings* (n 37).

[39] *Virgin Atlantic* (n 24); *Re Gategroup Guarantee Ltd* [2021] EWHC 775 (Ch) and *Hong Kong Airlines* (n 36).

[40] *Re Hawk Insurance Co Ltd* [2001] EWCA Civ 241.

[41] *Virgin Atlantic* (n 24).

[42] *Re Noble Group Ltd* [2018] EWHC 2911 (Ch).

[43] *AGPS Bondco* (n 37) [120].

[44] *Re Smile Telecoms Holdings Ltd* [2022] EWHC 740 (Ch) [53]–[55].

explained in evidence why the terms of the plan might be considered unfair to them.[45] *Adler*[46] has partially changed this approach.

Readers should remember that, in restructuring plans, creditors are divided into classes. All classes should vote on the plan, with a majority in each class voting in favour,[47] except in the case of a cross-class cram-down. This mechanism has the potential to yield unfair results, as it involves the vote of a class of creditors being overturned by the court. As a result, when a cross-class cram-down is invoked, the law prescribes additional criteria for sanctioning a plan.[48] Additionally, in the exercise of their discretion, the courts should at least use the same approach as with schemes of arrangement.[49]

Quite sensibly, the courts exercise more scrutiny when a cross-class cram-down is invoked. Case law agrees that the discretion granted by the law should not be used as 'an invitation to [...] act capriciously, arbitrarily or on [the judge's] own individualised view of the merits [of the case], untethered to legal principles'.[50] The appellate court in *Adler* suggests that the concepts of "vertical" and "horizontal" comparison, which were developed in relation to company voluntary arrangements,[51] could be modified and applied to the sanctioning of restructuring plans involving dissenting classes of creditors.

Vertical comparison relates to the position of a particular class of creditors under the plan and under the relevant alternative. Horizontal comparison relates to the position of a class of creditors compared with other creditors or classes of creditors under the plan. In exercising its discretion to impose a plan on a dissenting class, a court has to identify whether the plan provides for differential treatment of classes of creditors and, if so, whether those differences

---

45 *Re ED & F Man Holdings Ltd* [2022] EWHC 687 (Ch) [55]–[56].

46 *AGPS Bondco* (n 37). For an analysis: E Vaccari, 'The Adler Restructuring Saga: Fair Wind for Dissenting Creditors?' (2024) 35(6) ICCLR 293.

47 75% in value of the creditors or class of creditors or members or class of members, present and voting either in person or by proxy at the meeting: CA 2006, s 901F(1). As stated above *sub* [5.2.1], if no such majority is achieved in all classes, the debtor can ask the court to sanction the plan despite the opposition of one or more classes of creditors. This is called "cross-class cram-down".

48 CA 2006, s 901G.

49 *Re Telewest Communications Plc (No.2)* [2004] EWHC 1466 (Ch); *Noble Group* (n 42); and *Virgin Atlantic* (n 24).

50 *AGPS Bondco* (n 37) [107].

51 These expressions were first used by Mr Justice Etherton in the context of an unfair prejudice challenge to a CVA in *Prudential Assurance Co Ltd v PRG Powerhouse Ltd* [2007] EWHC 1002 (Ch).

could be justified.[52] This judgement[53] defines vertical and horizontal comparison as mechanisms for ensuring fairness whenever a cross-class cram-down is invoked.

Accordingly, fairness requires that departures from the strict implementation of the principle of equal treatment of creditors are possible only if sound reasons are provided.[54] Lord Snowden refrained from providing a list of situations in which a departure could be justified. However, he mentioned that promoting the restructuring goals might be enough to meet this requirement.[55] He equally considered that the full payment of essential trade creditors and employees could be a valid, justifiable reason.[56]

These developments suggest that courts are taking it upon themselves to use the terms of restructuring plans to identify and measure imbalances in compromised creditors' interests.[57] This is particularly the case where the plan appears to have been approved quickly, and where subordinated creditors and shareholders have been allocated part of the restructuring surplus.[58] In the past, the absence of creditor opposition justified a lighter touch exercise of the court's prerogatives.[59] However, this trend seems to have been reversed by the appellate judgment in *Adler*, at least for cases where a cross-class cram-down is invoked. This suggests a tiered approach to the exercise of fairness, in which ESG considerations could become part of the restructuring procedures conducted under CA 2006, Part 26A.

5.2.2.2 Administration

An administration must pursue one of three objectives:[60]

1. rescue the company as a going concern;

---

52 *AGPS Bondco* (n 37) [156].

53 Similar points were made by Mr Justice Trower in *Deep Ocean* (n 23) [63] and by Mr Justice Zacaroli in *Houst* (n 38).

54 In other words, the departure from the principle of *pari passu* treatment of creditors should be "justified": *AGPS Bondco* (n 37) [166].

55 Ibid [167].

56 Ibid [170].

57 de Vries and Trottier (n 35) 201. Other valid examples of this trend are *Great Annual Savings* (n 37) (where the plan was opposed by one key creditor) and *Hong Kong Airlines* (n 36) (where no creditors opposed the plan).

58 J Hewitt, J Holley and T Rayfield, 'Atento: The Final Restructuring Plan of 2023—A Case Study' (2024) 17(1) C.R. & I. 3, 4.

59 *Re Chaptre Finance plc* [2023] EWHC 2276 (Ch) and *Re Yunneng Wind Power Co Ltd* [2023] EWHC 2275 (Ch).

60 IA 1986, sch B1, para 3(1).

2. achieve a better result for the company's creditors as a whole than would be likely if the company were wound-up;[61] or
3. realise the property and distribute the proceeds.

Fairness concerns are frequently addressed as part of traditional administration procedures. In this context, the common law principle known as the rule in *Ex parte James*[62] holds that the court will not permit its officers to act in a way which, though lawful and in accordance with enforceable rights, does not accord with the standards which right-thinking people would think should govern the conduct of the court or its officers. The principle applies to a failure to act, as much as it applies to positive acts.[63] Furthermore, statutory rules[64] allow the court to grant relief where an administrator is acting, has acted or is proposing to act in a way which unfairly harms the interests of the applicant.

The unfair treatment of certain creditors was a contentious issue in *Lehman Brothers Australia Ltd (in liq.) v MacNamara*.[65] In the first instance case,[66] Mr Justice Hildyard adopted a light touch approach to the court's discretion in assessing whether an administrator's behaviour was unfair.[67] A restrictive approach to both the common law test (by reference to an "unconscionability test") and the statutory test was adopted.

This approach was modified on appeal. The Court considered that courts and administrators, who are both officers of the court,[68] are expected to apply standards of conduct that go beyond mere abidance by legal duties. Analysing the relevant case law,[69] including the Supreme Court's judgment in *Re Nortel*

---

61 This basically means transferring the "good" part of the business to a new buyer.

62 (1873–74) LR 9 Ch App 609.

63 *Re Hall* [1907] 1 KB 875.

64 IA 1986, sch B1, para 74.

65 [2020] EWCA Civ 321. For an analysis, see (among others): J Lewison, 'Lehman Brothers Australia Ltd (in liquidation) v MacNamara' (2020) 13(2) C.R. & I. 60; Clifford Chance, 'Unfair Administrators: The Rule in *Ex parte James*' (2020) 31(4) PLC Mag. 73; and Shearman & Sterling LLP, 'United Kingdom: Administrators' Powers and Duties—Court's Power to Control its Officers' (2020) 35(7) JIBLR N87.

66 *Lehman Brothers Australia Ltd (in liquidation) v Lomas* [2018] EWHC 2783 (Ch).

67 The judge's view on the threshold test for the application of the principle in *Ex parte James* was *obiter*.

68 Trustees in bankruptcy, liquidators in compulsory liquidations and administrators are all officers of the court. As a result, they are all subject to this rule.

69 *Re Tyler* [1907] 1 KB 865; *Re Thellusson* [1919] 2 KB 735; *Re Wigzell* [1921] 2 KB 835; *Re Clark (A Bankrupt)* [1975] 1 WLR 559; *Re Multi Guarantee Co Ltd*

GmbH (in administration),[70] the court observed that, whilst unfairness had been articulated as part of the *Ex parte James* test from an early stage, few authorities supported the unconscionability test.[71] As a result, the restrictive interpretation of the common law rule adopted by the lower court was reversed in favour of an interpretation based on the broader concept of fairness. Under the revised approach, the standard is that of a right-thinking person representing the current views of society.[72] The appellate court also reiterated that statutory rules allow courts to rely on an 'objective standard of fairness'.[73]

It follows that, under the revised guidance provided on appeal, English courts will not permit their officers to act in a way that would be clearly wrong for the court itself to act.[74] Such an interpretation is consistent with the interventionist, objective,[75] and expansive view of fairness later followed by the Court of Appeal in *Adler*.[76]

With reference to pre-packaged administration procedures, concerns over fairness are heightened by additional issues. These include the need to address information asymmetries, and the need to prevent time constraints from being used by insiders[77] (debtors and negotiating creditors) to promote individual priorities at the expense of the collective interest of creditors.[78] Successive

---

[1987] BCLC 257; *Re TH Knitwear (Wholesale) Ltd* [1988] Ch 275; *Re Lune Metal Products Ltd* [2006] EWCA Civ 1720, [2007] 2 BCLC 746.

70 Also known as *Bloom v Pensions Regulator* [2013] UKSC 52.

71 Notably, it was argued that *Wigzell* (n 69) was binding authority in favour of a test of unconscionability, which—if followed—meant that the rule in *Ex parte James* reached the point at which it might never be successfully invoked.

72 As noted by the court, this standard is flexible because it is not laid down by statute. The advantage of such a flexible approach is that it can adapt in line with the evolution of collective thinking. The drawback is one of predictability: 'Lehman Brothers v MacNamara' (n 65) [37].

73 Ibid [84].

74 Ibid [68].

75 Ibid [38].

76 *AGPS Bondco* (n 37).

77 However, testing this hypothesis and finding no evidence of this problem, see: A Polo, 'Secured Creditor Control in Bankruptcy: Costs and Conflict' (2012) <https://papers.ssrn.com/sol3/papers.cfm?abstract_id=2084881>.

78 On pre-packaged administrations, see (among others): P Walton, 'Pre-packaged Administrations—Trick or Treat?' (2006) 19 Insolv. Int. 113; Vaccari (n 20); C Umfreville, 'Pre-packaged Administrations and Company Voluntary Arrangements: The Case for a Holistic Approach to Reform' (2020) 30(11) ICCLR 581; B Adebola, 'Transforming Perceptions: The Development of Pre-pack Regulations in England and Wales' (2023) 43(1) OJLS 150. For a comparative overview of pre-packaged approaches to corporate rescue, see: J Payne, 'Debt

investigations into pre-packs suggest that most of these concerns are grossly exaggerated.[79]

Several reports have been produced to assess how pre-packaged administration operates in practice.[80] The most recent report[81] forms the basis of the new regulations enacted in 2021. These regulations significantly restrict pre-packaged sales to parties connected with the debtor, and provide better protection to unsecured creditors.[82]

The changes introduced in the Statement of Insolvency Practice (SIP) 16 in 2009, and subsequently in the law, suggest that the legislator wants the parties to focus on two different sets of questions. The issue most frequently discussed is the valuation of distressed debtors, and whether a pre-packaged "fire" sale represents the best value for all affected parties. The second issue, which is strictly connected with the topic of this chapter, is whether a decision to pre-pack has been rightly made.[83]

Most scholarship considers pre-packaged procedures to be fair when they achieve good value for company creditors.[84] The desire to preserve the key

---

Restructuring in English Law: Lessons from the United States and the Need for Reform' (2014) 130 LQR 282; A Gurrea-Martinez, 'The Rise of Pre-Packs as a Restructuring Tool: Theory, Evidence and Policy' (2023) 24 EBOR 93.

[79] S Frisby, 'A Preliminary Analysis of Pre-packaged Administrations' Report to R3—The Association of Business Recovery Professionals (August 2017, R3—The Association of Business Recovery Professionals) 5; A Bloom and S Harris, 'Pre-packaged Administrations—What Should Be Done Given the Current Disquiet?' (2006) 8 Insolv. Int. 122, 122–123.

[80] Frisby (n 79); Graham (n 19).

[81] Insolvency Service, 'Prepack Sales in Administration Report 2020' (8 October 2020) <https://www.gov.uk/government/publications/pre-pack-sales-in-administration/pre-pack-sales-in-administration-report>.

[82] Against, see Gurrea-Martinez (n 78) [6.2.3.2]. The author's argument that the new framework has several weaknesses and may lead to "suboptimal outcomes for creditors" and to a problem of "opinion shopping" is theoretically sound but practically baseless. One in three administrations continue to be carried out through a pre-pack sale after the Regulations 2021: A Plainer et al, 'Legislative Developments: The New Pre-Pack Regulations' (4 March 2022) Global Restructuring Review <https://globalrestructuringreview.com/guide/the-art-of-the-pre-pack/edition-2/article/legislative-developments-the-new-pre-pack-regulations) [5.1] and suggests that pre-packs are a needed and not abused marked practice, and that the Regulations 2021 did not unduly restrict the parties' freedom to use this process.

[83] Adebola (n 78) 159.

[84] V Finch, 'Pre-packaged Administrations: Bargains in the Shadow of Insolvency or Shadowy Bargains?' (2006) JBL 568; M Parkhouse and K Scott,

features of pre-packs (confidentiality, information asymmetries and quick turnaround) has resulted in the legislator waiving any requirement for a fairness test in such procedures. As a result, no leeway is left in pre-packs either for fairness tests or for mandatory ESG considerations, even if parties nonetheless consider such factors on a voluntary basis.

Other legal systems such as the US bankruptcy law require plans to be "fair and equitable",[85] meaning that they must not discriminate unfairly and must comply with the statutory order of distribution of assets in insolvency.[86] This is currently not the case in the UK, even though the objective fairness test in traditional administration procedures is not too dissimilar from the US approach.

5.2.2.3 Company voluntary arrangements

CVAs are statutory contracts between a debtor and its creditors. They result in agreements—which take the form of reorganisation plans—that involve delayed or reduced debt payments or capital restructurings. Such agreements cannot modify the rights of secured creditors except with the consent of the creditor concerned.

This procedure does not require active involvement of either the courts (who are not required to sanction a plan) or insolvency practitioners (who do not run the debtor's business but simply supervise the implementation of the plan). Nevertheless, a fairness test is also present in CVAs. Interested parties may challenge an approved CVA on two grounds:

1. the CVA unfairly prejudices the interests of a creditor, member, or contributory of the company;[87]

'A Fair Deal?' (2009) 159 New Law Journal 421; E Vaccari, 'Pre-pack Pool: Is It Worth It?' (2018) 29(12) ICCLR 697 (arguing that fairness could be achieved through a system of mandatory referrals to external monitors—the Pre-pack Pool—later partially effected by the Regulations 2021); B Adebola, 'The Case of Mandatory Referrals to the Pre-pack Pool' (2019) 32(2) Insolv. Int. 71; Umfreville (n 78).

[85] On this point, see: chapter 3, *sub* [3.2.2].

[86] Payne (n 78); B Adebola, 'Proposed Feasibility Oversight for Pre-pack Administration in England and Wales: Window Dressing or Effective Reform?' (2015) 8 JBL 591. Reference is made to 11 US Code, § 1129(b): 'the court, on request of the debtor, shall confirm the plan [...] if the plan *does not discriminate unfairly*, and *is fair and equitable*, with respect to each class of claims or interests that is impaired under, and has not accepted, the plan' (emphasis added). This test only applies in case one class of creditors has not accepted the plan and it is impaired (affected) by it.

[87] IA 1986, s 6(1)(a).

2. there has been some material irregularity at or in relation to the meeting of the company or in relation to the relevant qualifying decision procedure.[88]

If a court is satisfied that one of the grounds has been met, it may revoke or suspend the CVA. A court may also order that a new creditors' meeting be held, with the new vote again having to be by means of a qualifying decision procedure.[89]

The issue of whether the CVA was unfairly prejudicial is to be determined based on the information available at the time the CVA was approved (i.e. with no benefit of hindsight).[90] There is no unfair prejudice if a reasonable and honest person in the same position as the creditors would have approved the CVA.[91]

In the absence of a single and universal test for judging unfairness,[92] general guidance has been provided in cases like *SISU Capital*,[93] *T & N Ltd*,[94] and *Lazari v New Look*.[95] In the latter case, the court held that providing for differential treatment of sub-groups of creditors is not, for that reason alone, unfairly prejudicial.[96] The court accepted that its authority was constrained by the broader principle of equality of treatment. As a result, for a proposal to be considered "fair", the court considered it necessary that the statutory majority shared sufficiently similar rights with the minority it sought to bind.[97]

Previous case law clarified that, where an approved proposal conflicts with a statutory provision (e.g. a distribution rule), and where that statutory provision refers to the substance of the proposal and results in a clear prejudice, a court should not approve the proposal, except in circumstances where this differential treatment is justified.[98] This is, for instance, the case where the debtor is

---

88 Ibid s 6(1)(b).

89 Ibid s 6(4).

90 *Prudential Assurance* (n 51) [71].

91 Ibid [96].

92 Ibid [74].

93 *SISU Capital Fund Ltd v Tucker* [2005] EWHC 2170 (Ch).

94 *Re T & N Ltd* [2004] EWHC 2361 (Ch).

95 *Lazari Properties 2 Ltd v New Look Retailers Ltd* [2021] EWHC 1209 (Ch).

96 On this point, see also: *Mourant & Co Trustees Ltd v Sixty UK Ltd (in administration)* [2010] EWHC 1890 (Ch).

97 *Lazari Properties 2* (n 95) [197].

98 *Re a debtor (No. 101 of 1999)* [2001] 1 BCLC 54 [63e] (arguing that differential treatment, which is not assented to by a creditor who considers that he has been less favourably treated, may well give cause for an enquiry, but it does not necessarily prove unfair prejudice); *Prudential Assurance* (n 51) [103] (arguing that guaranteed landlords cannot receive the same return as non-guaranteed

able to demonstrate that differential treatment is necessary to ensure fairness[99] or to enable the company to continue trading.[100]

Courts are inclined to follow the professional judgements of insolvency practitioners[101] without deferring all of their discretion to them. In *Carraway*,[102] Mr Justice Zacaroli held that it was appropriate to revoke a CVA despite it already having been terminated. The CVA treated one of the creditors as critical to the company's ability to continue trading. However, this "critical creditor" was a shareholder. The proposal envisaged the company paying its shareholders almost twice as much as *all* impaired creditors under the CVA—despite offering no justification for this payment.

To assess whether conduct is unfair, courts look at all of the circumstances surrounding a case.[103] They look suspiciously when a CVA's approval has been achieved only because of the votes of a large swathe of creditors who are unaffected by the plan.[104]

Overall, the case law agrees that the unfair prejudice must be affected by the terms of the arrangement itself, not by some external agreement. Unfair prejudice must be the result of the challenging party being in a position that is *significantly* worse than:

- the outcome they would have achieved in the relevant alternative (vertical comparison), usually a winding up procedure;[105]
- the position of a class of creditors compared with other creditors or classes of creditors under the plan (horizontal comparison).[106]

---

ones); *Lazari Properties 2* (n 95) [170] (arguing that differential treatment is not inherently prejudicial).

99 *Sea Voyager Maritime Inc v Bielecki* [1999] 1 BCLC 133.

100 *SEA Assets Ltd v Perusahaan Perseroan (Persero) PT Perusahaan Penerbangan Garuda Indonesia* [2001] EWCA Civ 1696 [45]–[46]; *IRC v Wimbledon Football Club Ltd* [2004] EWHC 1020 (Ch) [18]; *SISU Capital* (n 93) [69].

101 *SISU Capital* (n 93).

102 *Carraway Guildford (Nominee A) Ltd v Regis UK Ltd* [2021] EWHC 1294 (Ch).

103 *Re a debtor (No. 101 of 1999)* (n 98) 63d; *SISU Capital* (n 93) [71]; *Re Mizen Design/Built Ltd* [2023] EWHC 127 (Ch) [45].

104 *Re Mizen Design* (n 103) [46].

105 This point was made in the Cork Report itself (Report of the Review Committee on Insolvency Law and Practice (1982) Cmnd 8558), at paras 264(4) and 378. There have been cases where the comparison was with an alternative scheme of arrangement: *Re T & N Ltd* (n 94) [81]; *Prudential Assurance* (n 51) [95]; and *Re Mizen Design* (n 103) [27].

106 *Prudential Assurance* (n 51).

The returns to creditors in the counterfactual have been termed the "irreducible minimum" below which the return in the CVA cannot go.[107] Though relevant and potentially important, the fact that a particular class of creditors could and might have blocked a scheme does not necessarily mean that they have been unfairly prejudiced.[108] Equally, the fact that a CVA could (or could not) have been approved using a Part 26A restructuring plan is also not a reason to dismiss a claim for unfair prejudice.[109]

Additionally, it is not for the court to speculate whether the terms of the proposed CVA were the best that could have been obtained, or whether it would have been better if it had not contained all of the terms it did contain.[110] This represents a significant difference from the discretion that courts can exercise in sanctioning a restructuring plan. This difference in the exercise of the court's discretion can be explained by the more limited efficacy of CVAs. Compared to restructuring plans, CVAs require higher majority thresholds, cannot bind secured creditors without their consent, and cannot be imposed on dissenting classes of creditors (as creditors are not divided into classes). Hence, it is only reasonable for courts to exercise a less interventionist role given the comparatively small risk of unfairly prejudicial treatment against minority creditors.

5.2.2.4 Discretion and fairness under the law

Except for pre-packaged sales, English courts are more likely to challenge a rescue deal whenever information asymmetries,[111] confidentiality, time constraints, or strategic use of the procedure[112] suggest that an unfair outcome has been imposed on dissenting and/or non-participating creditors. Such a challenge is conducted based on an objective standard of assessment that relies on the concept of fairness.[113]

---

107 *Mourant & Co Trustees* (n 96) [67].

108 *SISU Capital* (n 93) [134]; *Prudential Assurance* (n 51) [95].

109 *Re Mizen Design* (n 103) [48].

110 *SISU Capital* (n 93) [73]; *Prudential Assurance* (n 51) [82].

111 See *Re Sunbird Business Services Ltd* [2020] All ER (D) 39 (Sep) with reference to schemes and *Virgin Active* (n 23) with reference to restructuring plans.

112 In *Re Prezzo Investco Ltd* [2023] EWHC 1679 (Ch) [91] and *Nasmyth Group* (n 37) [116], the courts held that they need to be satisfied that the plan is not going to be used as an "instrument of abuse".

113 The circumstance that different judges might reach different views on the instant case should not be used to justify that fairness is ultimately a subjective standard, as it was wrongly asserted in *Lehman Brothers v Lomas* (n 66) [70] and in *Heis v Financial Services Compensation Scheme Ltd* [2018] EWHC 1372 (Ch) [143(1)].

This substantive, as opposed to procedural, test has grown significantly in relevance and scope since the early cases in the area were decided. The contentious nature of restructuring procedures means that expert evidence must be provided regarding the valuation of debtor's assets and regarding the treatment of all affected parties. Especially in procedures like CVAs and restructuring plans, it is essential to demonstrate that the "restructuring surplus"[114] is divided among interested parties—as these procedures are not subject to the usual statutory order of priorities.

The next section assesses to what extent such powers have resulted or could result in ESG being considered in English restructuring proceedings.

5.2.3 An ESG Critique of English Insolvency Law

This sub-section determines if and to what extent an objective notion of fairness, grounded on the standard of a right-thinking person representing the current views of society, has accommodated or can accommodate the inclusion of ESG considerations in the assessment of rescue plans.

5.2.3.1 ESG considerations

Chapter 2 has discussed ESG through a broader analysis of corporate social responsibility (CSR) issues and their relevance for the topic of insolvency and restructuring law. It demonstrated that sound ESG performance reduces a firm's likelihood of becoming financially distressed.[115]

Much like courts, English insolvency practitioners (trustees, liquidators, and administrators) have wide discretion in exercising their powers. At times, they are faced with a conundrum: should they prioritise environmental concerns over the maximisation of creditors' returns? This is a problem particularly where debtor companies operate in a highly regulated environment, due to the environmentally impactful nature of their operations and the hazardous materials they use in their business activities. Courts have held that preferential consideration should be given to environmental issues where insolvency practitioners are appointed not only for the purpose of maximising the return to creditors, but also to address any health, safety, and environmental concerns that could possibly arise from the dispute.[116] This approach shows that whilst

---

[114] This term refers to any value or potential future benefit that arises post restructuring, which is allocated to low-ranking or subordinated pre-petition creditors and shareholders through debt-for-equity swaps.

[115] Among others, see: AM Habib, 'Do Business Strategies and Environmental, Social, And Governance (ESG) Performance Mitigate the Likelihood of Financial Distress? A Multiple Mediation Model' (2023) 9 Heliyon e17847.

[116] *Re Baglan Operations Ltd* [2022] EWHC 647 (Ch) [55].

the English framework is flexible enough to prioritise environmental concerns in insolvency disputes, it may only do so where the insolvency practitioner's appointment clearly reflects such concerns. In all other instances, interested parties face an uphill battle to hold practitioners accountable for breaches of environmental duties.

One way of prioritising environmental issues is by granting preferential treatment to environmental claims in insolvency procedures.[117] However, the preferential treatment granted to landfill taxes and climate change levies under IA 1986[118] was removed by the Enterprise Act 2002 and was not reinstated when the tax authority was granted preferential creditor status in 2020.[119] There are no plans to introduce any new preferential treatment rights into the English corporate insolvency framework.

Similar considerations broadly apply to social issues. For instance, if an insolvent employer fails to pay money owed to their employees, the Employment Rights Act 1996 (ERA 1996) and the IA 1986 will try to ensure that these employees are not unduly and detrimentally affected by this circumstance. However, the insolvency protections are rather limited.[120] This preferential treatment is limited to £800 in total, whilst the amount due for accrued holiday pay is not capped (but limited to a period of six weeks).[121] In addition, employees can claim for any unpaid contributions towards occupational pension schemes and state scheme premiums, all within certain limits.[122] On the contrary, the ERA 1986 protects employees to a greater degree. The ERA 1986 allows employees to claim, from the Redundancy Payments Service, sums due for statutory redundancy payments, arrears of pay (up to £538 per week for eight weeks), payments for failure to give statutory notice, holiday pay.[123] Consequently, employees' rights are protected under the law as a whole. The same cannot be said for tort claimants, who do not enjoy any sort of special treatment in insolvency law—despite their position having been significantly

---

[117] World Bank, 'Insolvency and Climate Change: Considerations for Policy Makers' (2024) (forthcoming).

[118] IA 1986, sch 6, paras 3B–3C.

[119] Finance Act 2020, effective from 1 December 2020.

[120] IA 1986, sch 6, para 9.

[121] Ibid sch 6, para 10.

[122] Ibid sch 6, para 8.

[123] L Conway and D Ferguson, 'Employment Rights and Insolvency' *House of Commons Library* (24 April 2020) 4 <https://researchbriefings.files.parliament.uk/documents/SN00651/SN00651.pdf>.

elevated by recent judgments in seminal tort cases concerning breaches of environmental obligations.[124]

Finally, in terms of governance considerations, reference could be made to English law's stance on the exercise of third-party releases in restructuring procedures. Third-party plan releases are provisions in a restructuring plan that release or limit the liability of non-debtor parties (e.g. guarantors) to other non-debtor parties (e.g. the debtor's creditors). They potentially present serious governance and accountability issues. Guarantees are usually provided by the company's owners or by other insiders who are aware of potential governance breaches within the debtor company. Unrestricted use of such releases may result in the promotion of poor governance practices.

Third-party releases of non-proprietary rights are common in English law schemes of arrangement and, more recently, restructuring plans. In most cases, third-party releases are necessary to ensure the effectiveness of a plan. Imagine that a company agrees to reduce the rent paid under a tenancy agreement as part of a restructuring plan. If another entity acts as a guarantor for such an agreement, the landlord could claim the balance from the guarantor, and the guarantor could claim back the amount paid against the restructured entity. A "ricochet" claim such as this may well undermine the restructuring because it would indicate that the affected claim had not been compromised.

Whilst commercially sensible, third-party releases may frustrate the legitimate expectations of creditors who are relying on cross-guarantees and/or other forms of cross-liability arrangement.[125] Unsurprisingly, English courts[126] held that, for a third-party release to be effective, it needs to appear necessary, it must be expressly referred to in the scheme/plan, and its inclusion must be disclosed in the explanatory statement. In the context of a scheme/plan, a third-party release can never be implied. At the same time, the focus on the release being "necessary" and "disclosed" means that, if a scheme/plan is "fair",[127] governance considerations may be set aside, and third parties may not be held accountable for the debtor's breaches of contractual, tortious or environmental duties (among others).

Overall, the traditional pro-creditor attitude embedded in English law does little to prioritise ESG concerns in insolvency and restructuring procedures.

---

[124] *Chandler v Cape plc* [2012] 3 All ER 640 (CA); *Lungowe v Vedanta Resources plc* [2019] UKSC 20; *HRH Okpabi v Royal Dutch Shell* [2021] UKSC 3.

[125] I Kokorin, 'Third-Party Releases in Insolvency of Multinational Enterprise Groups' (2021) 18(1) ECFR 107, arguing that third-party releases are a matter of commercial necessity.

[126] *Oceanfill Ltd v Nuffield Health Wellbeing Ltd and Cannons Group Ltd* [2022] EWHC 2178 (Ch).

[127] See above *sub* [5.2.2.1] on the meaning of "fairness" in restructuring plans.

However, this section has also evidenced that such considerations can be accommodated in the current framework. As a result, it is now appropriate to investigate to what extent courts do actually consider ESG criteria in the adjudication of insolvency and restructuring cases.

5.2.3.2 Lessons from practice

In *ClientEarth v Shell*,[128] an English court ruled that the non-profit environmental law organisation, ClientEarth, which held a minority share in Shell, failed to establish a *prima facie* derivative claim against the directors concerning the company's climate change risk management strategy. This case highlights the challenges minority shareholders face in influencing company boards, especially regarding ESG goals. Directors are not legally bound by self-imposed ESG goals during solvent times, which raises questions about the enforceability of such goals in restructuring or insolvency without statutory mandates.

Statutory regulations can help shareholders monitor corporate activities. For example, the UK's Companies (Miscellaneous Reporting) Regulations 2018 require large companies to report on various matters, including the environmental impact of their operations (CA 2006, section 172(d)).[129] Whilst some research indicates that directors have incentives to promote ESG goals,[130] other studies suggest that companies may alter their ESG reporting to satisfy raters, potentially leading to superficial improvements aimed at pleasing investors and consumers.[131] Due to the risk of "cosmetic compliance" with

[128] *ClientEarth v Shell plc* [2023] EWHC 1897 (Ch). For a comment, see: D Gibbs-Kneller, 'Corporate Strategy on Climate Risk in The Courtroom: Not Worth Powder in Shot' (2023) 25(4) Env. L. Rev. 326.

[129] See, among others: SF Copp, 'S.172 of the Companies Act 2006 Fails People and the Planet?' (2010) 31(12) Comp. Law. 406; E Lynch, 'Section 172: A Ground-Breaking Reform of Director's Duties, or the Emperor's New Clothes?' (2012) 33(7) Comp. Law. 196; A Jones, 'For the Greater Good? Directors' Duties to Manage Environmental Liabilities during Insolvency Proceedings' (2021) 34(4) Insolv. Int. 108.

[130] M Barzuza, Q Curtis and D Webber, 'CEOs Have Real Incentives to Promote ESG' (26 October 2023) <https://www.promarket.org/2023/10/26/ceos-have-real-incentives-to-promote-esg/>. The authors of this study suggest that there are five powerful factors that influence directors to pursue ESG goals. These include personal risks (risk of termination; undiversifiable risks; and mitigation costs not borne by directors); the need to attract socially inclined investors and hedge funds; and market pressure.

[131] K Albitar and T Abdoush, 'Do Corporate Governance Mechanisms and ESG Disclosure Drive CSR Narrative Tones?' (2023) 28(4) IJFE 3876.

ESG standards,[132] more comprehensive ("narrative") reporting approaches are being developed to provide better ESG context.[133]

Theoretically, ESG standards can be integrated into distressed asset investing and restructurings by incorporating them into business plans, operations, reporting requirements, board composition, executive compensation, and financial modelling.[134] In the US, restructuring proceedings have addressed environmental liabilities.[135] However, in the UK, such liabilities are often discharged through liquidation,[136] incentivising companies to liquidate rather than restructure businesses with environmental burdens. If restructured, the buyer might need to address these liabilities to continue operations.

Social issues like employment protection are typically considered in restructuring procedures, but there is hesitation to apply ESG criteria. There is scant scholarship on using ESG criteria in insolvency, and the Supreme Court's decision in *BTI 2014 v Sequana*[137] clarified that directors' prioritisation of external considerations triggers only upon insolvency,[138] not before. Directors do not owe fiduciary duties to creditors.[139]

Credit rating agencies like Moody's and Standard & Poor's incorporate ESG risk assessments into their evaluations,[140] and there has been a rise in

---

[132] J Cornaggia and K Cornaggia, 'ESG Ratings Management' (18 August 2023) <https://ssrn.com/abstract=4520688>.

[133] G Michelon, G Trojanowski and R Sealy, 'Narrative Reporting: State of the Art and Future Challenges' (2022) 19(1) Accounting in Europe 7 <https://doi.org/10.1080/17449480.2021.1900582>.

[134] B Mirchandani, 'Distressed Credit and the ESG Opportunity' (*Forbes*, 5 August 2021) <https://www.forbes.com/sites/bhaktimirchandani/2021/08/05/distressed-credit-and-the-esg-opportunity/?sh=627912d128bc>; Mayer Brown, 'How ESG May Affect Refinancing and Restructurings of COVID-Era Debt' (April 2021) <https://www.mayerbrown.com/-/media/files/perspectives-events/publications/2021/04/how-esg-may-affect-refinancings-and-restructurings-of-covidera-debt_apr21.pdf>.

[135] *In re PG&E Corporation*, Bankruptcy Case No. 19-30088 (DM) (US Bankruptcy Court for the Northern District of California, San Francisco Division).

[136] E Vaccari and D Ehmke, 'Environmental Liabilities in Insolvency' in E Ghio and E Vaccari (eds), *The Perpetual Renewal of European Insolvency Law* (INSOL Europe 2024).

[137] *BTI 2014 LLC v Sequana SA* [2022] UKSC 25.

[138] IA 1986, ss 123(1)(e) and 122.

[139] S Sheikh, 'Serving Two Masters: Balancing Shareholders' and Creditors' Competing Interests' (2023) 34(6) ICCLR 305.

[140] Moody's, 'ESG Credit and Sustainable Finance' (2023) <https://www.moodys.com/newsandevents/topics/ESG-Credit-00702C>; S&P Global, 'ESG in

ESG-linked loans by institutional investors.[141] An Ernst and Young report indicated that three-quarters of institutional investors might divest from companies with poor environmental records.[142] Similarly, within restructuring, lenders and investors increasingly scrutinise a company's ESG policy, influencing funding decisions.[143]

The concept of fairness in restructuring is used to prevent the coercing of a minority of creditors into promoting adverse interests and is assessed based on available information at decision time. Courts have the authority to investigate better alternative plans, and minority creditors can express governance concerns within this fairness test. Environmental concerns, whilst less prominent, could be considered if raised by creditors.

Fairness allows deviations from equal creditor treatment if justified, and ESG considerations might validate differential treatment among creditors. As ESG concerns gain prominence, courts are likely to incorporate them into fairness and reasonableness tests. Integrating ESG goals into restructuring could offer new opportunities for distressed firms but requires multidisciplinary expertise among professionals and investors. Understanding regulatory changes, technological developments, reputational risks, climate-related litigation, and insurance costs is crucial for effective restructuring decisions.[144]

In conclusion, ESG considerations can be part of fairness and rationality tests in rescue procedures.[145] However, the English insolvency framework prioritises creditor protection over societal concerns, and judges may lack the expertise for independent ESG analyses. Thus, there is an argument for independently stress-testing restructuring deals against ESG considerations. Legislators should consider mandating that courts assess both fairness and ESG factors when approving or challenging restructuring plans.

Credit Ratings' (2023) <https://www.spglobal.com/ratings/en/research-insights/special-reports/esg-in-credit-ratings>.

141 K Fulton-Fleming, 'UK Distressed Restructuring: Why Are ESG Issues Important?' (2023) 16(6) C.R. & I. 225, 225.

142 Available at: <https://go.ey.com/482jFpD>.

143 Fulton-Fleming (n 141).

144 J Sarra, 'Insolvency Risk and Climate' (2019) Annual Review of Insolvency Law 279 <https://law-ccli-2019.sites.olt.ubc.ca/files/2020/02/Janis-Sarra-Insolvency-Risk-and-Climate.2019.pdf>.

145 Fulton-Fleming (n 141) 226–227. These include customer retention; long-term value enhancement; avoidance of breaches of directors' duties; mitigation of litigation risk; and divestment opportunities in areas with acute ESG risks.

5.3 LOCAL PUBLIC ENTITIES

5.3.1 Legal Framework

This part looks at the statutory framework that regulates local authorities in England only. The focus is on getting the "bigger picture" before detailing what happens when a local authority experiences financial distress.

5.3.1.1 Local authorities

Elected local authorities across England were established as early as the nineteenth century. They were corporate bodies incorporated either by a charter granted under the royal prerogative or by statute.[146] As there is no formal written constitution in England, there is no constitutional protection guaranteed for local government in England, neither for their existence nor for their powers or funding.

However, the principle pertaining to local authorities' power is now contained in section 1(1) of the Localism Act 2011, which provides that a local authority 'has [the] power to do anything that individuals generally may do'.

Following demographic changes after World War II, the Redcliffe-Maud committee (1969) recommended organising local government across England into a number of one-tier entities.[147] However, a change of government meant that statutory reforms went in the opposite direction and divided England into a number of two-tier entities. Although amended, the Local Government Act 1972 still sets out the basic framework of local authorities in England.

A local authority (often called a local council) is an elected body that provides a range of services for a geographical area. Local authorities in England can be divided into county councils (upper tier) and district, borough, and city councils (lower tier).

At a very local level, England has town and parish councils. These all have limited powers. At the opposite end of the spectrum, large cities tend to organise all of the services into one tier of local government. For instance, in London, services such as the fire service, police, and public transport are

---

[146] S Bailey, *Cross on Local Government Law* (Sweet & Maxwell, London, regularly updated) para 1-03.

[147] The Redcliffe-Maud commission recommended a system of single-tier unitary authorities for the whole of England, apart from for three metropolitan areas of Merseyside, Selnec (Greater Manchester), and the West Midlands (Birmingham and the Black Country). This report was accepted by the Labour Party government of the time despite considerable opposition. However, the Conservative Party won the June 1970 general election on a manifesto that committed them to a two-tier structure.

provided through a "joint authority" (the Greater London Authority). Besides the Greater London Authority, there are 32 borough councils[148] in London that deal with the services usually allocated to county and district councils, such as education, adult social care, refuse collection, and tax collection.

However, this distinction has lost some of its relevance today as the two-tier system has been replaced by a unitary one—predominantly in large cities. Where it exists, this single tier carries out all of the functions of county and district councils. In recent times, there has been a growing demand for the creation of more unitary authorities.[149]

The process of changing from a two-tier to a unitary local government system is normally referred to as "restructuring" or "reorganisation". The legal procedure can be found in sections 1 to 7 of the Local Government and Public Involvement in Health Act 2007. A separate procedure, under sections 8 to 10 of the same act, applies to the merger of different district councils. For the moment, access to this procedure is elective, and there is no obligation to merge the responsibilities of county and district councils into unitary entities.

As of May 2024, there are 317 local authorities in England. Of these, 21 are county councils, 164 are district councils, and 132 are single-tier authorities. Of the latter, 32 are London boroughs and 36 are metropolitan boroughs.[150] Besides that, 10 combined authorities have been established in England via the Local Democracy, Economic Development and Construction Act 2009. These are not local authorities but joint legal bodies through which groups of authorities can work together.

Local governance is organised around periodic elections for local councillors. There are three models of local governance: mayor and cabinet, leader and cabinet, or the committee system.[151] Local governance can deviate from these models, so that local residents can directly elect their mayor after a referendum on the matter or if a resolution is adopted to this effect. At present, there are 13 directly elected mayors in local government.[152] However, the system has

---

148 <https://directory.londoncouncils.gov.uk/>.

149 M Sandford, 'Unitary Local Government' *House of Commons Library* (22 July 2021) <https://researchbriefings.files.parliament.uk/documents/CBP-9056/CBP-9056.pdf>.

150 M Sandford, 'Local Government in England: Structures' *House of Commons Library* (15 September 2021) <https://researchbriefings.files.parliament.uk/documents/SN07104/SN07104.pdf>.

151 The Local Authorities (Committee System) (England) Regulations 2012.

152 M Sandford, 'Directly Elected Mayors' *House of Commons Library* (Research Briefings, 2024) appendix A <https://researchbriefings.files.parliament.uk/documents/SN05000/SN05000.pdf>.

not been accepted unanimously, as the process of directly electing mayors has been reversed in six cases.[153]

5.3.1.2 Functions and missions

Councils have core statutory obligations to deliver certain services,[154] such as social care, schools, housing, planning, and waste collection. Councils are also under a statutory obligation to deliver additional services such as licensing, business support (including trading standards), fire and public safety, libraries, registrar services and pest control. These duties span numerous statutes. This makes it difficult for local government to know the exact scope of its powers and duties, so much so that the UK government agreed to compile a list of these statutory duties.[155]

Whilst these are core requirements, councils are unable to provide services of the same standard across the country for a variety of reasons, including the political agenda of the party controlling the council, but also (and more importantly) the needs of the council's users.

Under section 101 of the Local Government Act 1972, counties and districts may agree to undertake functions for one another. If they do so, the responsibility for the function remains with the council to which it legally belongs. In England, the government retains the legal power to replace a local authority in delivering the functions attributed to it.[156]

The rules on reporting financial results have changed over the last 30 years. According to the Audit Commission Act 1998, the auditors appointed by a local authority had to be satisfied that the authority had made proper arrangements to use its resources in an economical, efficient, and effective manner;[157] had a statutory right to documents and information underpinned by criminal sanction;[158] had considered whether to make a report in the public interest;[159] and had sought a judicial declaration in respect of any items of account that

---

153 Ibid 13.

154 The list of essential services provided by local authorities can be found here: House of Lords, 'Local Authority Provision of Essential Services—Debate on 29 January 2019' (2019) <https://researchbriefings.files.parliament.uk/documents/LLN-2019-0006/LLN-2019-0006.pdf>.

155 <https://www.data.gov.uk/dataset/01171494-e40b-463f-9967-56d158412321/statutory-duties-placed-on-local-government>.

156 Local Government Act 1999, s 15.

157 Audit Commission Act 1998, s 5.

158 Ibid s 6.

159 Ibid s 8.

were contrary to the law.[160] This system was perceived as being burdensome and was deeply reformed when the Coalition Government came to power in 2010.

The Local Audit and Accountability Act 2014, currently applicable, introduced a decentralised audit regime for local authorities and abolished the pre-existing Audit Commission.[161] Currently, six different entities have a statutory role in overseeing and monitoring the framework for local authority accounting and auditing. However, none of them has a statutory responsibility to act as a system leader. This complicated system led to audit delays and to high fees being charged to audit local accounts.[162] Consequently, the Redmond review (2020) suggested introducing significant changes to the auditing system.[163] These recommendations had not been implemented at the time of writing. The Conservative government was also considering a significant overhaul of the structure, mandate and funding of local authorities.

In England, there has been increasing pressure to merge county and district councils. This pressure is spearheaded by independent reports,[164] as well as the Levelling Up, Housing and Communities Committee.[165] Mergers between different local entities may result in long term financial savings and better services for citizens. However, they also carry financial and performance risks, especially where the new unitary authority has to operate alongside other trusts and entities to provide local services to the communities it is tasked

[160] Ibid s 17. See N Dobson, 'Local Authority Corporate Law' (2003) 6(3) JLGL 50, 55.

[161] L Ferry, H Midgley and A Murphie, 'Local Government Auditing in England' in L Ferry and P Ruggiero (eds), *Auditing Practices in Local Governments: An International Comparison* (Emerald 2022) 57–64.

[162] M Sandford, 'Local Audit and Accountability in England' *House of Commons Library* (Research Briefing, 20 February 2024) 26 <https://researchbriefings.files.parliament.uk/documents/CBP-7240/CBP-7240.pdf>.

[163] T Redmond, 'Independent Review into the Oversight of Local Audit and the Transparency of Local Authority Financing Reporting' (September 2020) 10 <https://assets.publishing.service.gov.uk/government/uploads/system/uploads/attachment_data/file/916217/Redmond_Review.pdf>.

[164] PwC, 'Evaluating the Importance of Scale in Proposals for Local Government Reorganisation' (August 2020) <https://www.countycouncilsnetwork.org.uk/new-analysis-reveals-that-single-unitary-councils-could-deliver-3bn-saving-over-five-years-and-maximise-the-benefits-of-economic-growth-and-housing-policy/>.

[165] Housing, Communities and Local Government Committee, 'Progress on Devolution in England. Fourth Report of Session 2021–22' (HC 36, 1 October 2021) <https://committees.parliament.uk/publications/7467/documents/78200/default/>.

with overseeing. In the Levelling Up White Paper,[166] the Conservative government confirmed its intention to deal with this issue. It also announced that negotiations have begun in respect of two new or revised Mayoral Combined Authorities, as well as revealing that negotiations were taking place to agree on "trailblazer" devolution deals with the West Midlands and Greater Manchester. Mergers are difficult to negotiate, as evidenced by the attempted deal between Stratford-on-Avon and Warwick. Despite the councils being of similar size and financially in good condition, and despite an independent report raising no major objections to the merger,[167] the deal was ultimately unsuccessful due to concerns over a joint venture that one of the councils was participating in.[168] This suggests that there might be insufficient incentives for councils to move to a one-tier system on a voluntary basis. The White Paper called for the introduction of a stricter "accountability framework" for mayors. However, there was no provision for a mandatory move to a one-tier system. The future of these reforms needs to be reassessed under the Labour government.

5.3.1.3 Funding

Local authorities can rely on diverse sources of funding. Besides receiving central government funding and a portion of business rates, local authorities rely on council tax, fees and charges for the services that they provide (such as planning applications), and loans.

Government funding is allocated through grants, the largest of which is the annual Revenue Support Grant. This grant is not ring-fenced, whilst some additional grants are ring-fenced (e.g. the Public Health Grant). Additional grants are distributed between authorities according to separate criteria.

The government's standard annual funding, which has been cut dramatically in recent years, is complemented by funding from the Public Works Loan Board (PWLB) to go towards more significant capital projects. In recent years, councils have increasingly relied on loans from the PWLB. Furthermore, local authorities retain 50% of the business rate, even if the government intends to

---

166 HM Government, 'Levelling Up the United Kingdom' (White Paper, CP 604, 2022) <https://assets.publishing.service.gov.uk/government/uploads/system/uploads/attachment_data/file/1052706/Levelling_Up_WP_HRES.pdf>.

167 C West, 'Stratford-on-Avon DC and Warwick DC Financial Disclosure Review' (Local Government Association, 24 May 2021) <https://www.southwarwickshire.org.uk/doc/210677/name/Financial%20Review.pdf>.

168 O Rudgewick, 'Authorities Scrap Merger amid Council-Owned Company Concerns' (Public Finance, 22 April 2022) <https://www.publicfinance.co.uk/news/2022/04/authorities-scrap-merger-amid-council-owned-company-concerns?utm_source=Adestra&amp%3Bamp%3Butm_medium=email&amp%3Bamp%3Butm_term=>.

increase this percentage to 75%. Some areas have retained 100% of business rates since 2017–2018.

With reference to council tax, local authorities can set their own rates, and they may retain all of the revenues they receive from council tax. However, rates need to sit within the council tax bands fixed by the government. Additionally, annual rises in council tax are subject to "referendum principles" set by the Secretary of State. Finally, fees and charges are not really an additional source of revenue. In most cases, fees must not exceed the cost of providing services, and in many cases, fee levels are set nationally.

Local authorities may also derive commercial income from their ownership of assets or from their investments. In recent years, some councils have sought to generate alternative sources of revenue by borrowing money to invest in commercial property. This results in uncertain revenue streams and may also expose the council to huge losses should these investments prove unsuccessful and unprofitable.[169]

Each year, local authorities in England are allocated funding through central government grants. The amount of funding offered is determined by the annual Local Government Finance Settlement. In December 2015, the government published indicative funding levels for the following four financial years (2016–2020), but there have been no more multi-year settlements for local government since 2020.

The funding landscape of local government is thus highly fragmented and complex. In 2023, the government decided to simplify it, in particular by making funding available in larger pots geared to strategic purposes.[170]

5.3.1.4 Other bodies

Not all public services are delivered by local authorities. Some are delivered at a local level by national organisations that are not accountable to local government. An example would be health services, which are delivered via the National Health Service (NHS). Other examples include welfare benefits and employment services, and probation and prison services.

All parts of England are covered by (at least) one local enterprise partnership (LEP). LEPs were established in 2010–2011 to coordinate local economic

---

169 M Loughlin, 'Innovative Financing in Local Government: The Limits of Legal Instrumentalism' (1990) Public Law 372 (part 1) and (1991) Public Law 568 (part 2).

170 Department for Levelling Up, Housing and Communities, 'Guidance: Simplifying the Funding Landscape for Local Authorities', last updated 10 January 2024. https://www.gov.uk/government/publications/simplifying-the-funding-landscape-for-local-authorities/simplifying-the-funding-landscape-for-local-authorities>.

development and growth. Whilst they work closely with local and combined authorities, and often include councillors on their boards, they are not formally accountable to these authorities.[171] LEPs are in the process of being integrated into local authorities, and government funding of these entities has ceased. However, local authorities can decide to continue operating LEPs as private enterprises.[172] The rules outlined in this part of the book do not apply to partnerships or to any other public–private corporate entities. However, based on the considerations made *sub* 5.4.3 with reference to utility companies providing essential services, there might be an argument to extend special administration regimes to cover private LEPs in financial distress.

Hospitals in the UK are not funded in the same way as local authorities. The NHS is funded through taxes and a portion of national insurance contributions. Funding for health services in England is provided by the budget of the Department for Health and Social Care. A small portion of the money is generated by patient charges. Individual NHS organisations—such as hospital trusts—can generate additional income, for example, through parking charges, land sales and treating private patients.

To ensure that the service provided by NHS trusts is financially viable, the government created NHS Improvement (NHSI). NHSI seeks to reduce the proportion of NHS trusts in deficit from the peak of 66% reached in the 2015–2016 financial year.[173] In any case, the rules governing NHS trusts are separate from the laws regulating local authorities in distress.

5.3.2 Legal Framework of Local Authorities in Distress

The insolvency procedures discussed *sub* 5.2.1 are not available to local authorities, and no legal framework tailored to the insolvency of a local authority currently exists.

---

171 The Government is conducting a review on the role, structure and functioning of local enterprise partnerships. This may lead to councils losing their role of governance in these partnerships.

172 Department for Business and Trade, and Department for Levelling Up, Housing and Communities, 'Guidance for Local Enterprise Partnerships (LEPs) and Local and Combined Authorities: Integration of LEP Functions into Local Democratic Institutions' (4 August 2023) <https://www.gov.uk/government/publications/local-enterprise-partnerships-integration-of-lep-functions-into-local-democratic-institutions/guidance-for-local-enterprise-partnerships-leps-and-local-and-combined-authorities-integration-of-lep-functions-into-local-democratic-institutions>.

173 See <https://www.kingsfund.org.uk/projects/nhs-in-a-nutshell/trusts-deficit>.

Local authorities are required by law to balance their budgets. Technically, they cannot become insolvent. Whilst no insolvency procedures are available to local authorities, several measures are available to them when they are facing financial difficulties. When all other remedies have proven ineffective, local authorities can request their chief financial officer (CFO) to issue a section 114 notice.[174] This notice bars all new expenditures, except for those that safeguard vulnerable people and statutory services.

A CFO leads the authority's financial plans. CFOs must be qualified accountants. They have statutory duties, including a duty to report any unlawful financial activity involving the authority (past, present or proposed) and a duty to report failure to set or keep to a balanced budget. They also have several statutory powers to perform this role. CFOs have the power and legal responsibility to suspend a local authority's spending for a period if they consider that the council does not have a balanced budget or if there is an imminent prospect of default.

CFOs can issue two types of notices. The first is a notice under section 114(2) of the Local Government Finance Act 1988 (LGFA 1988), also known as an advisory notice. This advisory notice is only issued when the local authority is about to make a decision that would be unlawful. Its effect is to prevent a local authority from pursuing such conduct.[175]

Secondly, section 114(3) LGFA 1988 grants CFOs with a more general power to stop a local authority from entering into new transactions and from performing some of its existing ones:

> if it appears to him that the expenditure of the authority incurred (including expenditure it proposes to incur) in a financial year is likely to exceed the resources (including sums borrowed) available to it to meet that expenditure.

Before issuing a section 114 notice, the CFO is likely to have formed the view that future expenditure cannot be brought under control, that the authority is projected to end the financial year with a deficit, and that there is no way of brokering a solution without issuing a section 114 notice.

---

[174] Local Government Finance Act 1988, s 114(3). Section 114 does not apply to Scotland. In Scotland, the requirement to set a balanced budget is established in s 108(2) of the Local Government (Scotland) Act 1973 and s 93(3) of the Local Government Finance Act 1992. In Northern Ireland, the equivalent duty—whilst not specified in statute—would rest with the authority's CFO in keeping with the statutory responsibility under s 54 of the Local Government Act (Northern Ireland) 1972.

[175] Local Government Finance Act 1988, s 115(5).

The procedure[176] will most probably result in the appointment of new independent commissioners for the local authority in debt. Newly appointed, independent commissioners will deal with the local authority's financial distress without liquidating it. There is no statutory duty to agree on a restructuring plan with creditors, or even to impose it on dissenting parties. As a result, the procedure has been compared to a Part A1 moratorium with monitorship.[177] However, where under general insolvency law the moratorium is a step towards a solution, for public authorities the moratorium is not followed by any specific, mandatory mechanism to reach an agreement with the council's creditors. Claims against a council cannot be abandoned or compromised.

5.3.2.1 Rules and procedures

Key differences between existing procedures for local public entities in distress and the corporate insolvency procedures discussed *sub* 5.2.1 needs first to be outlined. The section 114 notice does not provide comprehensive answers to the typical legal questions arising from insolvency procedures. This technique primarily aims at preventing unbalanced budgets. It is not a collective procedure involving negotiations with creditors under the direction of a third party. This technique also plays out against a backdrop of political dynamics that can develop between local and central government or between two successive local governments run by different parties. As the law is succinct, room exists for varying degrees of interpretation when implementing section 114.

Whilst the LGFA 1988 does not mandate managerial changes, the existing management will likely have to relinquish control of a local authority as soon as a CFO issues a section 114 notice. This is because the supervising executory authority is likely to appoint new management to implement the financial restructuring of the distressed entity, as the relationship of trust with the old management is likely to have been detrimentally affected. This new management does not have to be in possession of specific qualifications under the law, meaning that governance aspects are not heightened by the local authority's "bankruptcy".

No automatic stay is granted because creditors are usually repaid in full. However, it is possible to terminate some executory contracts such as employment contracts. In fact, most councils resort to collective redundancies when section 114 notices are issued. Creditors do not participate in restructuring efforts and cannot influence a restructuring plan.

---

176 See the outline of the procedure *sub* [5.3.2.1].

177 D French et al, '"Insolvent" Councils: When Is an Insolvency Not an Insolvency?' (2023) 16(5) C.R. & I. 195, 196.

These are not judicial or court-supervised procedures. Their nature is purely politico-administrative. Key powers are given to the CFO, as well as to the (new) management of a local authority, who both operate under the supervision of the Secretary of State.

There are no specific rules on interim finance, but the government frequently steps in to provide additional funding to allow local authorities to restructure their debt and provide the essential services they are legally bound to provide. Additionally, there are no special rules applicable to a distressed local authority's assets.

Moving on to the analysis of the current framework,[178] the procedure for dealing with section 114 notices is outlined in section 115 LGFA 1988. Similar rules apply to elected local policing bodies (such as councils and districts), fire and rescue authorities, and the police in section 115A LGFA 1988.

Once a section 114 notice is issued, an issuing council has 21 days to convene a meeting and discuss the implications of the notice.[179] This is also known as the "consideration" or "prohibition" period. During this time, the notice prevents any new expenditure, except for expenditure designed to fund statutory services. However, existing commitments and contracts continue to be honoured, and local authority officers continue to carry out their duties. Only certain expenditures are permitted under an emergency protocol (which lasts until a different arrangement is agreed upon among the parties involved in the procedure). The only payments that may be made whilst an emergency protocol is in operation are those that constitute:

- existing staff payroll and pension costs;
- expenditure on goods and services which have already been received;
- expenditure required to deliver the relevant local authority's provision of statutory services at a minimum possible level;
- urgent expenditure required to safeguard vulnerable citizens;
- expenditure required by existing legal agreements and contracts;
- expenditure funded through ring-fenced grants; and
- expenditure necessary to achieve value for money or mitigate additional in-year costs.

---

178 See also: E Vaccari, L Coordes and Y Marique, 'What Happens when Your Local Council Goes Bankrupt' (*The Conversation*, 4 July 2022) <https://theconversation.com/what-happens-when-your-local-council-goes-bankrupt-185539>; E Vaccari and Y Marique, 'One in Five Councils at Risk of "Bankruptcy"—What Happens after Local Authorities Run out of Money' *(The Conversation*, 14 February 2024) <https://theconversation.com/one-in-five-councils-at-risk-of-bankruptcy-what-happens-after-local-authorities-run-out-of-money-222541>.

179 Local Government Finance Act 1988, s 115(1D).

During a prohibition period, a local authority may only incur new expenses where prior authorisation has been granted by its CFO. A CFO may only authorise new expenditures if they believe that such expenditures would prevent the situation (that resulted in the section 114 notice) from worsening or reoccurring, or if these expenditures would improve the situation.

A full council meeting marks the end of a prohibition period. In that meeting, an elected body must consider the relevant report, decide whether it agrees or disagrees with the views contained in the report, and what action (if any) it proposes to take in consequence of the report.[180]

Following such a meeting, a report will be produced in alignment with section 115(1)(E) LGFA 1988. This report includes:

(a) what action (if any) that body, authority or chief officer has taken in response to the initial report;
(b) what action (if any) that body, authority or chief officer proposes to take in response to the initial report; and
(c) the reasons for taking the action specified or, as the case may be, for taking no action.

In accordance with section 115 LGFA 1988, a CFO of an elected local policing body must notify the body's auditor of any decisions taken by the body. At a meeting, council members and auditors should work together to produce a shared solution. In this context, the Secretary of State may intervene and appoint new commissioners to advise on or take over the functions originally allocated to the elected members of the local authority.

Where a shared solution is found, a plan for ongoing management is sent to the government for approval. If the plan is green-lighted, it is implemented by the elected officials of the local authority or by the independent commissioners appointed by the government. Where a solution is not found, the CFO is likely to issue a second s 114 notice (although there is no legal requirement to do so), and the government will step in to ensure that creditors are paid.

The government retains the legal power to replace the local authority in delivering the functions afforded to them.[181] Formal government interventions in the running of local authorities are rare. They usually take the form of a formal direction notice. More serious interventions are typically only triggered by dramatic events capable of undermining the public's confidence in that elected local authority.

---

180 Ibid s 115(1B).
181 Local Government Act 1999, s 15.

To date (May 2024), twelve interventions have taken place since this power was granted to the government by the Local Government Act 1999 (see Figure 5.1). The most recent appointments of independent commissioners occurred at Birmingham City Council (2023)[182] and Nottingham City Council (2024).[183] Previously, commissioners were appointed to run Liverpool City Council (2021) because of reports of failures in governance, a lack of scrutiny of the use of and regard for public funds, and a culture of intimidation at the council.[184] In some cases (e.g. Woking Borough Council), the Secretary of State had to replace existing commissioners with new commissioners.[185] According to guidelines published in May 2020, interventions of this kind are limited to cases where the Secretary of State is satisfied that the authority is failing to comply with the "best value duty".[186]

Failure to set a balanced budget or allowing a service to fail is likely to breach the best value duty, even in the absence of a section 114 notice. If this occurs, the Secretary of State has the power to appoint an independent commissioner to inspect the non-compliance (and alleged offending) of the local authority. Under section 15 of the Local Government Act 1999, the Secretary of State can impose a range of measures, including directing the authority to take any action necessary to meet its best value requirements.

Exercise of such powers is usually accompanied by financial assistance from the government. This is because, under the current framework, local authorities cannot fail, and creditors need to be paid in full. Lenders can appoint a receiver where their claim exceeds £10,000 and has gone unpaid for two

---

[182] Department for Levelling Up, Housing & Communities, 'Birmingham City Council: Intervention' (5 October 2023) <https://assets.publishing.service.gov.uk/media/651eab6779fc580014639641/Max_Caller_CBE_Appointment_Letter.pdf>.

[183] Nottingham City Council, 'Government Announces Commissioners for Nottingham City Council' (22 February 2024) <https://www.nottinghamcity.gov.uk/government-announces-commissioners-for-nottingham-city-council/council-response-on-commissioners-appointment/>.

[184] Press Release, 'Local Government Secretary Appoints Commissioners to Support Liverpool City Council' (10 June 2021) <https://www.gov.uk/government/news/local-government-secretary-appoints-commissioners-to-support-liverpool-city-council>.

[185] Woking Borough Council, 'Richard Carr Appointed Managing Director of Woking Borough Council' (13 December 2023) <https://www.woking.gov.uk/news/richard-carr-appointed-managing-director-woking-borough-council>.

[186] Ministry of Housing, Communities and Local Government, 'Statutory Intervention and Inspection: A Guide for Local Authorities' (7 May 2020) <https://www.gov.uk/government/publications/statutory-intervention-and-inspection-a-guide-for-local-authorities>.

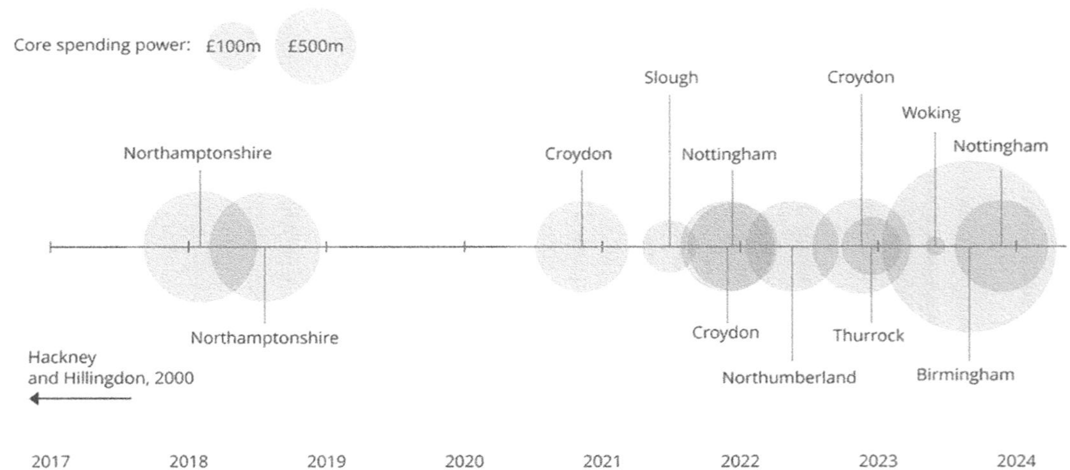

Source: Institute for Government analysis of various sources including local authority press releases and media reports.
Note: Section 114 notices for Nottingham (the first time) and Northumberland were issued as a result of unlawful expenditure, as opposed to being unable to balance their budget.

Figure 5.1 Section 114 Notices in England, 2017–23, as at 29 Nov 2023 (2023/24 prices)

months or more, even though security cannot be provided by local authorities. Under the Local Government Act 2003, the High Court has the authority to confer on the receiver the power to collect revenues destined for the local authority, to issue levies or precepts, and to set and collect council tax.

5.3.2.2 Alternative procedures

Local authorities cannot be subject to other debt resolution mechanisms (for example, state oversight, active supervision, or financial assistance from other authorities) apart from those outlined in this section. However, other entities that provide public services are subject to a special resolution regime.

English law recognises the existence of a variety of special administration regimes that apply in relation to organisations that provide critical services. These include electronic money institutions, investment banks, further education institutions, pension firms, and utility companies. Much attention has been paid to the treatment of railway and water companies (see below *sub* 5.4.3), as both sectors have experienced difficult market conditions.

With reference to water companies, the government implemented new rules[187] by means of the Water Industry Special Administration Regulations 2024. The 2024 Regulations introduced a pre-packaged exit procedure for insolvent or overindebted water companies. These regulations modify the provisions of schedule B1 to IA 1986 in relation to a water company that enters administration.

The new procedure allows the special administrator to discharge unprofitable assets, and even to compromise creditors' claims. None of these remedies are available to councils experiencing financial distress. In practice, these changes extend the scope of restructuring plans so that they apply to special administration procedures, thus giving insolvent companies that provide critical services a way out of their financial problems.

Special administrators now have the option to transfer the business by hive-down.[188] Hive-downs are commonly used in restructurings, especially as part of merger and acquisition strategies, as they allow an administrator to ring-fence value. The Water Industry Act 1991 (Amendment) Order 2024 provides that, in a special administration procedure, the administrator can transfer all or part of the company's undertaking to a wholly owned subsidiary. Later, this subsidiary is sold to another company.

---

[187] Special administration was governed by Part IV of the Water Industry Act 1991 (WIA 1991) and the Water Industry (Special Administration) Rules 2009 (SI 2009/2479).

[188] In a hive-down, the seller transfers assets into a new company within the seller's group as part of a wider restructuring and the new company is then sold to the buyer.

Hive-downs come with tax savings, and they are less complex and expensive than asset sales. Hive-downs effected through a special administration procedure result in the company being sold free of liabilities.

5.3.2.3 Principles and purposes

English law seeks to provide mechanisms that allow local authorities to deal with their financial difficulties before they become insolvent. There is, in other words, a preventive restructuring framework, whose measures include reducing costs, sharing services with other local authorities, and mergers between local authorities. For instance, Northamptonshire was forced to merge with a neighbouring council in 2018.[189] It is also possible for councils to rely on loans from PWLB, loans from other sources, bonds, as well as revenues from local taxes.[190]

Local authorities are little encouraged to deal with a situation of financial imbalance at an early stage. They have perverse incentives for not disclosing any ongoing financial difficulties. This is because disclosure of such problems will likely lead to the local authority's existing management being supervised and eventually replaced by independent commissioners appointed by the government.

Not everyone agrees with this assessment. In oral evidence presented to the Housing, Communities and Local Government Committee in 2021, Richard Watts (Chair of the Local Government Association) argued that the punitive nature of the statutory provisions has resulted in 'very significant engagement by local authorities under real financial pressure to effectively take the kinds of measures you would undertake in a section 114 process, but without formal issuing of the notice'.[191] Watts provided no evidence in support of this statement. Additionally, punitive corporate insolvency frameworks have traditionally pushed companies to delay dealing with their issues rather than promoting the adoption of timely restructuring measures. It is not clear why local public entities would react differently when subject to the same (dis)incentives for

---

189 H Siddique, 'Northamptonshire Proposes Replacing Councils with Two Unitary Authorities' *The Guardian* (London, 17 August 2018) <https://www.theguardian.com/uk-news/2018/aug/17/northamptonshire-councils-two-unitary-authorities>.

190 For a clear outline of the preventive restructuring solutions, see N Gavin-Brown, 'Restructuring Options for UK Local Authorities' (20 August 2018) <https://www.pinsentmasons.com/out-law/analysis/restructuring-options-uk-local-authorities>.

191 Housing, Communities and Local Government Committee, 'Oral Evidence: Local Authority Financial Sustainability and the Section 114 Regime' (HC 309, 2021) Q42.

early filing or restructuring. In fact, in the case of Croydon, the local representative acknowledged that the council should have issued a notice sooner.[192]

To summarise, section 114 notices are late warning signals. The consequences of issuing these notices are severe for the councils issuing them. All but essential expenses are frozen, and councils may be forced to merge with neighbouring ones.

5.3.2.4 Players

A key role is entrusted to the management of a local authority in distress. Courts and creditors do not play an active role in procedures dealing with local authorities in distress. There is no statutory leeway for the involvement of other figures such as mediators, arbitrators, and company doctors—even if the latter may be hired by the existing management to attempt to rescue a local authority before it files for statutory protection.

Balancing a local authority's budget is a crucial aspect of a CFO's role. Under the law, section 114 notices should be issued whenever there is a significant imbalance in a local authority's accounts. However, this does not frequently happen in practice. On multiple occasions during the Covid-19 pandemic, the government intervened to prevent councils from issuing such notices.[193]

When these notices are issued, the government steps in to ensure that the local authority addresses the issues that largely caused its financial difficulties. Usual measures include the appointment of new management (including a new CEO and CFO), cost-cutting actions, the provision of additional interim funding, and long-term policies such as a merger with neighbouring local authorities.

Besides CFOs and the government, auditors also have a prominent role in these procedures. A recently published review on how the audit system operates concluded that it was in dire need of reform, as 'none of the six entities with responsibility for the different elements of the framework has a statutory responsibility, either to act as a system leader or to make sure that the framework operates in a joined-up and coherent manner'.[194] Other reports also

[192] Housing, Communities and Local Government Committee, 'Oral Evidence: Local Authority Financial Sustainability and the Section 114 Regime' (HC 1054, 2021) Q107.

[193] Anonymous, 'Whitehall Has Waived Financial Rules to Save Councils from S114' *Inside Croydon* (London, 20 July 2020) <https://insidecroydon.com/2020/07/20/whitehall-has-waived-finance-rules-to-save-councils-from-s114/>.

[194] Redmond (n 163) 10.

suggest that the local audit regime is not fit for purpose,[195] partially due to a shortage of experienced auditors willing to carry out work for local authorities.

The Conservative government sought to follow these recommendations. In 2021, a White Paper detailed the government's proposal to establish a new regulator (the Audit, Reporting and Governance Authority (ARGA)) to replace the Financial Reporting Council (FRC).[196] This change should have become effective in 2023,[197] but legislation to establish ARGA was still not forthcoming at the time of national elections that saw the Labour party come to power (July 2024).

Additionally, a reform that may have broader consequences is the removal of local authorities' ability to choose their own auditors.

5.3.3 ESG when English Local Entities Are in Financial Distress

English local entities have long supported policies that seek to alleviate ESG concerns. This is the case even though their track record of success varies, and despite the fact that reforms undertaken in the 1980s encouraged local entities to be more speculative. For instance, on the one hand, local English entities have taken pay considerations into account since the early twentieth century,[198] and have sought to use public procurement and public contracts to tackle social and environmental issues.[199] On the other hand, in cases such as *Hammersmith* the courts decided that some local councils had acted *ultra vires* when entering into high-risk business ventures.[200] As a result, the Local Government Act was adapted in 2000 to specify that local councils had so-called "well-being

---

195 National Audit Office, 'Timeliness of Local Auditor Reporting on Local Government in England, 2020' (HC 2019–20 1243) <https://www.nao.org.uk/wp-content/uploads/2021/03/Timeliness-of-local-auditor-reporting-on-local-government-in-England-2020-.pdf>.

196 Department for Business, Energy and Industrial Strategy, 'Restoring Trust in Audit and Corporate Governance' (March 2021) CP 382 <https://assets.publishing.service.gov.uk/government/uploads/system/uploads/attachment_data/file/970676/restoring-trust-in-audit-and-corporate-governance-command-paper.pdf>.

197 S Bouvier, 'FRC Officials Detail ARGA Transition Timetable, Upcoming Workplan Priorities' *IPE News* (London, 24 September 2021) <https://www.ipe.com/news/frc-officials-detail-arga-transition-timetable-upcoming-workplan-priorities/10055122.article>.

198 C McCrudden, *Buying Social Justice: Equality, Government Procurement, and Legal Change* (OUP 2007) 42–51.

199 A Davies, *The Public Law of Government Contracts* (OUP 2008) ch 9.

200 *Hazell v Hammersmith & Fulham London Borough Council* [1992] 2 AC 1 (HL); *Credit Suisse v Allerdale Borough Council* [1997] QB 306.

powers",[201] i.e. powers that they can use to promote the economic, social, and environmental well-being of the local community.[202]

This thus leads to a contrasting picture in solvent times. What happens when councils are financially distressed? This section analyses the extent to which ESG is taken into account when turnaround strategies are being devised for local entities in financial distress.

5.3.3.1 Environmental goals

There are no specific rules on interim or restructuring finance. However, when a council is in financial trouble, it must cut essential services to the bare minimum. This may affect environmental considerations as rubbish collection becomes less frequent, or related services such as access to recycling centres or garden waste collection are either not offered or must be paid for. This contrasts with what happens for companies providing other essential services, such as electricity, gas, or water. These companies are subject to special administration regimes (SARs) that ensure that the service being provided to customers is not affected, and that the costs of the corporate failure are spread across users, creditors and taxpayers.

Moreover, local authorities oversee planning applications. Potentially, they could play a huge role in adopting climate change mitigation and adaptation strategies, either before, or even during and after a restructuring procedure. If an authority is financially distressed, staff numbers in the planning department may be reduced and, as a result, their proactive role in the adoption of climate change mitigation and adaptation strategies might be affected. Alternatively, as the local government is strapped for cash, it may be tempted to grant planning applications more generously. Tensions arise in this respect, as local government operates within a tightly regulated planning system that is controlled at the national level.[203] Local government may also be tempted to obtain financial benefit by entering into planning development agreements,[204] under which the local government requires developers to pay for public amenities. Equally, local government could set up schemes akin to the ultra-low emission zone (ULEZ) in London, which result in charges being paid to the local government. The local government would however need to be careful in its cost–ben-

[201] Local Government Act 2000, s 2 (no longer applicable in England since the Localism Act 2011).

[202] Local Government Act 2000, Explanatory Note, para 14.

[203] M Lee, 'English Planning Law: An Outline' in M Lee and C Abbot (eds), *Taking English Planning Law Scholarship Seriously* (UCL Press 2022) 10–32.

[204] E Mitchell, 'Contracting in the Public Interest? Re-examining the Role of Planning Obligations in Contemporary Town Planning Processes' (2024) XX CLP 1.

efit analysis, as such a scheme may deter and/or attract residents with varying capacities to pay council taxes and varying needs for public services (such as schools, social housing, care homes).

In the absence of special rules applicable to local entities in financial distress, some general provisions continue to apply to distressed entities. One of them is the Environment Act 2021. This act introduces a legal duty to consider the environmental implications of any proposed policies. In other words, policymakers should apply the following five environmental principles[205] when making policy decisions:

1. the principle that environmental protection should be integrated into the making of policies;
2. the principle of preventative action to avert environmental damage;
3. the precautionary principle, so far as the policy relates to the environment;
4. the principle that environmental damage should as a priority be rectified at source; and
5. the polluter pays principle.

On 29 March 2024, the government issued the "Environmental Principles Assessment Guide".[206] This statutory document explains how to interpret and proportionally apply the five environmental principles. It includes a series of questions that policymakers should answer as part of the design and implementation of new policies. The answers to these questions should be recorded, but they are for internal use only and not available to residents or local associations unless they submit a freedom of information (FOI) request.

Moreover, principles are not rules, and do not dictate policy outcomes. The assessment guide also states that policymakers are not expected to carry out a "deep-dive" assessment of all environmental effects. Therefore, it remains to be seen whether the new principles and assessment guide will affect how councils operate before and during a period of financial distress.

5.3.3.2 Social issues

In terms of social considerations, councils have to reduce their fixed costs, and they usually do so by employing some headcount reduction strategies. These usually include: (i) hiring and wage freezes; (ii) postponement of wage increases; (iii) reducing fringe benefits; (iv) reducing work hours with

---

[205] Environment Act 2021, s 17(5).

[206] <https://www.gov.uk/government/consultations/sprinklers-in-care-homes-removal-of-national-classes-and-staircases-in-residential-buildings/outcome/environmental-principles-assessment-guide>.

proportionate pay cuts; and (v) discontinuing the use of temporary and part-time employees and redistributing their work to permanent employees. There are no significant differences with private corporations as to the redundancy process. Moreover, where more than 20 redundancies are proposed, protections are subject to a mandatory consultation period.

Remaining on the topic of social considerations, whilst secured charges are enforced as part of any restructuring procedure involving a council in financial distress, no other examples of preferential treatment are recognised under the law. This is good news, as the main preferential creditor under English law (besides employees) is the tax authority, and there is no need to grant HMRC a preferential treatment over general unsecured creditors.

One of the first and most obvious consequences of triggering a section 114 notice is that the affected councils have to lay off staff, scale back any expenditure (including capital expenditure), and increase local revenue. A council under a section 114 notice is forced to only provide services that are statutorily required under the law. However, those who rely on the services provided by the council are the most vulnerable citizens. These cuts to services and increases in local taxes may push more citizens into financial difficulty. This may have a domino effect on citizens' ability to pay taxes, and on the council's ability to provide essential services.

As people need electricity, water and heating in their homes, most families in financial need decide not to pay their council tax, which is the main source of income for most councils. According to the latest available figures,[207] as of 31 March 2023, the total amount of council tax still outstanding amounted to £5.5 billion. This is a cumulative figure and includes arrears that may stretch back several years. This is £510 million more than what it was at the end of 2021–2022. In other words, cuts to essential services and increases in local taxes risk triggering a vicious cycle that operates only to the advantage of private collection agencies.

5.3.3.3 Governance considerations

Governance is a complex and very current issue in the public sector. A report on the financial sustainability of local authorities and the section 114 regime outlines that these measures are triggered at the very last moment, and that the regime makes it difficult for local authorities to act in a timely manner. As a result, it advises the government to introduce an intermediary "yellow card" which, when issued by a CFO, would force a council to confront the

---

207 <https://www.gov.uk/government/statistics/collection-rates-for-council-tax-and-non-domestic-rates-in-england-2022-to-2023/collection-rates-for-council-tax-and-non-domestic-rates-in-england-2022-to-2023#:~:text=At%2031%20March%202023%2C%20the,the%20end%20of%202021-22>.

seriousness of its financial position much sooner.[208] The report also recommends that CFOs report on the financial state of (and, in particular, any potentially serious financial problems affecting) the local authority to which they are appointed. Their findings must be presented to both the executive and the appropriate scrutiny committees, and should be updated on a quarterly basis.

Another aspect related to governance is the statutory attitude towards financially distressed entities. The Cork Report (1982)[209] advocated for a novel approach to corporate and personal insolvency in this country. It advised viewing corporate failure as a fact of life rather than a sin committed by those controlling a failing company. These recommendations were later implemented through a series of statutory reforms, which have neglected local authorities.

Councils will be keen to make timely decisions, not only to avoid more serious financial difficulties but also because the consequences of being issued a section 114 notice are particularly harsh. Yet, the reduced transfers from central government coupled with a lack of expert auditors to supervise a council's activities may lead to local authorities experiencing serious financial difficulties with draconian consequences for councils, their workers, the services they provide, and their existing procurement contracts.

This punitive approach towards failure has no equivalent in the English insolvency framework and lacks proper theoretical justification. Rather than punishing local authorities for being in debt, reforms aimed at supporting indebted local authorities are needed to realign the treatment of local public entities in distress with the rest of the English insolvency framework.

In many recent cases involving section 114 notices, the government commissioned independent reviews to understand if mistakes were made in the decision-making process which led to the notice. Similar investigations have also been carried out by the Local Government Association.[210] Unsurprisingly, most of these reports showed serious governance failures in the years preceding the section 114 notice. Croydon is one of many cases of egregious governance failures as the case study section below details.

Finally, it is noteworthy that the continued provision of water and sewerage services to customers and the discharge of environmental obligations are the main objectives of alternative SARs provided to critical service companies. Taking as an example the rules governing the special administration of water companies, the special administrator must prepare and submit a report to the High Court within three months of the appointment, setting out proposals to

---

[208] Ibid 32–33.

[209] Cork Report (n 105).

[210] Local Government Association, 'Learning from Councils Which Faced Finance and Governance Challenges' (27 February 2024) <https://www.local.gov.uk/publications/research-councils-experience-finance-S114>.

achieve the objectives of the special administration. SARs are now applicable to a variety of sectors and organisations, including investment banks,[211] energy supply companies,[212] postal services,[213] the water industry,[214] and payment and electronic money institutions.[215] Similar rules could be applied to local entities in financial distress as they also provide essential services to local communities and their most vulnerable members. In addition, the UK is part of the Council of Europe, which has adopted soft law guidance on the continuity of local public services.[216]

5.3.3.4 Concluding remarks

To conclude, from a long-term sustainability perspective, preventive intervention is considered preferable to reactionary measures.[217] Alternative procedures such as SARs embed ESG considerations. Unfortunately, the procedure outlined in the LGFA 1988 lacks any reference to environmental and social factors. It is also questionable whether the procedure laid out in the act is capable of transforming governance practices, due to how late on in the process intervention can be made and also due to the procedure's punitive approach to financial distress. The next section outlines to what extent ESG considerations have played a role in recent high-profile cases of basic and hybrid local authorities[218] in financial distress.

---

211 The Investment Bank Special Administration Regulations 2011.

212 Energy Act 2011.

213 Postal Services Act 2011 (PSA 2011), which allows for the application of a postal administration order (PAO) and the appointment of a postal administrator to manage the affairs of a universal service provider (Royal Mail) that is in financial difficulty.

214 Regulated by Part IV of the Water Industry Act 1991 (WIA 1991) and the Water Industry (Special Administration) Rules 2009 (SI 2009/2479), as amended by The Flood and Water Management Act 2010 (Commencement No. 10) Order 2024, which became effective on 12 January 2024, and The Water Industry Act 1991 (Amendment) Order 2024 and The Water Industry (Special Administration) Regulations 2024, each of which came into effect on 22 February 2024.

215 The Payment and Electronic Money Institution Insolvency Regulations 2021.

216 Guidelines to Recommendation No. R (97)7 of the Committee of Ministers to member states on local public services and the rights of their users.

217 T Linna, 'Company Purpose in the Context of Business Sustainability and Insolvency Proceedings' (2021) 18 European Company Law 162.

218 On the distinction between "basic" and "hybrid" local authorities, see LN Coordes, Y Marique and E Vaccari, *When Liquidation is NOT an Option: A Global Study on the Treatment of Local Entities in Financial Distress* (INSOL International, 2022) vii. A basic local authority is a municipality, city, district,

5.4 LOCAL PUBLIC ENTITIES IN FINANCIAL DISTRESS—LAW IN PRACTICE

In recent years, local government has faced successive challenges to its financial sustainability. The rising demand for services has led to higher costs for local authorities. Notably, successive governments have failed to provide adequate funding to address the burden of social care costs. The social care requirements are the most significant stressor on local authority budgets, as these expenses account for 40% of local councils' budgets.[219] Changes to the level of funding equalisation between councils, the introduction of the Business Rate Retention Scheme, and, more recently, the Covid-19 pandemic have made these issues more pressing.[220] As a result, following encouragement from the government, councils have adopted creative revenue-generating practices. A few of them backfired. Examples of such failures include the tiny Surrey borough of Spelthorne buying BP's campus headquarters,[221] Thurrock in Essex bankrolling solar farm developments,[222] and Labour-run Warrington buying shares in a bank controlled by a former Conservative Party treasurer.[223]

---

province, or other political subdivision that provides essential services to local communities. At times, essential public services are provided by hybrid entities. These are either state- or privately-owned entities that either carry out fundamental services or are responsible for the production or distribution of essential goods at a local, territorial or regional level.

[219] National Audit Office, 'Financial Sustainability of Local Authorities Visualisation: Update (20 July 2021) <https://www.nao.org.uk/reports/financial-sustainability-of-local-authorities-visualisation-update/>.

[220] P Butler, 'Cost-of-living Crisis for Councils Will Make Levelling Up a Distant Dream' *The Guardian* (London, 17 June 2022) <https://www.theguardian.com/society/2022/jun/17/cost-of-living-crisis-for-councils-will-make-levelling-up-a-distant-dream>.

[221] T Wall, 'Tory Leader's £1bn Office Buying Spree "Leaves Dangerous Legacy" for Council' *The Guardian* (London, 25 October 2020) <https://www.theguardian.com/society/2020/oct/25/tory-leaders-1bn-office-buying-spree-leaves-dangerous-legacy-for-council>.

[222] A Lawson, 'Solar Farm Owner Toucan Energy Enters Administration amid Thurrock Scandal' *The Guardian* (London, 11 November 2022) <https://www.theguardian.com/business/2022/nov/11/solar-farm-owner-toucan-energy-enters-administration-amid-thurrock-scandal>.

[223] R Partington, 'Austerity-hit Council Defends Its "High-risk" Investment Strategy' *The Guardian* (London, 15 January 2022) <https://www.theguardian.com/society/2022/jan/15/austerity-hit-council-defends-its-high-risk-investment-strategy>.

Unsurprisingly, some councils (including Northamptonshire County Council in 2018, Croydon Council in 2020, Slough Borough Council in 2021,[224] Northumberland County Council in 2022, Birmingham City Council,[225] and Nottingham City Council both in 2023) have been forced to issue section 114 notices declaring that they had run out of money.

This chapter covers three case studies: Croydon, Birmingham, and Thames Water. Croydon is a seminal case. It is one of the first significant local authorities in England to have issued a section 114 notice in recent times. Due to the council's mismanagement, the case commanded extensive media and parliamentary attention. Changes have been discussed because of the shortcomings of the statutory framework.

Birmingham is a significant and evolving case. It is the largest local authority in the UK. The failure of Birmingham is allegedly and primarily due to social issues. Birmingham found itself unable to cover the costs associated with an equal pay judgment that resulted in the council having to pay approximately £2 billion to existing and former female employees.

Thames Water is a large private utility company, incorporated as a limited liability enterprise. Its inclusion in this book may appear inappropriate, as the company has not formally entered into insolvency (at the time of writing), even if restructuring experts have allegedly been appointed to explore potential rescue options.[226] However, this case study is significant for two reasons. Firstly, it shows that existing restructuring rules can be applied (with modifications) to entities that provide essential public services, such as water supply and sewage treatment. Secondly, the corporate crisis at Thames Water (and arguably many other utility companies) epitomises the long-term damage to the environment caused by corporate greed (and by regulators and legislators being asleep at

---

[224] The situation in Slough is evolving, with news that the council is proposing to restructure the finance department (O Rudgewick, 'Slough Proposes Financial Department Restructure' *Public Finance* (15 June 2022) <https://www.publicfinance.co.uk/2022/06/slough-proposes-finance-department-restructure?utm_source=Adestra&amp%3Butm_medium=email&amp%3Butm_term=>) and that most of the council's properties may be sold (O Rudgewick, 'Slough Urged to Sell Most of Its Properties' *Public Finance* (London, 27 May 2022) <https://www.publicfinance.co.uk/news/2022/05/slough-urged-sell-most-its-properties?utm_source=Adestra&amp%3Butm_medium=email&amp%3Butm_term=>).

[225] E Vaccari and Y Marique, 'Birmingham's Bankruptcy Is only the Tip of the Iceberg—Local Authorities across England Are at Risk' (*The Conversation*, 6 September 2023) <https://theconversation.com/birminghams-bankruptcy-is-only-the-tip-of-the-iceberg-local-authorities-across-england-are-at-risk-212912>.

[226] G Plimmer and J Pickard, 'Thames Water Owners to Begin Urgent Restructuring Talks' *The Financial Times* (London, 31 March 2024) <https://www.ft.com/content/b892d786-5dd5-44ab-8bdd-42c0d8d438f5>.

the wheel). Therefore, it is essential that ESG considerations are included as part of the discussion on the restructuring options available to Thames Water.

5.4.1 Case Study 1: Croydon

The financial condition of the London Borough of Croydon has deteriorated since the 2017–2018 tax year.[227] This was caused by growing spending pressures stemming from both child and adult social care, low levels of financial reserves, financial mismanagement, and poor auditing records. Additionally, the local authority was made financially responsible for many unaccompanied asylum-seeking children, whose maintenance was not fully covered by the government.

As evidenced in a later emergency strategic review conducted by PwC, several financial issues were attributed to Croydon's commercial subsidiaries. Notably, their lack of proper governance and accountability, as well as significant underperformance against their business plans, were deemed to have caused the financial issues.[228]

The scale of corporate dysfunction at Croydon Council prior to its collapse was serious enough to warrant police investigation into potential misconduct in public office. A report (Penn Report) revealed a 'highly dysfunctional organisation characterised by a culture of poor decision-making and conduct of some of the Council's most senior managers'.[229]

In other words, Croydon's financial difficulties were the result of poor money management by the council and its subsidiaries. However, their job was made particularly difficult by the Covid-19 pandemic and by pressures associated with an ageing population and a growing number of asylum seekers. Governance failures included: management's inability to follow a prudential code of conduct in investing funds; management's lack of accountability;

---

227 G Thornton, 'London Borough of Croydon. Report in the Public Interest Concerning the Council's Financial Position and Related Governance Arrangements' (October 2020) <https://www.croydon.gov.uk/sites/default/files/2021-03/Report%20in%20the%20Public%20Interest%20-%20London%20Borough%20of%20Croydon.pdf> ("Report in the Public Interest").

228 PwC, 'Independent Strategic Review of Brick by Brick Croydon Ltd, Growth Zone, Croydon Affordable Homes LLP, the Revolving Investment Fund and the Assets Investment Fund' (13 November 2020) <https://democracy.croydon.gov.uk/documents/s26083/Appendix%201%20-%20PwC%20Report.pdf> ("Strategic Review Report").

229 R Penn, 'Report for the Interim Chief Executive' (March 2021) 129 [14.5] <https://www.croydon.gov.uk/sites/default/files/2023-02/penn-report-24-02–23.pdf> ("Penn Report"). This report was only published on 24 February 2023.

over-optimistic forecasts from the management team of one of the council's debtors; and a lack of incentives to promote the early restructuring of the debtor's finances.[230]

The Penn Report and other reports[231] observed that whilst the council's governance looked fit for purpose on the surface, in practice no governance controls were in place for loan agreements in excess of £200 million, information was not shared among key cabinet figures, and there was widespread tolerance for overspending.[232] Senior officers were allowed to run the council in disregard of the governance structures that should have prevented this outcome.[233]

Despite Croydon authority's members, the government, and the public being aware of the borough's financial (and governance) issues for some time, the borough was allowed to approve risky investments, and secure additional funding through loans, even when the levels of reserves were too low to sustain such investments. Some of these, such as the purchase of the Croydon Park Hotel, resulted in a significant loss (with the holding company going into administration in 2020). Others failed to generate satisfactory returns, as in the case of the delayed Brick by Brick property developments, and the council's investment into the town centre regeneration project.

Despite these warning signs, the council operated "as usual" until mid-2020, when it approached the Ministry of Housing, Communities and Local Government (MHCLG) for support. Eventually, the CFO was forced to issue a section 114 notice on 11 November 2020 when it became clear that the council faced a predicted budget shortfall of between £30 million and £67 million by the end of 2020–2021. At that time, the government was not willing to cover the council's deficit without a change of management. This was followed by a second section 114 notice on 2 December 2020.

As no further cost-cutting or revenue-generating measures could be adopted in late 2020, the existing directors of the council were gradually replaced by professionals appointed by the MHCLG. Finally, in March 2021, the government issued a capitalisation direction allowing the council to borrow £70 million in 2020–2021 and £50 million in 2021–2022 to support its revenue budget position.[234]

---

230 Ibid 129–132.

231 Report in the Public Interest (n 227); Strategic Review Report (n 228); C Wood, 'Non-statutory Review London Borough of Croydon' (November 2020) <https://assets.publishing.service.gov.uk/media/601962738fa8f53fc62c58b2/Croydon_Rapid_Review_Report.pdf> ("Rapid Review Report").

232 Penn Report (n 229) 129 [14.5].

233 Ibid 130 [14.8].

234 MHCLG, 'Croydon Capitalisation Direction' (16 March 2021) <https://assets.publishing.service.gov.uk/government/uploads/system/uploads/attachment

During the restructuring process, the government decided not only to replace the existing management, but also to appoint an improvement panel.[235] These steps mark a significant departure from the previous governance arrangements. They are designed to address the governance problems which led to the council's dire financial situation.

Despite these governance changes, cost-cutting actions and revenue-generating measures, the council was forced to issue a third section 114 notice in November 2022. At that time, the council stated that it faced an "existential question" having collapsed under the weight of a toxic debt burden running to more than £1 billion.[236] This led the government to conclude—two years into the section 114 procedure—that the council was still not meeting its "best value duty"[237] as required under Part I of the Local Government Act 1999. In March 2023, the government exercised its powers of direction under the same act to grant statutory powers to the Improvement and Assurance Panel (established in 2021).[238] As a result of this measure, the council must follow the panel's recommendations if ever the panel's members are not satisfied with progress being made.

_data/file/970303/Croydon_Capitalisation_Direction_16_March_2021.pdf>. A capitalisation direction is a tool that allows a council to use the proceedings generated from asset sales to fund day-to-day costs. This is generally not possible, unless with previous authorisation from the Government.

235 <https://assets.publishing.service.gov.uk/government/uploads/system/uploads/attachment_data/file/1143274/Max_Soule_Letter_to_London_Borough_of_Croydon_Chief_Executive.pdf> (March 2023).

236 P Butler, 'Croydon Council Declares Effective Bankruptcy for Third Time in Two Years' *The Guardian* (London, 22 November 2022) <https://www.theguardian.com/society/2022/nov/22/croydon-council-declares-effective-bankruptcy-for-third-time-in-two-years>.

237 The "best value duty" relates to the statutory requirement for local authorities and other public bodies defined as best value authorities in Part 1 of the Local Government Act 1999 to 'make arrangements to secure continuous improvement in the way in which its functions are exercised, having regard to a combination of economy, efficiency and effectiveness'. In practice, this covers issues such as how authorities exercise their functions to deliver a balanced budget (Local Government Finance Act 1992, Pt 1), provide statutory services, including adult social care and children's services, and secure value for money in all spending decisions.

238 <https://assets.publishing.service.gov.uk/government/uploads/system/uploads/attachment_data/file/1143274/Max_Soule_Letter_to_London_Borough_of_Croydon_Chief_Executive.pdf>.

In February 2023, Croydon obtained preliminary approval for a capitalisation direction and further flexibilities worth a total of £225 million.[239] Croydon also obtained a further £38 million in financial support from the government for the financial year 2024–2025.[240] Notwithstanding the constant need for further funding to balance its books, the Improvement and Assurance Panel chair announced that the authority has adopted a culture of transparency. The chair concluded that the council is focused on improving its finances, thus making it likely that the panel will not be needed after 2025.[241]

It is clear, therefore, that governance considerations were, and still are, part of Croydon's restructuring efforts, and that arguably previous governance failures justified the change of management. However, environmental and social concerns were never part of the restructuring efforts. Croydon never discussed the adoption of green policies as a mechanism to attract new investment in the beleaguered borough. Additionally, the cuts in staff numbers at the council, in the services provided to the local population, and a record-high 15% council tax rise,[242] suggest that no leeway was given for social considerations as part of the restructuring effort.

5.4.2 Case Study 2: Birmingham

The "bankruptcy" of Croydon shows that a lack of proper governance and inadequate independent oversight from external auditors may have dire consequences for local communities. It also shows the general disregard that the "restructuring" process triggered by a section 114 notice has for social and environmental issues.

---

239 O Rudgewick, 'Government Signals further Flexibility for Thurrock, Croydon & Slough' (*Public Finance*, 3 March 2023) <https://www.publicfinance.co.uk/news/2023/03/government-signals-further-flexibility-thurrock-croydon-slough>.

240 O Rudgewick, 'Councils Given £2.5bn in Exceptional Financial Support' (*Public Finance*, 29 February 2024) <https://www.publicfinance.co.uk/news/2024/02/councils-given-ps25bn-exceptional-financial-support>.

241 O Rudgewick, 'Croydon Improvement Team Plans 2025 Exit' (*Public Finance*, 18 October 2023) <https://www.publicfinance.co.uk/news/2023/10/croydon-improvement-team-plans-2025-exit>.

242 A Elgueta, 'Croydon Approves Council Tax Rise of 15%' *BBC News* (London, 9 March 2023) <https://www.bbc.co.uk/news/uk-england-london-64892461>.

On 5 September 2023,[243] Birmingham issued a section 114 notice. This was followed by a second section 114 notice on 21 September 2023, partially as a wake-up call to the council to deal with the causes of the authority's financial failure.[244]

Several explanations were given for this notice. The Labour-run council was quick in blaming the Conservative-run government for failing to adequately fund local authorities, arguing that the largest council in the country had suffered a £1 billion cut in funding over the last decade.[245] The government rejected this narrative, arguing that they had actually increased funding for Birmingham in the last financial year.[246]

Political bickering aside, unlike in the case of Nottingham, which issued a section 114 notice shortly after Birmingham,[247]cuts in central transfers and funding were not the main causes of Birmingham's financial distress. Birmingham's financial collapse was mainly due to three issues: problems with the installation of a new IT system (£100 million), the debt legacy of the 2022 Commonwealth Games (£184 million), and significant ongoing liability for equal pay claims.[248]

According to statements from the council, as of June 2023, the local authority had paid out £1.1 billion in equal pay claims over the past decade, and had current liabilities of £650 million to £750 million, accruing at a rate of £5 million to £14 million per month.[249] This is because thousands of women employed by the council were granted compensation in 2012, after a successful equal pay claim in which they argued that they had missed out on bonuses

---

243 <https://www.birmingham.gov.uk/download/downloads/id/27684/section_114_notice.pdf>.

244 O Rudgewick, 'Equal Pay Delay Prompts Second Birmingham S114 Notice' (*Public Finance*, 21 September 2023) <https://www.publicfinance.co.uk/news/2023/09/equal-pay-delay-prompts-second-birmingham-s114-notice>.

245 J Murray, 'Birmingham City Council Declares Itself in Financial Distress' *The Guardian* (London, 5 September 2023) <https://www.theguardian.com/society/2023/sep/05/birmingham-city-council-financial-distress-budget-section-114>.

246 Ibid.

247 <https://www.nottinghamcity.gov.uk/media/jmzb22b0/report-made-under-part-viii-s114-3-of-the-local-government-finance-act-1988-291123.pdf>.

248 French et al (n 177); Vaccari and Marique (n 225).

249 These figures are actually disputed, and there is evidence that the equal pay liability bill might have been significantly overstated: J Murray, 'Birmingham City Council Accused of Basing Drastic Cuts on "Imagined" Data' *The Guardian* (London, 1 May 2024) <https://www.theguardian.com/uk-news/2024/may/01/birmingham-city-council-accused-of-making-cuts-based-on-imagined-data>.

awarded to men on the same paygrade, with claims stretching back several years.[250]

At the core of Birmingham's financial distress is a story of social and equality issues, as well as gender discrimination within the council. Similar problems are being experienced by other councils across the country, thus threatening the financial stability of more authorities.[251] Therefore, it would seem appropriate for any restructuring of the council's finances to address the reasons that made the council "bankrupt" in the first instance.

To date, this has not entirely been the case. To address the financial shortfall, the council approved a programme of £300 million in cuts (to highways spending and streetlights, as well as to other essential services such as youth services[252]), up to 600 redundancies,[253] and a 21% council tax rise over two years.[254] Therefore, the current administration is adopting the same strategies as all other financially distressed councils: cuts coupled with increases in local taxation. Like Croydon, central government is stepping up its financial support, and has announced additional financial support worth £685 million for the next financial year.[255] It is also acting to ensure that the new funds are not misspent, having appointed a commissioner to supervise the council's activities.[256]

At the same time, the council started negotiating for a new job evaluation scheme that would remove any discriminatory elements from staff salaries.[257] This was urgently needed, as the council's auditors estimated that if the authority did not have a non-discriminatory pay structure in place by the start of 2025–2026, it could cost between £5 million and £14 million in additional

---

250 *Birmingham CC v Abdulla and others* [2012] UKSC 47.

251 O Rudgewick, 'Sheffield Faces Equal Pay Claim from GMB' (*Public Finance*, 25 September 2023) <https://www.publicfinance.co.uk/news/2023/09/sheffield-faces-equal-pay-claim-gmb>.

252 K Lorrimer, 'Cuts to Youth Services Are "Inevitable", Birmingham Warns' (*Public Finance*, 8 February 2024) <https://www.publicfinance.co.uk/news/2024/02/cuts-youth-services-are-inevitable-birmingham-warns>.

253 O Rudgewick, 'Birmingham Warns of 600 Redundancies' (*Public Finance*, 17 January 2024) <https://www.publicfinance.co.uk/news/2024/01/birmingham-warns-600-redundancies>.

254 C Gall and S Gilbert, '"Bankrupt" Birmingham Reveals 21% Council Tax Rise' *BBC News* (London, 19 February 2024) <https://www.bbc.com/news/uk-england-birmingham-68342493>.

255 Rudgewick (n 240).

256 Department for Levelling Up, Housing & Communities (n 182).

257 O Rudgewick, 'Birmingham Agrees Big Step Towards Fixing Pay Issues' (*Public Finance*, 13 October 2023) <https://www.publicfinance.co.uk/news/2023/10/birmingham-agrees-big-step-towards-fixing-pay-issues>.

funds every month.[258] However, the authority also delayed the payment of the equal pay claims, prompting unions to call for industrial action.[259]

Compared to the case of Croydon, Birmingham presents less pressing governance issues—at least at the time of writing. Nevertheless, a review found that Birmingham City Council has been plagued by poor relationships between officers and councillors.[260] This led to a "deep-seated blame culture", where failures were blamed on individuals and not on inadequate governance principles. The government-appointed commissioners embraced the findings of the review and stated that they would be working with the council to make the appropriate governance changes.[261] However, this topic has not played a significant role in the restructuring process so far.

Unfortunately, the same could be said for both environmental and social issues. The absence of consideration for environmental issues can be explained by the lack of any incentives in the statutory framework to consider such concerns. The government could have made the issuance of new funds and/or capitalisation directions contingent upon changes being made to local policies, guaranteeing the long-term sustainability of the local authority. They decided not to pursue that avenue. More disappointingly, the latest developments suggest that this crisis is going to be paid for by the council's workers, the very group that the 2012 Supreme Court judgment aimed to protect. In other words, this restructuring makes a mockery of the social issues that triggered it.

5.4.3 Case Study 3: Thames Water

Water companies in the UK are under immense financial and operational pressure for several reasons, including high debt burdens, long-term underinvestment, rising operational costs, and penalties for failing to monitor storm

---

[258] Grant Thornton, 'External Audit 2020–21 to 2023–24' (29 September 2023) <https://www.birmingham.gov.uk/downloads/file/28033/external_audit_2020-21_to_2023-24>.

[259] O Rudgewick, 'Birmingham Strike Vote a "Major Escalation"' (*Public Finance*, 5 March 2024) <https://www.publicfinance.co.uk/news/2024/03/birmingham-strike-vote-major-escalation>.

[260] Centre for Governance and Scrutiny, 'Birmingham City Council. Report to Cabinet' (12 December 2023).

[261] O Rudgewick, '"Deep-seated Blame Culture" Contributed to Birmingham S114, Says CfGS' (*Public Finance*, 5 December 2023) <https://www.publicfinance.co.uk/news/2023/12/deep-seated-blame-culture-contributed-birmingham-s114-says-cfgs>.

overflows.[262] Thames Water is in a particularly difficult predicament, although problems are spread across the sector.[263]

Thames Water Utilities Ltd (Thames Water) is—at the time of writing—not an insolvency case, even if bailout is looming[264] and its investors are writing off their investments in the company.[265] It may never result in an insolvency case, for instance if the company's shareholders, its creditors, and the Water Services Regulation Authority (Ofwat) reach an agreement to restructure the company's ballooning debt. Unlike the local entities' failures discussed above, the Thames Water saga is taking place in a heavily regulated environment. Should a utility company become insolvent, the company will be restructured through a water industry special administration regime (WISAR)—unless either a nationalisation process or an informal restructuring agreement of the company's debt is organised.

Thames Water is a British private utility company responsible for water supply to, and wastewater treatment in, Greater London and the neighbouring areas. It is owned by the Kemble Water Group (Kemble), which is in turn owned by some of the biggest pension and sovereign wealth funds in the world.[266]

When Thames Water was privatised in 1989, the company was debt-free.[267] The previous owner, Australian firm Macquarie, took out nearly £3 billion in

---

[262] Hill et al, 'Navigating Troubled Waters: Updates to Water Insolvency Legislation amid Growing Concerns about the Sector' (23 February 2024) <https://www.dlapiper.com/en/insights/publications/2024/02/navigating-troubled-waters-updates-to-water-insolvency-legislation-amid-growing-concerns-about-the>.

[263] PA Media, 'South East Water Says It Needs Cash Injection to Stay Afloat' *The Guardian* (London, 10 July 2024) <https://www.theguardian.com/business/article/2024/jul/10/south-east-water-says-it-needs-cash-injection-to-stay-afloat>.

[264] M Kleinman, 'Thames Water Investors to Quit Boards amid Spectre of Bailout' *Sky News* (London, 15 May 2024) <https://news.sky.com/story/thames-water-investors-to-quit-boards-amid-spectre-of-bailout-13136327>.

[265] G Plimmer and J Cumbo, 'Thames Water's Biggest Shareholder Writes Off Investment' *Financial Times* (London, 17 May 2024) <https://www.ft.com/content/aa0a8179-27ce-42aa-9687-b4a61360c907>.

[266] Two of the company's main shareholders are the Ontario Municipal Employees Retirement System (c. 31.7% of shares) and the Universities Superannuation Scheme (c. 19.7% of shares). The ownership structure is available here: <https://www.thameswater.co.uk/about-us/governance/our-structure#:~:text=Thames%20Water%20is%20part%20of,been%20in%20place%20since%202006.>.

[267] For an outlook of the privatisation process of water utility companies in the UK, see (among others): N Pratley, 'Cheap Sales, Debt and Foreign Takeovers: How Privatisation Changed the Water Industry' *The Guardian* (London, 10 July

dividends and allowed its debt pile to triple between 2006 and 2017. The current shareholders have taken dividends,[268] with the last payment effected soon before they refused to provide emergency funding to the company.[269]

Both Kemble and Thames Water are struggling financially due to the excessive debt accumulated over the years.[270] Kemble has defaulted on interest payments on existing loans. It negotiated with Ofwat to pump cash into Thames Water.[271] Ofwat agreed to increase water bills by 22.5% for the period 2025–2030, but also imposed a Turnaround Oversight Regime on the company and considered appointing an independent monitor to oversee the company's compliance to a turnaround plan.[272] As a result, both Kemble and Thames Water—which have debt approaching £18.3 billion[273]—are at risk of financial default.

Several options are on the table, including the nationalisation of the company[274] or a debt-to-equity swap that would allow Kemble's bondholders to acquire a stake in the company.[275] The newly elected Labour government has not committed to a renationalisation strategy, preferring to advocate for a pol-

2024) <https://www.theguardian.com/business/article/2024/jul/10/cheap-sales-debt-and-foreign-takeovers-how-privatisation-changed-the-water-industry>.

268 A total of £195.8 million was paid in dividends in the financial year 2023/24: Thames Water, *Annual Report 2023–24* (2024) 45 <https://www.thameswater.co.uk/media-library/home/about-us/investors/our-results/2024-reports/thames-water-annual-report-2023–24.pdf>.

269 A Lawson and A Isaac, 'Thames Water Board Approved £150m Payout Hours before Funding U-Turn' *The Guardian* (London, 28 June 2024) <https://www.theguardian.com/business/article/2024/jun/28/thames-water-board-150m-dividend-payout-funding-u-turn>.

270 According to figures released in a parliamentary debate, Southern Water and South East Water have also been using up to 25% of customer bills to service their debts: HC Deb 6 February 2024, vol x, col 5 (per Emma Hardy); HL Deb 19 February 2024, vol 836, col 74GC (per Baroness Hayman of Ullock).

271 S Jack, 'Can Troubled Thames Water Avoid Collapse?' *BBC News* (London, 5 April 2024) <https://www.bbc.co.uk/news/business-68738410>.

272 Ofwat, 'Ofwat Sets Out record £88 billion Upgrade to Deliver Cleaner Rivers and Seas, and Better Service for Customers' *Ofwat* (London, 11 July 2024) <https://www.ofwat.gov.uk/pr24-draft-determinations-press-notice/>.

273 G Plimmer, 'Thames Water's New Boss Faces Task of Persuading Investors over Turnaround Plan' *Financial Times* (London, 8 January 2024) <https://www.ft.com/content/fe8f6796-7be8-4778-9f20-26843f7fd319>.

274 A Isaac, 'Thames Water Nationalisation Plan Could Move Bulk of £15bn Debt to State' *The Guardian* (London, 18 April 2024) <https://www.theguardian.com/business/2024/apr/18/whitehall-blueprint-for-thames-water-nationalisation-could-see-state-take-on-bulk-of-15bn-debt>.

275 A Lawson, 'Thames Water Owner Bond Slumps to Record Lows amid Uncertainty over Firm' *The Guardian* (London, 2 April 2024) <https://www

icy of higher fines on water companies, blocking the bonuses of executives, and improving independent monitoring.[276]

The main rules in the area are now the Water Industry (Special Administration) Regulations 2024[277] (WISAR 2024) and the Water Industry (Special Administration) (England and Wales) Rules 2024. The Water Industry Act 1991 (Amendment) Order 2024 includes provisions relating to transfers by hive-down. All of them came into force in March 2024 and apply only to England and Wales. The Flood and Water Management Act 2010 (Commencement No. 10) Order 2024, which also includes updates to the WISAR, came into force on 12 January 2024.

Calls for a more proactive approach to the use of the regulator's powers emerged as a result of parliamentary investigations into the water industry.[278] In response, Ofwat considered that it would most likely use the special administration powers against inefficient companies that would otherwise fail.[279] However, the government's response was more cautionary, and it highlighted that the special administration powers are the "ultimate enforcement tool" at Ofwat's disposal and should be used only where other means are inadequate.[280] This point was later reiterated in the explanatory memorandum to the WISAR.[281] The existing WISAR also had to be updated to take into account changes made to the IA 1986 by the Enterprise Act 2002; the Small Business,

---

.theguardian.com/business/2024/apr/02/thames-water-owner-bond-slumps-to-record-lows-amid-uncertainty-over-firm>.

276 Labour's Party, 'Labour's Manifesto (2024): Make Britain a Clean Energy Superpower', sub-heading "Clean Water" <https://labour.org.uk/change/make-britain-a-clean-energy-superpower/#clean-water>.

277 This most significant instrument applies, disapplies, and modifies general insolvency provisions to water companies under the Water Industry Act 1991.

278 HL, Industry and Regulators Committee, 'The Affluent and the Effluent: Cleaning Up Failures in Water and Sewage Regulation' (HL Paper 166, 22 March 2023). See the call for Ofwat to be more proactive in using the powers to change management of continued poor performers: para 267 of the Report and para 43 of the recommendations.

279 Ofwat response to the HL Industry and Regulators Committee Report: The Affluent and the Effluent (22 May 2023) 7 <https://committees.parliament.uk/publications/40087/documents/195590/default/>.

280 Government Response to the HL Industry and Regulators Committee Report: The Affluent and the Effluent: Cleaning Up Failures in Water and Sewage Regulation (June 2023) 6–7 <https://committees.parliament.uk/publications/40187/documents/196307/default/>.

281 At para 7.1 <https://www.legislation.gov.uk/uksi/2024/205/pdfs/uksiem_20240205_en_001.pdf>.

Enterprise and Employment Act 2015; the Insolvency (England and Wales) Rules 2016; and CIGA 2020.[282]

There are several key differences between a traditional administration procedure and the WISAR applicable to water companies. Firstly, the procedure can only be commenced by the Secretary of State for Environment, Food and Rural Affairs (DEFRA), the Welsh ministers, or Ofwat, when they are satisfied that one of these conditions has been met:

1. the company is unable to pay its debts ("insolvency ground");
2. the company is unable or likely to become unable to meet its statutory or license obligations ("performance ground").

The new law did not change the two main grounds on which a water company can enter special administration. When a special administration order is made, a special administrator is appointed, and a court must dismiss any petition for the winding up of the company.[283] The company is granted a moratorium on all executory actions against them or their property. These actions cannot be continued unless consent is given by the special administrator or permission is given by the court.[284]

The special administrator is an insolvency practitioner appointed by the High Court. Unlike the commissioners for local authorities, special administrators are highly qualified and regulated professionals, who are subject to clear statutory duties and obligations. Whilst the special administrator has the same powers and duties as "traditional" administrators,[285] they must exercise them to ensure the continued provision of services and fulfilment of the company's environmental obligations.[286] Achieving the best result for the company's creditors remains a goal of the procedure, but is subordinated to the main objective described above.

---

[282] This point was expressly mentioned in the parliamentary debate: HL Deb 19 February 2024, vol 836, col 69GC. The latter statute is not expressly mentioned in the official parliamentary debate.

[283] The Water Industry (Special Administration) Regulations 2024, regulation 11, amending IA 1986, sch B1, para 40.

[284] Ibid regulation 13, amending IA 1986, sch B1, para 43.

[285] The powers of traditional administrators are outlined by IA 1986, sch B1, paras 59–64. For an overview of the relevant case law, see (among others): M Weaver, 'Administrators: Rights and Responsibilities' (2018) 11(5) C.R. & I. 177.

[286] *Re Bulb Energy Ltd* [2021] EWHC 3735 (Ch), outlining the administrator's powers (and duties) with reference to a special administration involving an energy company.

Before this reform, special administrators could only transfer the assets of the regulated business to a new owner. The old water company would then be liquidated or dissolved, and the existing shareholders would be wiped out. The new regulations expand the scope of the existing rules to cover the restructuring of company debt and to allow the company to exit administration as a going concern. Rescue can be pursued through modified rules on company voluntary arrangements, schemes of arrangement and restructuring plans.[287] The rescue route is only possible where the debtor company is insolvent. As a result, the transfer route can be pursued only if rescue is not possible or if a transfer is more likely to secure better performance of the water company's functions and activities than if the company was rescued as a going concern.[288]

The new rules also allow special administrators to hive-down the regulated business.[289] Through a hive-down, the regulated business is separated from the unregulated business and from other liabilities. The portion of the business that is essential to supply water and wastewater treatment services is transferred to a business fully owned by the debtor, whilst the existing debt and non-essential assets are not transferred. The shares in this subsidiary are then sold to a third-party buyer. The hive-down approach is particularly attractive to new investors, as this allows them to buy an entity which is free of, or has very few, liabilities and which has no surplus assets. There are also tax efficiencies associated with a sale following a hive-down, as compared to a sale of assets.[290] At the time of writing (July 2024), Thames Water is in advanced talks to conduct a series of hive-downs and divide the company into smaller entities.[291]

The grounds upon which a special administrator's conduct can be challenged by a creditor or member are narrower than in a standard administration. In the traditional procedure, these parties can challenge any decision by

---

287 WISAR 2024, regulation 56.

288 Ibid regulation 17, amending IA 1986, sch B1, para 49.

289 The Water Industry Act 1991 (Amendment) Order 2024, art 5, amending the Water Industry Act 1991, sch 2, para 2.

290 J Houghton and R Cheetham, 'Changes to the Special Administration Regime for UK Water Companies' *GreenbergTraurig* (14 February 2024) <https://www.gtlaw.com/en/insights/2024/2/changes-to-the-special-administration-regime-for-uk-water-companies>; K Stephenson, 'New UK Legislation to Facilitate Special Administration of Water Companies' *Kirkland & Ellis* (17 January 2024) <https://www.kirkland.com/publications/kirkland-alert/2024/01/new-uk-legislation-to-facilitate-special-administration-of-water-companies>.

291 L Mucklejohn, 'Thames Water Explores Radical Restructuring Plan in Fight for Survival' *City A.M.* (London, 7 April 2024) <https://www.cityam.com/thames-water-explores-radical-restructuring-plans-in-fight-for-survival/>.

the administrator on the basis that the administrator is 'not performing his functions as quickly or as efficiently as is reasonably practicable'.[292] In the new WISAR, challenges can only be made on the basis that the special administrator is 'conducting the special administration in a way that is preventing its purposes from being achieved as quickly and efficiently as is reasonably practicable'.[293] Additionally, courts cannot grant a remedy unless the relevant authority and Ofwat have been given a reasonable opportunity to make representations about the claim and the proposed remedy, relief or order. No order can be made if it is likely to prejudice, impede or prevent the purposes of the WISAR from being achieved.[294] Special administrators thus have more freedom to exercise their powers to protect public services, even if this means providing a lower return to the company's creditors.

Finally, the new WISAR allows the administrator to dispose of fixed charge property without the consent of the charge holder. The charge holder will only receive "appropriate value" for, rather than the "market value" of, the collateral.[295] Appropriate value is described as 'the best price that could be reasonably available on a sale which is consistent with the achievement of the purposes of the special administration'.[296] Whilst this formulation may lead to litigation,[297] it also signals the government's preference for prioritising social and public interests over the maximisation of returns to creditors.

The special administrator is required to send a report to DEFRA, the regulator and other interested parties containing a statement of the company's financial position, the reasons for the special administration, potential ways to transfer the company or its assets, and the likely impact on customers, the environment, and creditors. The report must also invite representations from recipients within a specified period, meaning that these parties collectively devise a solution for the distressed debtor which promotes the common good. At the same time, the debtor's creditors do not vote on the administrator's proposal, and the administrator cannot dispose of protected land without the regulator's consent. The regulator can provide its consent subject to any appropriate conditions.[298] In practice, any sale of the company's protected land requires the regulator's support.

---

[292] IA 1986, sch B1, para 72(2).

[293] WISAR 2024, regulation 25, amending IA 1986, sch B1, para 74.

[294] Explanatory Memorandum to the WISAR 2024, para 7.18.

[295] WISAR 2024, regulations 22 and 23, amending IA 1986, sch B1, para 71(3)(b) and 72(3)(b).

[296] Ibid regulation 40, amending IA 1986, sch B1, para 71.

[297] HL Deb 19 February 2024, vol 836, col 73GC.

[298] WISAR 2024, regulation 20, amending IA 1986, sch B1, para 60(1).

In conclusion, whilst the original WISAR was already preferable to the current statutory framework for local authorities in financial distress, it included little in terms of ESG-orientated measures. By broadening out the purpose of the statutory intervention and by providing the special administrator with a greater array of restructuring options compared with the previous legislative framework, the revised WISAR allows more latitude to design and implement effective restructuring solutions that ensure the long-term viability of the affected company.

Overall, the WISAR is designed to protect the interests of customers and the environment when a water or sewage company is in financial distress or at risk of insolvency. This is done by mandating that the public service be provided pending rescue or transfer to new owners. A secondary purpose of this WISAR is to ensure that consumers are—as much as possible—protected from the impacts of the corporate distress affecting the water company.

In other words, the framework puts the E and S in ESG at the centre of the restructuring efforts. This is also evidenced by the (questionable) choice to prioritise grants, loans, and the repayment of government guarantees over the ordinary expenses of the special administration (which include the special administrator's remuneration).[299]

This development came at a time when there was a reasonable prospect that the law would be needed to rescue a troubled entity. This indicates that, when the public interest is at stake, environmental and social concerns take on a central role in shaping the restructuring process. At the same time, the government failed to apply for a WISAR order where a water company breached consistently and flagrantly its environmental duties. Finally, the law does not require the special administrator to continue to discharge the company's investment plans beyond what is strictly necessary to comply with the relevant environmental obligations.

Unfortunately, governance issues do not feature as prominently under the current law. For instance, the WISAR 2024[300] allows either a relevant authority (i.e. the Secretary of State or a Welsh Minister) or Ofwat to appoint a special administrator to aid the insolvency practitioner that is running the procedure. The law does not include any requirement for this person to be independent and unconnected with the previous management of the water company.

Additionally, the hive-down procedure allows a financially distressed water company to be sold (free of debt) to a new buyer, much like when the privatisation process started in the late 1980s. Nothing prevents the new owners from behaving like the existing ones, in using the water companies to reap profits

[299] Ibid regulation 35, amending IA 1986, sch B1, para 99.
[300] Ibid regulation 37, amending IA 1986, sch B1, para 103.

whilst neglecting maintenance obligations and polluting the environment.[301] Actually, nothing prevents new owners connected to the previous ones from buying (at a discount) a slimmed-down and debt-free utility company as part of a hive-down, pre-packaged sale. This process is now subject to additional requirements when it occurs as part of a traditional administration procedure.[302] However, the same safeguards have not been applied to the hive-down of water companies.

Finally, neither Ofwat nor the Environment Agency has sufficiently effective powers to tackle the unlawful discharge of untreated sewage water into English rivers and seas, or to hold the managers of the water companies accountable for these failures. The parliamentary debate in the House of Commons highlighted that the regulators are under-funded and under-resourced, and are thus unable to tackle poor environmental performance by the water industry.[303]

To conclude, the heightened protection of customers marks a significant deviation from the traditional liberal, creditor-friendly approach of the Conservative government (which was governing the country at the time this legislation was introduced) and of much insolvency law from before 2006. However, as evidenced above, a statutory framework truly informed by ESG criteria would require the treatment of financially distressed water companies to be significantly changed.

5.5 CONCLUSIONS—AN ESG CRITIQUE OF THE LAW IN PRACTICE

ESG discussions are increasingly present in the public domain, and may result in controversial forms of protest.[304] They are also polarising, as tensions pertaining to the extension of the Ultra Low Emission Zone (ULEZ) in London[305] arguably had a knock-on effect on local by-election results.[306] Clean air pitches

---

301 HL Deb 19 February 2024, vol 836, col 72GC.

302 The Administration (Restrictions on Disposal etc. to Connected Persons) Regulations 2021.

303 HC Deb 6 February 2024, vol x, col 7 (per Wera Hobhouse).

304 See the measures adopted by the NGO/charity *Just Stop Oil* <https://juststopoil.org/>.

305 J Warren, 'London Mayor Sadik Khan Rules Out ULEZ changes' *BBC News* (London, 24 March 2024) <https://www.bbc.com/news/uk-england-london-68645199>.

306 G Wright and C Geiger, 'Uxbridge By-election: Khan defends ULEZ after Starmer Blames It for Poll Setback' *BBC News* (London, 21 July 2023) <https://www.bbc.co.uk/news/uk-politics-66264893>.

long-term health versus affordability of mobility. English elections are lost and won[307] on these stark choices. Judicial battles are waged around them also.[308]

If long-term ESG considerations matter in the ballot box, local councils may wish to consider them in their day-to-day operations, and in the process of dealing with financially distressed budgets. This chapter has shown that, whilst ESG considerations play an increasing role in judicial practice and the operational restructuring of the "English corporate", they have yet to scratch the surface of "public England".

This chapter has illustrated the shortcomings of the current framework for dealing with local entities in financial distress. The current rules are based on outdated punitive practices that incentivise poor auditing, late acknowledgment of financial distress, and *ad hoc*, *ex post* and fragmented intervention. Such intervention usually takes the form of central, one-off (but extended) financial support, and government-appointed commissioners who lack special qualifications and are not subject to statutory duties. In this creditor-friendly, taxpayer-funded bonanza, creditors are paid in full, no-one is held accountable for gross mismanagement decisions, public services are cut, local taxes are increased, local workers are made redundant, and vulnerable people are left behind.

New rules are urgently needed to encourage long-term, fair and equitable funding practices. They need to ensure local budgets promote prudent and ESG-orientated local capital investments, independent and effective monitoring of local finances by external auditors, the early acknowledgment of financial distress in local authorities, and the adoption of long-term ESG-informed turnaround practices when budgets are unbalanced.

In the turnaround phase, political bickering should play no role, as any name-and-shame exercise goes against the very interests of local communities. New rules based on successful corporate restructuring plans and the recently revised special administration rules should be implemented and used as a blueprint for negotiating a restructuring agreement with a local authority's creditors.

The new restructuring framework should prioritise debtor-in-possession mechanisms. These should be modelled on restructuring plans made in respect of councils that have been upfront about their financial difficulties, have called for statutory protection at an early stage and did not face allegations of gross mismanagement or governance failures. In all other cases, restructuring

---

307 T Mackintosh, 'Green Party: Co-leaders Hail Highest Number of Councillors' *BBC News* (London, 5 May 2024) <https://www.bbc.co.uk/news/uk-68956733>.

308 H Low, 'ULEZ: London Mayor Sadiq Khan Hails High Court Ruling' *BBC News* (London, 28 July 2023) <https://www.bbc.com/news/uk-66327961>.

options could be based on a modified version of the debtor-in-possession special administration regime, with additional safeguards to ensure the independence of the special administrator and the absence of collusion as part of the hive-down process.

When weighing up whether to restructure or reorganise, the existing management and/or the government-appointed commissioners must be familiar with the fast-changing regulatory and policy environment, any technological developments that may affect the cost and quality of services provided by local authorities, reputational risks and the risks of being litigated against for climate-related damages, and the impact of climate change and deepening economic inequality on local communities and their surroundings.

Turnaround plans should include reasonable cuts to local services, acceptable increases in local taxes, and even radical restructuring options (such as mergers with neighbouring authorities). The financial burden of local crises cannot be borne by national taxpayers. However, turnaround plans must be devised as part of a rescue strategy aimed at ensuring the long-term resilience and sustainability of the local authority. That strategy should ring-fence essential services and ESG-orientated capital investments and result in meaningful reductions in creditors' claims against the distressed local entity.

The mandatory, ESG-informed and non-arbitrary nature of the plan should be assessed by the creditors and—in the case of debtor-in-possession mechanisms—as part of a court's sanctioning process. Both routes should include mechanisms to overcome the dissenting, blocking vote of one or more classes of creditors.

To conclude, an ESG-informed overhaul of the legal framework regulating financially distressed local authorities presents the opportunity to apply the same principles to special administration regimes, LEPs and—more generally—corporate restructuring options.

6. A comparative analysis

6.1 INTRODUCTION

This book argues that to ensure the long-term financial recovery of a municipality in financial distress, the decision-making process must be tailored to include environmental, social, and governance (ESG) considerations in the interest of the local community it serves. As stated before, the turn to ESG strategies signals an alignment between long-standing corporate social responsibility (CSR) business practices and the pursuit of sustainability as a prevailing societal objective, especially in light of major international agendas such as the United Nations' Sustainable Development Goals (SDGs).[1]

The implementation of SDGs relies at least partly on local governments' actions and their financing. Local government finance has been recognised as the "missing link" in fostering development.[2] However, as local governments receive more attention for supporting SDGs, they face increasing financial pressures. Central governments have assigned them more responsibilities. Some local governments have, over the years, expanded their activities.[3] Simultaneously, central governments have restricted or conditioned funding to local authorities.

Budgetary restraints have pushed local governments to develop—where possible under national law—innovative means to access finances. These strategies are frequently dependent on financial markets. Access to favourable financial conditions is tied to good credit ratings. Credit ratings are generally positively affected by the promotion of ESG-orientated and sustainable policies. Consequently, ESG considerations impact local policies even when they

[1] See chapter 2, *sub* [2.1.3].

[2] J Roig, 'Financing Subnational and Local Governments: The Missing Link in Development Finance', in *OECD Regional Outlook 2016: Productive Regions for Inclusive Societies* (OECD Publishing 2016).

[3] M Moses, *The Municipal Financial Crisis. A Framework for Understanding and Fixing Government Budgeting* (Palgrave MacMillan 2022) ch 2.

do not directly affect funding and financing, such as in the case of tax-funded services.[4] Neglecting these factors can contribute to financial difficulties.

The book centred on three countries: the US, South Africa, and the UK (namely, England). In all three systems, the local governments are primarily responsible for identifying and addressing their financial problems. Only when they fail (South Africa) or do not seem in a position to succeed (England) will a superior entity (the national/federal or the state/province) intervene. In the US, such an intervention may indeed materialise, but it will be seen with suspicion as an interference with the locally elected representatives.[5] Financial distress in local government is addressed from inside the Bankruptcy Code in the US, from a tailored statutory perspective in South Africa, and according to a mostly politico-administrative process in England. In all three countries, there is recognised room for creativity, and traditional liquidation and rescue procedures are adapted. However, the specific adaptations vary by country. In the US, judges take a less hands-on approach to the financial distress of municipalities than they do with debtors under other chapters of the Bankruptcy Code. In South Africa, procedures are modified to accommodate the unique nature of local government. In England, the system differs significantly from standard liquidation and rescue practices, even in areas where there is no strong legal justification for the divergence, such as in the case of liquidation of the entity's assets. For this reason, it is a misnomer to speak about "municipal bankruptcy" in countries other than the US.

Although similar concerns and the need for resilience emerge during financial distress at the local level in all three systems (6.3), they arise within vastly different constitutional frameworks (6.2), accountability processes (6.4), and institutional contexts (6.5). The extent of these differences, alongside the shared concerns, allows us to propose approaches to municipal financial distress that incorporate ESG considerations to build resilience and support sustainable long-term recovery (6.6).

6.2 DIFFERENT CONSTITUTIONAL BACKGROUNDS

The US, South Africa, and the UK are *prima facie* very different economic systems. The US and the UK are G7 members[6] representing the epitome of the

---

4 Conditionality can be more or less closely connected to one activity or can extend to the general profile of an entity.

5 There is one exception to this principle: in North Carolina, there is an embedded state oversight role such that one could argue that the state government has put itself in the position of being primarily responsible (see chapter 3, *sub* [3.3]).

6 The Group of Seven (G7) is an informal grouping of advanced democracies that meets annually to coordinate global economic policy and address other

Global North and OECD members,[7] whilst South Africa is a BRICS member.[8] The economic differences are reflected in some main financial indicators. The debt-to-GDP ratio varies from 75.4% in South Africa,[9] to 97.9% in the UK,[10] and 123% in the US.[11] Nevertheless, South Africa's average annual income in 2024 (US$ 9,338) is much lower than the OECD average (US$ 30,490) or the average annual income in the UK (US$ 33,049) and the US (US$ 51,147).[12]

Regarding social indicators, reference should be made to the Gini factor, which assesses income, wealth, and consumption inequalities within specified communities. The latest available data show that inequality levels range from moderate (32.4 for the UK and 39.8 for the US, both in 2021) to extremely high (63.0 for South Africa in 2014).[13]

Related to social considerations are governance indicators. Data from the "Rule of Law" index rank the UK (15th out of 142 countries) and the US (26th out of 142 countries) as high or well-performing countries, whilst South Africa is ranked 56th out of the same pool of countries.[14] Similar results are evidenced with reference to transparency issues, with Transparency International ranking the UK (20th out of 180 countries) and the US (24th out of 180 countries)

---

transnational issues. Its members include Canada, France, Germany, Italy, Japan, the UK, and the US; additionally, the European Union is a "non-enumerated member".

[7] The Organization for Economic Co-operation and Development (OECD) is a unique forum where the governments of 37 democracies with market-based economies collaborate to develop policy standards to promote sustainable economic growth. The full list of member countries is available here: <https://www.oecd.org/en/countries.html>.

[8] BRICS is an intergovernmental organisation comprising Brazil, Russia, India, China, South Africa, Iran, Egypt, Ethiopia, and the United Arab Emirates.

[9] 'Government Debt (% of GDP)' (*International Monetary Fund*, 2024) <https://www.imf.org/external/datamapper/GGXWDG_GDP@AFRREO/SSA/OEXP/OIMP/COM/ZAF>.

[10] M Keep, 'Public Finances: Key Economic Indicators' (*House of Commons Library*, 19 July 2024) <https://commonslibrary.parliament.uk/research-briefings/sn02812/>.

[11] 'What Is the National Debt?' (*US Treasury Department*, 30 November 2023) <https://fiscaldata.treasury.gov/americas-finance-guide/national-debt/#tracking-the-debt>.

[12] All this information has been retrieved from the OECD 'Better Life Index': <https://www.oecdbetterlifeindex.org/#/11111111111>.

[13] 'Gini Index' (*World Bank*, 2024) <https://data.worldbank.org/indicator/SI.POV.GINI?skipRedirection=true&view=map>.

[14] Data is available on the World Justice Project website: <https://worldjusticeproject.org/>.

among the best-performing countries, whilst South Africa is lower in the ranking (83th out of 180 countries) with a significantly lower transparency score.

These figures suggest that the countries analysed as part of this study are economically, socially, and culturally different, meaning that our findings could potentially be influential for a wide range of jurisdictions. However, such differences are not the only factors to consider when comparing how local government financial distress is addressed in these three jurisdictions. This section highlights the first major difference: the constitutional background within which local governments operate. This can be further divided into formal constitutional differences (6.2.1) and economic constitutional differences (6.2.2).

6.2.1 Formal Constitutional Differences

Local government is often "forgotten" in constitutional theories,[15] even if their regulation is not necessarily as often forgotten in constitutional texts. Despite all being common law countries (at least in part), the role of the Constitution in the US, South Africa, and the UK is strikingly different. These differences result in distinctive frameworks for the interactions between law and politics in managing local entities, including those facing financial distress.

Among the countries considered in this study, South Africa boasts the most detailed constitutional framework on local government, as local entities were seen as one of the avenues for reconstructing democracy after Apartheid.[16] As a relatively recent creation from 1996, local governments in South Africa are still defining their appropriate role within the country's constitutional framework. They are also operating against a backdrop of ongoing urbanisation, which results in fewer people inhabiting rural areas. This shift places pressure on land use management, service delivery (including water, energy, food, waste, and sanitation), and social cohesion.[17] The constitutional provisions relating to local government in the South African Constitution have been hailed as 'the most comprehensive and successful endeavour to date to grant cities constitutional status and standing'.[18] The Constitution provides that all

---

[15] R Hirshl, *City, State, Constitutionalism and the Megacity* (OUP 2020), critically reviewed by M Loughlin, 'The City in the Constitutional Imagination' (2022) 72(3) UTLJ 356.

[16] The term "Apartheid" is used to refer to a system of institutionalised racial segregation that existed in South Africa and South West Africa (now Namibia) from 1948 to the early 1990s.

[17] L Nhamo et al, 'Urban Nexus and Transformative Pathways towards a Resilient Gauteng City-Region, South Africa' (2021) 116 Cities 103266.

[18] R Hirshl, 'The City as an Anti-Canonical Concept in Constitutional Law (and Recent Attempts to Change That)' in S Choudhry, M Hailbronner and M

spheres of government are 'distinctive, interdependent and interrelated',[19] and extensively details the principles governing municipalities.[20] These objectives include ensuring democratic and accountable governance for local communities; delivering services in a sustainable manner; promoting social and economic development; fostering a safe and healthy environment; and encouraging the active involvement of communities and community organisations in local government affairs.[21] Despite their broad constitutional powers, South African municipalities often lack the financial and administrative means to deliver on such duties.[22] Furthermore, municipalities have developmental duties.[23] In particular, they are required to 'structure and manage [their] administration and budgeting and planning processes to give priority to the basic needs of the community, and to promote [...] social and economic development'.[24] Finally, the South African Constitution recognises a highly developed set of socio-economic rights, including environmental protection rights. Local governments have a prominent role to play in protecting the environment,[25] although they are only able to allocate a small portion of their financial commitments (approximately 3.5% of their expenses in 2022) to the

Kumm (eds), *Global Canons in an Age of Contestation: Debating Foundational Texts of Constitutional Democracy and Human Rights* (OUP 2024) 504.

19 South African Constitution, s 40(1).

20 Ibid ss 151–164.

21 Ibid s 152(1). For problems arising from the definitions of these powers and possible overlaps with other institutions, see (among others): N Steytler and YT Fessha, 'Defining Local Government Powers and Functions' (2007) 124(2) SALJ 320; J de Visser, 'Developmental Local Government in South Africa: Institutional Fault Lines' (2009) 2 CJLG 7; M Mathenjwa, 'Contemporary Trends in Provincial Government Supervision of Local Government in South Africa' (2014) 18(1) LDD 178; M Pieterse, 'Development, the Right to the City and the Legal and Constitutional Responsibilities of Local Government in South Africa' (2014) 131(1) SALJ 149; M Mathenjwa, 'The Legal Status of Local Government in South Africa Under the New Constitutional Dispensation' (2018) 33(2) SAPL 1; O Fuo, 'Local Government and the Conundrum of Constitutional Competencies in South Africa: The Tussle Between City of Tshwane Municipality and the Gauteng Health Department Over Ambulance Services' (2022) 33(3) Stellenbosch L. Rev. 484.

22 South African Constitution, s 152(2).

23 S Mosala and T Nxumalo, 'The Inability of Municipalities in South Africa to Fulfil Their Developmental Agenda: The Case of Ngaka Modiri Molema District Municipality' (2023) 58(4) Public Admin. 1065.

24 South African Constitution, s 153.

25 A du Plessis, 'South Africa's Constitutional Environmental Right (Generously) Interpreted: What is in it for Poverty?' (2011) 27(2) SAJHR 279; A du Plessis, '"Local Environmental Governance" and the Role of Local Government

fulfilment of such duties.[26] Overall, the South African Constitution provides extensive justiciable rights that could contribute to including ESG considerations in local governments and the management of their financial distress. However, the Constitution seems to be less effective in ensuring that adequate financial resources are allocated to local governments to fulfil such tasks.[27]

Among the countries examined in this study, the US prides itself on the oldest constitutional framework. This framework is notably detailed, reflecting the country's historical context and organisational structure (federalism). However, the US Constitution does not mention local government. This is a "de-regulated topic", meaning that the federal states enjoy significant freedom in regulating this matter. Whilst some state constitutions cover certain socio-economic rights, the US Constitution is silent on this issue.[28] However, these considerations do not make it less relevant for governing the treatment of municipalities in distress, as the US Constitution reserves bankruptcy matters to the competency of the federal legislature.[29] This creates a fertile environment for testing federalist jurisprudence, as municipal bankruptcies challenge the boundaries of state sovereignty in managing potential fiscal crises at the local level.[30]

In contrast to South Africa and the US, English local entities operate in a much more fluid legal context. The absence of a formal written constitution in the UK results in a constitutional silence on the key powers, functions, and resources granted to local entities. Equally, socio-economic rights do not

in Realising Section 24 of the South African Constitution' (2010) 21 Stellenbosch L. Rev. 265.

[26] More information is available here: <https://www.sng-wofi.org/country-profiles/south_africa.html>.

[27] NJ Schoeman, 'Rethinking Fiscal Decentralization in South Africa' (2006) 41(2) Public Admin. 110; MH Kanyane, 'Financial Viability of Rural Municipalities in South Africa' (2011) 46(2) Public Admin. 935; DN Magagula et al, 'The Role of District Municipalities in Service Provision in South Africa: Dissecting Challenges Faced by Ehlanzeni District Municipality' (2022) 10(1) APSDPR 1; LBG Manuel and LJ Erasmus, 'A Sustainable Differentiated Funding Model for South African District Municipalities' (2024) 5 JOLGRI a163.

[28] CR Sunstein, 'Why Does the American Constitution Lack Social and Economic Guarantees?' (2005) 56 Syracuse L. Rev. 1; J King, 'Social Rights in Comparative Constitutional Theory' in G Jacobsohn and M Schor (eds) *Comparative Constitutional Theory* (EE Publishing 2018) 144.

[29] US Constitution, art I, § 8, cl. 4.

[30] JA Livingston, 'Defining the Relationship Between Municipal Bankruptcy and Modern Federalism Jurisprudence' (2024) 18 FIU L. Rev. 879.

enjoy any constitutional or entrenched status.[31] Finally, insolvency procedures, which have become increasingly complex, only apply to individuals and corporations. Whilst laws regulate the institutional framework of local entities and enforce fiscal discipline, the absence of detailed and comprehensive regulations in this area allows for considerable flexibility. This gap provides room for creativity, pragmatism, and political influences to contribute to, and potentially interfere with, the management of local authorities in financial distress. There are no formal constitutional mechanisms specifically addressing this issue, and even potential constitutional techniques fall under the realm of what is known as the "political constitution".[32] In cases of local government financial distress, judges are not involved. Instead, the central government intervenes through an entirely "administrative" process, which is subject to parliamentary oversight.[33]

To conclude, our three jurisdictions span a spectrum. South Africa has a clearly defined constitutional role for local government as an autonomous sphere of government, including justiciable socio-economic obligations that may encompass ESG considerations. The US Constitution grants bankruptcy regulation powers to the federal government, thereby ensuring judicial oversight of municipal bankruptcies. In the UK, the constitution provides only for parliamentary control over the financial support extended by the central government to struggling local governments.

---

31 The situation is very much in the political discussions in the UK. In 2023, the Scottish Government proceeded with a consultation on a future human rights bill for Scotland that would include economic, social, cultural (ESCR) and environmental rights (Scottish Government, 'A Human Rights Bill for Scotland: Consultation' (June 2023) <https://www.gov.scot/binaries/content/documents/govscot/publications/consultation-paper/2023/06/human-rights-bill-scotland-consultation/documents/human-rights-bill-scotland-consultation-june/human-rights-bill-scotland-consultation-june/govscot%3Adocument/human-rights-bill-scotland-consultation-june.pdf>). Among various reforms discussed prior to the 2024 UK national elections, the former Prime Minister Gordon Brown's Commission on the UK's Future recommended constitutional protection of social rights (Commission on the UK's Future, 'A New Britain: Renewing our Democracy and Rebuilding our Economy' (2023) <https://labour.org.uk/wp-content/uploads/2022/12/Commission-on-the-UKs-Future.pdf>). However, the political or legal nature of the "constitution" in the UK remains contested.

32 A political constitution means a constitution which is mainly enforced and the respect of which is mainly ensured by political organs: JAG Griffith, 'The Political Constitution' (1979) 42(1) MLR 1.

33 See below, *sub* [6.5].

6.2.2 Economic Constitutional Differences

The countries considered in this study do not simply differ on formal constitutional aspects; the differences extend to economic constitutional aspects.

"Economic constitution" refers to the idea that 'various arrangements for economic management form a coherent whole, and in particular with the extent to which they permit effective communication within different parts of government, with market actors and with others who may be affected by decisions'.[34] The economic constitution encompasses principles relating to taxation, expenditure, and property rights, and the institutional arrangements through which these principles operate. Whilst most of the attention in this area focuses on what central governments do, local governments also have a role to play. This is because they have the authority to levy taxes, manage public funds, own and invest in assets, and sell them. Such powers, however, are affected by the macro-economic and political conditions of their countries.

In the UK, liberal thinkers from the nineteenth century considered local government as a key laboratory to educate citizens.[35] This led to a period of prosperous municipal socialism, which terminated with World War II. Since then, centralisation trends have led to a weakening of local democracy, legitimacy, and financial resources.[36] Nowadays, it could be argued that the UK has a reasonable number of multi-purpose local government entities (374 at the local level and 35 at the intermediate level)[37] compared to its population. Special purpose and multi-purpose local government entities (such as fire brigades or police authorities) co-exist. Other special purpose entities operate at the local level, but are under tight control by the central government (NHS trusts, schools, and the care industry). The financial status of both special and multi-purpose entities varies from type to type, with some known to be struggling.[38] This also explains the presence of tailored insolvency regimes for some of them.[39]

---

34 T Prosser, *The Economic Constitution* (OUP 2014) 8.

35 JS Mill, *Considerations on Representative Government* (Gutenberg Project 2004) ch XV.

36 M Elliott and S Bailey, 'Taking Local Government Seriously: Democracy, Autonomy and the Constitution' (2009) 68(2) CLJ 436.

37 For more information: <https://www.sng-wofi.org/country-profiles/>.

38 See the case of Thames Water, discussed in chapter 5, *sub* [5.4.3].

39 Monitor, 'Statutory Guidance for Trust Special Administrations Appointed to NHS Foundation Trusts' (February 2015) <https://assets.publishing.service.gov.uk/media/5a809b20e5274a2e8ab511b1/TSA_guidance_final_for_publication.pdf>; Health and Social Care Act 2012, ch 5.

In the US, the history of municipal bankruptcy law begins in the mid-nineteenth century, during a period when the role of local governments was still being defined. At that time, the Supreme Court prioritised national policies, such as the development of railways funded by municipal bonds, over local interests.[40] Since then, local entities have used their tax levy powers and their municipal budgets to attract firms to their territories. Economists such as Tiebout argued that competition between local governments was an effective way to allocate resources across the territory.[41] Currently, these approaches are contested[42] as US local governments are extremely fragmented—both horizontally and vertically.[43] Numerous[44] general and special purpose[45] local government entities coexist, leading to accountability issues and resulting in overlapping or competing services within the same area. Whilst this fragmentation may raise concerns about efficiency and economies of scale, it also means that financial distress in one entity does not necessarily impact all services in a given area. Instead, the effects of a default are generally limited to the specific services managed by the distressed entity, mitigating the overall impact.

In South Africa, local governments have proven essential to boosting economic and social development.[46] They have a crucial role in implementing and delivering a democratic welfare state in the aftermath of the political transition and social transformations that followed the end of Apartheid. In contrast to the US and UK, the relatively young local government system in South Africa is a streamlined one with wall-to-wall municipalities falling into one of three

40 D Schleicher, *In a Bad State—Responding to State and Local Budget Crisis* (OUP 2023) 42–56.

41 C Tiebout, 'A Pure Theory of Local Expenditures' (1956) 64 J. Polit. Econ. 416.

42 S Calabrese, D Epple and R Romano, 'Inefficiencies from Metropolitan Political and Fiscal Decentralisation. Failures of Tiebout Competition' (2012) 79(3) *REStud* 1081.

43 CB Goodman, 'Local Government Fragmentation: What Do We Know?' (2019) 51(2) SLGR 134.

44 In 2017, the total number of general and special purpose municipalities in the US was 91,126: Goodman (n 43) 134.

45 For the importance of these special purposes in the development of some parts of the USA, see the Pulitzer Prize winning book by R Caro, *The Power Broker: Robert Moses and the Fall of New York* (Knopf Publishing Group 1974). For the municipal bankruptcy that followed, see Schleicher (n 40) 70–74.

46 E Nel and T Binns, 'Initiating "Developmental Local Government" in South Africa: Evolving Local Economic Development Policy' (2001) 35(4) Reg. Stud. 355; CM Rogerson, 'Local Economic Development in South Africa: Strategic Challenges' (2010) 27(4) Dev. South. Afr. 481.

clearly defined types (metropolitan, district, and local). All other local public entities exist as subsidiaries of these municipalities and hence under their direct control. Since local government is created as one of the three spheres rather than levels of government in South Africa,[47] municipalities stand in a partnership relationship with national and provincial governments, rather than subordinate to them. This also applies to the financial relationship between municipalities and other spheres of government. Local governments are constitutionally entitled to an equitable share of revenue raised nationally.[48] They can raise their own revenue, but only within set parameters, which include limitations on the type of rates and taxes that may be levied[49] and on municipal borrowing.[50] The partnership structure also means that municipalities are exclusively responsible for their financial distress and intervention by other levels is only possible under strict conditions.[51]

In normal times, local governments in the three countries considered in this study operate in a challenging environment. Tight budgets force them to make short-termist decisions (such as when the UK government stopped investing in critical infrastructure like flood protection).[52] Local municipalities are generally unable to absorb central cuts or dwindling revenues, as their long-term cost structure is inflexible (and generally on an upwards trajectory). In the US, local governments often face challenges when dealing with "acute fiscal shocks"—unexpected emergencies that are difficult to prepare for due to their low probability but potentially severe consequences. For example, wildfires can drastically alter municipal revenues and expenses,[53] posing significant management challenges. Local governments may struggle to justify maintaining large reserves of idle funds for such rare events,[54] leading them to seek state or federal assistance. However, this funding is not always guaranteed. Federal aid may be unavailable for disaster recovery, such as after a hurricane,

---

47 South African Constitution, s 40.

48 Ibid s 214.

49 Ibid s 229.

50 Ibid s 230A.

51 Ibid s 139.

52 See, among others: J Tapper, 'Charity Criticises "Crazy" Rules for Flood Defence Funding in England and Wales' *The Guardian* (London, 6 January 2024) <https://www.theguardian.com/uk-news/2024/jan/06/charity-criticises-crazy-rules-for-flood-defence-funding-in-england-and-wales>.

53 Y Liao and C Kousky, 'The Fiscal Impacts of Wildfires on California Municipalities' (2022) 9(3) JAERE 455.

54 R Kravchuk, 'Municipal Budgets, Balance Sheets, and Acute Fiscal Shocks' in C Johnson, T Moldogaziev and J Ross (eds), *Research Handbook on City and Municipal Finance* (EE Publishing 2023) 204.

or for public investments like railways that benefit broader regions beyond local jurisdictions. In South Africa, local governments encounter pressures from increasing urbanisation and the need to develop adequate infrastructure.[55] However, the central government has imposed strict borrowing limits on municipalities to promote fiscal responsibility.[56] Such limits—which are common across all jurisdictions studied in this book—make it challenging for local entities to deal with the needs arising from urbanisation levels.

In all three countries, the economic situation has worsened in the aftermath of the Global Financial Crisis. English local entities faced two main issues. First, their central funding has traditionally been linked to local business rates, which do not account for the actual needs of local communities. This means that the funds they receive from the central government may not match the services required locally.[57] Second, the central government has not updated the land valuations used for local taxes since 1991.[58] This out-of-date valuation affects how much money local councils can raise. Additionally, local governments have been under increasing pressure to fund social care and special needs education.[59] This has led them to fiscally imprudent measures, such as relying on reserves and short-term borrowing, at times ignoring regulatory guidelines.[60]

---

[55] Pieterse (n 21) 150.

[56] R Wandrag, 'The Quest for Financial Discipline at Local Government Level: The Regulation of Municipal Borrowing and Financial Emergencies' (2003) 7(2) LDD 243.

[57] M Sandford, 'Public Services and Local Government: The End of the Principle of "Funding Following Duties"' (2016) 42(4) Local Gov. Stud. 637.

[58] For more information on the UK council tax, see <https://obr.uk/forecasts-in-depth/tax-by-tax-spend-by-spend/council-tax/>. On the matter of revaluation, see (among others): S Adam et al, 'Revaluation and Reform: Bringing Council Tax in England into the 21st Century' (Institute for Fiscal Studies 2020) <https://ifs.org.uk/publications/revaluation-and-reform-bringing-council-tax-england-21st-century>; Local Government Association, 'Reforming Revenues—Options for the Future Financing of Local Government' (13 January 2022) <https://www.local.gov.uk/publications/reforming-revenues-options-future-financing-local-government>. Valuation is also discussed in the US chapter, and it raises difficult technical issues: J Youngman, 'Property Taxes and Municipal Finance' in C Johnson, T Moldogaziev and J Ross (eds), *Research Handbook on City and Municipal Finance* (EE Publishing 2023) 24.

[59] See, among others, the case of Croydon, discussed in chapter 5, *sub* [5.4.1]. See also: Levelling Up, Housing and Communities Committee, *Financial Distress in Local Authorities* (HC 2023–24, 56).

[60] H Dagdeviren and E Karwowski, 'Impasse or Mutation? Austerity and (de) financialisation of Local Governments in Britain' (2022) (22) J. Econ. Geogr. 685.

The Covid-19 pandemic also affected local finances, albeit in different ways. In the US, the central government released unprecedented subsidies to local governments.[61] A similar trend was observed in England, where the central government increased funding, including earmarked funding (e.g. the Levelling Up fund),[62] or tied it to devolution deals for some major cities, such as Manchester.[63] In South Africa, the central government provided additional funding and support through emergency and debt relief measures, as well as special grants.[64] However, many local entities still faced significant challenges due to the scale of the pandemic's impact and ongoing financial constraints.

The consequences of austerity policies on local government have been chronicled in the US,[65] South Africa,[66] and England.[67] This has pushed local governments to find creative ways to obtain funding and to gain access to financial markets through loans, municipal bonds, structured loans, swaps, and tax increment financing, among others. These all appear to be regular means of

---

[61] Y Kim, 'The Role of Cities and Public Health Expenditures in the Covid-19 Era' in C Johnson, T Moldogaziev and J Ross (eds), *Research Handbook on City and Municipal Finance* (EE Publishing 2023) 105, 118–119; Schleicher (n 40) 20–22; E Mildred et al, 'Challenging Austerity under the Covid-19 State' (2023) 16(1) CJRES 197. This can be compared with the policies carried out in a previous austerity period: LM Lobao and L Adua, 'State Rescaling and Local Governments' Austerity Policies Across the USA, 2001–2008' (2011) 4(3) CJRES 419.

[62] More information is available here: <https://www.gov.uk/government/collections/new-levelling-up-and-community-investments>.

[63] M Sanford, 'Trailblazer Devolution Deals' House of Commons Research Briefing Paper (24 November 2023) 32–34 <https://researchbriefings.files.parliament.uk/documents/CBP-9901/CBP-9901.pdf>.

[64] A Zweni et al, 'Municipal Special Budget Adjustments in Response to Negative Impact of COVID-19 in South Africa' (2023) 25(1) SAJAAR 85.

[65] J Peck, 'Pushing Austerity: State Failure, Municipal Bankruptcy and the Crises of Fiscal Federalism in the USA' (2014) 7(1) CJRES 17.

[66] T Matlala, 'An Assessment of the Challenges Facing Municipalities Going Into the 2022/2023 Financial Year' (2022) 22(4) CIGFARO Journal 14, 14–16; T Ajam et al, 'The Impact of the Covid-19 Pandemic on District Municipalities in the Western Cape' (2021) 16(4) Local Government Bulletin 1; T Ajam et al, 'The Impact of the Covid-19 Pandemic on Local Municipalities in the Western Cape' (2021) 16(4) Local Government Bulletin 1; D Petterson, 'Enabling Service Delivery' (2020) 15(6) WSA 3.

[67] M Gray and A Barford, 'The Depths of the Cuts: The Uneven Geography of Local Government Austerity' (2018) 11(3) CJRES 541.

financing local entities in the US,[68] the UK,[69] and South Africa.[70] Whilst these techniques are not all new,[71] the academic literature has recently questioned whether this wave of local government financialisation is positive.[72]

Differences arise in relation to the instruments developed in each country. For instance, issuing debts is a widespread borrowing method in the US,[73] where municipal bonds are a highly developed and effective form of finance.[74] Conversely, municipal bonds are relatively uncommon in South Africa, where direct lending remains predominant.[75] They had flourished in the nineteenth century in England,[76] but their use is now highly differentiated. Only a small number of local entities continue to make use of them.[77] To encourage their use, a UK Municipal Bond Agency was established in 2014.[78] Although only

---

[68] A Janssen, 'Financial Officers, the Municipal Swap Industry and the Rise of Risky Innovations among States' (2022) 20(3) SER 1287.

[69] A Pike, *Financialization and Local Statecraft* (OUP 2023); K Muldoon-Smith and M Sandford, 'Grasping the Nettle: The Central–Local Constraints on Local Government Funding in England' (2023) 11(8) Territory, Politics, Governance 1709.

[70] M Glasser, 'Municipal Bonds in Three Countries: India, South Africa and the United States' (2020) 4 JCULP 96.

[71] See examples in the US in the nineteenth century, in Schleicher (n 40) ch 3. See also the examples from the UK in the 1980s: M Loughlin, *Legality and Locality—The Role of the Law in Central–Local Government Relations* (Clarendon Press 1996) ch 6 (on swaps); J Braithwaite, 'Thirty Years of *Ultra Vires*: Local Authorities, National Courts and the Global Derivatives Markets' (2018) 71(1) CLP 369.

[72] H Hasenberger, 'What Is Local Government Financialisation? Four Empirical Channels to Clarify the Roles of Local Government' (2024) 61(11) Urban Studies 2039 <https://doi.org/10.1177/00420980231222133>; H Dagdeviren, 'Austerity Urbanism, Local Government Debt-Drive, and Post Covid Predicaments in Britain' (2024) 24(1) J. Econ. Geogr. 79.

[73] For details, see (among others): WB Hildreth and J Jose, 'The Security, Structure, and Market of Municipal Debt: Recent Trends, Research and Developments' in C Johnson, T Moldogaziev and J Ross (eds), *Research Handbook on City and Municipal Finance* (EE Publishing 2023) 271.

[74] 'Investor Bulletin: The Municipal Securities Market' (*US Securities and Exchange Commission*, 1 February 2018) <https://www.sec.gov/resources-for-investors/investor-alerts-bulletins/ib_munibondsmarket>.

[75] Glasser (n 70).

[76] I Webster, 'Making the Municipal Capital Market in Nineteenth-Century England' (2022) 75(1) Econ. Hist. Rev. 56.

[77] Pike (n 69) 175.

[78] For more information, consult this website: <https://ukmba.org/>. See also Pike (n 69) 175–176.

rarely used,[79] this Agency has developed a bond for sustainable finance, which includes social and environmental dimensions.[80]

In response to funding crises, local governments have financialised public assets and services. They have applied financial principles to land use and borrowed against public assets. They have used bonds and derivatives to manage borrowing risks and costs, and have sought to generate income through financial investments.[81]

This dire financial situation underscores the need for long-term strategies to enhance local government resilience and capacity. Local governments now face the scrutiny of credit-rating agencies.[82] These agencies rely on ESG matrices to assess the creditworthiness of the municipality, making it essential that local governments embrace "responsible investment" (rather than creative borrowing strategies).[83]

6.3 SIMILAR CONCERNS AND NEEDS: RESILIENCE IN ACTION

Despite the major differences discussed above in relation to the formal and economic constitutions, the local governments of the US, South Africa, and England share similar concerns and needs in times of financial troubles. These are often encapsulated by the legal[84] and economic[85] scholarship under the umbrella term of "resilience".

---

79 R Shamseen, 'The Application of Municipal Bonds to Fund Local Authorities Projects in England; Barriers and Solutions' (PhD thesis, University of Sheffield 2022).

80 For more information, consult this website: <https://ukmba.org/sustainable-finance/>.

81 Hasenberger (n 72).

82 RA Greer, 'Local Government Risk Assessment: The Effect of Government Type on Credit Rating Decisions in Texas' (2016) 36(2) Public Budgeting & Finance 70; AC Allen and DM Dudney, 'The Impact of Rating Agency Reputation on Local Government Bond Yields' (2008) 33 J. Finan. Serv. Res. 57; S Park, C Maher and S Deller, 'The Impact of Fiscal Rules on Local Debt: Credit Ratings, Borrowing Costs, and Debt Levels' in C Johnson, T Moldogaziev and J Ross (eds), *Research Handbook on City and Municipal Finance* (EE Publishing 2023) 335, 339–341.

83 C Bruno and W Henisz, 'ESG Factors in Municipal Finance' (*PRI Blog*, 24 February 2022) <https://www.unpri.org/pri-blog/esg-factors-in-municipal-finance/9550.article>.

84 Schleicher (n 40).

85 C Barbera et al, 'Government Financial Resilience—A European Perspective' in C Johnson, T Moldogaziev and J Ross (eds), *Research Handbook*

If local governments were to "disappear"[86] or reduce their services, the local community could face significant disruptions. Financially, formal creditors could incur losses if the local government defaults. Essential services like waste collection and emergency response might suffer, affecting public health and quality of life, particularly for those in vulnerable situations. Social services might become inadequate, worsening inequalities. The local economy could also be harmed by reduced support for businesses and infrastructure. The broader public might see a decline in confidence in local institutions and stability. The impact would extend to surrounding areas, which could face increased pressure from displaced residents or businesses. The position of each of these groups is analysed in turn below.

6.3.1 Debtor–Creditors Relationship: Equality Revisited

Creditors vis-à-vis financially distressed municipalities are usually treated rateably, unless their claims are secured by collateral or they enjoy a contractual or legal preferential status. ESG considerations may help distinguish creditors that otherwise would share *pari passu*. When assessing resilience, there are two key legal aspects to consider: procedural and substantive. These aspects help evaluate how creditors of local entities in financial distress are treated across our legal systems, revealing similarities and differences in their approaches.

When it comes to creditors' procedural involvement, their rights are generally more limited than under ordinary insolvency/rescue procedures. In the US, creditors in chapter 9 procedures have less ability to influence the content of a restructuring plan compared to a chapter 11 procedure. For this reason, they will often fight strenuously to prevent the debtor from being declared eligible for chapter 9.[87] In South Africa, the Municipal Finance Management Act (MFMA) regime provides very limited protection to creditors. Only "principal suppliers and creditors" need to be consulted on the financial recovery plan, and only if they requested it, which means that not all creditors are contacted. The plan is approved by the competent provincial member of the executive council (MEC) for finance, not by the creditors. Unsurprisingly, scholarship

---

on City and Municipal Finance (EE Publishing 2023) 408.

86 In the US, 19 states in 2020 had introduced laws allowing the state to intervene in local government financial distress. Some of these laws grant the state the power to dissolve the municipality: S Hughes, A Dick and A Kopec, 'Municipal Takeovers: Examining State Discretion and Local Impacts in Michigan' (2021) 53(3) State and Local Government Review 223, 224.

87 LN Coordes, 'Gatekeepers Gone Wrong: Reforming the Chapter 9 Eligibility Rules' (2017) 94 Wash. U. L. Rev. 1191.

criticises this approach.[88] In England, creditors are not formally included in the process of a section 114 notice but *ad hoc* negotiations may follow to facilitate the restructuring of the indebted entity. Once again, the creditors' involvement is a possibility, not a right.

Moving to substantive matters, the focus shifts to repayment rights. Are creditors entitled to full payment because the debtor is a local entity? If they are not entitled to full payment, are creditors at least treated in a manner that is comparable to what happens in corporate insolvency procedures?

Evidence suggests that local governments, due to their public nature, are less risky investments than for-profit economic entities.[89] This is mainly because another public entity—either directly or indirectly (bailouts)—guarantees the municipality's debt. In the US, investors do not seem concerned about municipal defaults—discounting them as negligible risks—even in the absence of a formal guarantee mechanism.[90] Equally, English municipal debts are not protected by such guarantees,[91] yet investors are generally confident that obligations will be honoured. In most cases of municipal crises, the question is whether the national government can afford not to intervene.[92] A negative answer leads to a rise in informal bailouts.[93] In most of the recent section 114 notice cases that occurred in England, the government has generally (but not systematically) issued capitalisation directions—which are basically an exceptional financial support—and increased the funding opportunities for distressed entities.[94] By contrast, in South Africa, there is no duty on national

---

[88] R Roos and L Stander, 'Insolvent Municipalities? An Analysis of the Debt Relief Mechanisms at the Disposal of Municipalities and the Disappearance of the "Advantage of Creditors"' (2007) 22 SA Public Law 166, 173.

[89] R Doty, 'Diversity and Default Risks of Municipal Bonds' (2013) 34(2) MFJ 55; and M Schwert, 'Municipal Bond Liquidity and Default Risk' (2017) 72(4) J. Finance 1683.

[90] M Gulati and RC Schragger, 'Do Investors Care about Municipal Debtors' Access to Bankruptcy? Evidence from Bond Disclosures' (2023) 50 Fordham Urb. L.J. 657.

[91] M Allers and J de Natris, 'Preventing Local Government Defaults: No-Bailout Policy and Its Alternatives' in R Geissler, G Hammerschmid and C Raffer (eds), *Local Public Finance: An International Comparative Regulatory Perspective* (Springer 2021) 187, 190.

[92] The question also arises in relation to problems in the water sector, to the failure of the London public–private partnerships in the late 2000s, or some ailing NHS trusts.

[93] D de Widt, 'Top-Down and Bottom-Up: Institutional Effects on Debt and Grants at the English and German Local Level' (2016) 94 Public Admin. Rev. 664.

[94] Department for Levelling Up, Housing and Communities, 'Financial Distress in Local Authorities: Government Response to the Select Committee

or provincial government to provide funding to local governments in financial distress.[95] Overall, it can be argued that while creditors may have a legitimate expectation that governments will not ignore municipal distress, there is insufficient evidence to argue that the special nature of local entities justifies a full repayment of their claims.

With this in mind, the level of repayment to creditors in cases of municipal financial distress varies depending on the secured or preferred status of their claims. In the US, the process of maximising asset values during municipal bankruptcies is moderated by the rule that only the local government can decide whether to sell assets; neither creditors nor judges can compel such sales. This autonomy aims to preserve essential public functions and services. Conversely, in South Africa, there are provisions for a "cram-down", where a reorganisation plan can be imposed on creditors if certain conditions are met, though, similar to the US, only the municipality can decide on asset sales. The hierarchy of creditor payments is clearly defined, prioritising secured claims and essential services. In England, the situation is somewhat different, with fewer restrictions on the sale of local assets, even to fund service provision.[96] For example, since 2010, authorities have sold off thousands of assets, returning £1.2 billion each year,[97] with the previous Conservative government encouraging local authorities to dispose of assets to meet budget shortfalls,[98] despite this causing them subsequent troubles.[99] Consequently, creditors are generally paid in full.

Report' (25 March 2024) <https://www.gov.uk/government/publications/financial-distress-in-local-authorities-government-response-to-the-select-committee-report/financial-distress-in-local-authorities-government-response-to-the-select-committee-report>.

[95] *Member of the Executive Council for Local Government, Mpumalanga v Independent Municipal and Allied Trade Union* 2002 (1) SA 76 (SCA).

[96] W Eichler, 'Nineteen Councils Allowed to Sell Assets to Pay for Services' *BBC News* (London, 29 February 2024) <https://www.bbc.co.uk/news/uk-politics-68439624>.

[97] Z Billingham et al, *Parallel Lives. Regionally Rebalancing Wealth, Power and Opportunity* (IPPR 2023) <https://ippr-org.files.svdcdn.com/production/Downloads/1695291479_parallel-lives-sept-23.pdf>.

[98] Ministry of Housing, Communities & Local Government, 'Call for Views on Local Authority Capital Flexibilities' (19 December 2023) <https://consult.levellingup.gov.uk/local-government-finance/17f61919/>.

[99] J Shaw, 'Is Selling Off Assets the Right Solution to the Crisis in Local Government Finance?' (*UK in a Changing Europe*, 11 January 2024) <https://ukandeu.ac.uk/is-selling-off-assets-the-right-solution-to-the-crisis-in-local-government-finance/>.

Despite these regulations governing debtor-creditor relationships, the pervasive challenge of municipal financial distress necessitates significant reorganisation of local government activities, assets, and priorities. In the US, this reorganisation often includes controversial measures such as pension cuts, which are legally permissible under certain conditions to balance budgets and reduce liabilities. In South Africa, the MFMA provides for the retrenchment of municipal employees, except those affordable within the scope of projected revenues outlined in an approved financial recovery plan, aiming to align labour costs with the municipality's financial capacity. Similarly, in England, financial distress often leads to staff lay-offs and asset sales as local governments strive to manage expenditures and liabilities responsibly.

6.3.2 Public Services: Continuity under Pressure

Local residents benefit from the public services provided, subsidised, or paid for by the local government. For some vulnerable residents, such public services are vital. Some services are essential by nature (e.g. the provision of utility services). For most residents, a paramount concern is that the municipality's insolvency does not affect the continuity of public services.

Whilst continuity of essential services is recognised in all the countries considered in this study, the way in which this principle is operationalised varies.

The starting point is always to establish what services are essential. Here, there are many contrasts. On the one hand, US law provides no definition of "minimum public services" because municipalities vary in size and functions, and the matter is generally devolved to the states. On the other hand, South Africa's Constitution makes it clear that the whole *raison d'être* of municipalities is the provision of basic services to residents. Their continuation in the case of financial distress is paramount and is informed by the socio-economic rights provided for in the Constitution. These include everyone's right to have access to adequate housing,[100] the right to have access to health care services, sufficient food and water, and social security;[101] the right of children to family or parental care, or to appropriate alternative care, to basic nutrition, shelter, basic health services, and social services.[102] The aim of the South African legislative framework is to secure the continuation of public services despite the local entity's financial distress. The financial recovery plan aims to ensure that the municipality meets its obligation to provide basic services or its financial

[100] South African Constitution, s 26.
[101] Ibid s 27.
[102] Ibid s 28.

commitments.[103] In this vein, assets may be sold under the plan, but not those needed for the provision of the minimum basic municipal services.[104] England occupies a middle ground between these extremes. The country distinguishes between discretionary and statutory powers, with discretionary powers being subject to discontinuation whilst statutory powers are not. Nevertheless, no constitutional or legal protection for the level of public services exists.

The statutory differences suggest that the operationalisation of the principle of continuity of public services would be much weaker in the US than in South Africa and (to a lesser extent) England. Yet, in the Detroit case study, the provision of essential services to residents outweighed the general obligations towards bondholders.[105] Operationally, some local governments in South Africa, such as Mangaung, have faced widespread service disruptions across all departments, leading to violent protests. This undermines the principle of continuity of public services as mandated by the Constitution.[106] In England, the situation is blurred. On the one hand, discontinuing discretionary powers may be undertaken with prior consultation of the local residents, as happened in the case of Woking.[107] On the other hand, statutory powers are numerous and arcane. However, the consequences of failing to discharge them fall more readily in the realm of the ombudsman than the one of liability.

In addition, public services face sector-specific issues, as illustrated by the water industry. In the US, South Africa, and England, problems with access, quality, and affordability of water—a vital public resource—are acute during financial distress, leading to service cuts and price hikes.[108]

In Flint, Michigan, an emergency manager switched from a safe water source to the contaminated Flint River to cut costs, resulting in severe public health consequences. Similarly, Jefferson County, Alabama, went bankrupt due to the enormous costs of repairing and upgrading its sewer and water treatment infrastructure.[109] In South Africa, although the Constitution guarantees access to water, rapid population growth has hindered efforts to realise this

---

[103] Local Government: Municipal Finance Management Act 56 of 2003 (MFMA), s 142.

[104] Ibid s 142(1)(b).

[105] See chapter 3, *sub* [3.3.1].

[106] See chapter 4, *sub* [4.4.1].

[107] Woking Borough Council, 'Time is Running Out to Help Shape the Future of Discretionary Council Services' (31 July 2023) <https://www.woking.gov.uk/news/time-running-out-help-shape-future-discretionary-council-services>.

[108] Hughes et al (n 86).

[109] L Yang, 'Negative Externality of Fiscal Problems: Dissecting the Contagion Effect of Municipal Bankruptcy' (2019) 79(2) Public Admin. Rev. 156.

right.[110] Disputes over significant debt between Mangaung and Bloemwater (a local water utility) led to water restrictions in the city and threatened water supply to other municipal areas. In England, the water sector, privatised in the 1980s, now faces significant challenges. Insufficient investment has led to widespread leakage and the discharge of untreated water into rivers and the sea. Thames Water, one of the UK's most financially distressed water companies, exemplifies these issues.

Our analysis, therefore, shows a significant disconnect between the statutory formulation of the principle of continuity of public services and its actual implementation.

6.3.3 Public Health and Safety: Reaching Beyond the Local Area

A key role recognised for local governments is ensuring public health and safety within their jurisdiction.[111] This includes preventing the spread of disease, maintaining street cleanliness, closing dangerous buildings near collapse, regulating polluting activities with negative externalities on the neighbourhood, and policing protests. The Covid-19 pandemic highlighted the crucial role that local governments play in this regard.[112]

Public health and safety intersect with the services local governments provide, such as rubbish collection or fire services. These services fall within their powers to inspect, patrol, and detect issues within their territory. This role can partly overlap with environmental considerations under ESG, but not necessarily. Local governments exercise their powers primarily within their own territories, but their effective performance impacts wider constituencies. For instance, tourists or business travellers should not contract illnesses due to poor hygiene, and neighbouring local authorities benefit if local environmental issues, like pollution or disease in cattle, are managed effectively.

These public health and safety challenges are present in the US, South Africa, and England. In the US, protections ensure that in cases of imminent danger to public health and safety, burdensome assets may be abandoned to

---

110 G Murwirapachena, 'Capital Expenditure, Population Growth and Access to Water Services in South Africa' (2022) 8(131) Sustain. Water Resour. Manag. 1.

111 The original powers of local government in France, stemming directly from the French Revolution, are focused on maintaining "public order", which encompasses public health and safety: J Bell and F Lichère, *Contemporary French Administrative Law* (CUP 2022) 37.

112 C Nunes Silva (ed), *Local Government and the COVID-19 Pandemic—Local and Urban Governance* (Springer 2022); N Steylter, 'Introduction' in N Steylter (ed), *The Forum of Federations Handbook on Local Government in Federal Systems* (Palgrave Macmillan 2024) 3.

the state or state regulators as part of a settlement. In addition, during the Detroit bankruptcy, a significant factor in determining the city's eligibility for bankruptcy was the judge's finding that Detroit could not provide a minimum level of health and safety services to its residents and was therefore "service delivery insolvent". In South Africa, the legislative framework defines a "basic municipal service" as essential for maintaining an acceptable quality of life and safeguarding public health, safety, or the environment.[113] Failures in these services can lead to violent protests, as seen in Mangaung. In England, the failing water sector poses significant health risks, making governmental intervention almost indispensable.

6.4 VARIATIONS BETWEEN DEMOCRATIC ACCOUNTABILITY AND FINANCIAL EXPERTISE

The US, South Africa, and England have experienced different levels of municipal distress in recent times. In the US, there have been approximately 500 municipal bankruptcy cases since chapter 9 entered into force (1938). However, most of these cases pertain to special-purpose local entities. Local financial problems have been common in South Africa over the past two decades, with nearly half of the local authorities facing precarious situations as of 2019–2020 and the situation worsening. Between 1998 and 2017, there were 140 provincial or national interventions in municipalities, with new issues continually emerging. Section 114 notices had been barely used in England until 2018. Since then, there have been approximately 13 cases of section 114 notices, some of them affecting high-profile municipalities. Close to 20% of local governments had considered issuing one such notice within a year in autumn 2023.[114]

Despite the quantitative differences among them, no legal system seems to effectively restore the long-term financial viability of local governments with ease. Whilst some cases have achieved relatively successful recoveries, overall, it remains difficult for local governments in the three jurisdictions under comparison to overcome financial distress. In the US, Detroit stands out as an anomaly for exiting bankruptcy after 18 months, whereas cases like Vallejo show that not all recovery procedures are equally effective.[115] In South Africa,

113 MFMA, s 1.

114 Levelling Up, Housing and Communities Committee (n 59) 5.

115 Other examples include Moffett, Oklahoma, and Washington Park, Illinois, each of which filed for bankruptcy twice. See J Chapman, 'By the Numbers: A Look at Municipal Bankruptcies Over the Past 20 Years' (*The Pew Charitable Trusts*, 6 July 2020) <https://www.pewtrusts.org/en/research-and-analysis/articles/2020/07/07/by-the-numbers-a-look-at-municipal-bankruptcies-over-the-past-20

limited progress has been made after lengthy procedures exceeding five years in Mangaung and Kannaland. In England, local governments such as Croydon and Nottingham have issued multiple section 114 notices, highlighting ongoing financial challenges.[116]

Against this factual backdrop, two distinct accountability systems are in place: one based on democratic accountability (6.4.1) and the other on financial expertise (6.4.2). These systems can either complement each other or be in tension (6.4.3), and they vary significantly across the US, South Africa, and England.

6.4.1 Democratic Accountability

Democratic accountability is a key factor for the legitimacy of local policies and for the public to trust in local institutions. Democratic accountability generally operates retrospectively at the ballot box. However, there are numerous examples of continuous democratic accountability at the local level, for instance through referendums and consultations (e.g. on increases of council tax in England and adoption of integrated development plans in South Africa).[117] Democratic accountability can be general and hence include the financial management of the local government (e.g. local elections); it can have a specific financial dimension (e.g. consultation on public services); or it can directly relate to public finances (e.g. referendum on local taxation,[118] local approbation of municipal bonds[119] or community consultation on amendments to existing procurement contracts).[120]

-years>: '[T]he [municipal] bankruptcy process can be costly and time-consuming and can cause long-term damage to a locality's reputation. Bankruptcies also commonly result in increased taxes, higher fees for services, reduced benefits for workers, payments to receivers and emergency managers, lawyers' fees, and elevated future borrowing costs.'

[116] For a list of the section 114 notices issued in England in the period 2018–2023, see <https://www.statista.com/statistics/1447315/england-section-114-notices/>.

[117] BC Mubangizi, 'Interplay between Civil Society and Local Government in South Africa: Conflict and Collaboration in the Delivery of Public Services' (2022) 22 (Special Issue 1) AJDS 39.

[118] M Sanford, 'Council Tax: Local Referendums' House of Commons Research Briefing Paper (4 January 2023) <https://researchbriefings.files.parliament.uk/documents/SN05682/SN05682.pdf>.

[119] Municipal Securities Rulemaking Board, 'Ways to Buy Municipal Bonds' (March 2023) <https://www.msrb.org/sites/default/files/Ways-to-Buy-Municipal-Bonds.pdf>.

[120] MFMA, s 116.

In addition, political accountability can arise from non-formalised practices, such as protests, demonstrations, or petitions for or against specific local decisions with financial consequences. Civil society movements are keen on exercising media pressure on (local) government to exercise the right to bid for community assets[121] or to disinvest from economic sectors they deem harmful (e.g., for social or environmental reasons). Civil society may be able to mobilise campaigns to make socio-economic rights effective at the local level. Examples of such legal mobilisation pertain to rights to water in Johannesburg and Detroit, despite prior judicial failures.[122]

A local government's financial distress disturbs the ordinary avenues of political accountability, raising key questions about state or central interference in local decision-making processes, which may culminate with the removal of elected officials. In the US, such state interference is highly contested. Residents are sometimes able to strike down the powers of a state's mandatory emergency manager system. This happened in Michigan, where a referendum repealed the legislation that granted extensive powers to emergency financial managers.[123] States have adopted laws to remove financial emergency managers, including by means of a referendum within 18 months from appointment.[124] The case of Flint evidenced the need to put non-elected, albeit professional, managers under stricter control.

In South Africa, provincial governments must intervene when a municipality experiences serious financial problems (with a statutory list of the factors pointing towards such problems).[125] This obligation to intervene is triggered when a crisis in the financial affairs of the municipality leads to serious or persistent failures to provide basic services or to meet its financial obligations. Under such an intervention, the provincial government must dissolve the elected council should the council fail to implement the required financial measures under a recovery plan and appoint an administrator to replace the council until a new council is elected. Since both the intervention itself and the dissolution of the council under such intervention are stated as obligatory in instances of financial crisis, affected parties (such as residents) have the

[121] For more information about asset sales in England, see <https://locality.org.uk/local-authority-finances#asset-sales>.

[122] J Dugard, 'Water Rights Struggles in Johannesburg and Detroit Revisited: Looking beyond Courts at the Politics and Power of Rights-Based Legal Mobilization in a Neoliberal Global Order: A "Powerpack" Analysis' (2023) 15 J. Hum. Rights Pract. 46.

[123] Hughes et al (n 86) 226.

[124] Ibid 227.

[125] See chapter 4, *sub* [4.4.2].

power to force such steps by way of application to courts.[126] These mechanisms can thus be enforced from either another level of government or from local stakeholders.

In England, tension arises when the central government appoints commissioners to address financial distress, formalising its quasi-hierarchical control over local governance. This move signals a lack of confidence in local authorities. The central government is not required to justify its decision to appoint commissioners, which typically follows a section 114 notice and failed attempts to resolve financial issues locally. While the central government can also issue capitalisation directions and may need to explain its choices to a House of Commons committee such as the Public Accounts Committee, it does not have to answer to the local constituency.

Overall, state interference in local governments' democratic processes is generally viewed with suspicion. In response, US law has established stringent procedures to limit national interference, even in cases where municipalities are financially distressed. This legal framework seeks to preserve local autonomy and ensure that local governance remains insulated from excessive federal control. In South Africa, both politically elected officials and centrally appointed managers may collaborate, reflecting a more integrated approach to managing local government issues, and courts are empowered to oversee the limits of interventions. Conversely, in England, limitations on central interference in local governments' democratic processes primarily rely on self-restraint. Central authorities are expected to respect local autonomy, although this reliance on self-regulation can vary in practice.[127]

6.4.2 Financial Expertise

Political accountability for financial management cannot exist in isolation; it requires significant expertise, especially when local governments deal with complex, multi-faceted issues and governance structures. Decisions in these contexts often have both immediate and long-term consequences that are difficult to reverse. Financial expertise is crucial not only for tracking funds and identifying early signs of financial distress but also for addressing and rectifying financial challenges once they arise.

The availability of relevant (financial) expertise in the local government to make the necessary decisions to ensure its resilience in the face of uncertainty and risks varies within each of our jurisdictions. In South Africa, only 28% of

[126] *Unemployed Peoples Movement v Premier Province of the Eastern Cape* [2020] ZAECGHC 1.

[127] As evidenced in the cases of Croydon and Birmingham in chapter 5, *sub* [5.4.1]–[5.4.2].

local governments submitted audit statements without errors in 2019–2020,[128] which in itself may reveal a lack of relevant expertise at the local level. At the end of the 2021–2022 financial year, municipal finance units had an average vacancy rate of 18%, and 22% of municipalities had a vacancy in the chief financial officer position (up from 15% in the previous year).[129] Overall, it appears that a major issue in South Africa is municipalities' excessive reliance on consultants to do a large part of their financial management work.[130] In England, there is a strong differentiation in the practice of financial innovation, with approximately half of the local governments not engaging with it in 2020.[131] The reason for such disengagement may be diverse, but lack of familiarity and expertise seems to be one reasonable explanation for such a state of affairs.[132]

The need for financial expertise is pervasive and particularly relevant for auditors and insolvency professionals.

In the US, municipal audits are a state matter, resulting in variations across different states. Nonetheless, local governments' extensive reliance on municipal bonds is linked to local expertise in two significant ways. First, local governments typically avoid unfamiliar and complex financial instruments, opting instead for municipal bonds, which, despite some variations, have a long history with well-documented issues. This allows local expertise to become specialised and well-practised. Second, rating agencies for the bond market consider various indicators when assessing municipal bonds. The ability of a local government to demonstrate professional accreditation in financial reporting contributes to a positive rating. Consequently, local governments have a direct incentive to ensure that their staff possess professional expertise in financial reporting.[133]

---

128 Auditor-General of South Africa, 'Consolidated General Report on the Local Government Audit Outcomes MFMA 2019–20' (2021) <https://www.agsa.co.za/Reporting/MFMAReports/MFMA2019-2020.aspx>.

129 Ibid 35.

130 Auditor-General of South Africa, 'Consolidated General Report on Local Government Audit Outcomes MFMA 2021–22' (2023) 111 <https://mfma-2022.agsareports.co.za/>, with comments on the extensive and wasteful use of consultants due to lack of financial skills within the local governments (e.g. at 5, 7, 28, 30, 31–35). The report shows that 85% of municipalities relied on financial reporting consultants in the 2021–2022 financial year and that 53% of these relied on consultants to provide finance skills that the municipality did not have.

131 Pike (n 69) 219.

132 Ibid.

133 J Park et al, 'The Effects of High-Quality Financial Reporting on Municipal Bond Ratings: Evidence from US Local Governments' (2020) 47(5) Local Gov. Stud. 836.

In South Africa, the Auditor-General annually audits compliance with local government financial management rules. In cases of non-compliance, they issue recommendations. The Auditor-General also has the power to take remedial action, which includes recovering any loss from the responsible person.[134] In England, the local audit system was centralised before 2010. Reforms undertaken since the early 2010s led to the adoption of a hybrid accounting system, which created a 'symbiotic relationship between auditors and their client firms' (i.e. the local government).[135]

Whilst not being a recommended strategy,[136] (financial) expertise can be brought in at the time of financial distress. In the countries considered in this study, normally the democratically elected officials are not automatically set aside when financial distress arises, at least on paper. In practice, this is frequently the case. However, the appointment of expert financial advisors presents some challenges. First, the law does not necessarily require special expertise for the person appointed following the municipal financial distress (if any). In South Africa, the MFMA provides that "any suitably qualified person" may be appointed by the provincial government to prepare the financial recovery plan. No further rules exist regarding the qualifications, appointment, or remuneration of such a person. In the US, an emergency manager or member of a financial control board need not have any particular qualifications. Their regulation is not consistent across the US states.[137] In England, there are no requirements when it comes to the commissioners appointed following a section 114 notice.

Secondly, even if the person is an expert, there is only a limited pool of expert people with relevant expertise in local public finances.[138] In South

---

[134] Public Audit Act 25 of 2004 (South Africa), ss 5A, 5B. For a detailed explanation of the audit system in South African local government, see (among others): M McKenzie and B Marx, 'Turnaround for Municipal Distress Resolution: An Audit Outcomes Approach' (2024) 38(2) SAJAR 174.

[135] T Ehrmann and A Prinz, 'The Auditing Game: The Dark Side of the Private Provision of a Public Good' (2023) Eur J Law Econ <https://doi.org/10.1007/s10657-023-09785-6>.

[136] It is generally preferable to avoid the insurgence of a problem by following considerate financial practices rather than intervening *ex post* by appointing expert financial advisors to remedy the issues caused by financially inept administrators.

[137] The most extensive system is in Michigan (US): Hughes et al (n 86).

[138] See for instance calls from the Local Government Association (UK) to enhance the expertise of local professionals: Local Government Association, 'Local Government White Paper' (7 June 2024) <https://www.local.gov.uk/publications/local-government-white-paper>. See also Government Finance Officers Association, 'Meeting Demand for State and Local Public Finance Jobs' (2024) <https://www.gfoa.org/meeting-demand-public-finance>: '[D]emand for state

Africa, there is scant information and regulation concerning the qualifications, requirements, powers, duties, and remuneration of those responsible for preparing and overseeing financial recovery plans. This lack of transparency raises concerns about potential professional capture.

In England, a small pool of experts serves a lucrative market. The central government decides the role of commissioners, which can vary in specificity.[139] For example, Max Caller was appointed lead commissioner for Birmingham[140] after serving in Slough between December 2021 and March 2023,[141] along with other roles related to local financial distress.[142] Margaret Lee was appointed financial commissioner for Slough and finance lead on the Improvement and Assurance Panel for the London Borough of Croydon.[143] The government can appoint commissioners with different roles, such as in Nottingham, where there is a lead commissioner, a financial commissioner, and a commissioner for transformation.[144] Remuneration rates are £1,200/day for the lead commissioner and £1,100/day for other commissioners.[145] The

---

and local public finance officers is outstripping the current supply of workers in the sector'; P Ntuli, 'Towards a Functional Local Government: Tools to End a Crisis' (2023) <https://www.sahrc.org.za/index.php/sahrc-media/opinion-pieces/item/3486-towards-a-functional-local-government-tools-to-end-a-crisis>: '[T]he capacity of municipalities to implement government policies and programmes, and deliver services and manage finances, has gradually and tremendously been weakened by ... a shortage of skills to implement financial management'.

[139] A Gill and I Kavanagh, 'S114 Update: Appointment of Commissioners' *Local Government Lawyer* (13 October 2023) <https://www.localgovernmentlawyer.co.uk/governance/314-governance-a-risk-articles/55326-s114-update-appointment-of-commissioners>.

[140] For more information, see <https://www.birmingham.gov.uk/info/50306/commissioners_intervention_and_improvement/2768/intervention_and_commissioners>.

[141] Slough Borough Council, 'Best Value Commissioners' <https://www.slough.gov.uk/council/best-value-commissioners/7>.

[142] M Caller, 'Last Call: Max Caller on Council Governance and Finance' *Local Government Lawyer* (14 September 2023) <https://www.localgovernmentlawyer.co.uk/governance/314-governance-a-risk-articles/55051-last-call-max-caller-on-council-governance-and-finances>.

[143] Slough Borough Council (n 141).

[144] G Watson, 'Nottingham: Commissioners Brought in to Help Run "Bankrupt" Council' *BBC News* (London, 22 February 2024) <https://www.bbc.com/news/uk-england-nottinghamshire-68369304>.

[145] Birmingham City Council, 'Cost of Commissioners and Expenses' <https://www.birmingham.gov.uk/info/50306/commissioners_intervention_and_improvement/2768/intervention_and_commissioners/5>.

total expenses for the commissioners in Birmingham amounted to approximately £93,000 as of March 2024.[146]

Thirdly, the laws in the countries considered in this study do not provide clear criteria for the displacement of existing managers with emergency ones. It could be argued that their appointment can lead to moral hazard, as the decisions of emergency managers affect local communities well beyond the tenure of such non-elected professionals.[147]

Overall, the challenges and costs of appointing expert financial managers only when an entity is already in financial distress highlight the need for their proactive use to help prevent distress and ensure better financial management. There is no case, however, for the pre-emptive displacement of local officials.

6.4.3 Complementarity and Tensions

In the context of local financial distress, the provision of financial expertise is inextricably linked to the accountability of a municipality's leaders to its stakeholders. How a local entity uses its money is often a primary focus of voters, residents, and taxpayers and is therefore a key area of focus when it comes to an entity's governance.

Democratic accountability and financial expertise can complement each other, especially when auditing practices bring data and information into the public domain. This means that local residents and voters can scrutinise the local government's accounts, raise questions, and potentially make more informed choices at the ballot box. In this virtuous circle, transparency is key. Some good practices have been developed, for instance that of fiscal dashboards[148] in North Carolina (US). That state developed a preventative system based on early warning and monitoring. Other states and municipalities have, so far, mostly resisted attempts to give access to such detailed information. In England, the Local Audit and Accountability Act 2014 sought to encourage local taxpayers to monitor local finances. However, the implementation of such a law fell short of its original ambitions. In South Africa, rampant corruption and opacity cut short this virtuous cycle.[149] Most recently, initiatives have been implemented to increase transparency in municipal finances, such as the 'Municipal Money' tool on the GoMuni online portal that aims to provide data

146 Ibid.

147 Ibid 225.

148 N Ermasova and T Guzman, 'Assessments of Municipalities' Fiscal Health: Comparative Analysis of State Online Dashboard Systems' (2023) 22(2) PFM 112.

149 See chapter 4, *sub* [4.3.3].

on all municipalities' financial performance in an accessible format, and also allows for comparison between municipalities on their financial standing.[150]

However, democratic accountability and financial expertise can also be at loggerheads, especially when the professionals bringing financial expertise do not collaborate with the democratically elected officials or their representatives. There have been cases where this conflictual relationship led to the reversal of state take-over laws by local referendums.[151] The South African chapter also discusses the difficulties that arose from a lack of co-operation between the technical team and the existing administration in Mangaung.[152]

6.5 DIFFERENCES ACROSS JUDICIARIES: FROM CREATIVITY TO ABSENCE

The US and South Africa have a formalised system to address financial distress at the local level, whilst England has a highly informal one. England's only relevant statutory provision is section 114 of the Local Government Finance Act 1988. The rest of the procedure lies in the hands of the chief financial officer (CFO) and the government.[153] This varying degree of "juridification" is reflected in a key difference between the three countries: the judicial nature of the third party overseeing the procedure to address municipal financial distress.

In the US and South Africa, judges contribute to policing the recovery procedure, even if in a different manner from what they would do for commercial insolvencies. In England, judges are conspicuously absent from the process. This mirrors the strongly political[154] nature of the English constitution, where political organs control the working of the state machinery.

In all three countries, creativity seeps into the rescue procedures. In the US, deviations from general standards may occur in practice when the judiciary takes a more hands-on approach to the management of financially distressed

---

150 See <https://lg.treasury.gov.za/ibi_apps/portal/Home>.

151 See chapter 3, *sub* [3.3.2.3].

152 See chapter 4, *sub* [4.4.1].

153 The latter intervenes with letters of appointments and terms of reference that can be tweaked, amended, and revised as needed.

154 In England, financial issues arising at the local level theoretically have both criminal and civil dimensions. A potential tort action for misconduct in public office exists but is rarely initiated. Scholars have called for making this action more effective and even expanding its criminal aspects: J Horder, *Criminal Misconduct in Office: Law and Politics* (OUP 2018). However, this would apply only to individuals and not to institutions, making comparisons with the legal techniques used in the US and South Africa inapplicable.

municipalities. In South Africa, judges are particularly concerned with ensuring respect for the country's constitutional values and typically approach the enforcement of the legislative rules on municipal distress from this perspective.[155] In England, lack of effective judicial oversight results in abundant space to devise creative solutions to address municipal financial distress.

This section discusses the scope of judicial creativity in relation to the US and South Africa (6.5.1). It also seeks to explain the varying degrees of judicial interventions in supervising the management of the financial distress of local governments in the US, South Africa, and England (6.5.2).

6.5.1 Scope of Creativity

In the US, bankruptcy judges have different roles in municipal and commercial procedures. Although they are experts in bankruptcy matters, judges are not typically specialists in local finances, as municipal bankruptcies arise infrequently. In municipal bankruptcy cases, judges maintain a supervisory role, assessing the municipal debtor's plan while creditors retain the right to object. However, municipalities have greater latitude in shaping their plans, and no one—neither the judge nor the creditors—can force them to sell assets. This relatively uncharted territory has allowed judges to exercise creativity in brokering solutions.

For instance, in Detroit, the judge deemed the municipality "service-delivery insolvent" and took steps towards including taxpayers as parties in interest in the bankruptcy—an innovative move without a clear basis in the Bankruptcy Code. Additionally, the judge in Detroit made bold decisions, such as accepting cuts to accrued pensions despite state constitutional protections. He then appointed another judge to mediate the "Grand Bargain", a negotiation that significantly improved the city's financial situation by securing funding from foundations, the state, and others to protect city pensions from severe cuts and preserve the Detroit Institute of Arts' collection from being sold. This inclusion of mediation as a central part of the case, not specified by law, exemplifies judicial creativity in addressing municipal financial distress.[156]

In South Africa, municipal and corporate insolvency rules pursue different goals. The ordinary High Court deals with insolvency and business rescue proceedings and exercises general oversight over them. The same High Court exercises oversight in cases involving municipal distress, but to achieve different goals. Courts have, for example, ordered other spheres of government to

155 South Africa has one of the most comprehensive sets of rules on local government in financial distress outside of insolvency: see MFMA, ch 13.

156 See chapter 3, *sub* [3.4.1].

intervene in municipalities where service delivery has failed due to financial distress[157] and have highlighted the intergovernmental obligations in cases where municipalities faced spiralling debts.[158]

In England, no judicial procedure is organised in relation to municipal financial distress. However, past experiences pertaining to financial commitments undertaken by local governments have shown that judges can take bold decisions, including quashing hugely speculative swap transactions[159] or imposing procedural duties of consultation on central government whenever they seek to terminate financial support to local government.[160] This strand of procedural fairness (i.e. the duty to undertake consultations) remains in current case law and illustrates the tensions arising between local government (in this case Birmingham's council) and central government.[161]

The scope of judicial creativity is significant because it indicates how judges might incorporate ESG considerations into their decisions. By linking ESG principles to existing legal doctrines or addressing specific needs in each situation, judges can influence outcomes in cases involving municipal financial distress. For example, if a local government takes on risks exceeding its turnover without adequate disclosure or proper investment testing processes, this could be seen as failing to meet governance criteria under ESG standards. Judicial creativity in such contexts can ensure that ESG factors are integrated into legal reasoning, potentially leading to either more responsible and sustainable financial management practices by local governments (*ex ante* effect) or a different distribution of assets across the affected stakeholders (*ex post* effect).

---

[157] J Wright, F Dube and A du Plessis, 'Judicial Enforcement of Mandatory Provincial Interventions in Municipalities in South Africa' (2022) 55 VRÜ 105, 114–117.

[158] *Eskom Holdings SOC Ltd v Resilient Properties (Pty) Ltd* [2020] ZASCA 185; *Eskom Holdings SOC Ltd v Lekwa Ratepayers Association* [2022] ZASCA 10.

[159] *Deutsche Bank AG London v Comune di Busto Arsizio* [2021] EWHC 2706 (Comm); *Banca Intesa San Paolo SpA v Comune di Venezia* [2023] EWCA Civ 1482.

[160] *R (Luton BC) v Secretary of State for Education* [2011] EWHC 217 (Admin).

[161] *Birmingham City Council v Secretary of State for Transport* [2024] EWHC 1487 (Admin).

6.5.2 Explaining the Differences

It is challenging to justify such remarkable differences in the judicial approaches to municipal cases in the countries considered in this study.[162] Judges play a different role in each of the jurisdictions considered in this study. However, this characteristic alone is insufficient to explain the differences evidenced in this section of the chapter. There are, however, some factors that might explain the role of the judiciary in each of the countries considered in the study. First, the legal basis for the jurisdiction of judges differs. In the US, judges have an explicit mandate to act as bankruptcy judges, with Congress establishing specialised bankruptcy courts to handle these cases. The importance of specialised bankruptcy expertise is also significant at the appellate level, where five circuits have created bankruptcy appellate panels that can hear appeals with the consent of the parties involved. This specialisation has led to a unique judicial approach, with courts developing a specific understanding of their mission to promote negotiation and resolve bankruptcy efficiently. Factors contributing to this include judicial discretion, the need for creative solutions to fill gaps in the bankruptcy code, and the pursuit of practical outcomes over strict adherence to formal provisions. Scholars have, therefore, observed that '[b]ankruptcy judges seek to do justice, as they understand justice in the distinctive context of bankruptcy'.[163] However this specificity of the bankruptcy judges is tempered in the case of chapter 9 procedures, as judges cannot interfere with the municipality's affairs (in particular, its political and governmental powers, its property or revenues and use or enjoyment of income-producing property). In South Africa and England, judges would exercise their general judicial review functions, and not one specific to insolvency. The difference between South Africa and England is that South African judges adjudicate with a strong mandate to realise socio-economic rights,[164] a characteristic which is currently wholly absent in England.

---

[162] A whole legal field analyses judicial behaviour, which requires specific methodologies: see, among others, L Epstein and K Weinshall, *The Strategic Analysis of Judicial Behavior: A Comparative Perspective* (CUP 2021). This book does not primarily aim to contribute to this discussion, though it certainly provides materials and insights that could do so. This section modestly focuses on comparing the findings generated by our comparison, without attempting to make broader claims.

[163] J Seymour, 'Against Bankruptcy Exceptionalism' (2022) 89(8) U. Chi. L. Rev. 1925, 1929–1930.

[164] For a more detailed discussion about how courts may use overlapping narratives to construct a notion of shared values, see R Dixon, *Responsive Judicial Review—Democracy and Dysfunction in the Modern Age* (OUP 2023) 254.

Secondly, the level and areas of specialisation acquired by judges vary. In the US, bankruptcy judges are experts in bankruptcy, and this expertise can assist them in developing a coherent and consistent body of law. This leads to increased efficiency.[165] However, these bankruptcy judges are not experts in local government financial matters, so they too must rely on experts in these cases. In South Africa, judges have gained specialised expertise in constitutional rights adjudication, and they appear quite comfortable in transferring their expertise to the financial distress of local government. However, the Constitutional Court primarily employs a reasonableness approach to the progressive realisation of socio-economic rights. It is cautious about becoming too involved in decisions on public spending, a recurring issue in the implementation of the International Covenant on Economic, Social and Cultural Rights, both in domestic courts and international monitoring bodies.[166] This approach is particularly evident in constitutional cases related to urban local governments, focusing on urban housing and service delivery.[167]

In England, judges face significant pressures to strike a delicate balance in their judicial roles. They are urged to exercise restraint and avoid engaging too critically with judicial review of administrative action.[168] They are equally discouraged from developing any robust protective jurisdiction concerning human rights, including socio-economic rights.[169] This dual pressure requires judges to navigate carefully between respecting the boundaries of their judicial mandate and ensuring the protection of the rule of law.

Thirdly, judges understand their institutional role in a different manner. Judges by their very nature are only "reactive", in that they respond to the cases that are submitted. However, over time they can see themselves as one cog in a wider machinery as they see it operating. Path dependency may to some extent

---

[165] Y Aran and M Ofir, 'The Effect of Specialised Courts over Time' in S Ranchordas and Y Roznai (eds), *Time, Law and Change: An Interdisciplinary Study* (Hart Publishing 2020).

[166] O de Schutter, 'Public Budget Analysis for the Realization of Economic, Social and Cultural Rights—Conceptual Framework and Practical Implementation' in K Young (ed), *The Future of Economic and Social Rights* (CUP 2019) 527, 529.

[167] S Liebenberg, 'The Participatory Democratic Turn in South Africa's Social Rights Jurisprudence' in K Young (ed), *The Future of Economic and Social Rights* (CUP 2019) 187, 191–192; S Liebenberg, *Socio-Economic Rights Adjudication Under a Transformative Constitution* (Juta 2010).

[168] See the many attempts at limiting judicial review in England: G Cowie and J Dawson, 'Judicial Review Reform' (House of Commons Library, 1 April 2021) <https://commonslibrary.parliament.uk/judicial-review-reform/>.

[169] M Amos, 'Democratic State, Autocratic Method: The Reform of Human Rights Law in the United Kingdom' (2024) 73(1) ICLQ 1.

explain the institutional trust judges generate by their decisions. For instance, in the US, judges understand their role as supportive of the market. This may result in judgments prioritising the municipal bond market over the interests of local government, even at times of financial distress.[170] Even if this case law is now old and superseded by the US Bankruptcy Code, the municipal bond market continues to flourish in the US, suggesting that the judicial attitude has not significantly shifted. In South Africa, some scholarship suggests that courts shape their case law around narrow, market-orientated views of fundamental rights. This perspective reduces entrenched socio-economic rights to mere formal or procedural guarantees, rather than recognising them as substantive material entitlements. This approach aligns with a neo-liberal conception of rights that emphasises individual responsibility and market principles over broader socio-economic protections.[171] Others argue that courts seek to foster a deepening of democratic engagement.[172] They argue that judicial activity 'focuses on strengthening institutions, systems and processes of urban service delivery, and on making these more accountable, open and accessible to urban residents'.[173] Pieterse elaborates on this by writing that

> [the] Court [is] preoccupied with ensuring that everyday governance and dispute resolution institutions and mechanisms exist, function and are strengthened, whilst simultaneously being accountable to citizens and responsive to their rights and concerns. This appears to be motivated by a concern not only for good governance, but also to ensure that rights work for *all* residents, rather than only for those who have access to litigation as means to enforce them. Furthermore, while the Court generally attempts to foster inclusive and participatory urban governance, it is clearly intent on preserving local government's ability to *govern*, in accordance with its democratic mandate and the rule of law.[174]

---

170 Schleicher (n 40) 45–52.

171 P O'Connel, 'The Death of Socio-Economic Rights' (2011) 74(4) MLR 532, 533.

172 B Ray, *Engaging with Social Rights: Procedure, Participation, and Democracy in South Africa's Second Wave* (CUP 2016) 187–190, 212–214.

173 M Pieterse, 'Socio-Economic Rights Adjudication and Democratic Urban Governance: Reassessing the "Second Wave" Jurisprudence of the South African Constitutional Court' (2018) 51(1) VRÜ 12, 14.

174 Ibid. This analysis could be compared to that offered to explain the role that the UK Supreme Court develops in respect of major infrastructure projects: see Y Marique and S Van Garsse, 'Public–Private Co-Operation and Judicial Review—A Case Study Drawn from European Infrastructure Projects' (2018) 24(3) EPL 515, 528 in relation to *R on the Application of HS2 Action Alliance Ltd v The Secretary of State for Transport* [2014] UKSC 3, involving the most expensive transport infrastructure project in Europe at the time. The Supreme Court also seemed to act as the "great clockmaker", ensuring that information flows between

The Kannaland case is a good illustration of this reasoning.[175]

In England, the role of the judiciary is more limited because public finances are controlled by the executive power. The legislature approves broad financial appropriations, which means that judges have limited scope to interpret specific legislation related to financial matters. This is because such appropriations are general and do not provide detailed guidance or specific criteria that judges can use to review the exercise of administrative powers. Consequently, judges' usual role of interpreting and controlling the implementation of administrative powers is less applicable in the context of broad financial allocations.

Except for taxation disputes,[176] courts have exercised limited scrutiny on executive decisions for principled but also practical reasons (due to the high technical complexity of the matters).[177] The principled reasons revolve around the doctrine of separation of powers,[178] and the political judgment that is supposed to be at play in public finance matters. This factor is compounded by a lack of judicial expertise and the difficulty in predicting the consequences of a judgment. This makes this matter highly "polycentric".[179] For example, public–private partnerships (PPPs)—often politically contentious—have been extensively examined by the National Audit Office and the Public Accounts Committee but have received minimal scrutiny from the courts.[180] Courts are

---

the different parts of the constitutional and administrative machinery, from the administration to Parliament and vice-versa, and from civil society to public actors and vice-versa. But it does not make any substantive or political judgments.

[175] *Executive Council of the Western Cape Province v Kannaland Local Municipality* [2021] ZAWCHC 208.

[176] W Bateman, *Public Finance and Parliamentary Constitutionalism* (CUP 2018) ch 8.

[177] Note that, although technical complexity is also true of EU public finances, the CJEU ventures into shaping this field with landmark cases such as *Pringle* (C-370/12 *Pringle v Government of Ireland* (2012)), for instance, re-interpreting the no-bailout clause of TFEU, art 125. A pending case to follow is the one initiated by the European Parliament against the Commission's decision to free the Polish funds frozen for breach of horizontal conditionality (C-225/24 *Parliament v Commission*, application submitted on 25 March 2024).

[178] *R (Hooper) v Secretary of State for Work and Pensions* [2005] 1 WLR 1681 [32]: '[i]n a […] system […] concerned with the separation of powers, […] decisions about social and economic policy, particularly those concerned with the equitable distribution of public resources […] are ordinarily recognised by the courts to be matters for the judgment of the elected representatives of the people'.

[179] LL Fuller and KI Winston, 'The Forms and Limits of Adjudication' (1978) 92(2) Harv. L. Rev. 353, 395.

[180] Y Marique, *Public–Private Partnerships and the Law—Regulation, Institutions and Community* (EE Publishing 2014).

also acutely aware of the potential economic and financial consequences that judgments on municipal matters may have on locals[181] and the national budget. In this sense, the *Hammersmith* case is particularly illuminating: the financial risks of the local government were so high that the Treasury would have had to intervene otherwise. In the current crisis facing English local government, some entities have taken on risks that are disproportionately large relative to their turnover.[182]

6.6 ESG AND A RESILIENT LONG-TERM RECOVERY: SUGGESTIONS

Municipal financial distress can vary significantly across the US, South Africa, and England. The legal frameworks for addressing it differ widely among these jurisdictions, and even within different regions of each country. Can a legal approach be proposed that offers both certainty and a roadmap for achieving long-term resilience for distressed local governments?

This section explores one such potential approach, focusing on three key dimensions: first, the necessity for a thorough diagnostic (6.6.1); second, the adoption of a flexible or modular approach to financial distress (6.6.2); and third, the integration of substantive ESG considerations (6.6.3).

6.6.1 First Dimension: Diagnostic of the Proximate and Systemic Causes of Financial Distress

Too often, local officials are blamed for municipal failures. However, it is important to pause and give due consideration to the root causes of municipal financial distress, to be sure that the proposed solutions are suitable.

In some cases, the financial distress is caused by external factors, such as the long-term economic decline of the local area and a decrease in the local population, compounded by increasing public expenses to face the environmental and social consequences of this long-term economic decline. Detroit is the best illustration of this scenario, when the long-term financial, industrial, social,

---

[181] As explained in chapter 5, *sub* [5.4.2], a significant part of the financial problems experienced by Birmingham originated from a Supreme Court's decision in a discrimination case.

[182] P Murphy, 'Intervention and Monitoring: How the UK Government Has Responded to Financial Service and Corporate Failings in Local Entities' Essex Business School seminar (29 May 2024), mentioning that Spelthorne has borrowed £1.1bn, i.e. 87 times its turnover, whilst Woking was allowed to borrow £2bn, equivalent to 62 times its turnover.

and demographic decline of the municipality was precipitated at one time with the GM/Chrysler bankruptcies during the Great Recession.

In other cases, municipal distress is caused by a major financial event, either directly financial in the case of bad financial investments, or indirectly in the case of a major accident with immense financial consequences such as wildfires or the equal pay dispute in Birmingham. In most cases, the causes of local distress are to be ascribed to financial management (for instance in the interactions between the local and the central government) or even a systemic lack of financial expertise (such as in South Africa).

To summarise, some problems, be they economic, financial, or political, are systemic, whilst others are case-specific. The interconnectedness of the issues discussed in this book is best illustrated by the Flint water crisis, which emerged as a consequence of the city's financial troubles.[183] The South African legal framework also acknowledges these interconnections. It considers a municipality's failure to meet its financial commitments as a serious breach if it affects or is likely to affect the availability or cost of credit for other municipalities. This triggers the obligation for provincial governments to intervene.[184] In the case of failing NHS trusts, the English National Audit Office (NAO) considers the impact on surrounding and related trusts before devising a restructuring strategy.[185]

Given the varied factors contributing to municipal financial distress, the diverse financial structures and recovery tools, and the differing future prospects—especially those revealed through an ESG analysis—a thorough assessment based on reliable and accurate information is essential. This assessment should be conducted by experts in both local governance and economic or financial matters.

6.6.2 Second Dimension: A Modular Approach to Financial Distress of Local Government

The differences in the problems faced by American, South African, and English systems to address municipal financial distress suggest that an appropriate strategy to secure a resilient recovery requires the adoption of a modular approach.

The modular approach is a promising technique to ensure the protection of vulnerable players.[186] If a legislator decided to apply a modular approach to

---

183 For an analysis of these case studies, see chapter 3, *sub* [3.4.1]–[3.4.2].

184 MFMA, s 140(2)(d).

185 National Audit Office, *The Financial Sustainability of NHS Bodies* (HC 2014–15 722) 39–40.

186 See chapter 2, *sub* [2.1.1.2].

devise principled strategies for the management of local entities in financial distress, they would seek inspiration in insolvency procedures as they exist and tailor them to the specificities of the financial distress encountered by local government. This would generally result in removing the procedures regulating municipal distress from the mostly politico-administrative realm that presides over them in a country such as England to "juridify" and formalise them in a manner closer to the experiences we encountered in the US and in South Africa. The municipal bond market requires greater legal certainty to develop properly, which would justify making this change.

A modular approach developed for micro- and small enterprises (MSEs) can be extended to local authorities in financial distress, as both often face revenue shortfalls that trigger financial difficulties. For MSEs, this may be due to decreased sales or loss of clients, while local authorities might suffer from reduced tax revenues, lower government funding, or diminished service fee collections. These revenue issues, coupled with cash flow problems, make it challenging for both MSEs and local authorities to meet their financial obligations, such as operational costs and public services, respectively. This situation necessitates effective cash flow management and strategic planning to navigate fiscal distress.

Both MSEs and local authorities must also address the concerns of vulnerable parties; for MSEs, these include funders and suppliers, whilst for local authorities, low-income residents and certain suppliers are affected. The modular approach to insolvency allows stakeholders to select the most suitable procedure to maximise the debtor's estate value based on a detailed report of the financial condition. This approach provides a core set of principles[187] and various "modules"[188] that can be adapted to specific jurisdictional issues.[189] Legislators are encouraged to create flexible tools for reorganising or

[187] These include a debtor-in-possession approach, giving the entrepreneur or entrepreneurs who run a distressed debtor the ability to restructure or liquidate their business; a mechanism that allows for the discharge of debts; and procedures that limit the involvement of courts and practitioners to cases where it is absolutely necessary or to settle disputes.

[188] These include the possibility for creditors to commence insolvency or restructuring proceedings should the entrepreneur fail to deal promptly with a situation of distress, the offering of a moratorium from executory actions against the debtor, and the provision of mechanisms to bind dissenting minorities (e.g. cross-class cram-down) or to promote negotiated solutions (e.g. mediation).

[189] J Sarra, 'Making Insolvency Law Responsive to the Needs of Financially Distressed Micro and Small Enterprises' in PJ Omar and JLL Gant (eds), *Research Handbook on Corporate Restructuring* (EE Publishing 2021) 250.

liquidating distressed entities and implement out-of-insolvency measures, with incentives and checks to prevent moral hazard.

No modular approach has been specifically tailored for financially distressed municipalities, despite international recognition of its utility. Local authorities face unique challenges due to their roles in public service provision and economic management, which a one-size-fits-all insolvency framework often fails to address. A modular approach could be tailored to accommodate the specific circumstances of local authorities, ensuring more effective and equitable financial resolutions.

The framework would start by identifying the unique requirements of local authorities, emphasising public welfare over mere financial recovery. Flexibility is key, allowing for different modules to be chosen based on the specific distress situation. For instance, if a local authority has liquidity issues but solid long-term prospects, a module for restructuring and debt rescheduling could be applied. If the authority is fundamentally non-viable due to mismanagement or debt, a module focusing on liquidation or a merger with a neighbouring authority might be prioritised, potentially involving state assistance for the provision of essential services.

Stakeholder involvement is another critical component, ensuring that all interests are considered in the insolvency process. Advisory committees with representatives from the community, unions, service providers, and creditors could ensure transparency and comprehensive decision-making.

Incentivising the correct use of a modular insolvency framework broadly compliant with internationally accepted guidance for corporate debtors[190] and specific principles for local authorities[191] would also be crucial. To promote the appropriate use of this modular framework, legislators could offer rewards for proactive engagement, such as grants or low-interest loans, while implementing strict audits to prevent financial mismanagement. The approach should also be culturally and socially sensitive, reflecting local traditions, and involving community-based restructuring efforts to foster local engagement and commitment to recovery.

In summary, a modular insolvency framework for local authorities would provide a flexible, inclusive solution tailored to local needs, ensuring the safeguarding of public welfare, financial recovery, and consideration of ESG

[190] World Bank Group, *Principles for Effective Insolvency and Creditor/Debtor Regimes* (2017) section C; European Bank for Reconstruction and Development, *EBRD Core Principles of an Effective Insolvency System* (2021).

[191] Local Government Association, *Navigating Financial Uncertainty and Building Resilience: Guiding Principles* (24 May 2024) <https://www.local.gov.uk/publications/navigating-financial-uncertainty-and-building-resilience-guiding-principles>.

principles. This comprehensive approach would address the complex nature of municipal distress, balancing financial stability with broader social and economic responsibilities.

6.6.3 Third Dimension: Including the ESG Considerations

Chapter 2 explained that, whilst there is no single definition of "ESG considerations", looking at the financial distress of a local government from an ESG perspective helps in breaking down possible causes for the poor financial situation of a local government and in developing strategies to address it going forward.

Overall, discussions of ESG considerations in municipal financial distress in the US, South Africa, and England are still in their early stages and can be strongly contested.[192] In the US, the inclusion of ESG factors in bankruptcy, particularly under chapter 9 of the US Code, is just beginning. South Africa's system, while taking a broader view on ESG than standard insolvency practices, still fails to adequately address ESG challenges in municipal disputes. In England, ESG considerations are largely missing from municipal restructuring processes. However, this is not unique to municipal financial distress, as this low integration of ESG considerations can also be noticed in general recovery procedures.

In addressing environmental considerations, it is crucial to align local policies with international law obligations and best practices across various environmental sectors, including mitigation and adaptation to climate change, pollution, and resource management (e.g. Flint and Thames Water). A comprehensive mapping of the pressure points on scarce resources such as health, water, biodiversity, and public infrastructure can provide a foundational understanding of the challenges faced by local governments. The goal is not merely to establish fixed targets but to highlight areas that require attention and develop a toolkit of best practices. This approach allows local governments to adopt strategies that suit their unique circumstances without the need to develop entirely new systems. Legal tools play a pivotal role in allocating risks and responsibilities, guiding the implementation of preventative, adaptive, and mitigative measures. The integration of ESG principles into local governance frameworks can enhance resilience to environmental crises, with legislatures

---

[192] For one example of discussion in the news at the time of writing, see S Woodman and J Robin, 'US Officials Are Investing Public Funds in Israeli Bonds in Deals That Raise Ethics Concerns' *The Guardian* (London, 25 July 2024) <https://www.theguardian.com/world/article/2024/jul/25/us-officials-israel-bonds-ethics>.

and the judiciary ensuring compliance and adaptability in the face of such challenges.

Social considerations in local governance encompass a wide range of issues, from ensuring equitable pension and pay structures (e.g. Detroit) to addressing mass torts and social crises (e.g. Birmingham). Local governments often serve as the first responders during crises, such as the Covid-19 pandemic or the influx of refugees (e.g. Croydon), requiring substantial financial and human resources. Ensuring the availability of these resources involves strategic planning and robust funding mechanisms. Furthermore, the preservation of public spaces is vital for community engagement and upholding rights such as peaceful protest. The privatisation of these spaces can undermine these rights and limit public access, which highlights the need for policies that protect public assets (e.g. South Africa's Constitution). Local governments must be equipped with the legal and financial tools to manage these challenges effectively, balancing social equity with fiscal responsibility.

Effective governance in local authorities requires robust internal and external systems to ensure efficiency, regularity, and legitimacy. Integrating ESG considerations into local decision-making processes is essential to ensure long-term sustainable outcomes, especially in times of financial distress. This can be achieved by embedding ESG criteria into the auditing systems that oversee local government operations. National and international auditing bodies and rating agencies (e.g. Moody's, S&P Global Ratings) are progressively encouraging the inclusion of ESG metrics, or at least the Sustainable Development Goals (SDGs), in their assessments. For instance, South Africa has made notable strides in this area, offering a model that other jurisdictions, including the UK, could emulate. The role of audits is not only to ensure compliance but also to guide local governments in meeting their ESG responsibilities. This requires a co-ordinated effort among various entities within a territory to harmonise ESG goals with local governance practices, ensuring that all stakeholders are aligned and that local governments can effectively navigate crises and shocks.

The role of ESG considerations in addressing municipal financial distress needs further clarification. ESG can serve as an analytical tool to evaluate the nature, causes, and extent of financial distress without necessarily prioritising claims related to ESG factors. This makes the ESG framework particularly relevant for diagnosing problems in the initial stages of the process, as outlined in *sub* 6.6.1.

An ESG framework also raises the question of whether and when ESG-related claims should be given preferential treatment. This question is ripe for further study. If this were to happen, legislative intervention would be required to establish clear priorities among competing claims. This would involve considering various legal and economic implications, such as the sources and scope of obligations, the nature of enforcement proceedings (administrative, civil, or criminal), and the guarantees and insurance backing these debts.

In the US, ESG considerations could disrupt the financial sector by introducing non-economic factors into a traditionally finance-focused area. However, the primary goal of addressing financial distress is to restore financial resilience, which involves developing both anticipatory and coping mechanisms to handle vulnerabilities and future financial shocks.

To achieve this, the procedure must first ensure that both internal and external governance structures are robust, including in-house expertise and anti-fraud systems. Long-term resilience also requires attention to social considerations, such as fair employment practices, anti-harassment policies, and whistle-blower protections. Developing a comprehensive vision for the local community that balances financial feasibility with social and environmental sustainability is crucial for effective local leadership and governance.

If local governments can become leaders in addressing ESG issues, they can pave the way for broader acceptance of ESG considerations in the commercial context as well. Indeed, to varying degrees, local governments have often innovated long before some practices become widespread in the corporate world.

6.7 CONCLUSIONS

Municipal financial distress manifests itself differently in the US, South Africa, and England due to varying constitutional frameworks, accountability procedures, and levels of in-house financial expertise. The disparities are most pronounced in the judicial oversight of municipal financial distress, with the US employing a more structured approach through chapter 9 bankruptcy, while England lacks comparable judicial mechanisms specifically tailored for municipal distress, and South Africa has opted for an administrative but court-supervised procedure. In the US, courts play a pivotal role in overseeing the reorganisation plans and ensuring that essential services continue. In South Africa, judicial involvement is more limited and typically focuses on administrative rather than financial interventions, as well as the preservation of constitutionally protected socio-economic rights. Judicial involvement is extremely limited in England. Nonetheless, across these jurisdictions, a common baseline exists concerning the legal implications for creditors, service users, and the wider community. This baseline includes the protection of municipal assets from forced liquidation, the continuity of essential services, and an overarching concern for public health and safety. The technicalities behind these protections may differ, yet the core principles align closely across all three systems.

Against this backdrop, a major consensus emerges: the necessity of developing a comprehensive system to manage municipal financial distress that mitigates human limitations, such as information asymmetries, over-optimism, and short-term thinking. This chapter proposes a framework encompassing three key dimensions: firstly, an in-depth diagnostic to identify the underlying causes of financial distress; secondly, a modular approach to financial recovery that provides tailored solutions depending on the specific circumstances of each case; and thirdly, a deeper integration of ESG considerations into the recovery process. The diagnostic phase would involve a thorough analysis of the municipality's financial health, identifying both immediate crises and structural issues. The modular approach would allow for flexibility, enabling the use of different strategies such as debt restructuring or austerity measures depending on the situation. Finally, integrating ESG considerations would ensure that financial recovery is not just fiscally sound but also socially and environmentally responsible, thus promoting sustainable long-term governance.

7. Conclusion to *Municipalities in Financial Distress*

This book posits that for a municipality experiencing financial distress to achieve long-term financial recovery and resilience, in the best interests of the local community it serves, it is essential that the decision-making processes addressing this distress be modularly tailored and incorporate environmental, social, and governance (ESG) considerations.

The conclusions first summarise this central argument of the book (7.1). They then draw lessons from the comparative analysis of the different legal systems, for local services, and for ESG considerations more broadly (7.2). The conclusions end with potential future steps and developments in the field (7.3).

7.1 THE END OF OUR JOURNEY: FINANCIAL DISTRESS, LOCAL GOVERNMENT, AND ESG

The comparison of the legal frameworks governing financially distressed local entities in the US, South Africa, and the UK (namely England) offers valuable insights into the processes and circumstances that lead to municipal financial distress, as well as the mechanisms for addressing these challenges. Our book highlights both successful interventions, such as in Detroit, and recurrent municipal failures, such as those in Mangaung and Croydon. Importantly, our analysis reveals that incorporating ESG considerations into the restructuring processes of local municipalities could lead to more sustainable, long-term solutions that minimise negative impacts on vulnerable stakeholders, including local residents, service users, and taxpayers.

The three legal systems under examination exhibit significant interconnections in their legal developments, primarily through their shared commitment to the principles of a democratic market economy. Nonetheless, their constitutional frameworks are notably distinct, particularly regarding the treatment of municipal financial distress. In the US, the Constitution assigns bankruptcy matters to federal jurisdiction, but it does not enshrine socio-economic rights, leaving local governments with a diverse array of responsibilities and the capability to issue municipal bonds. The sophisticated US municipal bond market is underpinned by credit rating agencies, which increasingly incorporate ESG considerations as a tool to inform investors.[1]

In contrast, South Africa's Constitution provides detailed provisions on local government, including the protection of socio-economic rights, which necessitates a more hands-on governmental approach to ensure their concrete implementation. However, the South African economic constitution relevant to local government is challenged by a lack of in-house financial expertise. This deficiency is further compounded by the country's rapid urbanisation, which demands substantial investments in public infrastructure to accommodate shifting demographics. Even during stable economic periods, South African local governments often struggle to secure adequate financing.

The UK, particularly England, operates under a constitution that remains largely political rather than legalistic, which impacts the management of municipal financial distress. The English economic constitution has historically eschewed financial instruments like municipal bonds, largely due to the setbacks experienced in the 1980s. This aversion to municipal bonds persists, despite a pressing need for financial innovation in local government finance.

These distinctions highlight the varying approaches and challenges each country faces in addressing municipal financial distress, shaped by their unique constitutional and economic landscapes. The US approach emphasises market mechanisms and financial instruments.[2] South Africa's model is constrained by socio-economic obligations and limited financial capacity. The UK's system is characterised by a cautious approach to financial innovation in local government finance.

7.1.1 Context and Comparative Analysis

In the US, the handling of municipal financial distress is primarily situated within the framework of the federal Bankruptcy Code, particularly through chapter 9 bankruptcy provisions. This process allows municipalities to restructure their debt while maintaining essential public services. However, the role of the judiciary typically focuses more on legal oversight than active involvement in financial decision-making.[3]

In South Africa, the approach is more bespoke, considering the specific challenges and legal context of local government. South Africa's Constitution

---

[1] See chapter 2, *sub* [2.1.3].

[2] National Association of Bond Lawyers, *Municipal Bankruptcy: A Guide for Public Finance Attorneys* (3rd edn, National Association of Bond Lawyers 2015).

[3] RC Picker and MW McConnell, 'When Cities Go Broke: A Conceptual Introduction to Municipal Bankruptcy', in *Municipal Bankruptcies: How to Handle a Chapter 9 from Start to Finish* (Practising Law Institute 1995).

mandates the provision of socio-economic rights, which influences the management of municipal financial crises. The South African model includes interventions tailored to the unique circumstances of local governments, often requiring a more hands-on approach to ensure compliance with these constitutional mandates. At the same time, this approach has often resulted in political interference in administrative matters.[4]

England, by contrast, relies on a politico-administrative process rather than a legalistic one. The handling of local government financial distress is embedded within a broader political framework, where decisions are often made with significant input from central government officials. This system does not conform to typical liquidation or rescue procedures seen in corporate insolvency, reflecting a distinctive approach that prioritises political and administrative solutions over judicial interventions.[5]

In all three countries, traditional notions of liquidation and rescue are adapted to fit the context of public sector entities. However, the use of bankruptcy, or its functional equivalent, is generally considered a last resort. Various administrative mechanisms are usually available before resorting to such drastic measures. Yet, the criteria and rationale for choosing to declare a municipality bankrupt, insolvent, or financially distressed often remain opaque and poorly articulated in the literature.

7.1.2 Tensions in Municipal Financial Recovery

The book identifies three critical tensions that frequently emerge in the context of municipal financial recovery. These tensions highlight the polycentricity, complexities, and competing interests that can arise during the restructuring and stabilisation processes of local governments.

7.1.2.1 Democratic accountability vs financial expertise

The first tension is the balancing act between democratic accountability and financial expertise. On the one hand, local governments are accountable to their constituents and must ensure that their decisions reflect the will and needs of the local electors. On the other hand, effective financial recovery often requires specialised knowledge and expertise that may not align with popular sentiment or immediate public preferences.

This tension can lead to challenges in implementing technically sound but potentially unpopular financial measures. The tension is underscored by the

---

[4] J de Visser, 'The Political-Administrative Interface in South African Municipalities: Assessing the Quality of Local Democracies' (2010) CJLG 87.

[5] T Travers, *The Politics of London: Governing an Ungovernable City* (Red Globe Press 2003).

need for transparent communication and inclusive decision-making processes that incorporate both expert advice and public input to ensure that local officials and external experts are held accountable for their decisions.[6]

7.1.2.2 Central/federal priorities vs local needs

The second tension involves the sometimes-conflicting priorities of central or federal governments and the needs of vulnerable local communities. Central governments often impose austerity measures that are intended to stabilise the broader economic environment and ensure the long-term viability of public debt. However, such decisions may not adequately consider the unique socio-economic conditions of specific localities. If taken in isolation, these decisions may actually result in short-term fixes that worsen the long-term viability of both local entities and nations.

This can result in policies that, while fiscally responsible from a macro-economic perspective, fail to address local vulnerabilities or even exacerbate them. For instance, austerity measures can disproportionately impact lower-income communities by cutting essential public services.[7] This dynamic underscores the importance of a nuanced approach that balances macro-economic stability with local social equity considerations.[8]

7.1.2.3 Short-term solutions vs long-term needs

The third tension relates to the tendency to prioritise short-term fixes over long-term planning and investment, partially due to the elective nature of local, regional/federal, and national officials.

In situations of financial distress, there is often a focus on immediate, reactive measures aimed at addressing pressing fiscal deficits. However, this can lead to the neglect of broader, long-term developmental needs, opportunities, and challenges. For example, the municipalities of Mangaung and Kannaland in South Africa, and Croydon in England, illustrate how short-term solutions can entrench financial difficulties, leading to cyclical crises rather than sustainable recovery. Similar tensions are also recorded in the US.[9] This underscores the necessity for recovery plans to incorporate a long-term strategic vision

---

[6] See generally: M Bovens, R Goodin and T Schillemans, *The Oxford Handbook of Public Accountability* (OUP 2014).

[7] M Blythe, *Austerity: The History of a Dangerous Idea* (OUP 2013).

[8] R Florida, *The New Urban Crisis: How Our Cities Are Increasing Inequality, Deepening Segregation, and Failing the Middle Class, and What We Can Do about It* (Basic Civitas Books 2017).

[9] RM Hendrick, *Managing the Fiscal Metropolis: The Fiscal Policies, Practices, and Health of Suburban Municipalities* (Georgetown University Press 2011).

that addresses structural issues and leverages local strengths and opportunities. Reliance on ESG indicators may prove useful to achieve such a purpose.

7.1.3 Recommendations for Municipal Financial Recovery

This book argues that effective management of municipal financial distress and the enhancement of long-term financial resilience require a thorough diagnostic approach. This involves identifying the root causes of financial distress[10] and implementing a modular, adaptable procedure that can be tailored to local cultures and the specific circumstances of the municipality in question. The involvement of an impartial third party, such as a judge or a qualified practitioner, is recommended to oversee the process, thereby ensuring transparency and credibility. This oversight is crucial for maintaining the trust of creditors, public service users, local taxpayers, voters, and both local and central government stakeholders.[11]

Additionally, a robust audit system is essential for assessing the financial health of local governments. Such a system should not merely focus on meeting targets or pursuing high-profile projects. It should also provide a comprehensive analysis of the financial stability of the municipality, taking into account both temporal and spatial dynamics. This includes making financial data accessible and comprehensible to the public, enabling timely identification and monitoring of financial red flags. It also includes providing better training opportunities on financial planning and budgeting for local elected officials.[12]

Crises should be seen as an opportunity to rethink the governance of municipal activities, asking critical questions about the necessity and methods of service delivery and pondering the costs and benefits of in-house provision and extensive monitoring of external provision. For example, by questioning why certain services are provided in a particular manner, municipalities can identify gaps, inefficiencies, and redundancies. Streamlining activities can lead to significant cost savings and better resource allocation. Furthermore,

---

[10] On this point, see also (albeit only with reference to the US jurisdiction): T Guzman and N Ermasova, *Municipal Fiscal Stress, Bankruptcies, and Other Financial Emergencies* (Routledge 2023).

[11] 'The State Role in Local Government Financial Distress' (*The Pew Charitable Trust*, 2013 updated in 2016) <https://www.pewtrusts.org/~/media/assets/2016/04/pew_state_role_in_local_government_financial_distress.pdf>.

[12] CF Symes, *Statutory Priorities in Corporate Insolvency Law: An Analysis of Preferred Creditor Status* (Routledge 2016). Whilst the book focuses on Australian law, it does refer to other selected common law jurisdictions, namely New Zealand, Canada, the UK, and the US.

establishing a clear financial link between the municipality's revenue and the costs of essential services ensures fiscal discipline and accountability. This alignment helps ensure that the entity lives within its means, providing services that are both necessary for the most vulnerable among the local community and financially sustainable. Ultimately, less can indeed be better, as focusing on the delivery of good quality core services that are subject to regular reviews allows for more efficient and effective governance.[13]

The development of sustainable recovery requires a new framework. This book advocates for the implementation of a comprehensive and conscious assessment and recovery framework that emphasises ESG considerations. Such a framework should incorporate specific legal mechanisms, which may include consensual third-party releases, deviations from general distribution rules, green finance, and tools designed to enhance both internal and external governance. The preferential treatment of vulnerable stakeholders, while controversial in general insolvency laws, could be pivotal in managing the diverse interests of creditors and other stakeholders in municipal bankruptcies, thus ensuring that the recovery plan is both equitable and efficient.

Moreover, the framework should prioritise the cultivation of robust governance practices. Good governance is critical in building the trust of stakeholders, including local residents, businesses, and potential investors. It involves not only transparency and accountability in decision-making processes, but also the establishment of clear lines of authority and responsibility. This can be achieved through the development of comprehensive governance codes and the regular auditing of financial and operational activities.[14]

An essential component of this framework is the motivation and retention of expert staff. Skilled personnel are indispensable for navigating the complexities of financial distress and implementing effective recovery strategies. It is crucial to establish incentives that attract and retain these experts, including competitive compensation, professional development opportunities, and a supportive work environment.[15] By ensuring that experienced staff are in place, municipalities can better manage the intricacies of financial recovery and long-term planning. The staffing dimension of the framework also calls for a focus on the particular type of expertise needed to steer recovery strategies in local governments and how a sufficient pool of such expertise can be developed in a country.

---

[13] M Moses, *The Municipal Financial Crisis. A Framework for Understanding and Fixing Government Budgeting* (Palgrave Macmillan 2022) 21.

[14] OECD, *OECD Corporate Governance Factbook* (2019).

[15] JD Ward, *Leadership and Change in Public Sector Organizations: Beyond Reforms* (Routledge 2017).

Finally, both before and during a municipal crisis, financial managers must collaborate closely with the entity's managers not only in drafting the budget but also in identifying and implementing more efficient service delivery methods. This partnership should extend beyond traditional budgeting processes to encompass a thorough analysis of current practices, identifying areas where resources can be optimised or reallocated. Financial managers can bring a critical perspective that highlights inefficiencies, cost overruns, or outdated practices that might otherwise go unnoticed. By leveraging financial data and analytical tools, they can provide actionable insights that help reshape operational strategies, streamline processes, and reduce costs. This collaborative effort may contribute to budgets not only reflecting financial realities but also strategic goals, ultimately leading to more sustainable and effective service provision.

The primary focus of any recovery framework should be the restoration and sustainable development of the local area. This involves not only financial stabilisation, but also initiatives aimed at socio-economic revitalisation, infrastructure development, and environmental sustainability. A recovery plan that prioritises these aspects can lead to a more resilient local economy and an improved quality of life for residents. It also has positive spill-over effects on neighbouring entities, fostering regional stability and economic growth.

In conclusion, a detailed and well-structured recovery framework that integrates ESG considerations, robust governance mechanisms, skilled staffing, and a focus on local area recovery is essential for enhancing the financial resilience of local governments. This approach not only addresses immediate financial challenges but also lays the foundation for sustainable long-term growth.

7.2 LESSONS FROM THE COMPARISON BETWEEN THE USA, SOUTH AFRICA, AND ENGLAND

7.2.1 Lessons for the USA

The comparative study of local entities in financial distress, with a particular focus on the US, offers several key lessons and recommendations aimed at enhancing the legal and administrative frameworks governing municipal bankruptcy.

A primary recommendation is to further develop the rich tradition of bankruptcy rules applicable to municipalities in distress. This tradition, primarily encapsulated in chapter 9 of the US Bankruptcy Code, provides a specialised mechanism for municipal entities (of varied size and type) to restructure their debts. However, there is an ongoing need to refine these rules to better accommodate the unique characteristics and challenges of municipal financial distress, ensuring that they remain effective in addressing contemporary issues.[16]

Another critical lesson from the study emphasises the importance of improving access to financial data at the local level. Transparent and comprehensive financial information is essential for the effective monitoring and management of municipal finances. This transparency not only aids in the early identification of fiscal distress but also facilitates informed decision-making by stakeholders, including creditors, policymakers, and the public. Enhanced access to financial data can be achieved through standardised reporting requirements and the use of digital platforms that make such data readily available.[17]

In addition to transparency, there is a need to develop the expertise of bankruptcy judges in the area of local government finance. Judges presiding over chapter 9 cases must possess a deep understanding of the unique aspects of municipal operations, including budgeting, public service delivery, and intergovernmental fiscal relations. Furthermore, the study highlights the importance of ensuring that qualified officials or external managers support the restructuring process, while being appropriately sensitive to concerns about the displacement of democratically elected officials. Such appointments are crucial for implementing effective recovery plans and restoring financial stability, particularly in municipalities lacking the necessary internal expertise.[18]

The study also calls for a better understanding of local audit systems across different states, advocating for the development of general principles that could standardise audit practices. This would help to ensure consistency and comparability in the financial oversight of local governments, thereby enhancing the reliability of financial reports and the accountability of municipal officials. Standardised audit principles would also facilitate cross-jurisdictional analysis and benchmarking, contributing to more effective fiscal management practices nationwide.[19]

---

[16] LN Coordes, 'Restructuring Municipal Bankruptcy' (2016) 2 Utah L. Rev. 307.

[17] 'State Strategies to Detect Local Fiscal Distress' (*The Pew Charitable Trust*, 2016) <https://www.pewtrusts.org/-/media/assets/2016/09/detecting_local_distress_report.pdf>.

[18] LN Coordes, 'Formalizing Chapter 9's Experts' (2017) 116 Mich. L. Rev. 1249.

[19] 'Standards for Internal Control in the Federal Government' (*General Accountability Office*, 2014) <https://www.gao.gov/assets/gao-14-704g.pdf> (which, however, looks at accountability in federal government rather than in local municipalities).

Furthermore, despite the growing ideological and politicised nature of the use of such concepts in US politics,[20] the study suggests that deviations from general bankruptcy law in chapter 9 proceedings should be justified by ESG considerations. For instance, social considerations may support maintaining collective bargaining rights and job security in financially distressed municipalities, recognising that these elements are vital for the social fabric and economic stability of local communities. Incorporating ESG considerations into bankruptcy proceedings aligns the financial restructuring process with broader societal goals, ensuring that recovery strategies are not solely driven by financial metrics but also by the well-being of residents and the sustainability of local economies.

Another significant recommendation is the encouragement of preventive restructuring and intervention measures. The study highlights the example of North Carolina, which employs proactive measures to address financial distress before it escalates to the need for chapter 9 bankruptcy, state intervention, or bailouts.[21] These early interventions can include financial oversight, technical assistance, and the implementation of corrective action plans. By addressing issues at an earlier stage, municipalities can avoid the more severe consequences of late-stage financial crises, leading to more sustainable and less disruptive recovery processes.[22]

Lastly, the study underscores the importance of fostering better communication and co-operation between local, state, and federal authorities in managing medium-to-large, general-purpose municipal bankruptcies. Effective intergovernmental collaboration is crucial for co-ordinating responses to financial distress, sharing best practices, and providing the necessary resources and support. A co-ordinated approach ensures that all levels of government are aligned in their efforts to stabilise and restore distressed municipalities, ultimately leading to more coherent and effective recovery strategies.[23]

---

[20] L Malone, E Holland and C Houston, 'ESG Battlegrounds: How States Are Shaping the Regulatory Landscape in the U.S.' (*Harvard Law School Forum on Corporate Governance*, 11 March 2023) <https://corpgov.law.harvard.edu/2023/03/11/esg-battlegrounds-how-the-states-are-shaping-the-regulatory-landscape-in-the-u-s/>.

[21] See chapter 3, *sub* [3.3.3].

[22] CK Coe, 'Preventing Local Government Fiscal Crises: Emerging Best Practices' (2008) 68(4) Public Admin. Rev. 759.

[23] O O'Donnell, 'Strategic Collaboration in Local Government' *Institute of Public Administration* (Local Government Research Series 2012) <https://www.ipa.ie/_fileUpload/Documents/StrategicCollaboration.pdf>.

By implementing these recommendations, the US can strengthen its framework for addressing municipal financial distress, promoting resilience and long-term sustainability in local governance.

7.2.2 Lessons for South Africa

The comparative study on local entities in financial distress, with a focus on South Africa, highlights several critical lessons and recommendations aimed at improving the legal and administrative frameworks governing municipal financial management.

A key recommendation is to build upon South Africa's established tradition of administrative rules applicable to municipalities in distress. This involves developing a more modular and flexible set of regulations that can adapt to the varying needs and circumstances of different municipalities. Moreover, there is a need for better co-ordination between different spheres of government—national, provincial, and local—to ensure a cohesive and comprehensive approach to managing municipal financial distress. This alignment is crucial for implementing consistent policies and providing the necessary support for distressed municipalities.[24]

Enhancing financial expertise at the local level is another crucial area of focus. Many South African municipalities lack the necessary in-house financial expertise to manage their finances effectively, leading to poor financial planning and execution. The study recommends bolstering the financial literacy and skills of municipal officials and promoting the use of preventive restructuring and intervention measures. By proactively addressing financial issues before they escalate, municipalities can avoid the need for more drastic and disruptive measures, such as provincial or national intervention or external management. This proactive stance not only stabilises municipal finances, but also enhances the overall capacity of local governments to manage their resources efficiently.[25]

A significant challenge facing South African municipalities is forward planning, particularly regarding social and environmental needs. Given that local

---

[24] C Tapscott, 'Intergovernmental Relations in South Africa: The Challenges of Co-Operative Government' (2000) 20(2) Public Admin. Dev. 119; I Uregu Ile, 'Strengthening Intergovernmental Relations for Improved Service Delivery in South Africa: Issues for Consideration' (2010) 7(1) Journal of US–China Public Administration 51; ML Tau, 'Intergovernmental Relations and Cooperative Governance in South Africa: Challenges and Prospects' (2015) 50(4) Public Admin. 1.

[25] M van Donk et al, *Consolidating Developmental Local Government: Lessons from the South African Experience* (Juta Publishing 2008).

governments are still in a constituting phase, there is a pressing need to develop tools and strategies for long-term planning. This includes addressing the root causes of municipal distress, such as inadequate infrastructure, uneven and unsuitable funding models, environmental degradation, and socio-economic inequalities. The study suggests adopting long-term solutions that are not only financially sustainable but also address the broader social and environmental challenges. By reducing the risk of prolonged or multiple restructuring processes, municipalities can focus on sustainable development and improving the quality of life for their residents.[26]

Balancing the protection of public interests and essential services with the rights of creditors is another critical consideration. This balance is particularly important when creditors are also service providers, such as utility companies. As a result, appropriate protection of creditors is essential for continued service delivery, not only in the distressed municipality but across a broader area. The study emphasises the need for a regulatory framework that protects the delivery of essential services while also safeguarding the interests of creditors. Such a framework would ensure that municipalities can continue to provide critical services like water and electricity, even during financial distress, while maintaining fair and equitable treatment for creditors given the close link between service delivery and creditors in many municipalities.

Furthermore, the study highlights the importance of preserving and enhancing the statutory link between environmental and social rights and the management of municipal financial distress, as outlined in the Municipal Finance Management Act (MFMA). This link is essential for ensuring that financial decision-making processes consider the socio-economic rights of citizens, such as the right to adequate housing, healthcare, food, water, and social security. The study recommends maintaining high standards for the provision of these basic municipal services and cautions against lowering these standards, even in the face of financial challenges. This approach aligns with the broader ESG framework, which emphasises the social dimension of financial management.

Additionally, the study underscores the importance of providing clear guidance on the courts' endorsement of a reasonableness approach to the realisation of socio-economic rights.[27] This principle, grounded in the paradigm of progressive realisation, requires that government actions be reasonable in both

---

[26] TA Koelble and A Siddle, 'Institutional Complexity and Unanticipated Consequences: The Failure of Decentralization in South Africa' (2013) 21(6) Democratization 1117.

[27] G Quinot and S Liebenberg, 'Narrowing the Band: Reasonableness Review in Administrative Justice and Socio-Economic Rights Jurisprudence in South Africa', in S Liebenberg and G Quinot (eds), *Law and Poverty: Perspectives from South Africa and Beyond* (Juta Publishing 2012).

intent and implementation when addressing socio-economic rights. By adhering to this standard, municipalities can ensure that their practices are just, even as they navigate financial constraints. It is thus imperative that as much clarity as possible be established on the reasonableness standard in this context in order to practically steer the formulation and implementation of municipal financial recovery plans. This legal and ethical framework helps safeguard the rights of vulnerable populations and promotes social justice.[28]

Finally, the study stresses the need to combat fraud and corruption, which are significant barriers to effective governance and financial management in South African municipalities. It recommends swift and decisive action, including the appointment of qualified external managers, when allegations of corruption or fraud are substantiated. Ensuring accountability and transparency in municipal governance is crucial for restoring public trust and fostering a culture of integrity. By taking these measures, South Africa can strengthen its municipal governance structures, enhance financial stability, and support sustainable development.[29]

7.2.3 Lessons for England

The comparative study on local entities in financial distress, with a specific focus on England, underscores several critical lessons and recommendations for enhancing the resilience of local governments.

One of the key findings is the necessity for long-term, adequate planning and enhanced subsidiarity in resource allocation. Austerity has actively reshaped the relationship between central and local government in Britain, shrinking the capacity of the local state, increasing inequality between local governments, and exacerbating territorial injustice.[30] The study suggests that "urban entrepreneurialism" could be a viable strategy for increasing revenue, provided it is approached with caution and keeps the local government within its legal obligation to have a balanced budget. This strategy should avoid speculative ventures and be subject to rigorous internal, as well as external and independent, auditing.

[28] KG Young, 'Socio-Economic Rights. Adjudication under a Transformative Constitution' (2013) 11(1) Int. J. Const. Law 270.

[29] S Dintwe and D Masiloane, 'Developing an Anti-Corruption Strategy for the South African Public Sector' (2014) 49(1) Public Admin. 180; N Gray, 'When Anti-Corruption Fails: The Dynamics of Procurement in Contemporary South Africa' (2021) 48(169) ROAPE 369.

[30] M Gray and A Barford, 'The Depths of the Cuts: The Uneven Geography of Local Government Austerity' (2018) 11(3) CJRES 541.

Municipal bonds to raise debt on a model such as the one successfully used in the US might be an interesting avenue to explore, provided that robust and reliable monitoring systems by an external third party are in place to ensure that risks are kept reasonably low and that the system instils confidence in the financial sector investing in the bonds.[31] Municipal bonds, whilst generally considered low-risk instruments if well-structured, require a reliable revenue stream to support the issuer's obligations. In the UK, local governments often lack sufficient commercial activities and revenue-generating mechanisms. This situation has historically deterred banks from underwriting municipal bonds, as they once incurred significant losses due to the ambiguous legal framework governing local government financial engagements.[32] To mitigate these risks, a clearly defined statutory framework and robust monitoring system are essential, ensuring that financial arrangements are legally sound and that there is a reduced likelihood of the agreements being deemed void. This would enhance the attractiveness and security of municipal bonds as an investment vehicle.

Furthermore, it is crucial that such initiatives are managed by individuals with appropriate financial expertise, rather than elected councillors who may lack the necessary knowledge. This recommendation highlights the need for a professional approach to financial management within local governments, ensuring that initiatives are grounded in sound financial principles and risk assessments.[33]

The current politico-administrative approach to managing financial distress in English municipalities, whilst potentially useful as a theoretical safeguard, reveals significant drawbacks when implemented in practice. The lack of democratic accountability and transparency in these procedures necessitates a reconsideration of the framework. The study advocates for introducing judicial or quasi-judicial supervision, drawing on the expertise of judges from commercial, civil, and administrative courts.[34] This approach could ensure a more balanced and accountable process, akin to the special administration regimes

---

31 Detroit defaulting on its bonds is one rare exception in such a large market in the US: D Cestau et al, 'Municipal Bond Markets' (2019) 11(65) Annu. Rev. Financ. Econ. 84.

32 J Braithwaite, 'Thirty Years of *Ultra Vires*: Local Authorities, National Courts and the Global Derivatives Markets' (2018) 71(1) CLP 369, 384–389.

33 See above *sub* [7.1.2].

34 Administrative courts in the UK, part of the High Court, play a key role in overseeing the lawfulness of decisions made by public bodies, ensuring they act within their legal powers and uphold individual rights. These courts handle judicial reviews, statutory appeals, and certain civil and criminal applications. They provide a crucial check on the exercise of public authority, ensuring that decisions affecting individuals and organisations comply with the law and principles

applicable to certain special-purpose entities, such as water companies.[35] A key aspect of this revised framework would include mechanisms to enforce financial compromises, such as "haircuts" on commercial creditors[36] and the imposition of plans on dissenting creditor classes, thereby providing a structured and equitable resolution process.

Enhancing in-house financial expertise at the local level is another critical recommendation. This enhancement is necessary both for municipalities not currently experiencing financial distress and during intervention procedures. The study recommends appointing qualified experts to support, rather than replace, existing management teams, except in cases where managers are found guilty of fraud, bribery, or gross negligence. This approach aims to shift the framework from a punitive and reactive stance to a more supportive and preventive one, helping municipalities to stabilise and recover without stigmatising or undermining existing administrative structures. Such a shift would promote a culture of improvement within local government, rather than fear and avoidance of addressing financial issues.

Furthermore, the adoption of long-term solutions that address the ESG root causes of municipal distress is crucial. The case of Croydon[37] highlights the dangers of short-term fixes that fail to address underlying issues, leading to recurrent financial instability. A focus on long-term, sustainable strategies that integrate social and environmental considerations will not only stabilise financial conditions but also promote broader community well-being and resilience.

Another important recommendation is the legal requirement to consider public interest factors in decision-making processes involving distressed local entities. This includes considerations affecting the environment, collective well-being, and social issues. A more comprehensive approach, as seen in Wales under the Well-being of Future Generations (Wales) Act 2015, offers a systematic framework for sustainability and community well-being, whilst allowing local governments flexibility in implementation. Currently, sporadic

---

of fairness. Statutory jurisdiction to review the functioning of public authorities is conferred on the Administrative Court by the Supreme Court Act 1981, s 31.

35 See, for instance, the discussion on the special administration regime that could potentially apply to Thames Water in chapter 5, *sub* [5.4.3].

36 In an insolvency procedure, a "haircut" refers to a reduction in the amount that creditors receive on their outstanding claims, often as part of a settlement agreement. This means creditors agree to accept less than the full amount owed to them, helping the debtor to resolve financial distress and potentially continue operations.

37 See chapter 5, *sub* [5.4.1].

inclusion of ESG is provided in the statute book.[38] By adopting a holistic approach—for instance, by mandating the inclusion of these considerations at the local level and providing for monitoring this inclusion—the legal framework can ensure that the management of municipal distress goes beyond financial metrics to incorporate broader societal impacts.

A municipal restructuring framework that aligns with the growing emphasis on ESG criteria in governance and financial management would better reflect a more holistic understanding of municipal responsibilities and the role of public institutions in fostering sustainable development.

7.2.4 Lessons for Specific Local Services

The comparative study of local entities in financial distress underscores the critical role of local services, particularly those provided by special-purpose governments, in maintaining essential public functions. While general-purpose governments encompass a wide range of responsibilities, special-purpose entities often manage specific services such as water, transportation, and healthcare. These services are fundamental to the well-being of residents and are also vulnerable to the repercussions of financial distress. The case studies of Flint and Detroit in the US,[39] and Mangaung in South Africa,[40] highlight the complexities and challenges associated with managing such vital services during periods of financial instability. These cases demonstrate that the financial health of special-purpose entities is not only crucial for the continuation of services but also intimately linked to the broader socio-economic stability of the communities they serve.

---

[38] For instance, under the 2021 Environment Act, UK government ministers and local authorities have a duty to consider environmental principles in policymaking, reflecting a commitment to sustainable and environmentally responsible governance. See chapter 2, *sub* [2.2.3]. The Public Services (Social Value) Act 2012 requires public authorities to consider the wider social, economic, and environmental benefits when commissioning and procuring services. The Public Sector Equality Duty imposes a duty to have due regard to protected characteristics to ensure that public decisions do not disproportionately impact vulnerable groups, aligning with the social component of ESG principles. While in the UK there was previously a more systematic and holistic approach through the Sustainable Development Commission, this approach continues to be adopted in Wales with the Future Generations Commissioner, emphasising social over environmental aspects. A middle way between this top-down approach and a more bottom-up approach could be explored fruitfully.

[39] See chapter 3, *sub* [3.4.1]–[3.4.2].

[40] See chapter 4, *sub* [4.4.1].

The provision of water, in particular, emerges as a critical issue during municipal financial crises. As highlighted in this study, water services are often among the first to experience the strain of financial distress due to their essential nature and the substantial infrastructure costs associated with their delivery. The Flint water crisis, for instance, was exacerbated by cost-cutting measures that ultimately compromised public health, illustrating the dire consequences of inadequate financial planning and oversight.[41] In a similar vein, the recent crisis at Thames Water in the UK revealed significant vulnerabilities in the management and financing of water services.[42] Likewise, in Mangaung, financial mismanagement and lack of resources severely impacted water provision, leading to widespread public dissatisfaction and highlighting the intersection between financial governance and basic human rights.[43] These examples underscore the importance of ensuring robust financial management and regulatory oversight for special-purpose entities, particularly in sectors as critical as water provision.

The study advocates for integrating ESG considerations into the financial and operational frameworks governing these services. In times of financial distress, the continuity and quality of essential services such as water need to be prioritised to protect human dignity and public health. This involves not only maintaining physical infrastructure and supply but also ensuring affordability and accessibility, especially for vulnerable users. The inclusion of ESG criteria can help safeguard these aspects by emphasising social equity, environmental sustainability, and accountable governance in the management of local services. For instance, regulatory frameworks could mandate that water utilities maintain service levels even during financial restructuring in order to minimise the kind of public health crises seen in Flint.

Furthermore, this analysis suggests that a rethinking of the financial and operational structures governing local services is necessary to prevent and mitigate the impacts of financial distress. It is recommended that local and central governments, along with regulatory bodies, develop more resilient financial models that include contingency planning and risk management strategies for essential services. The study emphasises that addressing the governance challenges of special-purpose entities, particularly in ensuring transparency and accountability, is crucial for maintaining public trust and securing the long-term viability of essential services. By adopting a holistic approach that integrates ESG considerations, local governments can better navigate financial

41 See chapter 3, *sub* [3.3.2].
42 See chapter 5, *sub* [5.4.3].
43 See chapter 4, *sub* [4.4.1].

crises whilst protecting the essential services that underpin community health and well-being.

7.2.5 Lessons for ESG Considerations

The integration of ESG considerations in the management of local entities in financial distress is crucial but often underdeveloped. ESG frameworks are typically designed to guide corporate governance and investment strategies, yet their application in public sector contexts, such as municipal governance, remains less clearly defined. This book underscores the need for a more structured and coherent application of ESG principles in the public sector, particularly during financial crises. Legal frameworks can incorporate specific provisions to ensure that ESG considerations are not overlooked during recovery efforts. For instance, environmental considerations, often neglected, should be a fundamental aspect of any restructuring plan, especially given the critical role local governments play in environmental stewardship. Such considerations can include mandates for sustainable infrastructure investments and climate resilience planning.

Social considerations are somewhat more visible in the management of local entities during financial distress, particularly concerning staff welfare, pay, and pensions. However, the treatment of these issues often lacks consistency and fairness. In many cases, financial recovery plans may involve renegotiating staff pay and pensions, potentially undermining employee welfare. Even where constitutional protections exist, as in some jurisdictions like South Africa or at the state level in the US (e.g. Michigan), these safeguards can be circumvented or renegotiated under the guise of financial necessity. The social dimension of ESG should therefore not only protect these rights but also actively promote social equity and inclusion. For example, restructuring plans could include provisions for retraining and redeployment of affected staff, thus supporting long-term employment stability and economic resilience within the community.

Governance reforms are frequently implemented as part of emergency financial interventions, such as the appointment of administrators/commissioners in South Africa and England or emergency managers in the US. Whilst these measures are often necessary to stabilise finances, they carry the risk of overly simplistic attributions of blame to existing management. This can lead to the neglect of deeper, systemic issues that contributed to the financial distress. Effective governance under an ESG framework requires a comprehensive analysis of the root causes of financial difficulties, beyond merely changing leadership. It involves strengthening institutional frameworks, ensuring transparency, and enhancing stakeholder engagement. For example, governance reforms could include establishing independent audit committees or improving mechanisms for public consultation and participation in decision-making processes.

Ultimately, the application of ESG considerations in the management of local entities in financial distress should aim for a holistic and sustainable recovery. This involves balancing immediate financial stabilisation with long-term social and environmental objectives. A more nuanced, modular, and integrated approach can help avoid short-term fixes that merely postpone underlying problems. For instance, by prioritising sustainable development and social justice in recovery strategies, local governments can lay the foundation for a more resilient and equitable community. Moreover, incorporating ESG principles into legal and regulatory frameworks can help ensure that these considerations are systematically addressed, providing a more stable and accountable basis for managing public sector entities in financial distress. This book advocates for such an integrated approach, recognising that the resilience of local governments depends not only on financial stability but also on their capacity to manage social and environmental challenges effectively.

7.3 NEXT STEPS

This book offers an initial exploration into how the US, South Africa, and England address municipal financial distress through the lens of ESG considerations. While it provides a valuable comparative analysis, it serves as a preliminary foundation for more nuanced and comprehensive studies aimed at achieving resilient financial recovery for municipalities.

To deepen the analysis presented, at least four areas warrant further investigation. Firstly, while the comparison between the US, South Africa, and the UK (namely, England) yields insightful similarities and differences, incorporating additional jurisdictions from Latin America, continental Europe, or Asia could significantly broaden the scope and impact of the findings. Such an expanded comparative framework would offer a more global perspective on municipal financial distress and recovery, revealing diverse approaches and potential cross-cultural lessons that could enhance the robustness of our conclusions.

Secondly, the collaborative effort of this project, which involved experts in insolvency law and administrative law, has provided a multifaceted view of municipal financial distress. Nevertheless, the research would benefit from a more interdisciplinary approach. Engaging methodologies and paradigms from fields such as history, sociology, economics, and political science would offer richer insights into the complexities of municipal financial management. Additionally, incorporating perspectives from human and economic geography, urban studies, and developmental studies could illuminate how demographic changes, financial innovation, climate change, and administrative capacity impact local governments. Integrating these disciplines could yield comprehensive tools and processes to bolster financial resilience in municipalities.

Thirdly, the focus of the book has predominantly been on general-purpose local governments, often treating them in isolation from broader economic, social, and environmental contexts. However, municipal financial distress also affects special-purpose local entities such as water companies, health trusts, hospitals, energy providers, and schools. These entities play crucial roles in delivering essential public services and directly impact the quality of life in local areas. Future research should explore the financial resilience and interconnections between these special-purpose local governments and their wider economic, social, and environmental contexts. Understanding how these entities interact and contribute to overall municipal well-being will provide a more comprehensive picture of local governance and its challenges.

Fourthly, the book has focused on one dimension of the legal treatment of local public entities in a commercial context, namely dealing with insolvency. However, there are many other dimensions of municipalities' operations in a commercial setting that warrant closer legal attention along similar lines to those applied in this book. Some of these settings have been subjected to legal study, such as municipal contracting for goods and services (public procurement), although not from the same perspective. Other settings, such as control over municipal assets, including disposals, corporate forms of subsidiary local entities, and business ventures of municipalities in competition with private enterprises, have received less attention. Exploring the legal treatment of municipalities across a wider range of commercial settings could provide a more holistic, integrated view of the legal conceptualisation of local public entities as commercial actors.

In conclusion, expanding the comparative scope, incorporating interdisciplinary perspectives, examining the roles of special-purpose local governments, and studying municipalities in more commercial settings are essential steps toward advancing the understanding and management of municipal financial distress. Such developments will not only enhance academic discourse but also offer practical insights for policymakers and practitioners working to foster resilient and sustainable local governance systems.

Index

Printed and bound by CPI Group (UK) Ltd, Croydon, CR0 4YY
17/06/2026
14902645-0003